FRENCH FOR COMMUNICATION

Bonjour!

H. Matisse

MATISSE, Henri. *Dahlias and Pomegranates.* 1947. Brush and ink, 30⅛ × 22¼″. Collection, The Museum of Modern Art, New York. Abby Aldrich Rockefeller Fund.

ANNE SLACK Harvard University

ELMER JULES MANDEL Los Angeles Unified School District

ELAINE M. HARDIE Concord-Carlisle High School

FRENCH FOR COMMUNICATION

ONE

HOUGHTON MIFFLIN COMPANY BOSTON

Atlanta Dallas Geneva, Illinois Hopewell, New Jersey

Palo Alto Toronto

ACKNOWLEDGMENTS

The authors and publisher would like to express their sincere appreciation to the teachers who fieldtested the **French for Communication** material during the developmental stages of the program, and to those who reviewed portions of the manuscript in first draft or final form.

FIELDTESTERS

Kathy Frieze, West High School, Wichita, Kansas

Renée Lamkie, Los Angeles High School, Los Angeles, California

Claire Fenn, Newton North High School, Newton, Massachusetts

Linda Healy, Central Regional High School, Bayville, New Jersey

Connie Hay, Southeast High School, Wichita, Kansas

Carol Jennings, West High School, Minneapolis, Minnesota

Carole Marissael, Hale Junior High School, Los Angeles, California

Arthur Summer, Parkman Junior High School, Woodland Hills, California

Virginia Worcester, Hale Junior High School, Woodland Hills, California

REVIEWERS

Laurel Briscoe, University of Texas, Austin, Texas

Sylvia Brown, Central Regional High School, Bayville, New Jersey

Enrique Lamadrid, University of New Mexico, Albuquerque, New Mexico

Edwin Little, Newton South High School, Newton, Massachusetts

Mildred Mortimer, Shipley School in Bryn Mawr, Bryn Mawr, Pennsylvania

William Moulton, Princeton University, Princeton, New Jersey

Mariette Reed, Educational Testing Service, Princeton, New Jersey

Mary Waters, Newton North High School, Newton, Massachusetts

Printed in the U.S.A.
Library of Congress Catalog Card Number: 77-87429
ISBN: 0-395-20159-4

ANNE SLACK, a graduate of the University of Algiers, currently teaches at Harvard University. Her activities in state, regional, and national language organizations include serving as an editor of the French Review and as national president of the American Association of Teachers of French. She was coordinator of FLES for the Schenectady, N.Y. public schools and taught the televised series **Parlons français,** of which she was the principal author. She also wrote and produced for five years a series of radio programs in French for station WGBH in Boston. She has taught and supervised language courses at NDEA Institutes, and has lectured extensively on pedagogy and foreign languages in the U.S., Canada, Great Britain, and France.

E. JULES MANDEL, a native of Cleveland, Ohio, has taught French, German, and Spanish at the secondary school and college levels. A graduate of the University of Chicago, the University of Geneva, Switzerland, and the University of California at Los Angeles, Dr. Mandel taught demonstration classes and applied linguistics at several NDEA Summer French Institutes. He also trained and supervised student teachers at UCLA and at California State University at Los Angeles. He is presently Instructional Specialist, Foreign Language, for the Los Angeles Unified School District.

ELAINE M. HARDIE, a graduate of Bates College and Middlebury College, currently teaches at Concord-Carlisle High School, Massachusetts, where she has twice served as Chairman of the Foreign Language Department. Miss Hardie has also taught in Rouen, France as a Fulbright Interchange Teacher and at an NDEA Institute in Athens, Georgia. She has served in various capacities in state and regional foreign language organizations, and as a member of the Executive Council of the American Association of Teachers of French.

To THE TEACHER

FRENCH FOR COMMUNICATION (FFC) is a two-level continuous sequence of teaching and learning materials designed for use in secondary schools. The components of FFC ONE consist of a student text, which is described below; a Teacher's Manual, containing the complete introduction to the program and a detailed set of class plans correlated with material in the student text; a set of audio-visual aids (posters, flash cards, grammar strips, and recordings); a workbook with a variety of supplementary exercises; and duplicating masters of the answer sheets for the Progress Tests.

The primary goal of FRENCH FOR COMMUNICATION is to provide students with information about how the French language works, and with practice in using it in context. Since individuals vary in the amount of time they need to understand a concept, most of the information about the French language is presented in self-instructional homework assignments called Preparations. In addition, the Preparations provide practice in reading and writing French, and supply cultural information. Each student can work at his or her own pace to absorb the information in a particular assignment. Class time, then, can be spent mostly in using the language. To that end, the class plans in the Teacher's Manual provide systematic re-entry of both grammatical structures and vocabulary, as well as detailed suggestions for many stimulating and contextually-oriented classroom activities.

FFC ONE is divided into eight Phases, each organized around a main theme: greetings, family and friends, sports, food, clothing, a journey to Senegal, a return to Paris. Each theme serves as a framework for introducing a set of grammatical structures and specific word sets.

A typical Phase of the student text contains the following:
1 a list of the Phase objectives
2 self-instructional Preparations, cultural notes, and a photo essay
3 the core dialogues and readings for the Phase
4 a summary of the major grammatical structures in the Phase
5 exercises intended for use in class.

A typical Phase of the Teacher's Manual contains:
1 a list of the Phase objectives; some suggested classroom procedures
2 Phase index and vocabulary; a list of quizzes and cultural notes
3 the core dialogues and readings for the Phase
4 a detailed set of suggested teaching plans for the Phase.

In addition, many optional activities and songs are included at the end of the Manual for use with each Phase.

FRENCH FOR COMMUNICATION is a realistic and flexible program. The variety of activities, both in class plans and in Preparations, the systematic re-entry, and the use of self-paced instruction are three outstanding features that help teachers and students make the most effective use of the time available for teaching and learning French.

See the Scope and Sequence chart on pp. x–xvii for a guide to the contents of each Phase.

ONTENTS

Scope and Sequence Chart

PHASE 1 *Salut!* 1

Objectives 2

STRUCTURE AND USAGE	DIALOGUES AND READINGS	CULTURAL CONTENTS

 For a detailed list of the contents of each Phase, see the Teacher's Manual

PHASE 3 **E**ntre nous 113

Objectives 114

PHASE 4 *Allez, les sportifs!* 185

Objectives 186

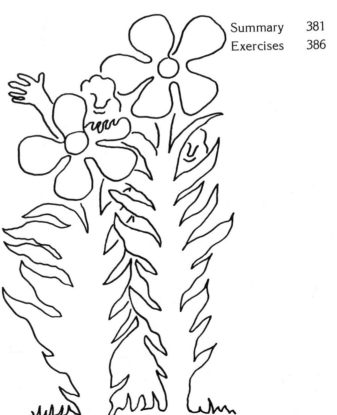

PHASE 7 En Afrique 389

Objectives 390

STRUCTURE AND USAGE

DIALOGUES AND READINGS

CULTURAL CONTENTS

PHASE 8  **Paris** 461

Objectives 462

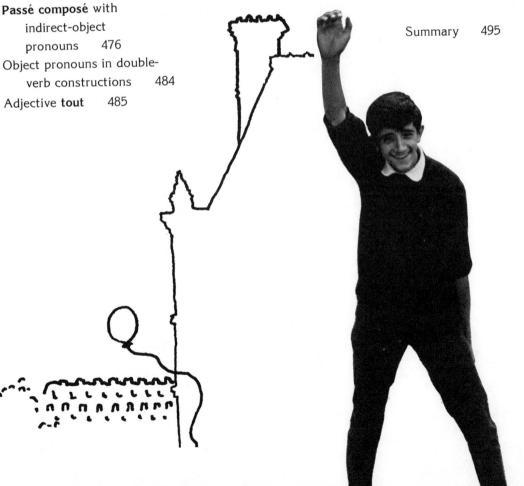

PHASE ONE OBJECTIVES

In this Phase you will learn to greet people in French, and to identify yourself, other people, and some common objects. Specifically, you will:

1 Learn to recognize and imitate the sounds of French words.

2 Practice greeting friends and strangers according to French custom, using the courtesy titles **Monsieur, Madame,** and **Mademoiselle,** and the two ways of saying "you" (the subject pronouns **tu** and **vous**).

3 Learn to tell someone your name.

4 Learn the French names for a number of school subjects and classroom objects and be able to identify them.

5 Be able to ask and answer questions about where things and people are by using the expression **où?** (where?).

6 Describe someone, using appropriate forms of the verb **être** (to be).

7 Practice carrying out a few commands.

8 Ask or tell what someone is looking for, using forms of the verb **chercher.**

9 Ask or tell what town someone is from, using the expression **être de.**

10 Tell who owns something, using **de** + a proper name.

11 Tell what someone is not looking for, or where someone is not from, using the negative **ne...pas.**

❃ The cultural notes describe the French-speaking world, French customs in greeting people, some famous French people, **Créoles** and **Acadiens,** and what French schools are like.

1 How to do a Preparation

A Preparation is an assignment whose main purpose is to prepare you to participate in classroom activities. It provides information that you need to know so that you can spend most of your class time communicating in French. Many Preparations also contain cultural notes and photographs that give you some information about the people and the customs of the French-speaking world.

Each Preparation is made up of two to four parts. Each part is made up of numbered frames. In a typical frame, the first section gives you information and asks you to supply an answer. The second section gives you the answer. You do not have to wait until the next class to find out if you were right.

Here is a sample frame, followed by a step-by-step explanation of how to work with it.

1 The French word for *green* is **vert.** The name of a New England state begins with **ver.** Its nickname is "The Green Mountain State." The name of the state is ——. I

Vermont

Here is how you actually work with a Preparation.

STEP 1: Get a sheet of lined paper on which to write your answers. This is your worksheet. Write your name and the Preparation number in the upper right-hand corner.

STEP 2: On the first line, write Part 1, then number 1. That's the number of the frame you're working on.

STEP 3: Cover the frame with a 5″ x 8″ card or a sheet of blank paper that you can't see through.

STEP 4: Slide the cover sheet down until you come to the mark I at the end of the final sentence.

STEP 5: Read the frame as far as the mark I, then write the answer on your worksheet. Your answer to frame 1 should look like this:
1. Vermont

STEP 6: Slide the cover sheet down past the answer (in color) and check to see if your response was correct. Now try the steps with frames 2–4.

2 The name of the country in Europe where French is spoken most widely is ——. (Write the missing part of the sentence on your worksheet.) I

France

3 Is a person most likely to hear French spoken in Chicago, Peking, or Paris? (Write the name of the city on your worksheet.) ❙

                    Paris

4 Is France the only country in the world where French is spoken widely? Write *yes* or *no* on your worksheet. ❙

                no (French is the first or second language in other countries in Europe, Africa, Asia, and in some parts of Canada and the United States.)

Notice that often additional information is given in parentheses after an answer, as in frame 4. You are not expected to supply this information.

STEP 7:   If you answered a frame incorrectly, draw a circle around the answer on your worksheet. This circle will tell you to look at the frame again when you have completed the Preparation. Now go on to frame 5.

5 The names of many American cities contain the French word for *city*. Three examples are Charlottesville, Jacksonville, and Nashville. What is the French word for *city* contained in each of these names? ❙

                ville

6 A major city in Missouri was named for a great king of France, Saint ____. ❙

                Louis (named for Louis IX, 1214–1270)

7 Two of the Great Plains states have capitals with French names. The capital of Iowa is D ___ M ___. The capital of South Dakota is P ___. ❙

                Des Moines; Pierre (*Pierre* is a common French name, equivalent to *Peter*.)

8 You've probably seen an expert baton twirler leading a parade. *Baton* comes from **bâton**, a French word meaning *stick*. (Notice that the French word **bâton** has a mark called a circumflex on the **â**.) The capital of Louisiana has a French name meaning *red stick*. What is the name of the capital? Refer to the map of Louisiana if you don't know. ❙

                Baton Rouge

9 If **bâton rouge** means *red stick*, then what is the French word for *red*? ❙

                rouge (It is believed that French settlers named the town after red cypress trees that formed the boundary between Indian tribes.)

10 There are many French place names in Louisiana because French colonists were among the first people from Europe to settle there. Look at the map.

One Louisiana city is known for its jazz bands and its Mardi Gras festival. This city is New ____. |

Orleans (The handsome wrought-iron balconies and French street names in the "old quarter" of the city are attractive reminders of the French colonists.)

11 Which city on the map has the same name as the French general who fought for the colonies during the American Revolution? |

Lafayette

How many frames did you get right? Look again at any frames you answered wrong and try to figure out your mistakes.

How long it takes to do a Preparation depends on you. Some students may finish an assignment in 15 to 20 minutes. Other students may take longer. Take the time *you* need to do each assignment well. Then you will be as well prepared as anyone else for the activities in the next class.

2 Sound versus spelling

The following frames will point out some of the differences between what you hear and what you see in a language. Before you start, position your cover sheet and write Part 2, number 1 on your worksheet. Remember to keep the answers covered until you have done what you are asked to do. It is important that you do not look at the answer until you have thought about the problem.

1 There are two ways of sending messages by words. One way is by putting words on paper. This is called writing. The other way is by sending sounds through the air. This is called ____. |

speaking

2 In English, a word you *hear* may be spelled in different ways. Say the words *write, right,* and *rite.* Can you tell how to spell these words by the sound of them? |

no (The three words sound alike.)

3 A word you *see* may be pronounced in different ways. For example, compare *record* as in *I have a new record,* with *record* as in *I record my voice on the tape recorder.* What tells you how to pronounce the word—the spelling or the meaning? |

the meaning (The spelling of a word doesn't always tell you how it sounds.)

In French, as in English, a word you *hear* may be spelled in different ways, and a word you *see* may be pronounced in different ways. The activities in class and in the Preparations will help you understand the relationship between the sounds of French and their spellings.

Your teacher will probably ask you to hand in your worksheets to see that you are doing the Preparations correctly and on time. You will not be graded on how many correct answers you write. Most people make mistakes when they are trying something new. What counts is that you do the Preparations regularly and learn from them.

NOTE ✳ *The French-speaking world*

From time to time in this text there are cultural notes that are marked by **une petite fleur rouge** (a little red flower). Read the cultural notes carefully. Your teacher may wish to discuss them in class.

See if you can think of five countries where French is a major language. Give yourself one full minute. Now turn to the map of the French-speaking world on p. 500. The place-names on the map are in French, but you can probably guess the English equivalents of most of them. In all the areas shown on the map, French is one of the main languages used in business, government, and often in the arts (film, painting, literature, theater).

French is a major language in over 35 countries. It is the official language for about 85 million people in France, in parts of Belgium, Switzerland, and Canada, in Haiti, in parts of North and West Africa, and some islands in the Pacific. It is an important second language for an additional 25 million people in other countries in the world, including parts of Asia.

In the United States, there are about two million French-Americans. Many of them have migrated to this country from Canada and, more recently, Haiti. In southern Louisiana and in New England there has been a strong revival of interest in the French language and culture in many French-American communities.

Magasin Prisunic à la Martinique

1 Recognizing cognates

Recently in class you saw the French names for a number of school subjects. The French words were quite similar to the English words, so chances are you found the French words fairly easy to understand.

1 Take a look at the French word **géométrie.** It is very similar to its English equivalent, which is ____. |

geometry

2 Write the English words that have the same meaning as **biologie** and **géographie.** |

biology, geography

3 Compare the English and French names of the school subjects you saw in frames 1 and 2.

geometry   biology   geography
géométrie   *biologie*   *géographie*

The English words end in the letter ____; the French words end in the letters ____. |

-y; -ie

4 Many English words ending in -*y* have a French equivalent ending in -***ie.*** How do you think the French word for *philosophy* is spelled? Write your answer on your worksheet. |

philosophie

5 Guess how the French word for *astronomy* is written. |

astronomie (Did you make a guess before you looked at the answer?)

6 Look at the English and French names for the following subjects.

music   gymnastics   mathematics
musique   *gymnastique*   *mathématiques*

Many English words ending in -*ic* or -*ics* have French equivalents ending in ____ or ____. |

-ique, -iques

7 What is the English equivalent of the French school subject ***physique?*** |

physics

8 Your study of French will be easier if you learn to recognize English and French patterns of spelling. Look at the following pairs of words and see if you can discover a spelling pattern.

senator   actor   doctor
sénateur   *acteur*   *docteur*

Many English words ending in -*or* have French equivalents ending in ____. |

-eur

Both English and French come in part from the same parent language: Latin. Thus many English and French words are related. Words that have the same parent word are called *cognates*.

Look at the relationship between the English and French cognates below, and the Latin words they came from.

LATIN	spiritus	adventurus
ENGLISH	spirit	adventure
FRENCH	esprit	aventure

English and French cognates are often easy to recognize in print because their spelling is similar or identical. They are harder to recognize in conversation because they do not sound alike in the two languages.

2 Accent marks and the cedilla

In written French, some letters have special marks that help to tell the reader how to pronounce them, for example *é, è, ê,* or *ç.* The mark on *é* is called an acute accent. The mark on *è* is called a grave accent. The mark on *ê* is called a circumflex accent. The mark attached to the bottom of the letter *ç* is called a cedilla.

1 Below are the names of French school subjects that are written with *é, è,* or *ç.* Copy each word carefully.

  a Words spelled with *é: géométrie, mathématiques, géographie.*

  b A word spelled with *è: algèbre.* (Make sure this accent goes in the opposite direction from the accent marks in *géométrie.*)

  c A word spelled with *ç: français.*

2 One word in each pair below needs an accent or cedilla. Pick out that word and rewrite it correctly. Use the model as a guide.

  Modèle: histoire, geographie **|**
       géographie

  a algebre, espagnol **|**
       algèbre (Make sure your accent mark goes in the correct direction.)

  b musique, mathematiques **|**
       mathématiques

  c anglais, francais **|**
       français

3 You have seen the circumflex in the French word *bâton,* meaning *stick,* and in the verb form *vous ____tes.* **|**
     ê (êtes)

4 In class, you will need to know the French names for the accent marks and the cedilla when you or your teacher spell aloud individual words.

Below are the French names with explanations of when they are used.

Accent aigu: ´ It occurs only on the letter *é.*
Accent grave: ` It occurs on the letters *è, à,* and on *ù* in the word *où* (where).
Accent circonflexe: ^ It occurs on the letters *â, ê, î, ô,* and *û.*
Cédille: ¸ It occurs only on the letter *ç.*

Copy the two French words that follow and add the correct accent marks. Two are **accents aigus,** one is an **accent grave.**

geometrie   algebre |

géométrie, algèbre

NOTE ✽

French ways of greeting

Americans observing French people often feel that they kiss and shake hands a lot. It is generally the custom for French people who are related, or who are close friends, to "brush cheeks" or give each other a light kiss on both cheeks when they meet and say good-by. In most French families, children—including teenagers and young adults—kiss their parents good morning and good night, and when leaving for or returning from school.

The French handshake
The French handshake consists of a light, firm grasp, a slight upward stroke, then one downward stroke—unlike the American handshake, which often includes a vigorous pumping up and down. In France, adults who are not close friends usually shake hands when they meet and say good-by. In business offices, some people shake hands every morning and at the end of a day. Young people greet adults who are not relatives or close friends of the family with a handshake. Most French teenagers greet each other with a simple **bonjour** or **salut.** If they are good friends, they may kiss on both cheeks or "brush cheeks."

3 Ways to say "you": tu *and* vous

1 Everybody has a name, like *Bob Smith* or *Mary Jones.* Names are used to identify people. When you speak directly to another person, however, it can be awkward if you use the name constantly.

If you were speaking on the phone to a friend named Henry, which would you say?

Hi, Henry! When is Henry coming over?
Hi, Henry! When are you coming over? |

Hi, Henry! When are you coming over?

2 In *When are you coming over?*, the noun *Henry* has been replaced by the pronoun ____ . |

you (A pronoun is a word used in place of a noun.)

3 Think for a minute about the use of *you*. Henry is your friend and you use *you* when you talk to him. But what if you were speaking to Henry's elderly aunt? You may never have met her before. Would you use *you* in speaking to her? |

yes (In English, *you* is used with both friends and strangers.)

4 In French, you have to choose between the pronouns *tu* and **vous** when you speak to a person. The choice depends on many conditions. Two important factors are the relationship between the speakers, and their ages.

a In France, a teacher normally uses **vous** in addressing a student. One student addressing another would use *tu.* If you were a student in France, would you say **Vous êtes en retard?** or **Tu es en retard?** to your classmate Paul? |

Tu es en retard?

b Judging by the situation in **a,** do you think *tu* shows a formal or informal relationship between the speakers? |

informal

5 *Vous* is usually used: with a person you don't know well; to indicate respect (toward an older person who's not related to you, for instance); in formal situations.

 Tu is usually used: by a child or a teenager talking with a friend; between a child and a parent or guardian; by an adult speaking with a child, a close relative, or a close friend; by anyone speaking to an animal.

 Use the information above to help you decide whether to use *tu* or *vous* in the following situations. Write *tu* or *vous* on your worksheet.

a You're speaking to the principal of the school. |

vous

b You're talking with a classmate. |

tu

c You're asking a policeman for directions. |

vous

d You're talking to your neighbor's dog Milou. |

tu

VOCABULARY

At the end of many Preparations, you will find a list of some of the French words and expressions you have used in class, together with their English meanings. Take a few minutes every day to study them.

madame	Mrs.; ma'am	*à demain*	until tomorrow, see you tomorrow
mademoiselle	Miss	*au revoir*	good-by
monsieur	Mr.; sir	*bonjour*	hello, good morning
absent, absente	absent	*bonsoir*	good evening
présent, présente	present		

1 *More on* tu *and* vous

In Preparation 2, you learned that the choice between *tu* and *vous* depends on a number of conditions, for example, how old the speakers are, how formal their relationship is, and how well they know each other.

1 Would the people in the following situations use *tu* or *vous* in speaking to you? Write *tu* or *vous* on your worksheet.

  a Your uncle asks you how you like school. |
tu (He's a close relative, and is probably older than you.)

  b You work as a sales clerk in a bakery. A teenager who has just moved to town comes in and asks you for some pastry. |
vous (The fact that you have a job in a public place classifies you as an adult.)

  c The new student in your class wants to borrow your pen. |
tu (You're both teenagers and students.)

  d You've won a national science contest, and the director of the sponsoring organization is about to give you an award before a large audience. |
vous (He doesn't know you well, and the situation is a formal one.)

2 So far, the situations have involved the speaker and one other person. Look at the following sentence, and then answer the questions below.

  Philippe et Marie, vous êtes en retard aujourd'hui.

  a What is the English meaning of *vous êtes?* |
you are

  b In the French sentence above, is *vous* used to speak to one person, or to more than one? |
more than one

3 In French, when you speak to more than one person, you always use *vous.* It doesn't matter what your relationship is to them. Would you use *tu* or *vous* in the following situations?

  a You are talking to your older brother about a soccer game. |
tu

  b You are talking to two older sisters about a soccer game. |
vous

  c You are talking to the owner of a pet shop. |
vous

  d You are talking to *two* owners of a pet shop. |
vous

  e You ask your mother if she will let you borrow the family car. |
tu

  f You ask your mother and father if they will let you borrow the family car. |
vous

4 The choice of *tu* or **vous** depends on many conditions. Sometimes it is difficult to tell if you know a person well enough to use *tu.* To avoid being rude, should you use *tu* or **vous** in a doubtful case? |

vous (It is better to use *vous* than to risk offending someone by using *tu*.)

2 *The indefinite markers:* un *and* une

1 Look at the following "sentences."

It's woman.   It's city.   It's shoe.

a Do the "sentences" make sense as they stand? |

no (Something is missing from each one.)

b Do the words *woman, city,* and *shoe* refer to three actions or to a person, a place, and a thing? |

a person, a place, and a thing

2 A word that refers to a person, a place, or a thing is called a *noun.* Look at the words in the list below. Write the nouns on your worksheet.

man   sing   restaurant   my   enter   tree |

man, restaurant, tree (*Man* refers to a person, *restaurant* refers to a place, and a *tree* is a thing.)

3 If you use certain words in front of a noun, you can give different kinds of information. For example:

It's *a* shoe.   (You identify the shoe as belonging to a group of things known as shoes.)

It's *the* shoe.   (You're talking about a shoe that you have referred to before.)

It's *my* shoe.   (You're talking about a shoe that belongs to you.)

The words *a, the,* and *my* are used in front of nouns. They belong to a group of words called *noun markers.*

Try to complete the sentence *It's ____ apple* with the words below. Which of the words can be used as noun markers for *apple?*

slowly   an   his   bread   this   the   run |

an, his, this, the

4 The remaining frames deal with the *indefinite marker.* In English, there are two forms of the indefinite marker that go with a singular noun: *a* and *an.*

a Write the indefinite marker that correctly completes each sentence below.

I see ____ car.   I see ____ airplane. |

a, an

b Do *a* and *an* have two different meanings? |

no (*A* and *an* are two different forms of the indefinite marker, but they have the same meaning.)

5 The choice of *a* or *an* depends on whether the noun begins with a vowel (*a, e, i, o,* or *u*) or a consonant (*b, c, d, f,* etc.). Compare the noun phrases *a car* and *an airplane.*

 a Which marker—*a* or *an*—is used before *car*? |

> a (*A* is used before a noun beginning with a consonant.)

 b Which marker—*a* or *an*—is used before *airplane*? |

> an (*An* is used before a noun beginning with a vowel.)

6 In French there are also two forms of the singular indefinite marker: **un** and **une.** The marker **un** is used with a noun that refers to a male. The other marker, ___, is used with a noun that refers to a female. |

> une (In French the choice of **un** or **une** depends on whether the noun is masculine or feminine. It doesn't matter whether the noun begins with a consonant or with a vowel.)

7 Would you use **un** or **une** if you were talking about the following people in French?

 a a boy, an uncle |

> un

 b a girl, an aunt |

> une

8 When words are referred to as being masculine or feminine, they are said to have gender. All nouns in French are either masculine or feminine in gender. This includes nouns that refer to things as well as nouns that refer to people. Is **un crayon** masculine or feminine? |

> masculine (A noun marked by **un** is masculine; a noun marked by **une** is feminine.)

9 In French, there is no simple way to tell whether a noun that refers to a thing is masculine or feminine. Therefore, it is very important to learn the marker when you learn the noun.

 Write the correct indefinite marker—**un** or **une**—for each picture of a classroom item you see below. Think before you look at the answers!

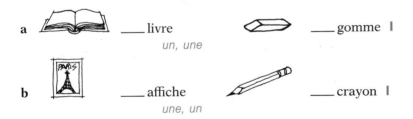

a ___ livre   ___ gomme |

> un, une

b ___ affiche   ___ crayon |

> une, un

3 *Practice using* je suis, tu es, vous êtes

1 You have been using **je suis, tu es,** and **vous êtes** in class. Read the following French sentences and answer the questions.

a *Je suis Philippe Boivin.* What is the English meaning of *je suis?*
I am *or* I'm

b *Tu es de Versailles?* What is the English meaning of *tu es?*
you are *or* you're

c *Vous êtes pressé aujourd'hui!* What is the English meaning of *vous êtes?*
you are *or* you're

2 In English, the words *I* and *you* are subject pronouns. The words *am* and *are* are verb forms. A verb form must "match" or go with the right subject pronoun. This matching is called *agreement*.

Which verb form matches the subject pronoun *I: are* or *am?*
am

3 In French, the words *je, tu,* and *vous* are subject pronouns. The words *suis, es,* and *êtes* are verb forms. Write the verb form that matches each subject pronoun.

a vous
êtes (Remember to put the *accent circonflexe* over the first e.)

b je
suis

c tu
es

4 Complete each sentence by writing the verb form that matches each subject pronoun.

a Je ____ de Versailles.
suis

b Vous ____ en retard aujourd'hui!
êtes (Remember to write the *accent circonflexe.*)

c Tu ____ de San Francisco?
es

5 Write the English equivalent of *Vous êtes en retard aujourd'hui!*
You are/you're late today!

VOCABULARY

ça va? how are things?
bien OK; well
et toi? and you?
merci thanks

pas mal OK; not bad
pas très bien not very well
très very
très bien very well

PHILIPPE EST PRESSÉ Philippe is in a Hurry
aujourd'hui today
en retard late
je suis I am
oh oui oh, yes
vous êtes you are

UNE RENCONTRE A Meeting
de from
je m'appelle my name is
moi I (emphatic); me
non no
salut! hi!
toi aussi you, too
tu es you are

1 *The subject pronouns* il, elle, ils, elles

1 You have been using *il, elle, ils,* and *elles* in class. Remember that pronouns replace nouns. Now read the pairs of sentences below.

> *Pierre est en retard.*   *Marie est en retard.*
> *Il est en retard.*   *Elle est en retard.*

a Is *il* used in place of a boy's name or a girl's name? |
> a boy's name

b What is the English meaning of *il?* |
> he

c Does *elle* replace a boy's name or a girl's name? |
> a girl's name

d What is the English meaning of *elle?* |
> she

2 Do the English pronouns *he* and *she* tell you whether the person referred to is male or female? |
> yes

3 Compare the subjects in each pair of sentences.

> *Guy et Jean sont de Versailles.*   *Sylvie et Jeanne sont de Versailles.*
> *Ils sont de Versailles.*   *Elles sont de Versailles.*

a What is the English meaning of *ils?* |
> they

b What is the English meaning of *elles?* |
> they

4 Does the English pronoun *they* tell you whether the people referred to are male or female? |
> no

5 French has two equivalents for *they.* Do *ils* and *elles* tell you whether the people referred to are male or female? |
> yes

6 Now look at this pair of sentences.

> *Georges et Marie sont en retard.*   *Ils sont en retard.*

a What is the meaning of *ils* in this situation? |
> they

b In this case, does *ils* refer to two males or to a male and a female? |
> a male and a female (*Ils* can refer to males only, or to a mixed group of males *and* females.)

c Suppose you're waiting for some people, and a friend says **Ils sont en retard aujourd'hui.** Does the word *ils* give you enough information to tell if there are females among that group? |
> no (You would need to hear the names of the people, or be able to see them.)

7 Write the subject pronoun—*il, elle, ils,* or *elles*—that would replace the following names.

a Madame Chenaud  |
elle

b Jean Dupont |
il

c Béatrice et Florence  |
elles

d Guy, Henri et Nathalie  |
ils

e Monsieur Fleury  |
il

f Jeanne, Sylvie, Suzanne et Laurent  |
ils

2 *The present tense of* être

The verb *être* (to be) is one of the most-used verbs in the French language. It would be difficult for two French speakers to carry on a conversation for very long without one of them having to use a form of *être.* In this section of the Preparation you'll practice using *être* in the present tense. The term *present tense* refers to *present time,* in contrast to future or past time.

Here is a chart showing the subject pronouns with the matching present-tense forms of *être.* Use the chart to help you do frames 1 and 2 below. Check your spelling carefully.

je	suis
tu	es
il/elle	est
ils/elles	sont
nous	sommes
vous	êtes

1 Write the subject pronouns with the matching form of *être*. With some verb forms, more than one subject pronoun can be used. Look at the model, and then begin with **a.**

Modèle: est |

il est, elle est

a êtes |

vous êtes (Remember the accent circonflexe over the first e.)

b est |

il est, elle est

c sommes |

nous sommes

d es |

tu es

e sont |

ils sont, elles sont

f suis |

je suis (Unlike English I, je is not capitalized unless it is the first word in a sentence.)

2 Write the English equivalents of each of the following sentences.

a Nous sommes d'Ivry. |

We're from Ivry.

b Vous êtes monsieur Chardin? |

You're Mr. Chardin? / Are you Mr. Chardin?

c Tu es très en retard! |

You're very late!

d Je suis très pressé! |

I'm in a big hurry!

Groupe de lycéens

3 For this frame, the answers are given in the answer key at the end of the book, starting on p. 503. Write all your answers before you check them against the key. This kind of exercise gives you a chance to practice French without seeing the answer immediately.

Write complete sentences to say where the people below come from, or whether they are late or in a hurry. Use the appropriate form of *être*.

Modèle: Pierre / pressé aujourd'hui. |
Pierre est pressé aujourd'hui.

a Je / de Chicago.
b Nous / d'Ivry.
c Tu / très en retard!

d Jeanne et Paul Dupont / d'Ivry.
e Vous / monsieur Chardin?
f Gérard / très pressé!

3 *Practice with* un *and* une

1 The singular indefinite markers in French are *un* and *une.*
 a Which marker goes with a masculine noun, like *livre?* |
  un
 b Which marker goes with a feminine noun, like *cassette?* |
  une
2 What are the English meanings for *un* and *une?* |
  a or an
3 Here are the classroom items you have been learning to identify.

affiche	*cassette*	*feuille de papier*	*règle*
bande	*crayon*	*gomme*	*stylo à bille*
cahier	*disque*	*livre*	*transistor*
caméra	*écran*	*morceau de craie*	

Identify each picture you see below by writing the correct indefinite marker and noun. If you do not remember which noun is masculine and which noun is feminine, look at the Vocabulary on p. 19 before proceeding. Answers are in the answer key.

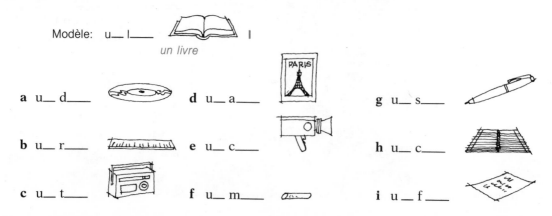

Modèle: u_ l___
un livre

a u_ d___

b u_ r___

c u_ t___

d u_ a___

e u_ c___

f u_ m___

g u_ s___

h u_ c___

i u_ f___

4 Write the English meaning of each phrase below.

a un cahier |

a notebook

b une bande |

a tape recording (a reel of tape)

c une cassette |

a cassette recording

d une feuille de papier |

a sheet of paper

e un écran |

a screen

f une gomme |

an eraser

CHECK-UP

From now on, many Preparations will include a short check-up section that will test your ability to answer questions using new structures and vocabulary. No answers will be given in the book for check-up sections. Your teacher will collect your answers as part of your homework, and may ask you to do the questions again in class. If you have worked with each part in the Preparation properly, frame by frame, you should have no difficulty in answering the questions.

Part 1

1 Which of these subject pronouns refers to a mixed group of males and females: *ils* or *elles?*
2 Write these names and the subject pronouns that would replace them: *Michel; Sylvie et Jacqueline.*

Part 2

Write these forms of *être* with their subject pronouns: *sommes, sont.*

Part 3

Write these nouns with their indefinite markers: *caméra, écran.*

VOCABULARY

une affiche poster
une bande tape recording
un cahier notebook
une caméra movie camera
une cassette cassette recording
un crayon pencil
un disque record
un écran screen

une feuille de papier piece of paper
une gomme eraser
un livre book
un morceau de craie piece of chalk
une règle ruler
un stylo à bille ballpoint pen
un transistor transistor radio

QU'EST-CE QUE C'EST? What is it?
un cadeau present, gift
pour moi for me
mais oui! well, yes! of course!
bien sûr of course, certainly
gentil nice

1 *Practice with* c'est *and* ce n'est pas

1 The expression *c'est* can be used with a name to help identify people, and with an indefinite marker and a noun to help identify things. Write the English equivalents of these two sentences: ***C'est Paul. C'est un transistor.*** |

It's/This is/That's Paul.

It's/This is/That's a transistor radio.

2 In class you have heard the questions ***Qui est-ce?*** and ***Qu'est-ce que c'est?***

a Which question means *Who is it?* |

Qui est-ce? (Remember to put the hyphen in *est-ce*.)

b Write the French for *What is it?* |

Qu'est-ce que c'est? (It's a tricky phrase, so check your spelling.)

3 To answer the questions below, write sentences with *c'est* + the name of the person or thing in parentheses. Use an indefinite marker—*un* or *une*—when appropriate.

Modèle: Qui est-ce? (Jean) |

C'est Jean.

a Qu'est-ce que c'est? (cassette) |

C'est une cassette.

b Qui est-ce? (Brigitte) |

C'est Brigitte.

c Qu'est-ce que c'est? (crayon) |

C'est un crayon.

d Qui est-ce? (Charles) |

C'est Charles.

4 In class you heard an exchange like this:

    –C'est Paul?

    –Non, ce n'est pas Paul. C'est David.

a Write the English meaning of ***Non, ce n'est pas Paul.*** |

No, it isn't Paul. / No, it's not Paul.

b In *ce n'est pas,* the French equivalent of *not* has two parts: *n'* and ____. |

pas

c In a negative sentence, the expression *c'est* becomes ____. |

ce n'est pas

5 Rewrite the following sentences in the negative.

a C'est Sylvie. |

Ce n'est pas Sylvie.

b C'est un tableau. |

Ce n'est pas un tableau.

c C'est Mlle Chenaud. |

Ce n'est pas Mlle Chenaud.

6 Answer each question below with **ce n'est pas** and tell what the pictured item is.

Modèle: C'est une règle? |

Non, ce n'est pas une règle, c'est un disque.

a C'est un transistor, n'est-ce pas? |

Non, ce n'est pas un transistor, c'est une caméra.

b C'est une chaise? |

Non, ce n'est pas une chaise, c'est une table.

c C'est une Peugeot, n'est-ce pas? |

Non, ce n'est pas une Peugeot, c'est une Renault.

d C'est une feuille de papier? |

Non, ce n'est pas une feuille de papier, c'est un morceau de craie.

Un lycéen français

2 Pre-quiz practice: indefinite markers

In your next class, you will have a written quiz on indefinite markers. This part of the Preparation will help you get ready for it.

Here are four of the nouns you learned recently: ***un bureau, un tableau, une chaise, une table.*** Be sure you know what they mean and how to spell them, as they will be part of the quiz.

Your teacher will hold up a flash card, and you will write a sentence to identify the object. For example:

You see: You write: ***C'est une chaise.***

Now write sentences to go with the following pictures. If you can't remember the names or the spelling of some words, study the Vocabulary on p. 19 and below. Check your answers in the answer key.

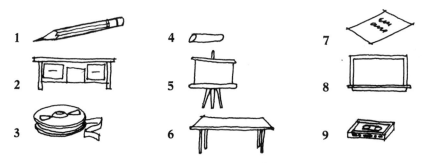

1

2

3

4

5

6

7

8

9

CHECK-UP
Part 1

1 What is the English meaning of *C'est Jeanne?*
2 Write the French equivalent of *It's a record.*
3 Write these sentences in the negative: *C'est un cahier. C'est monsieur Arnaud.*

VOCABULARY

une boîte   box
un bureau   desk
une chaise   chair
une étagère   open bookcase or shelf
une fenêtre   window
une porte   door
une table   student's desk; table
un tableau   chalkboard
derrière   behind, in back of
devant   before, in front of
entre   between

PREPARATION 6

1 More about subject pronouns

In any conversation, there is a speaker, a person spoken to, and often a person or thing spoken about. Because of this, it's often necessary to use a different subject pronoun and matching verb form in response to a question. In this part of the Preparation, you'll practice shifting pronouns and their verb forms in both English and French.

1 Read the following conversational exchanges, and then answer the questions about the use of subject pronouns in English.

John: Are you early?　　　　Mary (with Jack): Are we late?
Susan: Yes, I am.　　　　　　Alex: Yes, you are.

a John uses the pronoun *you* in his question. In her reply, Susan uses the pronoun ____.

b Mary uses the pronoun *we* in her question. In his reply, Alex uses the pronoun ____.

you (In English, speakers automatically shift pronouns and verb forms when they respond to a question. You must practice shifting pronouns and verb forms in French, too, until the procedure becomes automatic.)

2 If the conversation is about a third person or thing, what happens to the subject pronouns and matching verb forms? Read the following exchange between George and Marlene, who are talking about a new boy in school.

George: Is he in our class?
Marlene: Yes, he is.

Does Marlene use a different pronoun and verb form in her reply?

no (When the subject is *he, she,* or *it,* the same subject pronoun and matching verb forms are used in the question and answer.)

3 The chart below compares French and English subject pronouns. Notice which pronouns identify the person(s) speaking, the person(s) spoken to, or the person(s) or thing(s) spoken about.

	SINGULAR		PLURAL	
PERSON SPEAKING	je	I	nous	we
PERSON SPOKEN TO	tu/vous	you	vous	you
PERSON SPOKEN ABOUT	il/elle	he/she/it	ils/elles	they

4 Identify the French subject pronouns below as the person speaking, the person spoken to, or the person or thing spoken about.

a Je suis en retard.

person speaking

b Tu es gentil. |

person spoken to

c Il est d'Ivry? |

person spoken about

d La gomme? Elle est sur le bureau. |

thing spoken about

5 Write the English meaning of *La gomme? Elle est sur le bureau.* |

The eraser? It's on the desk. (When *il* or *elle* refers to a thing, the English equivalent is *it*.)

6 Write the complete answer to the following question: *Nous sommes en retard?* Begin your answer with *Oui...* |

Oui, vous êtes en retard.

7 The questions below ask if someone is late. Choose the correct answers and write them on your worksheet. Say the English equivalents of your answers.

Modèle: Je suis en retard, Irène?   —Oui, je suis en retard.
                                      —Oui, tu es en retard. |

Oui, tu es en retard. (Yes, you're late.)

a Marc et Suzanne, vous êtes en retard?   —Oui, nous sommes en retard.
                                                —Oui, vous êtes en retard. |

Oui, nous sommes en retard. (Yes, we're late.)

b Je suis en retard, Mme Longe?   —Oui, je suis en retard.
                                        —Oui, vous êtes en retard. |

Oui, vous êtes en retard. (Yes, you're late.)

c Nous sommes en retard, Sophie?   —Oui, je suis en retard.
                                         —Oui, vous êtes en retard. |

Oui, vous êtes en retard. (Yes, you're late.)

2 Pre-quiz practice: present tense of être

1 In your next class you will have a quiz in which you are to complete sentences with the correct forms of *être*. To prepare for it, write the correct form of *être* (*suis, es, est, sont, sommes, êtes*) for the following sentences. Check your answers in the answer key.

a Marie ____ une fille.
b Nous ____ derrière Marc.
c Tu ____ pressé?
d Robert et Marie ____ de New York.
e Je ____ Stéphanie Romain.
f Vous ____ en retard!

2 If you made any mistakes, go back to Preparation 4, Part 2, and spend a few minutes reviewing the forms of *être*. Then complete these sentences with the correct form of *être*. Answers are in the answer key.

a Je ____ de Paris.
b Vous ____ devant le tableau.
c Où ____ le crayon d'Alice?
d Nous ____ en retard aujourd'hui.
e La bande et le livre ____ là.
f Tu ____ de Chicago?

VOCABULARY

un élève	pupil (male)	*une femme*	woman
une élève	pupil (female)	*une fille*	girl
un enfant	child (male)	*un garçon*	boy
une enfant	child (female)	*un homme*	man

NOTE

Some famous French people

America has been influenced by French-speaking people since it was a young country. How many of the following people have you already heard of?

The explorers **Marquette** and **Joliet** mapped the Mississippi River in the 1670's.

Pierre L'Enfant served in the Revolutionary Army. In 1791, he designed Washington, D.C., which has parks and wide boulevards like those in Europe.

The emperor **Napoléon Bonaparte** sold the Louisiana Territory to the U.S. in the early 1800's, in order to have money to fight the British.

As a naturalized American citizen, **John James Audubon** observed and painted American birds and mammals from about 1810 to 1840.

The sculptor **Frédéric-Auguste Bertholdi** made the Statue of Liberty, which the French government presented as a gift to the United States in 1884.

The physicists **Marie** and **Pierre Curie** opened the atomic age by isolating the element radium in 1902.

Writer and philosopher **Simone de Beauvoir** has influenced American thought on the changing roles of women in society.

Oceanographer **Jacques Cousteau** has added much to our understanding of the oceans and their importance to human life.

1 *The definite markers* le, la, l'

1 The first noun marker you learned was the indefinite marker. It is often used to identify an item. The *definite marker* is often used to talk about an item that has already been identified or mentioned.

    a Compare the sentences below. Which sentence talks about a previously mentioned item?

        C'est un livre d'histoire.   *C'est le livre de M. Rochemont.* |

            C'est le livre de M. Rochemont.

    b Write the English meaning of ***C'est le livre de M. Rochemont.*** |

            It's Mr. Rochemont's book.

2 Compare the indefinite markers with the definite markers in these noun phrases.

        ***un** garçon,* **le** *garçon*   ***une** fille,* **la** *fille*

    a Which definite marker goes with ***garçon: le*** or ***la?*** |

            le (*Le* is used with a masculine singular noun.)

    b Does ***la*** go with a masculine singular noun or with a feminine singular noun? |

            a feminine singular noun

3 The singular definite marker has three forms in French: ***le, la,*** and ***l'.*** Compare the definite markers in these noun phrases.

        le cadeau   *la table*   *l'écran*   *l'affiche*

    a Is the marker ***l'*** used before a noun that begins with a vowel or a consonant? |

            a vowel (The dropping of the vowels *e* in *le* and *a* in *la* is a contraction. The French name for it is *élision*. This occurs in a few other one-syllable words.)

    b Can you tell by looking at the marker ***l'*** if the noun is masculine or feminine? |

            no (*L'* goes with any masculine or feminine singular noun that begins with a vowel sound.)

4 The letter ***h*** is always silent in French. When someone says the French word ***homme,*** the first sound you hear is a vowel sound. Is the marker ***le*** or ***l'*** used with ***homme?*** |

            l'

5 Here are some nouns with indefinite markers. Rewrite the nouns with the correct definite marker: ***le, la,*** or ***l'.***

    a une table |

            la table

    b un homme |

            l'homme

c un morceau de craie |

le morceau de craie

d une affiche |

l'affiche

e un cadeau |

le cadeau

2 Expressing possession with de + a name

1 In English we often express ownership with this pattern: name + *'s* + item owned, as in *This is Paul's workbook.* Look at the equivalent sentence in French: ***C'est le cahier de Paul.***

  a Which words in the French sentence represent the item owned? |

le cahier

  b Which word represents the owner? |

Paul

  c Which word is used to connect the item owned with the name of the owner? |

de (The preposition de is often used to connect one noun with another.)

2 Compare these two sentences to see what happens to *de* when it precedes a vowel sound.

   C'est la cassette de Pierre.   *C'est la cassette d'Alice.*

The preposition *de* becomes ____. |

d' (This dropping of e before a vowel is another example of élision.)

3 Imagine that you have borrowed some things, and now it's time to return them. Write sentences like the one in the model to tell who owns each item.

   Modèle: un écran / Charles |

C'est l'écran de Charles.

  a une règle / Marie |

C'est la règle de Marie.

  b un transistor / Georges |

C'est le transistor de Georges.

  c une gomme / Edouard |

C'est la gomme d'Edouard. (Did you remember to write d'?)

  d une caméra / M. Laval |

C'est la caméra de M. Laval.

4 Give the French equivalents for the following sentences. Answers are in the answer key.

  a It's Alain's camera.
  b It's Valérie's transistor radio.
  c It's Alice's poster.

✳

Creoles and Acadians in Louisiana

The French originally used the term **créole** to distinguish between French settlers in the New World and French people in France. In the strictest sense, the term was applied to the descendants of French settlers in the West Indies and the southern United States (especially Louisiana).

The French used the term **Acadien** (Acadian) to refer to French settlers in Canada. The **Acadiens** were driven out of Canada by the British in 1755 and sought refuge, for the most part, in Louisiana. The American name **Cajun** is a modified form of the word **Acadien.**

Today there are about 400,000 French-speaking people in Louisiana, many of them descendants of **Créoles** or **Acadiens,** and French is officially the second language of the state.

Jeune fille acadienne

3 *Using* ne...pas *with* être

You have learned that the French equivalent for *not* is **ne...pas,** as in *Je ne suis pas pressé,* or *n'...pas,* as in *Ce n'est pas une table.* This chart shows how the negative expression **ne...pas** combines with the present-tense forms of *être.*

je	ne	suis	pas
tu	n'	es	pas
il/elle	n'	est	pas
ils/elles	ne	sont	pas
nous	ne	sommes	pas
vous	n'	êtes	pas

1 *N'* is used before three of the verb forms. Which ones are they? �

  es, est, êtes (Ne becomes *n'* before a verb form beginning with a vowel.)

2 Rewrite each of these sentences in the negative, and write the English equivalent.

  a M. Rimbaud est de Paris. ▯

  M. Rimbaud n'est pas de Paris. Mr. Rimbaud isn't from Paris.

  b Vous êtes en retard. ▯

  Vous n'êtes pas en retard. You're not late.

  c Paul et Jean sont sous la table. ▯

  Paul et Jean ne sont pas sous la table. Paul and John aren't under the table.

  d Tu es gentil. ▯

  Tu n'es pas gentil. You're not nice.

3 Answer the following questions in the negative. Begin your answers with *Non.* Remember to change the subject pronoun and verb form when necessary.

  a Mlle Boivin, vous êtes de Versailles? (Non...) ▯

  Non, je ne suis pas de Versailles.

b Anne et Marie, vous êtes sous le bureau? (Non...) |

Non, nous ne sommes pas sous le bureau.

c C'est un cadeau? (Non...) |

Non, ce n'est pas un cadeau.

4 Write the French for the following sentences. The answers are in the answer key.

a We're not late.

b I'm not Sylvie Lemaître.

c Paul and Jean are not from Paris.

d The present is not on the table.

4 Basic intonation patterns

1 Intonation is the rise and fall of the voice in speaking. In both English and French, there are two basic intonation patterns for sentences: rising and falling. In rising intonation, your voice goes up at the end of a sentence. In falling intonation, your voice goes down. Say the following sentences aloud.

> Is it a present?   It's a present.

a Did your voice rise or fall at the end of the question? |

rise

b Did your voice rise or fall at the end of the statement? |

fall

2 The intonation pattern of a sentence helps to determine its meaning. For example, say the sentence *I'm going home* three times. The first time, say it as if you were very happy. Then say it as if you were very angry. Finally, say it as if you were very tired. Did you use the same intonation each time? |

no (Intonation will vary with the meaning you wish to convey.)

3 Here is a question with rising intonation in French: ***Vous êtes de Chicago?*** Would a one-word answer of ***oui*** or ***non*** make sense with this question? |

yes (It is called a *oui-non* question.)

4 Here is a question that has falling intonation in French: ***Où est Chicago?*** Would a one-word answer of ***oui*** or ***non*** make sense with this question? |

no (It asks for additional information. It is called an information question.)

5 In addition to information questions, there are two other kinds of sentences in French that have falling intonation: statements and exclamations. Identify each of the following sentences as a statement or an exclamation.

a Je m'appelle Jean Dupont. |

statement

b Bien sûr! |

exclamation

6 The sentences below are similar to those in the dialogues you have learned in class. Read each sentence aloud. Then say what kind of sentence each is (*oui-non* question, information question, statement, or exclamation). Also say whether the intonation would be rising or falling. You need not write the answers.

        Modèle: Tu es pressé? ⎮

                  oui-non question; rising intonation

a C'est un cadeau pour moi? ⎮

                  oui-non question; rising intonation

b Qu'est-ce que c'est? ⎮

             information question; falling intonation

c Zut, zut et zut! ⎮

             exclamation; falling intonation

d Qui est-ce? ⎮

             information question; falling intonation

e C'est Jean-Paul. ⎮

             statement; falling intonation

CHECK-UP **Part 1**	Replace each indefinite marker with the correct definite marker: *un écran, une caméra, un garçon.*
Part 2	**1** Write the French equivalent of *It's Jeanne's book.* **2** Write in French *It's Anne's book.*
Part 3	Change the following sentences to the negative: *Pascal et Pauline sont de Grenoble.* *Elle est en retard.*
VOCABULARY	*un singe* monkey *un tiroir* drawer *dans* in *sous* under *sur* on *de* of OÙ EST LE DISQUE? Where is the record? *Qu'est-ce qu'il y a?* What's the matter? *Qu'est-ce que tu cherches?* What are you looking for? *je ne sais pas* I don't know *pas possible!* you're kidding! *la télévision* television *là* there *où* where *ah, ça alors!* (shows annoyance or surprise) oh, good grief! *zut!* darn it! *que tu es bête!* boy, are you stupid!

Canada... **Terre des Hommes**

Grandeur et majesté

Charme et simplicité, jeunesse et

Joie de vivre

Le vieux monde

au Nouveau Monde

1 Verb forms

Verbs are an important part of a sentence. Some verbs express an action (like *to run* or *to swim*); some verbs express a state (like *to be* or *to rest*); some verbs express a process (like *to become* or *to think*). In this part of the Preparation, you'll learn a little about the present tense of action verbs in English, so that you can compare it with the present tense of action verbs in French.

1 a In the sentence *The children run,* which word tells who runs? |

children (*Children* is the subject of the sentence. The subject performs the action of the verb.)

b Which word tells what the subject does? |

run (*Run* is a verb. It tells what the action is.)

2 In *The children run,* does *children* refer to one person or to more than one? |

more than one (*Children* is a plural subject.)

3 Look at the sentences below to see what happens to the verb form when the subject changes from plural to singular.

The children run.   The child runs.

Is the verb form that goes with *children* the same as the verb form that goes with *child*? |

no (The form of the verb changes when the plural subject changes to the singular.)

4 Most verb forms are composed of two basic parts: a stem and an ending. In the present-tense form *runs,* the stem is *run* and the ending is *-s.* Which part tells you what the action is—the stem or the ending? |

the stem (run)

5 Compare *The child runs* with *The children run.* Does the *-s* ending of *runs* give you information about whether the subject is singular or plural? |

yes (The verb ending *-s* indicates that the subject is singular.)

2 The present tense of chercher

Most French verb forms, like English verb forms, are composed of a stem and an ending. Look at the chart of the present tense of **chercher** (*to look for*) to see which ending matches each subject.

je	cherch e
tu	cherch es
il/elle	cherch e
ils/elles	cherch ent
nous	cherch ons
vous	cherch ez

1 In French, a verb form that has one sound in speech may have several written forms. The *je-, tu-, il/elle-* and *ils/elles-* forms of ***chercher*** are all pronounced the same way. Their present-tense endings are silent. You just hear the stem ***cherch-***.

Write the endings that complete each written form of ***chercher*** below.

a tu cherch ____ ▌
-es

b Robert cherch ____ ▌
-e

c je cherch ____ ▌
-e

d Marie et Irène cherch ____ ▌
-ent

e Irène, Jean et Paul cherch ____ ▌
-ent

f Mlle Chenaud cherch ____ ▌
-e

2 The present-tense ***nous-*** and ***vous-***endings are heard in speech. Write the endings for those two forms of ***chercher.*** ▌
-ons, -ez

3 The verb ***chercher*** has three spoken forms in the present tense. How many written forms does it have? ▌
five (Note that the je- and il/elle-forms have the same endings.)

4 Write the subject and the matching form of ***chercher*** for each sentence.

Modèle: Je ____ la gomme de Marie. ▌
Je cherche

a Tu ____ un crayon? ▌
Tu cherches

b Vous ____ Philippe Verlut? ▌
Vous cherchez

c Lisette ____ un stylo. ▌
Lisette cherche

d Nous ____ l'écran. ▌
Nous cherchons

e Georges et Paul ____ le cahier de Paul. ▌
Georges et Paul cherchent

5 Write the English equivalents of these sentences.

a Tu cherches un crayon? ▌
Are you looking for a pencil?

b Guy et Paul cherchent le cahier de Paul. ▌
Guy and Paul are looking for Paul's notebook.

c Je cherche M. Blondin. ▌
I'm looking for Mr. Blondin.

3 *Practice with* ne...pas, être, *and* chercher

1 You know that *ne...pas* is used to make a sentence negative.
   a Write the English equivalent of *Je ne suis pas en retard.* |
   I'm not late.

   b When *ne* precedes a verb that begins with a vowel, *ne* changes
   form. Complete this sentence: *Tu ___ es pas de Paris.* |
   n'

2 a Do the present-tense forms of *chercher* begin with a vowel or a
   consonant? |
   consonant

   b Which negative expression is used with verb forms that begin with
   a consonant (like *cherche*): *n'...pas* or *ne...pas?* |
   ne...pas

   c How would you rewrite this sentence in the negative? *Je cherche le
disque de Paul.* |
   Je ne cherche pas le disque de Paul.

3 Rewrite these sentences in the negative.
   a Elles cherchent le transistor. |
   Elles ne cherchent pas le transistor.

   b Vous cherchez M. Dupont. |
   Vous ne cherchez pas M. Dupont.

4 Write a negative answer to each question below. Remember that you
may have to use a different subject and verb form in your answer.
   a Eric, vous êtes pressé? |
   Non, je ne suis pas pressé.

   b Anne cherche le stylo de Mme Chenaud? |
   Non, Anne ne cherche pas le stylo de Mme Chenaud.

   c Nous sommes entre Paul et Sara? (Reply with *vous.*) |
   Non, vous n'êtes pas entre Paul et Sara.

5 Write a negative answer to each question. Then check your answers
with the answer key.
   a Georges et Catherine, vous cherchez l'écran?
   b Robert est devant le tableau?
   c Le crayon et la feuille de papier sont sur le bureau?

4 Pre-quiz practice: definite markers

In the next class, you will have a short quiz on the definite markers *le, la,*
and *l'.* Your teacher will say the name of a thing or a person. You are to
write the correct definite marker.

1 You hear the word for this object: You write the
marker ____.

le

2 Write the correct marker for each of the following objects or people.
Answers are in the answer key.

a

b

c

d

e

f

g

h

i

j

k

l

CHECK-UP

Part 1

1 What are the two basic parts of most verbs?
2 Which part of a verb tells you what the action is?

Part 2

1 Which two endings of the verb *chercher* are the only endings that are
pronounced in speech?
2 Complete with the correct form of *chercher:*
    a Il ____ une feuille de papier.   **b** Tu ____ un stylo?

Part 3

Answer the following questions in the negative:
1 Jean-Claude et Laure cherchent le livre de Madame Robert?
2 Tu cherches la cassette de Suzanne?

VOCABULARY

américain, –e American
chercher to look for
français, –e French
grand, –e large, tall
petit, –e small, short

1 *Pre-quiz practice:* chercher

In your next class you will have a written quiz on the forms of *chercher.* In the quiz, you will see the present-tense forms of *chercher* on the board or on your answer sheet. You will hear a subject, and you are to write the form of *chercher* that matches the subject. For instance, when you hear *je,* you will be expected to write *cherche.*

Copy each of the following subjects, and write the form of *chercher* that matches it. Answers are in the answer key.

cherchons   cherchent   cherche   cherchez   cherches

1 je   **5** Marie et Hélène
2 André   **6** Marc
3 M. et Mme Dupont   **7** tu
4 vous   **8** nous

2 *Masculine and feminine forms of adjectives*

This part of Preparation 9 will help you learn how to describe someone or something in French. To do this, you need to learn how adjectives are used, both in English and French.

1 An adjective is a word that describes a noun (a person, a place, or a thing). An adjective may precede the noun it describes or follow it. What are the adjectives in the sentences below?

Mary is tall.   New York is large.   The small boy cried. |
tall, large, small

2 Look at the adjectives in each pair of sentences, then answer the question that follows.

John is nice.   The boy is absent.
Mary is nice.   The girl is absent.

In English, does an adjective change form to match the gender of the noun it describes? |
no

3 Most French adjectives have two different forms in the singular—a masculine form and a feminine form. Compare the adjectives in these two sentences.

Le garçon est petit.   La fille est petite.

a Which form goes with the masculine noun: *petit* or *petite?* |
petit

b Which form matches the feminine noun: *petit* or *petite?* |
petite

4 The written feminine form of many French adjectives is the masculine form + *e: petit* + *e* = *petite.* Write the feminine forms of the following adjectives: *absent, grand, américain.* |

> *absente, grande, américaine.* (Be sure to use a small letter *a* instead of a capital letter *A* for the adjective *américain,* and to write the *accent aigu* on the first *é.*)

5 The spoken feminine form of most French adjectives ends in a consonant sound. For example, *petite* ends in the consonant sound /t/. Say aloud each pair of adjectives below. Then copy the feminine form of the adjective and underline the pronounced consonant.

> Modèle: présent, présente |
>> *présen<u>t</u>e*

a absent, absente |
> *absen<u>t</u>e*

b française, français |
> *françai<u>s</u>e* (Remember to write the *cédille* under the ç.)

c américaine, américain |
> *américai<u>n</u>e*

6 Sometimes the written feminine form doubles a consonant before the final *e.* For example, *gentil* becomes *gentille.* Complete the following sentence with the feminine form of *gentil. Marie est très* ____. |
> *gentille*

7 With some adjectives, both the masculine and feminine written forms end in *e.* They are pronounced the same. Complete this sentence: *Paul est bête, et Marie est* ____ *aussi.* |
> *bête*

8 A masculine adjective that ends in *é* adds an *e* in the written feminine form, but there is no change in the spoken form. Complete each sentence with the correct form of *pressé.*

a Philippe n'est pas ____ aujourd'hui. |
> *pressé*

b Mme Chenaud est très ____ aujourd'hui. |
> *pressée*

9 Describe the people below in complete sentences, using the cues. Be sure to make all necessary changes. For example: change *être* to the form that matches the subject; use the correct form of *ne...pas* with the verb; use the form of the adjective that matches the subject in gender. If you are unsure about the feminine form of an adjective, refer to frames 4, 6, 7, and 8. Answers are in the answer key.

> Modèles: Véronique / être / gentil |
>> *Véronique est gentille.*
>
>> Pierre / ne...pas / être / absent |
>> *Pierre n'est pas absent.*

a Mlle Bonnard / être / pressé / aujourd'hui

b Philippe / être / très / grand

c Catherine / ne...pas / être / très / gentil

d Sheila / ne...pas / être / français.

NOTE *Comparing French and American schools*

The French school system is divided into two cycles: **le cycle élémentaire** (elementary school, ages 6–10 approximately) and **le cycle secondaire** (secondary school, ages 11–17 approximately).

The French do not number the grades as we do. For example, an eleven-year-old begins the **cycle secondaire** in **sixième** (sixth grade). Then there is a "countdown" to **troisième** (ninth grade), **seconde** (tenth grade), **première** (eleventh grade), and **terminale** (final year).

In the United States, schools serve as the center for many extracurricular activities, such as clubs and sports. The French think of their schools as academic centers only. If you visited a French **lycée** (high school), you would probably find the relationship between teacher and students somewhat formal and reserved. In France, the teacher's main purpose is to instruct and, if necessary, to discipline. Students rarely approach their instructors with personal problems, as they might in the United States.

Course load

The high-school program in France is rigorous; French students take a minimum of eight courses a year, most of which are required. For example, an eleventh-grader **(élève de première)** might take French literature, physics, chemistry, history, geography, two foreign languages, and gym. The student is also faced with the pressure of knowing that failing one course may mean repeating all the courses for that year. Thus, the time spent in class and on homework leaves very little opportunity for extracurricular activities.

3 Writing practice

In class you have been role-playing four different dialogues. This part of the Preparation gives you practice writing words from two of them.

Use the initial letters and the number of blanks to help you recall the words missing from the dialogues *Qu'est-ce que c'est?* and *Où est le disque?* Write the words on your worksheet and do your best to spell them correctly. Then check your spelling with the dialogues printed on p. 56.

Qu'est-ce que c'est?

MARTINE	Qu'est-ce que c'est?
PIERRE	C'est u _ c _ _ _ _ _ _.
MARTINE	Pour m _ _?
PIERRE	Mais oui, b _ _ _ s _ _!
MARTINE	Oh, c'est une cassette! Tu es g _ _ _ _ _ _! M _ _ _ _ _!

Où est le disque?

CHARLES	Z _ _ _, zut e _ zut!
IRÈNE	Qu'est-ce qu'il y a? Q _ '_ _ _ _-_ _ _ _ _ tu cherches?
CHARLES	Le disque de Paul. Je ne sais pas o _ il est.
IRÈNE	Que tu es b _ _ _ _! Il est là, sur la t _ _ _ _ _ _ _ _ _ _.
CHARLES	Pas p _ _ _ _ _ _ _ _! Ah, ça a _ _ _ _!

CHECK-UP
Part 2

Write complete sentences, using the cues given. Remember to make all necessary changes.

1 Marc/être/petit
2 Julie/être/très/pressé
3 Madame Benêt/ne...pas/être/gentil

VOCABULARY

gentille (f.) nice

1 Writing practice

1 Below are some of the words or expressions you have learned that require an additional mark in writing: **un accent grave** (as in **algèbre**), **un accent aigu** (as in **écran**), **un accent circonflexe** (as in **être**), and **une cédille** (as in **français**).

Write each word or expression with the correct accents or marks. Answers are in the answer key.

a Accent aigu: camera, present, presse, television
b Cédille: francais, garcon, ca alors!, ca va?
c Accent aigu: mathematiques, geographie, geometrie, americaine
d Accent circonflexe: bien sur!, vous etes, bete
e Accent grave: ou est...?, regle, tres bien, a demain
f Accents aigu et grave: eleve

2 In your next class your teacher will dictate some sentences for you to write. This is to give you practice in associating the sound of words with the way they are written.

Here are sentences similar to the ones you will hear. Some of the letters are missing. Try to decode each sentence and figure out which letters belong in the blanks. Then write the complete sentence. Answers are in the answer key.

a C'es_ l_ st_lo d_ Ph_lip___.
b C_ n'___t pa_ un_ gom___.
c J_ ch_rch_ _'af_iche d_ M_r_e.
d J_ _____ch_ u_ cra_o_.

2 Vocabulary round-up

In a few days you will have a progress test. This part of the Preparation will help you begin to review vocabulary in sets (nouns, prepositions, etc.). Notice that in the vocabulary lists below, the English is given first, then the French equivalent.

When you review, try the following technique: cover the English, look at the French, and see if you can give the English meaning. Then do the reverse: cover the French, look at the English, and try to give the French word or expression. Write the French words you don't know on a separate worksheet. Save it for use in Preparation 12.

NOUNS

monkey	*un singe*
child	*un/une enfant*
desk	*un bureau*
girl	*une fille*
drawer	*un tiroir*
woman	*une femme*
man	*un homme*
chalkboard	*un tableau*
table	*une table*
chair	*une chaise*
boy	*un garçon*
student	*un/une élève*

PREPOSITIONS

in front of	*devant*
under	*sous*
behind	*derrière*
on	*sur*
between	*entre*
in	*dans*

EXPRESSIONS

you're kidding!	*pas possible*
where is . . . ?	*où est...?*
oh, good grief!	*ah ça alors!*
in my opinion	*à mon avis*
my name is . . .	*je m'appelle...*

HIGHWAY Speed | **km/h**

 Metric Commission Canada   Commission du système métrique Canada

3 Practice with **ne...pas** *and adjectives*

1 Below are pictures of some people. Say that each has the first characteristic indicated in parentheses, but not the second one. Remember to use the correct masculine or feminine form of each adjective.

Modèle: Bob (américain / français) |
Bob est américain. Il n'est pas français.

a Irène (grand / petit) |
Irène est grande. Elle n'est pas petite.

b André (riche / pauvre) |
André est riche. Il n'est pas pauvre.

c Georges (présent / absent) |
Georges est présent. Il n'est pas absent.

d Stéphanie (absent / présent) |
Stéphanie est absente. Elle n'est pas présente.

2 Write the French equivalent of each sentence, using the correct form of *gentil, pressé,* or *bête.*

a Catherine isn't nice. |
Catherine n'est pas gentille.

b Marie-France isn't in a hurry. |
Marie-France n'est pas pressée.

c Max isn't dumb. |
Max n'est pas bête.

VOCABULARY   *pauvre* poor
                 riche rich
                 à mon avis in my opinion

1 *Pre-test practice:* être *and* chercher

Remember that in a few days there will be a progress test on the material you have been studying in Phase One. Take a moment now to look back at the Phase Objectives on p. 2 and see how much you have accomplished so far.

Preparations 11, 12, and 13 will help you get ready for the test. If you need help with a particular topic, you can refer to the Summary on p. 52 or go back to the specific Preparations mentioned at the beginning of each part. Now continue with the exercises in this Preparation. All answers are in the answer key.

Subject pronouns were presented in Preparations 2, 3, 4, and 6. The present tense of *être* was presented in Preparations 4 and 7. The present tense of *chercher* was presented in Preparation 8.

1 Write the subject pronoun that correctly completes each sentence below.

a ___ êtes américain?

b ___ suis derrière le bureau.

c ___ es pressé aujourd'hui?

d ___ est américaine.

2 Say what each person below is looking for. Write the correct form of *chercher* on your worksheet.

a Je ___ le cahier d'Hélène.

b Tu ___ la caméra de M. Delmas?

c Vous ___ la cassette de Philippe?

d Marie-Hélène ___ le livre de Pierre.

3 Answer the following questions according to the cues.

a Mlle Gaudin, vous êtes de Versailles?   (Non,...)

b Vous êtes français?   (Non, je...)

c Ils cherchent une bande?   (Oui,...)

d Tu cherches le cahier d'Isabelle?   (Oui,...)

2 *Pre-test practice: markers*

Indefinite markers were presented in Preparation 3. Definite markers were presented in Preparation 8.

1 Identify the missing form of the indefinite marker *un* or *une* on your worksheet.

a C'est ___ femme. Ce n'est pas ___ homme.

b Je cherche ___ cassette.

c Ce n'est pas ___ stylo. C'est ___ crayon.

d Le garçon cherche ___ morceau de craie.

e Nous cherchons ___ cadeau.

f C'est ___ garçon.

2 Write complete sentences, using the words given. Use the appropriate definite markers *le, la,* or *l',* and make all other necessary changes. You can check yourself by asking the following questions: Does the marker match the noun? Does the form of the verb match the subject? Should *ne...pas* or *n'...pas* be used? Does your sentence make sense?

> *Modèle:* affiche / ne...pas / être / dans / tiroir |
> *L'affiche n'est pas dans le tiroir.*

a femme / chercher / enfant
b nous / chercher / livre de Martine
c homme / ne...pas / être / en retard aujourd'hui
d feuille de papier / être / sous / chaise

3 Vocabulary round-up

Here are more words and expressions for you to review in preparation for your progress test. Use the same procedure for review as you did in Preparation 10, p. 42.

ADJECTIVES

big, tall	*grand, -e*
American	*américain, -e*
little, small, short	*petit, -e*
rich	*riche*
stupid, dumb	*bête*
poor	*pauvre*
French	*français, -e*
nice	*gentil, gentille*

EXPRESSIONS

darn it!	*zut!*
who is it?	*qui est-ce?*
thanks; thank you	*merci*
how's it going?	*ça va?*
very well	*très bien*
OK, not bad	*pas mal*
what are you looking for?	*qu'est-ce que tu cherches? (vous cherchez?)*

4 Pre-test practice: être *and adjectives*

Descriptive adjectives were presented in Preparation 9.

1 Describe each person below. Write a complete sentence with the correct form of the adjective in parentheses.

> *Modèle:* (gentil) Marie est ____. |
> *Marie est gentille.*

a (grand) L'homme est ____.
b (français) Anne est ____.
c (pauvre) Monsieur Martelli n'est pas ____.
d (riche) Madame Martelli est ____.

e (petit) La fille est ___ .

f (présent) Elisabeth n'est pas ___ aujourd'hui.

2 Use the cues given to describe each person below in a complete sentence.

> Modèle: L ___ fille / ne...pas / être / américain. **|**
> *La fille n'est pas américaine.*

a Jacques / ne...pas / être / pauvre.   **b** L ___ femme / être / grand.

VOCABULARY   *assez*   somewhat, rather

1 Pre-test practice: possession with de

If you need help with this topic, refer to Preparation 7. (Answers to all pre-test practice sections are in the answer key.)

1 Write a complete sentence to tell who owns the items mentioned.

> Modèle: règle / Georges **|**
> *C'est la règle de Georges.*

a affiche / Martine   **c** enfant / M. Marteau
b disque / Annick   **d** caméra / Bernard

2 Write complete sentences, using the cues given. In each case, you will have to connect a noun and a name by using *de* or *d'*. Make all other necessary additions and changes.

> Modèle: L ___ cassette / André / être / dans l ___ tiroir **|**
> *La cassette d'André est dans le tiroir.*

a où / être / l ___ gomme / Jacques?
b je / chercher / l ___ caméra / M. Teyssier
c tu / ne...pas / chercher / l ___ bande / Mme Legrand?

2 *Pre-test practice:* ne...pas, être, chercher

The negative expression **ne...pas** was presented in Preparations 7, 8, and 10. The present tense of *être* was presented in Preparations 4 and 7. The present tense of *chercher* was presented in Preparation 8.

1 Rewrite the following sentences in the negative form.

> Modèle: Stéphanie est petite. |
> *Stéphanie n'est pas petite.*

a Je suis de Boston.
b Elles cherchent le disque d'Hélène.
c La télévision de M. Moreau est très grande.
d Nous cherchons le transistor.

2 Write an English equivalent for each of the following sentences.

a Elles ne cherchent pas le disque d'Hélène.
b La télévision de M. Moreau n'est pas très grande.

3 Here are some questions to be answered in the negative. Be sure to change the subject pronoun and verb form when necessary.

> Modèle: Je suis en retard, Marie? |
> *Non, tu n'es pas en retard.*

a Paul, tu cherches le disque de Monique?
b Le stylo et la feuille de papier sont sur la table?
c Et vous, Nathalie et Yvonne, vous cherchez M. Legrand?
d Nous sommes en retard? (Answer with *vous.*)

3 *Pre-test practice:* tu *and* vous

If you need help with this section, refer to the Summary or go back to the Preparations. *Tu* and *vous* were presented in Preparations 2 and 3.

Tell whether you would use *tu* or *vous* in the following situations.

1 You are talking to both your parents.
2 You are talking on the phone to your best friend.
3 You are talking to a teller in the savings bank.
4 You are talking to a high-school student you have met at the beach.
5 You are talking to your little sister and her playmate.
6 You are talking to the manager of a supermarket about a job for the summer.
7 You are talking to your neighbor's cat.
8 You are talking to your neighbor, Mme Juillard.
9 You are talking to your neighbor's son Luc, who is your age.
10 You are talking to several people you play soccer with.

4 Pre-test practice: reading comprehension

Read the following sentences and the possible responses. Write the
letter of the logical response on your worksheet.

1 Salut, Philippe!
   a Bonjour, Jean-Paul, ça va?
   b Oui, je suis pressé.
   c Oui, je suis en retard.

2 Qu'est-ce que c'est?
   a C'est Mme Grandet.
   b C'est gentil.
   c C'est le livre de Jacqueline.

3 Où est le crayon d'Yvonne?
   a Il est sur la table.
   b Elle est dans le tiroir.
   c Elle est petite.

4 Je suis de Versailles. Et toi?
   a Je suis Robert.
   b Je suis d'Ivry.
   c C'est pour moi?

5 Vocabulary round-up

Review the words and expressions you missed in earlier round-ups.
Then study the words and expressions below.

NOUNS

tape	une bande
transistor radio	un transistor
television	une télévision
book	un livre
eraser	une gomme
screen	un écran
cassette recording	une cassette
pencil	un crayon
poster	une affiche
gift, present	un cadeau
record	un disque
movie camera	une caméra
ball-point pen	un stylo à bille
piece of paper	une feuille de papier
notebook	un cahier
piece of chalk	un morceau de craie

EXPRESSIONS

yes! (emphatic)	mais oui!
of course!	bien sûr!
for me?	pour moi?
what is it?	qu'est-ce que c'est?
hello	bonjour
good evening	bonsoir
hi!	salut!
today	aujourd'hui
in a hurry	pressé, -e
good-by	au revoir
late	en retard
you too?	toi aussi?
see you tomorrow	à demain
present (in class)	présent, -e
absent	absent, -e
somewhat (somewhat tall)	assez (assez grand)

Getting ready for a test

1 In the next class period, your teacher will give you a progress test to find out how well you use certain language skills. However, the results will not be accurate if you make mistakes because you don't know how to handle the test. This Preparation will give you practice with the kinds of questions in the test. Write your answers on your worksheet and check them with the answer key.

The purpose of the first two parts of the test is to find out how well you understand spoken French. In Part A, you will be tested on your ability to hear the difference between the masculine and feminine singular forms of adjectives. On your answer sheet, you will see two pictures—one male, and one female. You will hear a statement beginning with *vous êtes*. You are to write the letter of the picture that the statement refers to.

a For example, you see the pictures below.

  A   B

You hear: ***Vous êtes américaine.*** Will you write A or B on your answer sheet? (Check the key after finishing the Preparation.)

b You see the two pictures below.

  A   B

You hear: ***Vous êtes grand.*** Will you write A or B?

2 In Part B, you will see three pictures showing an item located in different places. You will hear two statements about the location of the item. You are to write the letter of the picture that corresponds to what you hear.

a For example, you see the pictures below.

  A    B   C

You hear: ***La caméra n'est pas sur le bureau. Elle est sur la télévision.*** Will you write A, B, or C on your answer sheet?

b You see the three pictures below.

 A B  C

You hear: *La chaise n'est pas devant la table. Elle est derrière le bureau.* Will you write A, B, or C on your answer sheet?

3 Part C of the test is designed to find out how well you understand what you read in French. You will see a question on your test sheet. It will be followed by three possible responses. You are to make a check mark in the box beside the logical response to the question. For now, copy the response on your worksheet.

    a Vous êtes français?
        ☐ Non, je suis américain.
        ☐ Oui, ça va bien.
        ☐ Non, je suis petite.
    b Qui est-ce?
        ☐ C'est une affiche.
        ☐ C'est Pierre.
        ☐ Il est sous la chaise.

4 Part D will measure how well you can match subject pronouns with forms of *être*. You will see a verb form. In the blank or blanks before the verb form, you are to write every subject pronoun that goes with that form.

    a ___, ___ est   **b** ___ êtes

5 In Part E, you will be tested on matching the correct forms of the verb *chercher* with the various subjects. You will see a subject pronoun followed by a blank. You are to fill in the blank space with the correct form of *chercher*.

    a tu ___   **b** Monique et Pierre ___

6 Part F will test you on the indefinite markers *un* and *une*. You are to write the correct form of the indefinite marker in the space before each noun.

    a ___ crayon   **b** ___ affiche

7 Part G will test how well you can match definite markers and nouns. You will be asked to fill in the blank before each noun with *le, la,* or *l'*.

    a ___ enfant   **b** ___ cassette

8 In Part H, you will be asked whether you would use *tu* or *vous* in addressing the person or persons mentioned. You are to write *tu* or *vous,* depending on the situation.

    a You are talking to a friend after school.
    b You are talking to your coach at basketball practice.
    c You are talking to your two younger sisters at breakfast.

9 Part I will measure how well you can match written adjectives with their nouns. You will see an adjective in parentheses, followed by an incomplete sentence. You are to complete the sentence by writing the correct form of the adjective.

    a (grand) Hélène est ____.

    b (français) Le garçon est ____.

    c (gentil) Madeleine est ____.

10 In Part J, you will be given a sentence and asked to change it to the negative. Change the following sentences to the negative.

    a Béatrice cherche le livre.   Béatrice ____ le livre.

    b Il est sur le bureau.   Il ____ sur le bureau.

11 In Part K, you will need to know how to use *de* and *d'* to show possession. You will see the name of an object and a proper name. Tell who owns the object by completing the sentence *C'est...* .

    a (le cadeau / Bernard)   C'est ____.

    b (le cahier / Annette)   C'est ____.

12 Part L will test your ability to write sentences in French. You will be given some cues with which to write a complete sentence. Make all necessary additions or changes and include accents and punctuation marks. You can check yourself by asking questions like these: Does the marker match the noun? Does the verb form go with the subject? Does the adjective match the noun?

    a u __ homme / chercher / l __ enfant

    b elle / ne...pas / être / américain

    c l __ caméra de Chantal / être / là

There will also be an extra-credit section in which you will be able to write a short sketch based on a dialogue you worked with in class.

    Now that you have gone over these sample test questions, you should be well-prepared for the test. If you want to review further, look at the Summary of grammatical structures on pp. 52–53 and the vocabulary round-ups at the ends of Preparations 10, 11, 12. ***Bonne chance!*** (Good luck!)

baseball

Ligue Nationale	Ligue Américaine
Jeudi	**Jeudi**
Los Angeles 8, Montréal 2	Texas 2, Kansas City 0
Atlanta 6, Pittsburgh 1	Détroit 9, Milwaukee 1
St-Louis 10, Cincinnati 1	Seattle 8, New York 6
Philadelphie 3, San Francisco 0	Californie 7, Baltimore 5
San Diego 5, New York 2	**Hier soir**
Hier soir	Texas à Kansas City
Chicago à Montréal	Toronto à Minnesota
St-Louis à Atlanta	Cleveland à Chicago
Los Angeles à New York	Détroit à Milwaukee
San Diego à Philadelphie	Boston à Seattle
San Francisco à Cincinnati	Baltimore à Oakland

Summary

1   Gender of nouns   *(Preparation 3)*

Nouns in French are either masculine or feminine in gender. This includes nouns that refer to males and females, like **homme** and **femme,** as well as nouns that refer to things, like **livre** and **cassette.**

2   Indefinite markers   *(Preparation 3)*

a. The indefinite marker **un** is used with a masculine singular noun.
b. The indefinite marker **une** is used with a feminine singular noun.

C'est un livre.	It's a book.
C'est une cassette.	It's a cassette.

3   Definite markers   *(Preparation 7)*

a. The definite markers used with singular nouns are **le, la,** and **l'.**
b. **Le** is used with a masculine singular noun beginning with a consonant.
   La is used with a feminine singular noun beginning with a consonant.
   L' is used with a masculine or feminine singular noun beginning with a vowel.

Le disque est sur le bureau.	The record is on the desk.
La chaise est devant la table.	The chair is in front of the table.
L'affiche est derrière l'écran.	The poster is behind the screen.

4   Subject pronouns   *(Preparations 3, 4, 6)*

a. The subject pronouns (pronouns used as the subject of a sentence) are shown in the chart below.

	SINGULAR		PLURAL	
Person Speaking	je	I	nous	we
Person Spoken To	tu/vous	you	vous	you
Person Spoken About	il/elle	he/she/it	ils/elles	they

b. In French, you have to choose between the pronouns **tu** and **vous** when you speak to a person. The choice depends on many conditions. Two important factors are the relationships between the speakers and their ages. **Vous** is always used when addressing more than one person.
c. **Ils** may refer to two or more males or to a group of males and females.

5   Possession with de *plus a name*   *(Preparation 7)*

Possession may be expressed with this pattern: *item owned* + **de** + *name of owner.* The preposition **de** becomes **d'** when it precedes a name beginning with a vowel.

*C'est le livre **de** Charles.*	It's Charles' book.
*C'est le livre **d'**Anne.*	It's Anne's book.

6 Present tense of être *(Preparation 4)*

The present-tense forms of *être* (*to be*) change to match the subject.

je	suis	I	am
tu	es	you	are
il/elle	est	he/she/it	is
ils/elles	sont	they	are
nous	sommes	we	are
vous	êtes	you	are

7 Present tense of chercher *(Preparation 8)*

a. Most French verbs consist of two parts: a stem, which gives the meaning of the verb, and an ending, which helps indicate the tense of the verb and the person.

b. The present tense of *chercher* is formed by adding the present-tense endings *-e, -es, -e, -ent, -ons,* and *-ez* to the stem *cherch-*. The endings must match the subject. This tense has five written forms and three spoken forms.

je	cherch	e	I'm looking for
tu	cherch	es	you're looking for
il/elle	cherch	e	he/she is looking for
ils/elles	cherch	ent	they're looking for
nous	cherch	ons	we're looking for
vous	cherch	ez	you're looking for

8 Negation with ne...pas *(Preparation 7)*

a. The French equivalent of *not* is *ne...pas.* *Ne* precedes the verb form and *pas* follows it.

   Il ne cherche pas le transistor.   He's not looking for the transistor radio.

b. When a verb form begins with a vowel sound, *ne* becomes *n'.*

   Ce n'est pas un stylo à bille.   It's not a ball-point pen.

9 Adjective agreement *(Preparation 9)*

An adjective in French matches the gender of the noun it describes.

a. Many adjectives that end in a written consonant in the masculine singular add an *-e* in the feminine singular.

   Il est petit.   *Elle est petite.*

b. Occasionally the written consonant is doubled before the final *-e.*

   Il est gentil.   *Elle est gentille.*

c. An adjective ending in *-e* in the masculine singular does not change form in the feminine singular: *Il est bête.*   *Elle est bête.*

d. An adjective that ends in *-é* in the masculine singular ends in *-ée* in the feminine singular: *Il est pressé.*   *Elle est pressée.*

Bonjour, tout le monde!

Philippe est pressé

Philippe Boivin is late for school. On his way, he exchanges a hurried greeting with a neighbor.

PHILIPPE	Bonjour, Madame!
MME CHENAUD	Bonjour, Philippe. Vous êtes pressé aujourd'hui!
PHILIPPE	Oh oui, Madame. Je suis en retard. Au revoir, Madame!

Philippe is in a hurry.

PHILIPPE	*Hello, Mrs. Chenaud!*
MME CHENAUD	*Hello, Philippe. You're in a hurry today!*
PHILIPPE	*Yes, Mrs. Chenaud. I'm late. Good-by!*

Une Rencontre

Gérard meets another boy at a party in Versailles.

GÉRARD	Bonjour!
JEAN	Salut!
GÉRARD	Tu es de Versailles, toi aussi?
JEAN	Non, je suis d'Ivry. Je m'appelle Jean Dupont.
GÉRARD	Moi, je suis Gérard Daumier.

A Meeting

GÉRARD	*Hello!*
JEAN	*Hi!*
GÉRARD	*Are you from Versailles, too?*
JEAN	*No, I'm from Ivry. My name is Jean Dupont.*
GÉRARD	*And I'm Gérard Daumier.*

Qu'est-ce que c'est?

Martine is opening a present that Pierre has just given her.

MARTINE   Qu'est-ce que c'est?
PIERRE   C'est un cadeau!
MARTINE   Pour moi?
PIERRE   Mais oui, bien sûr!
MARTINE   Oh, c'est une cassette! Tu es gentil! Merci!

What is it?

MARTINE   *What's that?*
PIERRE   *It's a gift!*
MARTINE   *For me?*
PIERRE   *Yes, of course!*
MARTINE   *Oh, it's a cassette! How nice of you! Thanks!*

Où est le disque?

Irène walks into the living room and sees her brother Charles looking everywhere for something.

CHARLES   Zut, zut et zut!
IRÈNE   Qu'est-ce qu'il y a? Qu'est-ce que tu cherches?
CHARLES   Le disque de Paul. Je ne sais pas où il est.
IRÈNE   Que tu es bête! Il est là, sur la télévision.
CHARLES   Pas possible! Ah, ça alors!

Where's the record?

CHARLES   *Darn, darn, darn!*
IRÈNE   *What's the matter? What are you looking for?*
CHARLES   *Paul's record. I don't know where it is.*
IRÈNE   *Boy, are you stupid! It's there, on the television set.*
CHARLES   *You're kidding! Oh, good grief!*

Zut! Je suis en retard!

PHASE TWO OBJECTIVES

In this Phase, you will learn to talk about a person's nationality, occupation, and interests. You will also learn the days of the week and the numbers 0 to 20. Specifically, you will be able to:

1 Ask or tell what someone's occupation or nationality is.

2 Say what you like or don't like to do.

3 Use adjectives to give a general description of a person.

4 Point out things and people by using the demonstrative markers **ce, cet, cette** or the expression **voilà**.

5 Describe a person or thing, using clauses that begin with the relative pronoun **qui.**

6 Ask and answer questions with **qui** (who), **qu'est-ce que** (what), **où** (where), and **n'est-ce pas** (isn't it? don't they? etc.).

7 Ask or tell what day of the week it is, was, or will be.

8 Use the numbers 0 to 20.

9 Say something about Québec, Martinique, Guadeloupe, and Haïti.

❊ The cultural notes describe the grading system in French schools, a Haitian hero, French-speaking Europe, a Caribbean statesman and poet, how the French write numbers, and what a **comptine** is.

1 What is a regular verb?

Now that you know the present-tense forms of **chercher**, you can apply the same knowledge to other French verbs. This section will show you how.

1 In English, the infinitive form of a verb usually consists of *to* and the basic form of the verb. Pick out the English infinitives in the following sentences. *She likes to sing. They hate to dance.* ▮

to sing, to dance

2 In French, the infinitive form of a verb is one word with two parts: a *stem* (which gives the meaning of the verb) and an *infinitive ending*.

  a The stem of **chercher** is **cherch-.** What is the infinitive ending? ▮

-er

  b The stem of **être** is **êt-.** What is the infinitive ending? ▮

-re

  c Give the English equivalents of the infinitives **chercher** and **être.** ▮

to look for, to be

3 In the next paragraph you will see two examples of a letter between slash marks: /e/ and /r/. These are called phonetic symbols. In the study of a language, a phonetic symbol is used to represent one sound that may have a variety of spellings. For example, one spelling for the sound represented by /e/ is *ez*, as in **cherchez.** Some of the other spellings could be *é, et,* and *er.*

The most common French infinitives are those that end in the sound /e/, spelled *-er* (as in **chercher**). Other French infinitives end in the sound /r/, spelled *-r* or *-re* (as in **être**).

It is important to know the infinitive form of a French verb. One reason is that in dictionaries and vocabulary lists, verbs are usually listed in the infinitive form. If you wanted to know the meaning of **cherchons,** you would have to look in the dictionary for the infinitive form ____. ▮

chercher

4 Another reason for knowing the infinitive of a verb is that it can often help you predict the other forms of the verb: the **je**-form, the **tu**-form, etc.

In Phase 1 you learned the present-tense forms of the verb **chercher.** The present-tense forms of every *-er* verb, except **aller** (*to go*), consist of the infinitive stem of the verb with one of the present-tense endings: *-e, -es, -e, -ent, -ons, -ez.* Because these verb forms follow a predictable pattern based on the infinitive, they are called regular verbs.

  a *Danser* is a regular *-er* verb. Write the stem of **danser.** ▮

dans-

b The *je*-form of *chercher* is *je cherche.* What is the *je*-form of *danser?* |

danse

c The *nous*-form of *chercher* is *nous cherchons.* What is the *nous*-form of *danser?* |

dansons

5 Not all French verbs are regular. Do the verb forms *suis, es,* and *sont* look like their infinitive *être?* |

no (*Être* is an irregular verb. You can't predict its forms by looking at the infinitive.)

2 *The present tense of* détester *and* aimer

Here is a chart of the present tense of the verb *détester* (*to hate*). If you need to, refer to the chart to answer frames 1–3.

je	détest e
tu	détest es
il/elle	détest e
ils/elles	détest ent
nous	détest ons
vous	détest ez

1 *Détester,* like *chercher,* is a regular verb whose infinitive ends in ____. |

-er

2 Rewrite the following phrases, and add the missing endings.
a je détest ____, il détest ____, elle détest ____ |

je déteste, il déteste, elle déteste

b nous détest ____, vous détest ____ |

nous détestons, vous détestez

c ils détest ____, elles détest ____ |

ils détestent, elles détestent

d tu détest ____ |

tu détestes

3 Which of these verb endings are usually silent in spoken French: *-e, -es, -e, -ent, -ons, -ez?* |

-e, -es, -e, -ent

4 Look at the chart of the present tense of *aimer* (to like). Refer to the chart to answer the questions below.

j'	aim e
tu	aim es
il/elle	aim e
ils/elles	aim ent
nous	aim ons
vous	aim ez

True or false? The present-tense endings of *aimer* are identical to the endings of *chercher* and *détester.* |

true

5 Do the forms of *aimer* follow a predictable pattern? |

yes (*Aimer* is a regular -er verb.)

6 Look at the subject pronouns in the chart of *aimer.* Which form is used with *aime: je* or *j'*? |

j'

7 When a verb begins with a vowel sound, as *aimer* does, the *e* of *je* is dropped. In writing, the *e* is replaced by an apostrophe: *j'aime.* You have observed this before, in noun phrases like *l'élève* and *l'enfant.*

a Which form of the definite marker is used with *affiche: la* or *l'*? |

l' (*l'affiche*)

b Which pronoun form should be used with the verb form *écoute: j'* or *je?* |

j' (*j'écoute*, I'm listening)

8 Look at the following verb phrases: *ils aiment, elles aiment, nous aimons, vous aimez.*

a The subject pronouns *ils, elles, nous,* and *vous* end with the written letter ____. |

s

b The *s* in *ils, elles, nous,* and *vous* is not pronounced when these pronouns are used with the forms of *chercher.* Is the *s* pronounced when they are used with the forms of *aimer?* |

yes (The written *s* is pronounced as part of the verb when these subject pronouns are used with any verb beginning with a vowel sound.)

c Does the *s* have the sound /s/ or the sound /z/? |

the sound /z/ (This /z/ sound is called a linking sound. The French term for the linking of a final consonant with a beginning vowel is *liaison.*)

9 To complete the dialogues below, write each subject and the matching form of *aimer.* Then say the dialogues aloud.

a –Vous ____ la télévision?
–Non, mais j'____ le cinéma. |

Vous aimez, j'aime

b –Tu ____ le rock?
–Non, mais j'____ la musique classique. |

Tu aimes, j'aime

c –Hélène et Marie ____ danser?
–Non, mais elles ____ écouter le jazz. |

Hélène et Marie aiment, elles aiment

d –Pierre et Claude, vous ____ la musique moderne?
–Pas tellement. Nous ____ la musique classique. |

vous aimez; nous aimons

10 Read this sentence: *Hélène et Marie aiment écouter le jazz.*

a Is the verb *écouter* in the infinitive form? |

yes (In the present tense, when a verb form like *aiment* is followed by another verb, the second verb is always in the infinitive form.)

b Write an English equivalent for the French sentence in 10. |

Hélène and Marie like to listen to jazz. / Hélène and Marie like listening to jazz.

3 Definite markers and school subjects

In this section you will practice using definite markers with the school subjects you learned in Phase 1.

1 Sort the following words into three groups, according to their markers: *le, la,* or *l'.*

la géométrie	l'algèbre	la physique
la géographie	le français	la musique
la biologie	l'espagnol	la gymnastique
l'histoire	l'italien	l'anglais ▌

Group 1: *le français*   Group 2: *la géométrie, la géographie, la biologie, la musique, la gymnastique*   Group 3: *l'histoire, l'algèbre, l'espagnol, l'italien, l'anglais*

2 The marker *l'* is used before a noun beginning with a vowel sound. Look at the answer to frame 1. Which noun in group 3 does *not* begin with a vowel letter (*a, e, i, o,* or *u*)? ▌

histoire (The letter *h* is never pronounced in French. The marker *l'* is used with most nouns that begin with *h*.)

3 Here are five school subjects, with some letters missing. Write the complete word, then say each word aloud: l'ital __ __ n, la g __ mnasti __ __ e, l'espa __ __ ol, l' __ ist __ __ re. ▌

l'italien, la gymnastique, l'espagnol, l'histoire

4 Write the English equivalent of ***Antoine et Michel aiment la physique, mais ils détestent la biologie.*** ▌

Antoine and Michel like physics, but they hate biology. (Notice that in the English sentence, no noun markers are used with *physics* and *biology*. The French equivalent, however, requires the use of the definite marker.)

5 Write the French equivalent of *I like gym, but I hate English.* ▌

J'aime la gymnastique, mais je déteste l'anglais.

6 In the following activity, tell which school subjects the persons indicated like and hate. Use each group of words to write a complete sentence. Answers are in the answer key.

Modèle: Paul et Frédéric / italien / anglais ▌
Paul et Frédéric aiment l'italien, mais ils détestent l'anglais.

a Monique / français / espagnol   **c** Antoine et Michel / physique / biologie
b Jean et moi, nous / algèbre / histoire

CHECK-UP
Part 2

Write French equivalents for:
1 I like history but I hate algebra.
2 Mariette and Pierre hate biology.
3 We like to listen to jazz.
4 You (*tu*) hate English.

VOCABULARY

lundi Monday		*samedi* Saturday	
mardi Tuesday		*dimanche* Sunday	
mercredi Wednesday		*moderne* modern	
jeudi Thursday		*aujourd'hui c'est...* today is...	
vendredi Friday		*demain c'est...* tomorrow is...	

ON AIME OU ON N'AIME PAS...! You like or you don't like...!

le jazz jazz	*écouter* to listen; to listen to
la musique classique classical music	*beaucoup* a lot
le rock rock music	*mais* but
adorer to love, to like a lot	*moi aussi* me, too
aimer to like	*moi non plus* me neither
danser to dance	*pas du tout* not at all
détester to hate	*pas tellement* not very much

PREPARATION 15

1 *Pre-quiz practice:* aimer

In your next class you will be asked to write subject pronouns and the corresponding verb forms of *aimer.* Your teacher will dictate a verb phrase, like *vous aimez,* and you will write it on your answer sheet. This section of the Preparation will help you with the spelling of the words. As you complete the frames, think of how the French words sound.

1 In some forms of *aimer,* there is a linking sound between the subject pronoun and the verb. This linking sound can be represented by the symbol /z/. In *vous aimez,* which letter represents the /z/ sound? ▌

s

2 One way to indicate linking visually is to use a link mark between the subject pronoun and the verb: for example, *nous aimons.* The link mark is *not* a part of French spelling. Read the following forms of *aimer* aloud. Write those which have linking sounds when they are spoken, and insert link marks in the correct places.

nous aimons	*elles aiment*	*tu aimes*	*j'aime*
il aime	*ils aiment*	*vous aimez*	*elle aime* ▌

nous aimons, ils aiment, elles aiment, vous aimez

3 The partial forms of *aimer* below have endings that are silent. Write the complete subject and verb.

a j'aim ____, tu aim ____, il aim ____, elle aim ____ ▌

j'aime, tu aimes, il aime, elle aime

b ils aim ____, elles aim ____ |

ils aiment, elles aiment

4 The **vous**-form of **aimer** sounds like the infinitive form, but it is spelled differently. Write the **vous**-form. |

aimez

5 The **nous**-form of **aimer** has a three-letter ending that represents one sound. Write the complete form with its subject pronoun. |

nous aimons

6 Here is a chart showing the forms of **aimer** in the negative.

je	n'	aime	pas
tu	n'	aimes	pas
il/elle	n'	aime	pas
ils/elles	n'	aiment	pas
nous	n'	aimons	pas
vous	n'	aimez	pas

When **ne...pas** is used with the forms of **aimer,** what happens to **ne?** |

it becomes *n'* (*Ne* contracts to *n'* before any verb form beginning with a vowel sound.)

7 Tell what the following people don't like by writing sentences with the present-tense forms of **aimer.** Say each sentence aloud before you write it. Answers are in the answer key.

Modèle: Je / ne...pas / l'histoire |

Je n'aime pas l'histoire.

a Ils / ne...pas / l'histoire
b Georges / ne...pas / la géographie

c Anne et moi, nous / ne...pas / l'espagnol
d Vous / ne...pas / tricoter, Madame?

2 French and English equivalents of verb forms

Sometimes it takes two or three English words to express the equivalent of a single French word, and vice versa. In this part of Preparation 15, you'll have a chance to practice with some French verbs whose English equivalents are longer and more complex than the single French form.

1 Compare the following French sentence with its English equivalent.
    Je cherche un crayon.   I am (I'm) looking for a pencil.
The French verb form is one word: **cherche.** The English equivalent is ____. |

am looking for (English often uses a form of *to be* and the *-ing* form of the verb where French uses a single verb form.)

2 Compare these French and English equivalents:
    Paul cherche un disque.   Paul is looking for a record.
The French verb form **cherche** is equivalent to English ____. |

is looking for

3 Now compare the following negative sentences:

Marie n'aime pas le jazz.   Marie doesn't like jazz.

The French negative verb form **n'aime pas** is equivalent to ___. |

doesn't like (In negative sentences, English sometimes uses *doesn't* or *don't* with the main verb.)

4 What happens in interrogative sentences? Compare the following:

Tu chantes?   Do you sing?

In the example above, the single French verb form **chantes** is equivalent to two English words: ___ + ___. |

do + sing

5 Write the French equivalent of *Does George sing?* |

Georges chante?

6 The following chart shows some of the English equivalents of the present-tense forms of **chanter**.

je chante	I'm singing / I sing
je ne chante pas	I'm not singing / I don't sing
tu chantes?	are you singing? / do you sing?

  a Give two English equivalents of **Paul chante.** |

Paul is singing, Paul sings

  b Give two English equivalents of **Paul ne chante pas.** |

Paul isn't singing, Paul doesn't sing

7 Write French equivalents for the sentences below, using the verbs **aimer** and **chercher.** Answers are in the answer key.

  a Do you (*tu*) like Marie-Hélène?
  b We're looking for Robert.
  c He doesn't like Marc.
  d Etienne and Charles, are you looking for Anne?
  e They aren't looking for Guillaume.

CHECK-UP
Part 2

1 Write the French equivalents for *Do they sing?* and for *Marc is singing.*
2 Write two English equivalents for *Vous chantez?* and for *Elle ne chante pas.*

VOCABULARY

l'algèbre algebra
l'anglais English
la biologie biology
l'espagnol Spanish
le français French
la géographie geography
la géométrie geometry
la gymnastique gym
l'histoire history
l'italien Italian
la musique music
la physique physics
chanter to sing
manger to eat
tricoter to knit

1 *Practice with* habiter *and other* -er *verbs*

1 In class recently you've been saying where people live by using the verb *habiter.* For example: *J'habite à Montréal. Vous habitez à Québec, n'est-ce pas?*

a Does *habiter* begin with a vowel sound or with a consonant sound? ▮

> a vowel sound (The *h* is not pronounced.)

b Why do you drop the *e* from *je* in *j'habite?* ▮

> When *je* precedes a verb form that begins with a vowel sound, the *e* is usually dropped. (In writing, the letter *e* is replaced by an apostrophe: *j'*.)

c When you say *vous habitez,* do you pronounce the *s* in *vous?* ▮

> yes (The subject pronouns *nous, vous, ils,* and *elles* link with a verb that begins with a vowel sound.)

d In *vous habitez,* is the *s* in *vous* pronounced as /s/ or /z/? ▮

> /z/ (like the sound of *s* in *chaise*)

This chart shows the present-tense forms of *habiter.*

j'	habit e
tu	habit es
il/elle	habit e
ils/elles	habit ent
nous	habit ons
vous	habit ez

2 *Habiter* is a regular *-er* verb. Are the endings of *habiter* the same as those of *aimer* or those of *être?* ▮

> *aimer*

3 Say where the following people live.

> Modèle: Serge: Paris ▮
>
> > *Serge habite à Paris.*

a Nous: Nice ▮

> *Nous habitons à Nice.*

b Tu: Bordeaux ▮

> *Tu habites à Bordeaux.*

c Paul: Montréal ▮

> *Paul habite à Montréal.*

d Je: Bruxelles ▮

> *J'habite à Bruxelles.*

e Louise et Michel: Genève ▮

> *Louise et Michel habitent à Genève.*

f Elles: Dijon ▮

> *Elles habitent à Dijon.*

CHATEAU

Chillon - Montreux
Suisse

4 In the remaining frames you will practice with *habiter* and the other regular *-er* verbs listed below. Remember that they all have the same endings as *habiter.* Answers are in the answer key.

    aimer   chanter   chercher   danser   détester   écouter

Write the subject pronouns and matching verb forms that complete the French equivalents of these sentences. Be sure to include *n'...pas* in the negative sentence.

      Modèle: *Does he like to dance?* ____ *danser?* |

                  Il aime

a Claire and Marcel, are you singing in French? *Claire et Marcel,* ___ *en français?*
b She's living in London. ___ *à Londres.*
c We don't listen to the radio. ___ *la radio.*
d Do you like living in New York? *Vous aimez* ___ *à New York?*

5 Write complete sentences with the cues below. Be sure to use the correct verb forms and to put all the words in the right order.

      Modèle: je / ne...pas / habiter / à Paris |

          Je n'habite pas à Paris.

a Jean-Claude et Philippe / écouter / la radio
b Richard et Martine / ne...pas / danser / le rock

c Tu / aimer / danser?
d Marc / détester / le jazz

6 Write affirmative or negative answers to the questions below.

      Modèle: Vous aimez danser? (non) |

          Non, nous n'aimons pas danser.

a Tu cherches un disque? (oui)
b Béatrice et Marie aiment la vie à la campagne? (non)
c Denis et Pierre, vous habitez à Saint-Louis? (non)
d Thierry aime habiter à Ivry? (oui)

2 Definite vs. indefinite markers

In this section, you'll learn more about when to use indefinite markers or definite markers in French.

1 Imagine that a friend is telling you what Marc is listening to: *Marc écoute un disque.*

    a In the sentence above, your friend tells you what type of thing Marc is listening to: a record. What marker does your friend use? |

        un (The speaker uses the indefinite marker to focus the listener's attention on the kind of thing being talked about.)

    b Your friend then gives you more information about the record: *Le disque est en anglais.* What marker is used this time? |

        le (Once the listener's attention has been focused on the kind of item, the speaker can use the definite marker to refer to the item just mentioned.)

2 Suppose a friend asks you what you're doing.

    a Say you're listening to a cassette. Use the indefinite marker *une* to focus attention on the kind of item you're talking about. |

        J'écoute une cassette.

    b Now tell your friend that the cassette is in French. Use the definite marker *la* to refer to the item again. |

        La cassette est en français.

3 Write pairs of sentences with the cues below. First call attention to the kind of thing you're talking about with *un* or *une.* Then use *le, la,* or *l'* to refer to the thing you just mentioned. Gender is indicated by *m.* (masculine) or *f.* (feminine). Answers are in the answer key.

        Modèle: disque (*m.*): J'écoute ____. ____ est en français. |

        J'écoute un disque. Le disque est en français.

    a garçon (*m.*): Nathalie aime ____. ____ est américain.
    b ville (*f.*): Eric habite dans ____. ____ est en France.
    c affiche (*f.*): Je cherche ____. ____ est de San Francisco.
    d transistor (*m.*): Nous écoutons ____. ____ est très petit.

4 The definite markers *le, la,* and *l'* are used in sentences expressing a like or dislike of something in general. In sentences like this, English doesn't use any noun marker. Look at this French sentence and its English equivalent.

        François déteste la musique.   François hates music.

    a What is the marker in the French sentence? |

        la

    b Write a complete sentence to say that Marie-France loves classical music: *Marie-France adore ____ musique classique.* |

        Marie-France adore la musique classique.

    c Say that Irène adores jazz. |

        Irène adore le jazz.

5 Express your feelings about the things listed below. Begin each sentence with one of these phrases: *J'adore, J'aime, Je n'aime pas,* or *Je déteste.* Use the appropriate forms of the definite marker—*le, la,* or *l'*.

    a base-ball (m.) ▌

                    J'adore / J'aime / Je n'aime pas / Je déteste le base-ball.

    b musique classique (f.) ▌

                    J'adore / J'aime / Je n'aime pas / Je déteste la musique classique.

    c français (m.) ▌

                    J'adore / J'aime / Je n'aime pas / Je déteste le français.

NOTE ✳

A Haitian hero: Toussaint L'Ouverture

Toussaint L'Ouverture was born a slave in 1743 in St. Domingue (Haiti's name under French domination). His owners favored him and provided him with a private tutor, which was almost unheard of at that time.

In 1791, when Toussaint was 48, a general slave revolt erupted. Toussaint joined the rebels and quickly became a leader. Meanwhile, Spanish and French forces were at war in the western part of the island. To obtain help from the blacks, the Spanish promised to free them as soon as the French were expelled. Although Toussaint doubted that they would honor their promise, he joined the Spanish forces in order to maintain a position of power. When, a short time later, the new French government declared the slaves free, Toussaint turned over Spanish forts and arms to the French army.

Success, betrayal, success

Toussaint's military and diplomatic genius allowed him to gain control of the colony and become Governor General of the island. He reorganized the agricultural production of the war-ravaged plantations, expelled the Spanish forces, and maintained friendly relations with the French government in Europe.

In 1801, French general Napoleon Bonaparte tried to re-establish French authority over the blacks in St. Domingue and sent an army from Europe. The black army resisted, and nearly succeeded. Some of the generals, however, joined the French after receiving promises that blacks would remain free. Toussaint then accepted a peace agreement, but he was soon betrayed.

The French arrested Toussaint in order to make the re-enslavement of blacks easier. But on boarding the prison ship to France, he said, "In overthrowing me, you have cut down in St. Domingue only the trunk of the tree of liberty. It will spring up again from the roots, for they are numerous and deep." He died in prison in 1803.

The black generals resumed their war against France. In 1804 one of the generals, Jean-Jacques Dessalines, wrested control of the island from France for the last time.

CHECK-UP
Part 1

Write the appropriate forms of the verbs in parentheses.

1 (habiter)   J' ____ à Marseille.
2 (écouter)   Nous ____ un disque de musique moderne.
3 (ne...pas / aimer)   Frédéric et Lise ____ danser.

Part 2

Write the appropriate markers to complete the following sentences.

Pierre adore ____ musique. Il écoute ____ disque de rock et ____ cassette de musique classique. Il aime ____ cassette mais il n'aime pas ____ disque.

VOCABULARY

une radio   radio
une télévision (*la télé*)   television (TV)

une école   school
le cinéma   movies

Ville ou campagne? City or country?
la campagne   country
la vie   life
un village   village
une ville   city
habiter   to live

je préfère   I prefer
pas beaucoup   not much
ou   or
à   in

1 Pre-quiz practice: -er verbs

In the next class you will have a dictation quiz to see how well you've learned to use the different forms of **-er** verbs. If you've done the Preparations regularly, the quiz shouldn't give you much trouble. This section gives you some more practice.

1 The present-tense forms of all regular **-er** verbs are made up of two parts: the stem and the ending.

  a Which part changes to agree with the subject? |
     the ending
  b Which part tells you the meaning of the verb? |
     the stem

2 For the quiz you will see sentences that are complete except for the verb forms. Your teacher will read the sentences aloud, including the missing verbs. You must listen carefully and write the correct verb forms on your answer sheet. For example, your teacher reads the complete sentence **Je n'habite pas à Montréal.** On the paper you see: **Je ____ à Montréal.** You write: ____. |
     n'habite pas

3 In the frames below, write the correct forms of the verbs in parentheses. Some of the sentences are in the negative. (Answers are in the answer key.)

  a (écouter)   Nous ___ la radio.
  b (nager)   Tu ___ bien!
  c (ne...pas / danser)   Nathalie et Alain ___ beaucoup.
  d (ne...pas / manger)   Je ___ aujourd'hui.
  e (patiner)   Il aime ___.
  f (tricoter)   Vous ___.
  g (aimer)   Elles ___ chanter en français.
  h (regarder)   Tu ___ l'affiche?

If you missed frames in this section, look again at Preparation 15, parts 1 and 2.

2   *Sound and spelling:* é, -er, -ez

This section will help you learn to write the forms of verbs when you hear them.

1 Say these three words aloud: *télé, regardez, danser.*

  a True or false? All three words end with the same vowel sound. |
            true (All three words end in the vowel sound /e/.)

  b The vowel sound /e/ is spelled in three different ways. Write the three words, and in each one underline the letters that spell this sound. |

          tél<u>é</u>   regard<u>ez</u>   dans<u>er</u>

2 Pick out the words below that contain the sound /e/ and write them on your worksheet.

  a cinéma   règle   cassette   élève   géographie   bête |
            cinéma, élève, géographie

  b chanter   habiter   monsieur   cahier   bonjour   fenêtre |
            chanter, habiter, cahier

  c cherche   mangez   aiment   assez   regardez   entre |
            mangez, assez, regardez

  d Hélène   Michel   Irène   Gérard   René   Michèle |
            Hélène, Gérard, René

  e patiner   adore   nagez   Roger   André   Laure |
            patiner, nagez, Roger, André

3 Read the following sentences aloud. Write the words from each one that contain the vowel sound /e/. Remember that the sound /e/ may be spelled in three different ways.

  a Qu'est-ce que vous tricotez? |
            tricotez

  b Gérard Leduc habite à Montréal. Il adore patiner. |
            Gérard, Montréal, patiner

4 Below are phrases with letters missing from certain words. The missing letters spell the sound /e/. Write the whole words, and be careful about spelling.

a un cahi_ _, la g_om_trie, vous n'_cout_ _ pas ▯
cahier, géométrie, écoutez

b une _cole, j'aime _cout_ _ la musique, vous tricot_ _ ▯
école, écouter, tricotez

NOTE ✳

French-speaking Europe

There are three European nations besides France where French is spoken: Belgium **(la Belgique),** Switzerland **(la Suisse),** and Luxemburg **(le Luxembourg).**

Belgium is a bilingual country. The Flemish-speaking **Flamands** live in the north; the French-speaking **Wallons** live in the southern part of the country. Belgium is densely populated, with much commercial and industrial activity. Brussels **(Bruxelles),** the capital, is a busy cosmopolitan city.

Switzerland's location in Europe has made it a natural international crossroads. French is one of four official languages; the others are Swiss German, Italian, and Romansch, a Latin-based language spoken by about 10,000 people. English, though not official, is also spoken widely. Geneva **(Genève),** one of the major cities, serves as a center for the United Nations, many summit conferences, and the International Red Cross **(la Croix-Rouge).**

Luxembourg, a tiny nation on France's northern border, has belonged to France, Holland, and Germany at different periods in history. French, German, and a Germanic dialect are the languages spoken by the citizens **(les Luxembourgeois).** Luxembourg has joined Holland and Belgium to form an economic union—**le Bénélux**—which is very important in world trade.

CHECK-UP
Part 1

The vowel sound /e/ is often represented by the letter *é*. Write two other common ways of spelling this sound. Write two words containing each spelling of this vowel sound.

VOCABULARY

nager to swim
patiner to skate
regarder to watch, to look at

c'était it was
hier yesterday

1 *More feminine forms of adjectives*

1 In Preparation 9 you learned that the feminine forms of some descriptive adjectives end in a consonant sound.

    a The feminine form of *petit* ends in the consonant sound /t/. The feminine form is written ____. **|**

        petite

    b Does the masculine form *petit* end in a consonant sound or a vowel sound? **|**

        vowel sound (The written combination -*it* represents the vowel sound /i/. In French, a written vowel plus a consonant at the end of a word may often stand for a spoken vowel sound.)

2 Read the sentences below.

    André est français. Marthe est française.

    a Write the feminine form of the adjective. **|**

        française (It ends in the consonant sound /z/.)

    b Which written combination contains a consonant sound when spoken—the masculine *-ais* or the feminine *-aise?* **|**

        the feminine *-aise*

3 Most French adjectives have a masculine form that ends in a written consonant. In the feminine form, all French adjectives end in the written vowel *e.*

    Write the correct form of the adjective in parentheses to complete the sentences below.

        Modèle: Vous êtes ____, Mademoiselle? (français) **|**

            française

    a Madeleine est ____. (grand) **|**

        grande

    b Est-ce que le garçon est ____? (américain) **|**

        américain

    c La fille est ____. (petit) **|**

        petite

4 Some adjectives have masculine and feminine forms that sound alike. Read the following pairs of sentences aloud.

    M. Dupont est riche. Mme Dupont est riche.

    M. Saunier est pauvre. Mme Saunier est pauvre.

    a Both forms of these adjectives end with the written letter ____. **|**

        e

    b Do these adjectives end in a vowel sound or a consonant sound? **|**

        consonant sound

5 In which pair of adjectives do both forms sound the same?

    américain, américaine   moderne, moderne   petit, petite |

        moderne, moderne

6 Write a short dialogue in French. Pretend that you are talking to a friend about Mr. Blondeau.

    a You ask your friend whether Mr. Blondeau is tall. Then your friend says no, he's very short. |

        –M. Blondeau est grand?   –Non, il est très petit.

    b Continue by asking whether Mrs. Blondeau is short. Your friend says no, she's very tall. |

        –Mme Blondeau est petite?   –Non, elle est très grande.

2 *Talking about occupations*

1   These sentences tell what two people do for a living: **M. Durand est dentiste. Mme Roule est comptable.**

    a Write the English equivalents of the sentences. |

        Mr. Durand is a dentist. Mrs. Roule is an accountant.

    b In English, an indefinite marker is used after a form of *to be* with the name of the occupation: He's *a* dentist; she's *an* accountant. Are indefinite markers used in the French equivalents? |

        no

2 When the name of an occupation follows a form of **être,** the marker is usually omitted. Write the French equivalents:

    a I'm an accountant. |

        Je suis comptable.

    b You (**Vous**) are a dentist. |

        Vous êtes dentiste.

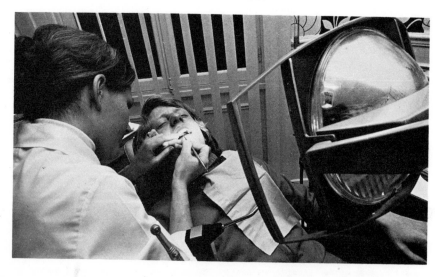

Dans un cabinet dentaire

3 The names of some occupations have feminine forms when they refer to women. (This also happens in English: *actor, actress.*) Look at these examples:

> *Alain est ouvrier. Alice est ouvrière.*
> *Jean-Paul est infirmier. Jeannette est infirmière.*

   a The feminine form of ***ouvrier*** is ___. ▮

             ouvrière (Remember the **accent grave**.)

   b The feminine form of ***infirmier*** is ___. ▮

             infirmière (There's that accent again—don't forget it.)

4 Use the picture cues below to write about what people do for a living. After you have written a sentence, say its English equivalent out loud. Check your spelling carefully with the answer in the book.

    Modèle: M. Labouche  ▮

           M. Labouche est dentiste. (M. Labouche is a dentist.)

  a Arthur Laprise ▮

           Arthur Laprise est photographe. (Arthur Laprise is a photographer.)

  b Tu  ▮

           Tu es pilote. (You're a pilot.)

  c Je  ▮

           Je suis médecin. (I'm a doctor.)

3 *Forming questions:* qui, où, qu'est-ce que

Questions that can be answered by ***oui*** or ***non*** generally have a rising intonation pattern. Questions that must be answered with information generally have a falling intonation pattern. Information questions often begin with a question word or expression like ***qui, où,*** or ***qu'est-ce que.***

1 Read the following questions aloud. ***Où est Marie-Claude? Qui habite à Paris? Qu'est-ce que tu regardes?***

   a Which question asks *what?* ▮

             Qu'est-ce que tu regardes? (What are you looking at?)

   b Which one asks *where?* ▮

             Où est Marie-Claude? (Where is Marie-Claude?)

   c Which question asks *who?* ▮

             Qui habite à Paris? (Who lives in Paris?)

2 Below are partial questions and the answers to them. Use the answers to figure out whether each question should begin with *qui, où,* or *qu'est-ce que,* and write the complete question.

a – ____ tu écoutes?   –J'écoute un disque de jazz. |

Qu'est-ce que tu écoutes?

b – ____ aime danser?   –Moi! J'adore danser! |

Qui aime danser?

c – ____ est le disque de rock?   –Il est sur la table. |

Où est le disque de rock?

3 Write French equivalents for the following questions.

a Where is Philippe? |

Où est Philippe?

b Who's singing? |

Qui chante?

c What are you eating? |

Qu'est-ce que tu manges? / Qu'est-ce que vous mangez?

CHECK-UP
Part 1

1 In spoken French, if you hear a consonant sound at the end of an adjective, is the adjective more likely to be masculine or feminine?
2 In written French, what letter do all feminine adjectives end in?
3 Give the appropriate forms of the adjectives in parentheses:
a (grand) Jacques est ____.   **b** (américain) Mme Warren est ____.

Part 2

Write the French equivalents for *Jean-Paul is a nurse* and *I'm a teacher.*

Part 3

Write the French equivalents for *Where are Georges and Charlotte?* and *What are you listening to?*

VOCABULARY

architecte architect
comptable accountant
dentiste dentist
infirmier, infirmière nurse
journaliste reporter
médecin doctor
ouvrier, ouvrière worker

pilote pilot
photographe photographer
professeur teacher, professor
secrétaire secretary
allemand German
parler to speak, to talk

1 *The demonstrative markers* ce, cet, *and* cette

1 In English, you often use the markers *this* or *that* to make clear which person or thing you're talking about. Sometimes you point or make a gesture at the same time. For example, here's a conversation that might take place at an auto show.

Paul: Do you like this sedan?

Jeanne: No, I like that station wagon better.

This and *that* are demonstrative markers. What kind of word follows a marker—a noun or a verb? |

a noun

2 Look at the French noun markers in the following sentences. They are equivalent to *this* and *that*.

Ce garçon est Jean-Michel.   *Cet homme est M. Giraud.*   *Cette fille est Marie-Claire.*

Which forms of the demonstrative marker occur in the sentences? |

ce, cet, cette (Each marker can mean either this or that, depending on the context.)

3 The demonstrative marker has three singular forms. There is a masculine form, a feminine form, and another form used before a masculine noun beginning with a vowel sound.

Look at the following noun phrases:

ce garçon   *cet homme*   *cette femme*
ce livre   *cet écran*   *cette étagère*

a Which form of the marker is used with a masculine noun beginning with a consonant sound? |

ce

b Which form is used with a masculine noun beginning with a vowel sound? |

cet (The h in homme is silent, so the word actually begins with a vowel sound.)

c Which form is used with a feminine noun? |

cette

4 Write the form of the demonstrative marker that correctly completes each of these statements.

a ＿＿ homme est de Bordeaux. |

Cet

b ＿＿ femme est Mme Rochemont. |

Cette

c ＿＿ garçon est américain. |

Ce

d ＿＿ enfant n'est pas français. |

Cet

5 Change the indefinite markers to demonstrative markers, and rewrite the noun phrases.

> Modèle: un stylo, un comptable ▮
>> *ce stylo, ce comptable*

a une classe, une secrétaire ▮
>> *cette classe, cette secrétaire*

b un écran, un homme ▮
>> *cet écran, cet homme*

c une étagère, une enfant ▮
>> *cette étagère, cette enfant*

d un ouvrier, une ouvrière ▮
>> *cet ouvrier, cette ouvrière*

6 *Cet* and *cette* sound alike in speech. How can you tell whether to write *cet* or *cette* when you hear *cet homme, cette étagère*—by the gender of the noun or by the sound you hear? ▮
>> *by the gender of the noun*

2   *The relative pronoun* qui

This section explains how to use the word *qui* to combine two statements.

1 You already know one use of the word *qui.* Write the English equivalent of *Qui est cet homme?* ▮
>> *Who is that man?* (*Qui* is used to ask questions about people.)

2 Here are two sentences that give information about a person.
>> Anne is talking with a man. The man is an architect.

It's possible to combine the two sentences into one. Write the word that is needed to join the two statements.

>> Anne is talking with a man ＿＿ is an architect. ▮
>>> who (The relative pronoun *who* refers to the word *man.*)

3 Here are the French equivalents of the sentences above.
>> *Anne parle avec un homme. L'homme est architecte.*
>> *Anne parle avec un homme qui est architecte.*

Which word in the second sentence corresponds to *who?* ▮
>> *qui* (The relative pronoun *qui* always replaces the subject of a sentence. Here, *qui* replaces *l'homme.*)

4 Combine these two sentences into one.
>> *Nathalie parle avec une femme. Elle est comptable.* ▮
>>> *Nathalie parle avec une femme qui est comptable.*

5 Give the French equivalent of *David is talking with a man who is a nurse.* ▮
>> *David parle avec un homme qui est infirmier.*

6 Read the following pair of sentences, then see how they are combined.

Monique is looking for the record. The record is under the chair.

Monique is looking for the record that is under the chair.

Here the relative pronoun is ____ instead of *who*. ▮

   that (*Who* is used only for people. *That* can refer to people or to things.)

7 Now look at the French equivalent of the sentence from frame 6.

 Monique cherche le disque qui est sous la chaise.

 a What is the relative pronoun? ▮

   qui

 b Which noun phrase does *qui* refer to? ▮

   le disque

 c True or false? The relative pronoun *qui* can refer either to people or to things. ▮

   true

8 Monique has a few friends who are as absent-minded as she is. Write complete sentences to tell what each is looking for and where it actually is.

 Modèle: Monique / le livre / sur la table. ▮

   Monique cherche le livre qui est sur la table.

 a Jacques / la cassette / derrière la télévision. ▮

   Jacques cherche la cassette qui est derrière la télévision.

 b Colette / la feuille de papier / sous le bureau. ▮

   Colette cherche la feuille de papier qui est sous le bureau.

 c Martine / le disque / sur l'étagère ▮

   Martine cherche le disque qui est sur l'étagère.

 d Guillaume / la chaise / entre le bureau et la porte ▮

   Guillaume cherche la chaise qui est entre le bureau et la porte.

9 Read the sentences below.

 Cette jeune fille est grande.

 La jeune fille qui chante maintenant est grande.

 a Does the adjective *grande* agree in gender with *jeune fille* in both sentences? ▮

   yes

 b Complete the French equivalent:

 The boy who is singing now is tall.

 Le garçon qui chante maintenant est ____. ▮

   grand (*Grand* must agree in gender with the masculine subject *le garçon.*)

10 Tell the nationality of a person living in the cities below.

 Modèle: homme / Milan / italien ▮

   Un homme qui habite à Milan est italien.

 a homme / Munich / allemand ▮

   Un homme qui habite à Munich est allemand.

 b femme / Wichita / américain ▮

   Une femme qui habite à Wichita est américaine.

NOTE

Statesman and poet: Aimé Césaire

Aimé Césaire is a poet, playwright, and statesman who has represented the Caribbean island of Martinique in the French Assembly, and has served as mayor of Fort-de-France, the capital. Born in 1913, Césaire was one of a number of black students who explored their heritage while they were enrolled in universities in France. Césaire coined the word **négritude,** which can be defined as the cultural values of black African and Caribbean people. Césaire's literary work reflects a quest for an authentic culture, and a reaction against the colonial experience which left his people in poverty.

Cahier d'un retour au pays natal ("Return to my native land"), one of Césaire's early works, is an angry rejection of the colonial policy that belittled African and Caribbean culture. His plays include **Le Roi Christophe,** based on the life of a black king who ruled Haiti in the 1800s, and **Une Saison au Congo,** which deals with the struggle of Patrice Lumumba, the leader of the Congolese independence movement in the 1960s.

CHECK-UP
Part 1

Complete the following sentence with the correct demonstrative markers.
_____ *femme est Mme Legrand,* _____ *homme est M. Legrand et* _____ *garçon est René Legrand.*

Part 2

Write the French equivalents.
1 The man who is listening to the radio is a doctor.
2 Joseph is looking for the present that is under the chair.
3 A woman who lives in Spokane is American.

VOCABULARY

un/une camarade   friend, pal

Une belle voiture, c'est important?   Is a beautiful car important?
une barbe   beard
une voiture   car
beau, belle   handsome, beautiful
jaloux   jealous
oh, ça va, ça va!   (shows annoyance) O.K., O.K.!
dis donc!   say!
hein?   huh? eh?
non, alors!   oh no!
tu plaisantes!   you're kidding!

Antilles...

Grâce et lumière

Espaces tièdes et bruyants,

Retraites fraîches et tranquilles

Après la lutte contre les éléments,

Labeur paisible et

Douceur de vivre

1 *The numbers* 0 *to* 10

Recently in class you learned how to say the numbers 0 to 10 in French. Here are the written forms of the numbers.

0 *zéro*	1 *un*	3 *trois*	5 *cinq*	7 *sept*	9 *neuf*
	2 *deux*	4 *quatre*	6 *six*	8 *huit*	10 *dix*

Some simple addition problems will help you practice with these numbers. For each sentence below, write the missing word on your worksheet, then write the equation in numerals. In these sentences *font*, which rhymes with *sont*, means equals.

Modèle: Un et un font ____. |
deux $1 + 1 = 2$

1 Deux et quatre font ____. |
six $2 + 4 = 6$

2 Quatre et ____ font sept. |
trois $4 + 3 = 7$

3 Un et huit font ____. |
neuf $1 + 8 = 9$

4 Trois et ____ font cinq. |
deux $3 + 2 = 5$

5 Quatre et ____ font quatre. |
zéro $4 + 0 = 4$

6 Neuf et ____ font dix. |
un $9 + 1 = 10$

7 Read aloud each equation that you have on your worksheet.

NOTE ❋   *French numbers*

The number **seven** was originally written *7*, to show seven angles. This came from the Arabic practice of writing a figure that showed the same number of angles as the number itself. Part of this symbol remains as the French **sept:** *7* . The French write the number **un** as *1* , and often interpret a handwritten American 7 as the number **one.** Here are the numbers 0 through 9 as a French person would write them. Which ones are different from the way you write?

2 Nasal consonants and nasal vowels

1 A nasal sound is one that is produced when air passes through the nose as you speak.

   a To find out if a word contains a nasal consonant, pinch your nostrils shut while you say the word. If there's a nasal consonant, you will have trouble saying the word because you are blocking the passage of air through your nose. Which of the following words contain nasal consonants?

       murmur   dawdle   noon   history   mystery **|**

         murmur, noon, mystery

   b The two nasal consonants are represented by the letters ＿＿ and ＿＿. **|**

         m, n (These two nasal consonants occur in both French and English.)

2 In French, there are *nasal vowels* as well as nasal consonants. Place your fingers lightly on the sides of your nose as you say these words aloud: ***beau, bon.***

   a Do you feel a strong vibration in your fingertips when you say ***bon?*** **|**

         yes (The vibration occurs because air is passing through your nose and mouth at the same time. The *-on* of ***bon*** represents a nasal vowel sound.)

   b Do you feel a strong vibration when you say ***beau?*** **|**

         no (When air passes through the mouth only, the sound is called an oral vowel. The *-eau* of ***beau*** represents an oral vowel sound.)

3 Look at these words with nasal vowels shown in boldface type.

    un   *médeci**n***   scie**n**ce   co**m**ptable
    a**n**glais   **bon**jour   ***im***porta**nt**   **em**pire

In written French, a nasal vowel sound is represented by a vowel (***a, e, i, o,*** or ***u***), plus the consonant ＿＿ or ＿＿. **|**

         m, n

4 Here are the same words with letters missing. Write the complete word by inserting the letters that represent the nasal vowels.

   a b＿＿jour, ＿＿pire, sci＿＿ce, ＿＿glais **|**

         bonjour, empire, science, anglais

   b ＿＿port＿＿t, médec＿＿, c＿＿ptable, u＿ **|**

         important, médecin, comptable, un

VOCABULARY			
	un éléphant elephant	*maigre* thin	*cinq* five
	une girafe giraffe	*stupide* stupid	*six* six
	un tigre tiger	*vieux* old	*sept* seven
	célèbre famous	*zéro* zero	*huit* eight
	gros fat, heavy	*un* one	*neuf* nine
	intelligent intelligent	*deux* two	*dix* ten
	jeune young	*trois* three	
	laid ugly	*quatre* four	

1 More practice with adjectives

This chart shows the adjectives you have used so far to describe people.

MASCULINE SINGULAR AND FEMININE SINGULAR FORMS OF ADJECTIVES

SOUND AND SPELLING ARE DIFFERENT	SOUND AND SPELLING ARE THE SAME	SOUND IS THE SAME; SPELLING IS DIFFERENT
américain, américaine	bête	pressé, pressée
beau, belle	célèbre	
français, française	classique	
gentil, gentille	jeune	
grand, grande	maigre	
gros, grosse	moderne	
intelligent, intelligente	pauvre	
jaloux, jalouse	riche	
laid, laide	stupide	
petit, petite		
vieux, vieille		

1 In giving the answers for this frame, write the masculine and feminine forms of each adjective.

   a In writing, the feminine form of many adjectives is made by adding *e* to the masculine form. Select those adjectives from the chart. ▌
   américain, américaine; français, française; grand, grande; intelligent, intelligente; laid, laide; petit, petite; pressé, pressée

b Sometimes the written feminine form is just like the masculine except that the final consonant is doubled before the final *e* is added. Which adjectives in the chart are like this? ▌
   gentil, gentille; gros, grosse

c Three of the adjectives in the list are irregular—that is, the sound or spelling of the feminine form is different from the masculine form, and the difference doesn't fit a predictable pattern. Write the three irregular adjectives. ▌
   beau, belle; vieux, vieille; jaloux, jalouse

2 You have learned nine adjectives that have the same sound and spelling in the masculine and feminine forms. They are shown below with some letters missing. See if you can write them all without looking at the chart.

b __ te   r __ ch __   st __ pid __
c __ lèbr __   m __ d __ rn __   cl __ s __ iq __ e
__ aigre   p __ uvr __   j __ __ ne   ▌
   bête, riche, stupide, célèbre, moderne, classique, maigre, pauvre, jeune

3 The first sentence in each frame below makes a statement about a person. Complete the second statement with the opposite adjective.

> Modèle: Henri n'est pas petit. Il est _____. |
> *grand*

a Philippe n'est pas stupide. Il est _____. |
intelligent

b Josette n'est pas laide. Elle est _____. |
belle

c Marcel n'est pas gros. Il est _____. |
maigre

d Monique n'est pas vieille. Elle est _____. |
jeune

4 Serge and Monique are a lot alike. Read each statement about one of them, and write the appropriate form of the same adjective to complete the description of the other.

> Modèle: Serge est grand. Monique est _____ aussi. |
> *grande*

a Monique est intelligente. Serge est _____ aussi. |
intelligent

b Monique est belle. Serge est _____ aussi. |
beau

c Serge est jaloux. Monique est _____ aussi. |
jalouse

5 Rewrite each sentence below so that it describes the person named in parentheses.

a Paul Bertrand est très beau et très célèbre. (Sylvie Duval) |
Sylvie Duval est très belle et très célèbre.

b M. Lesage est très vieux et très intelligent. (Mme Lesage) |
Mme Lesage est très vieille et très intelligente.

c Pierre est gros, laid et jaloux. (Christine) |
Christine est grosse, laide et jalouse.

2 *More on occupations: scrambled letters*

Unscramble the letters or complete the words to figure out the French occupations for the people described by the English cues.

1 a A male singer: ***un teuranch*** |
un chanteur

b A female singer: ***une chant_____*** |
une chanteuse

2 A person who writes books and articles: ***un ivécrain*** |
un écrivain

Agent de police à la place de l'Opéra

3 a A man who plays a role in a drama: **un teurac** |
     un acteur

b A woman who does the same: **une act____** |
     une actrice

4 a A woman who plays an instrument: **une ennimusice** |
     une musicienne

b A man who does likewise: **un music____** |
     un musicien

5 a A female dancer: **une ansdeuse** |
     une danseuse

b Her partner: **un dans____** |
     un danseur

6 a A man who helps a doctor: **un firminier** |
     un infirmier

b The female counterpart: **une infirm____** |
     une infirmière

7 a A woman who works in a factory: **une riouvère** |
     une ouvrière

b A man who works in a factory: **un ouvr____** |
     un ouvrier

8 Someone who flies a plane: **tilope.** |
     pilote

3 Pre-quiz practice: demonstrative markers

1 In your next class you will have a quiz on the demonstrative markers *ce, cet, cette.*

What are the two English equivalents for *ce, cet,* and *cette?* |

this, that

2 Which of the following conclusions is true, A or B?

The form of the demonstrative marker depends on . . .

A . . . the verb in the sentence.

B . . . the noun it introduces. |

B

3 Which form—*ce, cet,* or *cette*—is used with a singular noun that is:

a feminine? |

cette

b masculine and begins with a vowel sound? |

cet

c masculine and begins with a consonant sound? |

ce

4 For the quiz, you will see ten incomplete sentences. You are to complete each sentence with the correct demonstrative marker. For practice, write *ce, cet,* or *cette* to complete the sentences below. Answers are in the answer key.

a ___ fille est française.

b ___ enfant est anglais.

c ___ femme parle espagnol.

d ___ livre est beau.

e ___ garçon est de Québec.

f ___ enfant est belle.

g ___ homme est infirmier.

h ___ transistor est très petit.

5 Write a French equivalent for each of these sentences. Answers are in the answer key.

a This man is a laborer.

b That actress is beautiful.

CHECK-UP
Part 1

Rewrite these sentences with Mme Durand as the subject.

1 M. Durand est vieux.   **3** M. Durand est maigre.

2 M. Durand est intelligent.

VOCABULARY

acteur, actrice   actor, actress

chanteur, chanteuse   singer

danseur, danseuse   dancer

écrivain   writer, author

musicien, musicienne   musician

laide (f.)   ugly

grosse (f.)   fat, heavy

intelligente (f.)   intelligent

vieille (f.)   old

jalouse (f.)   jealous

1 Le voilà, la voilà

1 In a recent class you had some practice with the expressions *le voilà* and *la voilà.* Read this short dialogue.

　　–*Où est le livre?*
　　–*Le voilà.*
　　–*Ah, merci!*

What does *Le voilà* mean? ❙

　　　　There it is. / Here it is.

2 In the expression *Le voilà* in frame 1, *le* refers to the noun phrase *le livre.* If the noun phrase is *la cassette,* you use a different word before *voilà.* Give the word that is missing from this dialogue.

　　–*Où est la cassette?*
　　– ___ *voilà.* ❙

　　　　La (*Le* is used to replace a masculine noun; *la* replaces a feminine noun.)

3 Now look at this dialogue.

　　–*Où est Marie?*
　　–*La voilà.*

　a What's the English equivalent of *La voilà* this time? ❙

　　　　There she is. / Here she is.

　b How would you say *There he is* in French? ❙

　　　　Le voilà. (You can use *Le voilà* and *La voilà* to talk about things or about people.)

4 Suppose your teacher is sick, and a substitute has your class for the day. The substitute needs help finding people and things in the classroom, so you point them out. Write either *Le voilà* or *La voilà* in response to the following questions.

　a Où est la bande? ❙

　　　　La voilà.

　b Où est Michel Auriol? ❙

　　　　Le voilà.

　c Et Nancy Barbery? ❙

　　　　La voilà.

　d Où est le cahier de Mlle Roland? ❙

　　　　Le voilà.

　e Où est l'écran? ❙

　　　　Le voilà.

　f Et l'affiche? ❙

　　　　La voilà.

　g Où est le morceau de craie? ❙

　　　　Le voilà.

　h Et la règle? ❙

　　　　La voilà.

2 *Practice with* n'est-ce pas?

1 Complete the English equivalents for the questions below.

   a *C'est un disque, n'est-ce pas?* It's a record, ____? ▍
                   isn't it

   b *Daniel est français, n'est-ce pas?* Daniel is French, ____? ▍
                   isn't he

   c In the questions above, does **n'est-ce pas** have only one translation? ▍
                   no (The English meaning of *n'est-ce pas* depends on the context.)

2 Write the French equivalent for each sentence below, using **n'est-ce pas.**

   a They **(Ils)** are speaking Italian, aren't they? ▍
                   Ils parlent italien, n'est-ce pas?

   b She's listening to a Dany Leclerc record, isn't she? ▍
                   Elle écoute un disque de Dany Leclerc, n'est-ce pas?

3 Suppose that Jean-Luc, a French exchange student, is trying to remember things about his new American classmates, but he isn't having much luck. Write questions with **n'est-ce pas,** using the cues below. Then answer the questions in the negative.

      Modèle: Chuck / aimer le jazz ▍
               –Chuck, tu aimes le jazz, n'est-ce pas?
               –Non, je n'aime pas le jazz.

   a Bob / habiter à Clinton ▍
               –Bob, tu habites à Clinton, n'est-ce pas?
               –Non, je n'habite pas à Clinton.

   b Debbie / aimer patiner ▍
               –Debbie, tu aimes patiner, n'est-ce pas?
               –Non, je n'aime pas patiner.

   c What is the meaning of **n'est-ce pas** in items **a** and **b?** ▍
               don't you?

Emblems of Swiss cantons (states)

3 Getting ready for an oral test

During the next few classes you will be playing the game **Qui suis-je?** in which one person plays the role of a mystery guest and another guesses the identity by asking **oui-non** questions. This part of the Preparation will help you prepare to play the game.

1 You may want to know whether the mystery guest is a man, a woman, or a child. Write the indefinite markers that complete the following questions.

  a Tu es ＿＿ homme? ▮

  un

  b Tu es ＿＿ femme? ▮

  une

  c Tu es ＿＿ enfant? ▮

  un

2 You may want to ask the mystery guest whether he or she is American. Complete the questions and answers below with the correct form of **être.**

> –Tu ＿＿ américain?
> –Non, je ne ＿＿ pas américain. ▮

> *es, suis*

3 If you guessed the wrong nationality, you may want to try again. This time ask whether the mystery guest is French.

> –＿＿ ＿＿ français?
> –Oui, ＿＿ ＿＿ français. ▮

> *Tu es, je suis*

4 You'll probably want to know the occupation of the mystery guest. Remember that when **être** is followed by the name of an occupation, the indefinite marker is usually omitted. Write questions and answers with the cues provided.

> Modèle: architecte (non) ▮
>
> > *–Tu es architecte?*
> > *–Non, je ne suis pas architecte.*

  a comptable (non) ▮

  > *–Tu es comptable?*
  > *–Non, je ne suis pas comptable.*

  b écrivain (non) ▮

  > *–Tu es écrivain?*
  > *–Non, je ne suis pas écrivain.*

  c acteur (oui) ▮

  > *–Tu es acteur?*
  > *–Oui, je suis acteur.*

5 Ask the mystery guest the following questions in French.

   a Do you live in Paris? |

        Tu habites à Paris?

   b Do you speak French? |

        Tu parles français?

   c Do you like to sing? |

        Tu aimes chanter?

CHECK-UP
Part 1

Answer the following questions with *le voilà* or *la voilà*.

  1 Où est Jean-Paul?   **3** Où est Caroline?

  2 Où est le tableau?

Part 2

Write French equivalents for the questions, and write negative answers.

  1 You like to eat, don't you?   **2** Guy and René live in Spokane, don't they?

VOCABULARY

allemand, –e German
anglais, –e English
belge Belgian
canadien, canadienne Canadian
espagnol, –e Spanish
italien, italienne Italian

suisse Swiss
blond, –e blond-haired
brun, –e brown-haired
roux, rousse red-haired
la voilà here/there she (it) is
le voilà here/there he (it) is

Acteurs au festival du
Marais (Paris)

1 Practice with adjectives

1 You have had practice in class with these adjectives of nationality.

A	B	C
italien	belge	français
canadien	suisse	anglais
		allemand
		espagnol
		américain

a In which group does the written feminine form consist of the masculine form + *-e?* Write the letter A, B, or C. |

      C (français, française; anglais, anglaise, etc.)

b In which group are the masculine and feminine forms identical? |

      B

c In the feminine forms of *italien* and *canadien,* the final consonant is doubled and an *-e* is added. Write the feminine forms of *italien* and *canadien.* |

      italienne, canadienne

2 Philippe is identifying various students at a conference by their nationality. Write complete sentences using the cues provided. Remember to make the adjective agree with the subject.

    Modèle: Klaus (allemand) |

      Klaus est allemand.

a Nathalie (suisse) |

      Nathalie est suisse.

b Maria (espagnol) |

      Maria est espagnole.

c Linda (anglais) |

      Linda est anglaise.

3 Here are the adjectives you have been using in class to describe the way people look according to their hair color.

    blond, blonde   brun, brune   roux, rousse

State that the girl in each pair of sentences below has the same hair color as the boy.

a Alain est brun. Béatrice est ____. |

      brune

b Jean-Pierre est blond. Véronique est ____. |

      blonde

c Michael est roux. Caroline est ____. |

      rousse

4 Write a French equivalent for each sentence below.
  a That boy is a redhead. |
        Ce garçon est roux.
  b This dancer (*f.*) is German. |
        Cette danseuse est allemande.

5 a Read this sentence and complete the English equivalent: *Ce garçon brun est américain. This ___ is American.* |
        brown-haired boy

  b In the English phrase *brown-haired boy,* the adjective comes before the noun. Where does the adjective occur in the French phrase *garçon brun*—before or after the noun? |
        after (French adjectives of hair color always occur after the noun.)

6 Chantal wants a friend to identify some students for her. Write the questions that Chantal asks. Use *ce, cet,* or *cette* and the correct form of the adjectives.

        Modèle: fille / blond / être / anglais |
                Cette fille blonde est anglaise?

  a fille / roux / être / suisse |
        Cette fille rousse est suisse?
  b garçon / roux / être / allemand |
        Ce garçon roux est allemand?
  c fille / brun / être / italien |
        Cette fille brune est italienne? (Did you double the *n*?)

2 *Practice with* qui, où, qu'est-ce que

In this section you will have further practice asking information questions. Suppose a group of Americans are in Europe on vacation. In the frames below you see sentences telling which places they are visiting and some of their reactions. Write a question with *qui,* a question with *qu'est-ce que,* and a question with *où* based on each sentence. Be careful to use the correct word order, as in the model.

        Modèle: Donna visite le Kremlin à Moscou.
                a qui |
                    Qui visite le Kremlin?
                b qu'est-ce que |
                    Qu'est-ce que Donna visite?
                c où |
                    Où est le Kremlin?

1 Nancy visite le Louvre à Paris.
  a qui |
                    Qui visite le Louvre?

b qu'est-ce que |

Qu'est-ce que Nancy visite?

c où |

Où est le Louvre?

2 Robert aime Buckingham Palace à Londres.

    a qui |

Qui aime Buckingham Palace?

    b qu'est-ce que |

Qu'est-ce que Robert aime?

    c où |

Où est Buckingham Palace?

3 Mathieu admire le Parthénon à Athènes.

    a qui |

Qui admire le Parthénon?

    b qu'est-ce que |

Qu'est-ce que Mathieu admire?

    c où |

Où est le Parthénon?

VOCABULARY

un étudiant, une étudiante university student
martiniquais, -e from Martinique
ah bon! (shows mild surprise and interest) oh!; oh?
d'accord O.K.
pardon! excuse me!
tiens! (shows mild astonishment) hey! well!

Usine en Algérie

1 Pre-test practice: demonstrative markers

Soon there will be another progress test. Take a moment now to look at the Phase Objectives on p. 60 and see what you have learned to do in this Phase.

Preparations 24, 25, and 26 will help you get ready for the test. In addition, you can review the vocabulary for this phase by looking at the lists at the ends of the Preparations. All answers for the pre-test sections are in the answer key.

If you are unsure of something, you can use the Summary for review or go back to the specific Preparations mentioned at the beginning of each section. Demonstrative markers were presented in Preparations 19 and 21.

1 There are three singular forms of the demonstrative markers in French: c __, c __ __, and c __ __ __ __.
2 What are the two English equivalents for the markers in frame 1?
3 Before a masculine singular noun that begins with a vowel sound, like *écran* or *homme,* the marker ____ is used.
4 With which of the following nouns would you use the marker *cet?* Write the marker with each noun you choose.

      école   dame   écran   actrice   pilote   écrivain

5 Before a masculine singular noun that begins with a consonant sound, like *garçon* or *cahier,* the marker ____ is used.
6 With which of the following nouns would you use the marker *ce?* Write the marker with each noun you choose.

      musicien   architecte   dentiste   enfant   comptable

7 The demonstrative marker ____ is used before any feminine singular noun, whether it begins with a vowel sound, like *affiche,* or a consonant sound, like *gomme.*
8 Would you use *cet* or *cette* with each of the following nouns? Write the marker with each noun.

      actrice   écrivain   écran   école   enfant

9 Make complete sentences with the following cues. Use the demonstrative marker and the appropriate form of *être.*

    Modèle: femme / belle **|**
              Cette femme est belle.

a garçon / blond
b fille / rousse

c femme / grande
d enfant / beau

2 Pre-test practice: -er *verbs in questions*

Verbs were presented in Preparations 14, 15, and 16. Questions were presented in Preparations 15, 22, and 23.

1 In English, questions in the present tense often have two-part verbs.

Do you *speak* French?
Does she *live* in Paris?

Are you *watching* TV?
Is he *listening* to the radio?

If you were to express these questions in French, you would use a single verb form only.

*Vous **parlez** français?*
*Elle **habite** à Paris?*

*Tu **regardes** la télé?*
*Il **écoute** la radio?*

Express the following questions in French.

a Does she speak Italian?
b Do they (*ils*) speak German?
c Do you (*tu*) speak English?
d Does Robert live in New York?

e Do Pierre and Jean like to skate?
f Are you (*vous*) watching television?
g Is she listening to the radio?
h Are they (*elles*) eating now?

3 Pre-test practice: *descriptive adjectives*

Descriptive adjectives were presented in Preparations 18, 21, and 23.

1 René and his sister Renée are identical twins. State that Renée has the same characteristics as René.

Modèle: René est américain. |
Renée est américaine aussi.

a René est roux.
b René est gros.
c René est jeune.

d René est beau.
e René est jaloux.
f René est gentil.

2 Disagree with the speaker by using the appropriate form of the adjective in parentheses. Begin each response with **Non.**

Modèle: Jeanne est petite, n'est-ce pas? (grand) |
Non, elle est grande.

a M. Gardini est espagnol, n'est-ce pas? (italien)
b Mlle Dubois est intelligente, n'est-ce pas? (bête)
c Cette ville est belle, n'est-ce pas? (laid)
d Julie est belge, n'est-ce pas? (martiniquais)

VOCABULARY

onze eleven	*quinze* fifteen	*dix-huit* eighteen
douze twelve	*seize* sixteen	*dix-neuf* nineteen
treize thirteen	*dix-sept* seventeen	*vingt* twenty
quatorze fourteen		

1 Vocabulary round-up

Vocabulary for this Phase is listed at the ends of the Preparations. All answers for this Preparation are in the answer key.

1 Write complete sentences to say what you are doing during the coming week. Then write the English equivalents.

Modèle: lundi / nager / avec Paul ▮
Lundi, je nage avec Paul. (Monday, I'm swimming with Paul.)

a mardi / écouter / radio / avec Gabrielle
b jeudi / regarder / télévision avec Jean-François
c dimanche / patiner avec Daniel et Sylvie

2 Write sentences to say that you don't do the following things.
danser   patiner   tricoter

3 Complete the following dialogues with the correct name of an occupation.

a –M. Leroi est médecin?
–Non, il est d __ nt __ st __.
b –Mme Colbert est secrétaire?
–Non, elle est c __ mpt __ b __ e.
c –Roger est journaliste?
–Non, il est p __ ot __ g __ __ phe.
d –Denise est architecte?
–Non, elle est p __ o __ e __ s __ ur.
e –Et vous, vous êtes acteur à la télévision, Monsieur?
–Non, je suis __ cri __ __ __ n.

4 Alice has a pen pal. Describe her by using the feminine form of these adjectives: *martiniquais, grand, maigre, intelligent.*
Cette jeune fille est ____. Elle est ____, ____ et elle est ____.

5 Describe Jean-Pierre's pen pal by using the masculine form of these adjectives: *anglaise, petite, belle, rousse, gentille.*
Ce garçon est ____. Il est ____, ____, ____ et il est ____.

6 You have learned a number of names of occupations. Several of them have feminine forms that differ in spelling from the masculine form. Write the feminine forms of each occupation below.

infirmier   musicien   ouvrier
acteur   chanteur   danseur

7 Most feminine adjectives of nationality are spelled differently from masculine adjectives, but not all are. Look at the feminine adjectives below and write their masculine forms.

canadienne   italienne   anglaise   belge   suisse

2 Pre-test practice: je vs. j'

Je vs. *j'* was presented in Preparations 15 and 17.

1 The subject pronoun *je* becomes *j'* when used directly before a verb that begins with a ____ sound, like *aimer*.

2 Which of the following verbs begin with a vowel sound?

écouter   danser   regarder   habiter

3 Would you use *je* or *j'* with the verb forms indicated below? Write *je* or *j'* and the verb form.

a écoute

b danse

c n'écoute pas

d regarde

e ne danse pas

f ne regarde pas

g habite

h n'habite pas

4 Answer the following questions in the affirmative or negative, as indicated.

a Tu aimes tricoter? (Oui,...)

b Tu aimes nager? (Non,...)

3 Pre-test practice: reading comprehension

For each frame below, read the three French sentences that describe a person. Then write the letter of the English phrase that describes the person most accurately.

1 Chantal est danseuse. Elle est jeune et très maigre. Elle habite à Montréal.

Chantal is . . .

a a young singer from Montreal.

b a thin young dancer from Montreal.

c an intelligent young dancer from Montreal.

2 Jean-Pierre est suisse. Il est journaliste et photographe. Il est assez vieux.

Jean-Pierre is . . .

a a rather old Swiss reporter and photographer.

b a rather old Swiss lady who dislikes photographers and reporters.

c a young Swiss reporter and photographer.

3 Mme Lascala est musicienne. Elle est italienne et habite à Rome. Elle n'aime pas la vie à la campagne.

Mme Lascala is . . .

a an Italian architect who lives in the capital of Italy.

b an Italian musician who doesn't like to live in the country.

c an Italian musician who likes to live in the country.

Une Comptine

Une comptine is a rhyme spoken or sung by French children when they are playing. Like English rhymes (**One, two, buckle my shoe,** for instance), they sometimes help children learn numbers, months, and days of the week. Here is a **comptine** for the days of the week, and a translation of it.

Bonjour, Madame Lundi;	Hello, Mrs. Monday;
Comment va Madame Mardi?	How is Mrs. Tuesday?
–Très bien, Madame Mercredi;	–Fine, Mrs. Wednesday.
Dites à Madame Jeudi	Tell Mrs. Thursday
De venir vendredi	To come Friday
Danser samedi	To dance on Saturday
Dans la salle de Dimanche.	In Sunday's Hall.

PREPARATION 26

Getting ready for a test

In the next class you will have a test to measure your mastery of French language skills up to now. Everything in the test is something you have worked with, both in class and at home. This Preparation will describe the types of questions you will be asked. Go through it carefully and check your answers with the answer key.

1 Parts A, B, and C will test how well you understand spoken French. Part A consists of statements about people. You will hear each statement twice. On your answer sheet you will see two pictures—one male and one female. You are to decide whether the statement refers to a male or to a female, and circle the letter of the correct picture. For the frames below, write the correct letter on your worksheet.

a You hear: *Cet architecte est américain.*   A    B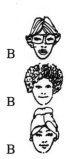

b You hear: *Tu es très grand!*   A   B

c You hear: *L'ouvrière est canadienne.*   A   B

2 In Part B, you will hear a statement twice. You will see a picture of one person and a picture of two people. You are to decide whether the statement is about one person or more than one, and circle the letter of the correct picture. For the frames below, write the correct letter on your worksheet.

a You hear: *Elles aiment écouter la musique.* A   B

b You hear: *Vous parlez français, Monsieur?* A   B

c You hear: *Il habite à New York.* A   B

3 In Part C, you will hear a question, followed by three possible answers. You will see the letters A, B, C for each answer. You circle the letter that corresponds to the correct answer. For example, you hear:

> Qu'est-ce que c'est, derrière le bureau?
> A C'est le tableau.
> B C'est dimanche.
> C Le stylo est sur la feuille de papier.

You see A, B, C. You circle A. For now, write the correct letter on your worksheet.

a Qui est-ce?
   A C'est lundi.
   B C'est dix.
   C C'est Marianne.

b Où est le disque?
   A Le voilà.
   B La voilà.
   C Voilà une cassette.

4 In Part D, you will see three French sentences that describe a person. Then you will see three descriptions in English. You will circle the letter of the English description that fits the French sentence most accurately. For now, write the letter on your worksheet.

Anne-Marie est suisse. Elle est petite et gentille. Elle aime patiner.
a A short, pretty Swiss girl who likes to skate.
b A short, nice Swiss girl who likes to skate.
c A short, nice Swiss girl who likes to swim.

5 In Part E, you will see a list of sentences with blanks. You will complete each sentence by writing the correct form of the adjective in parentheses. For now, write the adjectives on your worksheet.

a (roux) Jean-Pierre est petit et ___.
b (intelligent) Cette musicienne est ___.
c (anglais) M. Cabrini est italien mais Mme Cabrini est ___.

6 In Part F, you will see a list of sentences with blanks. You will complete each sentence by writing the correct demonstrative marker: *ce, cet,* or *cette.* Write the answers on your worksheet.

a ___ enfant est gentil.
b ___ fille est brune.

c ___ bureau est laid.
d ___ enfant est belle.

7 In Part G, you will see verb forms without subjects. You will fill in blanks with *je* or *j'*, whichever is correct. Write the answers on your worksheet.

    a ____ n'aime pas   **c** ____ mange

    b ____ écoute   **d** ____ habite

8 In Part H, you will see *-er* verb forms without subject pronouns. You are to write in the correct subject pronoun or pronouns. For now, write them on your worksheet.

    a ____ tricotez   **d** ____ manges

    b ____, ____ adorent   **e** ____ ne cherchons pas

    c ____, ____, ____ parle

9 In Part I, you are to complete each sentence with the correct form of the verb *être*. Write the answers on your worksheet.

    a Jacqueline et Pierre, vous ____ là?   **c** Les enfants ____ là.

    b Nous ____ ici, papa.

10 In Part J, you will use the cues provided to form questions.

        Modèle: Does she like TV? (aimer / télévision) |
                        Elle aime la télévision?

    a Is Jeannette looking for a record? (chercher / disque)

    b Do you like French? (aimer / français)

    c Do they (*ils*) like to swim? (aimer / nager)

11 Part K will test your ability to write French correctly. You will see a series of cues. Use each group of cues to write a complete sentence. For *c* __, *l* __, *u* __ write the correct demonstrative, definite, or indefinite marker. Follow the model.

        Modèle: c__ actrice / être / italien |
                       Cette actrice est italienne.

    a l__ dame / qui nager / être / espagnol

    b c__ garçon / ne...pas / aimer / l__ histoire

    c vous / regarder / l__ télévision aujourd'hui?

There will be an extra-credit section in which you can complete a dialogue. If you want to review further, look at the Summary and at the Vocabularies at the ends of the Preparations.

NOTE   ***The grading system in France***

One grading system used in France is based on letters, as in the United States. Another grading system is based on a range from 0 to 20. A grade of 10 is **passable** (passing), 12 is **assez bien** (fair), 14 is **bien** (good), and 16 or above is **très bien** (very good). As a student progresses through the **lycée,** grading becomes more and more strict. In classes of **première** and **terminale,** a grade of 15 is considered quite good.

SUMMARY

1 Regular -er verbs (*Preparations 14, 15, 16*)

a. In French, the infinitive form of a verb consists of one word with two parts: a stem (which gives the meaning of the verb) and an infinitive ending.

b. Many French infinitives end in the written ending *-er.* They are referred to as regular *-er* verbs because their forms follow a predictable pattern. Only one *-er* verb (**aller,** to go) is not regular.

<table>
<tr><td colspan="2">AFFIRMATIVE</td><td colspan="2">NEGATIVE</td></tr>
<tr><td align="right">j'</td><td>aime</td><td align="right">je</td><td>n'aime pas</td></tr>
<tr><td align="right">tu</td><td>aimes</td><td align="right">tu</td><td>n'aimes pas</td></tr>
<tr><td align="right">il/elle</td><td>aime</td><td align="right">il/elle</td><td>n'aime pas</td></tr>
<tr><td align="right">ils/elles</td><td>aiment</td><td align="right">ils/elles</td><td>n'aiment pas</td></tr>
<tr><td align="right">nous</td><td>aimons</td><td align="right">nous</td><td>n'aimons pas</td></tr>
<tr><td align="right">vous</td><td>aimez</td><td align="right">vous</td><td>n'aimez pas</td></tr>
</table>

c. When a verb begins with a vowel sound, as in the case of **aimer,** the subject pronoun *je* becomes *j',* and the negative particle *ne* becomes *n'.* In speech, there is a linking /z/ sound between *ils, elles, nous, vous,* and the matching affirmative verb forms.

d. An *-er* verb form usually has more than one English equivalent.

je patine	I skate / I'm skating
je ne patine pas	I don't skate / I'm not skating
tu patines?	do you skate? / are you skating?

e. In French, when a present-tense verb form is followed by another verb, the second verb is always in the infinitive form.

*Tu aimes **danser?*** Do you like *to dance?* (Do you like dancing?)

2 Uses of the indefinite and definite markers (*Preparations 14, 16*)

a. The indefinite marker is used to identify an item or to focus attention on someone or something. The definite marker is used to refer to an item already mentioned or identified.

*C'est **une** affiche. **L'**affiche est belle.*
***Une** femme parle avec Michel. **La** femme qui parle avec Michel est Mme Delacroix.*

b. The indefinite marker is usually omitted in French when the name of an occupation follows a form of *être.*

*Je suis **architecte.*** I'm *an architect.*

c. The definite marker is used in making general statements.

*Il écoute **la radio.*** He listens to *the radio.*

*J'aime **la musique moderne.*** I like *modern music.*

3 Le voilà, la voilà *(Preparation 22)*

The phrases *le voilà* and *la voilà* are used to point out a person or a thing. *Le* replaces a masculine singular noun; *la* replaces a feminine singular noun.

–Où est le garçon?	*–Le voilà.*	There he is.
–Où est la fille?	*–La voilà.*	There she is.
–Où est le cahier?	*–Le voilà.*	There it is.
–Où est la gomme?	*–La voilà.*	There it is.

4 *Forming questions* *(Preparations 18, 22, 23)*

a. There are two major kinds of questions in French: questions that require an answer with *oui* or *non* (*oui-non* questions) and questions that begin with a question word, such as *où, qui,* or *qu'est-ce que* (information questions).

b. *Oui-non* questions have a rising intonation pattern. Information questions have a falling intonation pattern.

OUI-NON QUESTIONS

Il est professeur?

Tu aimes le jazz, n'est-ce pas?

INFORMATION QUESTIONS

Où est Marie-Claire?

Qu'est-ce que tu écoutes?

The *que* of *qu'est-ce que* becomes *qu'* before a word beginning with a vowel: ***Qu'est-ce qu'elle aime?***

5 *The demonstrative markers* ce, cet, *and* cette *(Preparations 19, 21)*

a. The demonstrative markers *ce, cet,* and *cette* are used with singular nouns. Each marker can mean *this* or *that,* depending on the context.

b. *Ce* is used with a masculine singular noun beginning with a consonant. *Cet* is used with a masculine singular noun beginning with a vowel sound. *Cette* is used with any feminine singular noun.

c. *Cet* and *cette* sound alike in speech.

Ce garçon est gentil.	*Cette fille est gentille.*
Cet enfant est petit.	*Cette enfant est petite.*

6 *The relative pronoun* qui *(Preparation 19)*

The relative pronoun *qui* (who, that) is used to combine two statements. *Qui* replaces the subject of a sentence. It may refer to either a person or a thing.

Anne parle avec un homme. ***Cet homme*** *est photographe.*
Anne parle avec un homme ***qui*** *est photographe.*

7 *More about adjectives* *(Preparations 18, 21, 23)*

a. All feminine singular adjectives end in *-e.*
b. An adjective agrees in gender with the noun it describes.
c. Most feminine adjectives differ in sound and spelling from the masculine form. Some differ only in spelling. Some do not differ at all.

MASCULINE	canadien	beau	espagnol	belge
FEMININE	canadienne	belle	espagnole	belge

À Chacun son goût

On aime ou on n'aime pas...!

André and Valérie meet at a friend's house and talk about their mutual likes and dislikes.

ANDRÉ	Tu aimes danser?
VALÉRIE	Oui, beaucoup. Et toi?
ANDRÉ	Pas du tout. Je déteste danser.
VALÉRIE	Mais tu aimes la musique?
ANDRÉ	Ah oui, j'adore écouter le rock, le jazz...
VALÉRIE	Moi aussi! Et la musique classique, tu aimes?
ANDRÉ	Pas tellement.
VALÉRIE	Moi non plus.

You like or you don't like. . . !

ANDRÉ	*Do you like to dance?*
VALÉRIE	*Yes, a lot. Do you?*
ANDRÉ	*Not at all. I hate to dance.*
VALÉRIE	*But you like music?*
ANDRÉ	*Oh yes, I love to listen to rock, jazz. . .*
VALÉRIE	*Me too! Do you like classical music?*
ANDRÉ	*Not much.*
VALÉRIE	*I don't either.*

Ville ou campagne?

Véronique Lebeau, a young Canadian visiting the United States, is being interviewed for the school newspaper by Charles.

CHARLES	Vous habitez à Montréal?
VÉRONIQUE	Non, j'habite à Saint-Pierre.
CHARLES	C'est une grande ville?
VÉRONIQUE	Oh, non, c'est un petit village!
CHARLES	Vous aimez la vie à la campagne?
VÉRONIQUE	Pas beaucoup. Je préfère Montréal.

City or country?

CHARLES	*Do you live in Montreal?*
VÉRONIQUE	*No, I live in Saint-Pierre.*
CHARLES	*Is it a big city?*
VÉRONIQUE	*Oh, no, it's a small village.*
CHARLES	*Do you like living in the country (country living)?*
VÉRONIQUE	*Not much. I prefer Montreal.*

Une belle voiture, c'est important?

Jacques teases Roger about a young man who is standing near a car and talking with Roger's girlfriend.

ROGER	Qui est ce garçon qui parle avec Anne?
JACQUES	C'est François Galant. Il est beau, hein?
ROGER	Beau! Avec cette barbe? Ah non, alors!
JACQUES	Avec une belle voiture, un homme est toujours beau!
ROGER	Oh, ça va, ça va!
JACQUES	Dis donc, Roger, tu es jaloux?
ROGER	Moi, jaloux? Tu plaisantes!

Is a beautiful car important?

ROGER	*Who's that boy who's talking with Anne?*
JACQUES	*It's François Galant. He's handsome, isn't he?*
ROGER	*Handsome! With that beard? Oh, no!*
JACQUES	*With a beautiful car, a man is always handsome!*
ROGER	*(With annoyance) O.K., O.K.!*
JACQUES	*Say, Roger, are you jealous?*
ROGER	*Me, jealous? You've got to be kidding!*

Le Monde° est petit   world

Jean-Claude is at a get-together in New York for young people in an international exchange program. He bumps into a girl and makes her spill her beverage.

JEAN-CLAUDE	Oh pardon! Excusez-moi°! Euh...*excuse me!*	excuse me
MARIE-CLAIRE	Mais non, mais non, ce n'est pas grave°!	serious
JEAN-CLAUDE	Oh, vous parlez français! Vous êtes française?	
MARIE-CLAIRE	Oui, je suis de Paris. Et vous?	
JEAN-CLAUDE	Moi, je suis de Fort-de-France°.	capital of Martinique

5

MARIE-CLAIRE	Ah bon°! Qu'est-ce que vous faites° à New York?	oh / what are you doing
JEAN-CLAUDE	Je suis étudiant°. Vous aussi, je suppose?	university student
MARIE-CLAIRE	Oui, moi aussi, je suis étudiante. Je m'appelle Marie-Claire.	
JEAN-CLAUDE	Tiens°! C'est le nom° de ma sœur°! Moi, je m'appelle Jean-Claude.	hey! / name / my sister
MARIE-CLAIRE	Dites, je voudrais bien° un autre jus de fruit°. D'accord°?	I'd really like another fruit juice / O.K
JEAN-CLAUDE	Oui, d'accord. Allons-y°! Et encore° pardon.	let's go / again

EXERCICES

1 *Prepositions*

2 *Demonstrative markers*

Ce	1 actrice	est célèbre
Cet	2 acteur	
Cette	3 danseur	
	4 chanteuse	
	5 écrivain	

PHASE THREE OBJECTIVES

In this Phase you will learn vocabulary for family members, along with additional occupations, useful objects, and descriptive adjectives. By the end of this Phase you will be able to:

1 Speak about more than one person or thing, using plural nouns, adjectives, and markers.

2 Say who owns something by using possessive markers.

3 Say what people have and how old they are, using the verb **avoir.**

4 Say what people see, do, or are familiar with, using the verbs **voir, faire,** and **connaître.**

5 Say that people don't have certain things, using the construction **ne...pas de** + noun.

6 Use the direct-object pronouns **le, la,** and **les** for the English expressions **him, her, it,** and **them.**

7 Report or point out something, using the expressions **il y a** (there is, there are) and **voilà.**

8 Ask **oui-non** questions with the expression **est-ce que.**

9 Talk about family and friends.

10 Count from 21 to 69.

❀ The cultural notes discuss aspects of French farm life, relations between parents and children in France, French dating patterns, French expressions of courtesy, and Haiti, a French-speaking republic in the Caribbean.

1 The irregular verb avoir

This section will give you practice with a very common French verb, *avoir* (to have).

1 Yvette is asking her classmate Jacques about his family. Read this conversation.

> *Yvette:*   *Tu as un frère?*
> *Jacques:*   *Non, mais j'ai deux sœurs.*

a Write the English equivalent of the dialogue. |

–Do you have a brother?   –No, but I have two sisters.

b Write the subject-verb phrases that mean *I have* and *you have*. |

j'ai, tu as (*J'ai* and *tu as* are forms of the verb *avoir*.)

The chart at the right summarizes the present-tense forms of *avoir*. Refer to the chart when you answer frames 2–5.

j'	ai
tu	as
il/elle	a
ils/elles	ont
nous	avons
vous	avez

2 *Avoir* is called an irregular verb because its forms don't follow a pattern of infinitive stem + ending. Which of the following verbs is also irregular—*aimer, être,* or *parler?* |

être (In many languages, the verbs that are used most frequently are irregular. *To be* and *to have* are irregular in English, too.)

3 In the plural forms of *avoir,* a linking sound occurs between *ils, elles, nous, vous* and the matching verb forms. Is this sound like the /s/ in *salut* or the /z/ in *chaise?* |

the /z/ in *chaise*

4 Say that the following people have a brother by writing the subject and matching verb form. Read each complete sentence aloud.

> Modèle: Alain _____ un frère. |
> *Alain a*

a Nous _____ un frère. |

Nous avons

b Tu _____ un frère. |

Tu as

c Sylvie _____ un frère. |

Sylvie a

d Ils ___ un frère. |

Ils ont

e Je ___ un frère. |

J'ai (Remember that *je* becomes *j'* before a vowel sound.)

f Vous ___ un frère. |

Vous avez

5 Answer the questions below in the affirmative. Answers are in the answer key.

Modèle: Eric Duhamel a une sœur? |

Oui, il a une sœur.

a Tu as une sœur?

b Monique Dupré a une sœur?

c Vous avez une sœur, vous deux?

d Pierre et Robert ont une sœur?

2 *Plural nouns and the indefinite marker* des

The simplest definition of *plural* is *more than one.* In this section you will see how to say in French that there is more than one of something. First, consider how the plural works in English.

1 Complete the following "equations."
  a 1 chimpanzee + 1 chimpanzee = 2 ___. |

chimpanzees

  b 1 ostrich + 1 ostrich = 2 ___. |

ostriches

2 *Chimpanzee* is made plural by adding the ending ___. *Ostrich* is made plural by adding the ending ___. |

s, es

3 In written English, most plural nouns have the ending *-s* or *-es.* Are these plural endings pronounced in speech? |

yes

4 True or false? In spoken English, you can usually tell whether a noun is singular or plural by the sound of the noun itself. |

true

5 Compare the singular and plural forms of the following French nouns.

un garçon, deux garçons   un crayon, deux crayons
une fille, deux filles   une table, deux tables

  a What ending is added to the singular of the noun to form the plural? |

s (In spoken French, the plural ending *-s* is not pronounced.)

  b Rewrite these noun phrases with ***deux: une élève, un cousin.*** |

deux élèves, deux cousins

6 If you were buying school supplies, you might say to the clerk *I'd like a pencil and an eraser.*

    a Suppose, however, that you don't know how many pencils and erasers you want, but you need more than one. What word could you use to complete this sentence? *I'd like ___ pencils and ___ erasers.* |

        some (*Some* is the plural indefinite marker in English.)

    b Could you also say *I'd like pencils and erasers,* using no marker? |

        yes

7 In English, to indicate more than one without giving an exact number, you can use either the indefinite marker *some,* or a plural noun without a marker.

    French, like English, has an indefinite marker for use with plural nouns. In French, though, you *must* include the marker. Look at the French sentences below.

        Je voudrais un crayon et une gomme.
        Je voudrais des crayons et des gommes.

The plural form of **un** and **une** is ___. |

        des (There is only one plural indefinite marker—*des*. It is used with both masculine and feminine nouns.)

8 The marker **des** is pronounced as /de/ before nouns beginning with a consonant. Read aloud: **des crayons.** (Remember that the plural ending *-s* of a noun is not pronounced.)

    When **des** comes before a noun beginning with a vowel sound, there is a linking /z/ between **des** and the noun. Read aloud: **des affiches.**

    Read the following phrases aloud. Write the ones in which a linking /z/ is heard.

        des écrans   des livres   des hommes   des professeurs |

        des écrans, des hommes

9 Write sentences to say that you have more than one of the following items.

    Modèle: cassette |

        J'ai des cassettes.

    a chaise |

        J'ai des chaises.

    b étagère |

        J'ai des étagères.

10 Suppose a new student who has just come into your class asks for certain supplies. Tell this person that the teacher has some. Answers are in the answer key.

    Modèle: Je voudrais un crayon. |

        Le professeur a des crayons.

    a Je voudrais un cahier.   **b** Je voudrais une gomme.

NOTE

L'Argent de poche

Money is less available to young people in France than in the U.S. Children may be given **argent de poche** (pocket money) for getting exceptionally good grades in school and for doing household chores such as washing the car, doing the dishes, or cleaning their room or the yard. In some families they are expected to do these jobs without pay. Baby-sitting is not a source of revenue for most French teenagers because parents generally prefer to hire university students rather than students of junior

high or high school age. Pocket money is usually spent on books, records, and extra snacks, or saved in a piggy bank (**une tirelire**).

3 Ne...pas de + *noun*

1 Read the following sentences, and look closely at the markers.
> *Nous avons un frère, mais nous n'avons pas de sœur. Serge a une sœur, mais il n'a pas de frère. Chantal et Anne ont des cousins, mais elles n'ont pas de cousines.*

a Say the English equivalents of all three sentences. ▌

We have a brother, but we don't have a sister. Serge has a sister, but he doesn't have a brother. Chantal and Anne have (some) male cousins, but they don't have (any) female cousins. (The words in parentheses could be left out.)

b In the negative phrases *pas de sœur, pas de frère,* and *pas de cousines,* which marker replaces *un, une,* and *des?* ▌

de (The markers *un, une, des* are replaced by *de* in most negative sentences. The major exception occurs with *être: C'est un stylo? Non, ce n'est pas un stylo.*)

2 Compare these charts of the affirmative and negative forms of *avoir.*

j'	ai		je	n'	ai	pas
tu	as		tu	n'	as	pas
il/elle	a		il/elle	n'	a	pas
ils/elles	ont		ils/elles	n'	ont	pas
nous	avons		nous	n'	avons	pas
vous	avez		vous	n'	avez	pas

a Why is *n'* used instead of *ne?* ▌

because all forms of *avoir* begin with a vowel sound

b Why does the affirmative form *j'* become *je* in the negative? ▌

because *ne* begins with a consonant, not a vowel

c *De* also changes when it precedes a word beginning with a vowel sound. Complete this sentence: *M. Dufour n'a pas ____ enfants.* ▌

d'

3 Martin doesn't have many things. Write negative answers to these questions about him. Also write English equivalents of your answers for **a** and **b**.

Modèle: Martin a des stylos? |
Non, il n'a pas de stylos. No, he doesn't have any pens.

a Martin a une caméra? |
Non, il n'a pas de caméra. No, he doesn't have a movie camera.

b Il a un écran? |
Non, il n'a pas d'écran. No, he doesn't have a screen. (Did you remember that *de* becomes *d'* when it precedes a vowel sound?)

c Il a une voiture, n'est-ce pas? |
Non, il n'a pas de voiture.

d Il a des affiches? |
Non, il n'a pas d'affiches.

CHECK-UP
Part 1

Write the French equivalents:
1 I have two brothers.

2 They (*ils*) have a transistor.

Part 2

Write the French equivalents:
1 I'd like some books.

2 Do you have pencils?

Part 3

Express these ideas in the negative:
1 Tu as une voiture.

2 Ils ont des enfants.

VOCABULARY

vingt et un twenty-one
vingt-deux twenty-two
vingt-trois twenty-three
vingt-quatre twenty-four
vingt-cinq twenty-five
vingt-six twenty-six

vingt-sept twenty-seven
vingt-huit twenty-eight
vingt-neuf twenty-nine
trente thirty
avoir to have
ce sont these are, they are

ON N'EST JAMAIS CONTENT! People are never happy!
l'aîné, -e the oldest one
mon cousin my (male) cousin
ton frère your brother
une sœur a sister
pas de not any; no
beaucoup a lot
bien nice
malheureusement unfortunately
pourquoi? why?
mais but
hein? isn't it? huh?
bof! (shows indifference or mild impatience) well. . . !
oh là là! (shows surprise, pleasure, dismay, annoyance) oh my!
oh, oui alors! (shows enthusiastic agreement) oh yes! you bet!

1 *The plural definite marker* les

1 Take a look at the following noun phrases. Then use them to answer the questions below.

the boy	the girl	the man	the book
the boys	the girls	the men	the books

True or false? In English you can tell whether a noun is plural by the definite marker *the*. ▌

> false (*The* is used before both singular and plural nouns.)

2 Look at the French equivalents of the noun phrases in frame 1.

le garçon	*la fille*	*l'homme*	*le livre*
les garçons	*les filles*	*les hommes*	*les livres*

a Which forms of the French definite marker are used with singular nouns? ▌

> *le, la, l'*

b Which form of the definite marker is used with plural nouns? ▌

> *les*

c Is *les* used with both masculine and feminine nouns? ▌

> yes (There is only one plural form of the definite marker: *les*.)

3 In written French, how can you tell that the noun phrase *les garçons* is plural? ▌

> by the marker *les* and by the *s* at the end of *garçons*

4 In spoken French, how can you tell that *les garçons* is plural? ▌

> by the marker *les* (Remember that the plural noun ending *-s* is not usually pronounced.)

5 When *les* precedes a noun beginning with a vowel sound, there is a linking /z/ sound, as with the plural marker *des.* Read the following examples aloud: ***les garçons, les enfants, les mathématiques, les étagères.*** In which noun phrases is there a linking /z/? ▌

> *les enfants, les étagères*

6 Copy the following noun phrases in which a linking /z/ will occur, and put a link mark ‿ between the marker and the noun.

les éléphants	*les crocodiles*	*les girafes*	*les antilopes* ▌

> *les‿éléphants, les‿antilopes*

les frères Jacques

7 Write sentences to tell to whom the items below belong. Begin each sentence with *Ce sont* and the plural definite marker *les*. Write the English equivalent of frames **a** and **b**.

Modèle: cahier / Pierre |
> *Ce sont les cahiers de Pierre.*   They are Pierre's notebooks.

a frère / Marie-Claire |
> *Ce sont les frères de Marie-Claire.*   They are Marie-Claire's brothers.

b affiche / Agnès |
> *Ce sont les affiches d'Agnès.*   They are Agnès' posters.

c chaise / Mme Rimbaud |
> *Ce sont les chaises de Mme Rimbaud.*

8 Answer the following questions using the cues provided. Write complete sentences. Answers are in the answer key.

Modèle: Ce sont les disques d'Annette?  |
> *Non, ce sont les cassettes d'Annette.*

a Ce sont les tables de M. Roger?

b Ce sont les frères d'Henri?

2 Voilà *and* il y a

1 Suppose a friend has lost a pet snake and two mice in the back yard. If you see the snake, you might say: *There's the snake!* If you see the two mice, you might say: *There're the mice!*

a To point out one object or person, you can use the expression ____. |
> there is (there's)

b To point out more than one object or person, you can use the expression ____. |
> there are (there're)

2 Now read the French equivalents of the exclamations in frame 1.

Voilà le serpent!   *Voilà les souris!*

In French, to point out one or more than one item or person, you use the expression ____. |
> voilà (*Voilà* is used with a singular noun or a plural noun.)

3 Suppose you are able to catch your friend's snake. As you hand it over, you might say *Here's the snake.* In French, you would probably say **Voilà le serpent.**

    a Can **voilà** be used to point out something that's nearby as well as something that's far away? ▌

                    yes (*Voilà* can mean *here is / here are* or *there is / there are*.)

    b Write in French: *Here's a present.* ▌

                 Voilà un cadeau.

4 Use **voilà** and the following terms to write French equivalents for the sentences below.

          l'oncle   la tante   les parents   les grands-parents

    a Here're Charles' grandparents. ▌

                 Voilà les grands-parents de Charles.

    b There's Paul's aunt. ▌

                 Voilà la tante de Paul.

    c There're Véronique's parents. ▌

                 Voilà les parents de Véronique.

    d Here's Yvonne's uncle. ▌

                 Voilà l'oncle d'Yvonne.

5 Let's suppose you are in a restaurant in New York and you see a mouse running under the table.

    a The mouse is now out of sight, but you can still report this fact to the waiter by saying: ___ *a mouse under the table!* ▌

           There's (There is)

    b If you saw two mice disappear under the table, you would say: ___ *two mice under the table!* ▌

           There're (There are)

6 In English, you can use *there is* and *there are* to point out someone or something that you and your listener can see. You can also use these expressions to report the existence of a person or thing that may or may not be visible to your listener. In French, however, two different phrases are used.

    a Here are the French equivalents of the sentences in frame 5.

        Il y a une souris sous la table!

        Il y a deux souris sous la table!

What phrase is used in French to report that there are mice under the table? ▌

               Il y a (*Il y a* can be used with singular and plural nouns.)

    b If the mice poked their noses out from under the table, which expression would a speaker of French use to point them out? ___ **les souris!** ▌

               Voilà

7 To point out something or someone visible, the expression ___ is used in French. To report the existence of something or someone, the expression ___ is used in French. ▌

             voilà; il y a

8 Report to someone that there are two mice under the chair. |
Il y a deux souris sous la chaise.

9 Point out this animal to someone: ***un lion.*** |
Voilà un lion.

10 Report the location of this animal: ***lion / dans la salle de classe.*** |
Il y a un lion dans la salle de classe.

11 The negative of ***il y a*** is ***il n'y a pas.*** Complete the answer to the following question.

–*Il y a un zèbre dans la classe?*
–*Non, ____ zèbre dans la classe.* |
Il n'y a pas de (Did you remember that the indefinite marker *un* becomes *de* in a negative sentence?)

12 Write the English equivalent of ***Il n'y a pas de zèbre dans la classe.*** |
There is no (There isn't any) zebra in the classroom.

13 Imagine you have a little brother who is scared of finding strange animals in the house. Tell him that there aren't any. Answers are in the answer key.

Modèle: Il y a un tigre sous la table? |
Non, il n'y a pas de tigre sous la table!

a Il y a des crocodiles dans le tiroir?   **b** Il y a un lion sous la chaise?

CHECK-UP
Part 1

Write the plurals of the following nouns, using the definite marker *les.* Insert a link mark to indicate where liaison occurs.

la danseuse   l'ingénieur   l'actrice   le médecin

Part 2

1 Point out the following people: *Danielle; le professeur de gymnastique.*
2 Write a French sentence to point out Danielle's sister. Write a French sentence to report the following: *There are three boys who are talking with the gym teacher.*

VOCABULARY

le cousin, la cousine cousin
la famille family
la fille daughter
le fils son
le frère brother
les grands-parents grandparents
la grand-mère grandmother
le grand-père grandfather
la mère mother
l'oncle uncle
les parents parents; relatives
le père father

la sœur sister
la tante aunt
une antilope antelope
un crocodile crocodile
un lion lion
un zèbre zebra
une photo photograph
ce sont these are, those are, they are
il y a there is, there are
il n'y a pas de there is (there are) no. . .
qu'est-ce qu'il y a...? what is there. . . ?

1 Word sets: family vocabulary

1 You have been learning vocabulary in word sets since the beginning of your study of French; for example, classroom supplies, numbers, *-er* verbs, and adjectives of nationality. Here is the most recent set of words you have been practicing in class: family vocabulary.

la mère	*la fille*	*la sœur*	*la tante*
le père	*le fils*	*le frère*	*l'oncle*

la cousine	*la grand-mère*	*les parents*
le cousin	*le grand-père*	*les grands-parents*

a Which French word is a cognate of *uncle?* |
  oncle (Remember that a cognate is a word that is similar in spelling and meaning to a word in another language.)

b What is the French word for *aunt?* |
  tante

c What is the French equivalent for *daughter?* |
  fille

d What is the French equivalent for *son?* |
  fils (When the singular form of a noun ends in *s*, no *-s* is added to make the noun plural. The *s* in *fils* is pronounced: /fis/.)

2 Here is the family tree of Henri Dupont. Look to see how he is related to the other people, then answer the questions on the next page.

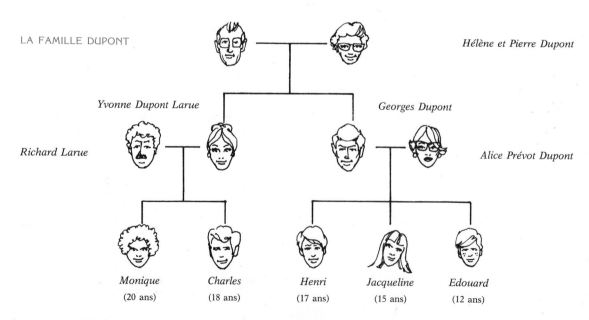

LA FAMILLE DUPONT

Hélène et Pierre Dupont

Yvonne Dupont Larue   *Georges Dupont*

Richard Larue   *Alice Prévot Dupont*

Monique	*Charles*	*Henri*	*Jacqueline*	*Edouard*
(20 ans)	(18 ans)	(17 ans)	(15 ans)	(12 ans)

a Henri et Edouard Dupont sont les ___ de Georges et d'Alice Dupont. |

fils

b Jacqueline Dupont est la ___ d'Henri et d'Edouard. |

sœur

c Edouard Dupont est le ___ de Jacqueline et d'Henri. |

frère

d Alice Dupont est la ___ d'Henri, de Jacqueline et d'Edouard. |

mère

e Georges Dupont est le ___ d'Henri, de Jacqueline et d'Edouard. |

père

f Alice et Georges Dupont sont les ___ d'Henri, de Jacqueline et d'Edouard. |

parents

g Hélène et Pierre Dupont sont les ___ de Georges Dupont et les ___ d'Henri, de Jacqueline et d'Edouard. |

parents, grands-parents

h Henri a une ___, Monique Larue, et un ___, Charles Larue. |

cousine, cousin

i M. et Mme Larue sont l' ___ et la ___ d'Henri. |

oncle, tante

NOTE ✳ ## *Relations between parents and children*

French families tend to be close-knit. In many families, keeping in touch with grandparents, cousins, aunts and uncles, is considered to be important. In smaller cities and towns, the members of the extended family may gather for dinner on Sundays or holidays.

French parents tend to expect more restrained behavior from their children than Americans do. Particularly when the children are with a group of adults, parents expect them to be polite and unobtrusive.

There are varying degrees of permissiveness regarding the use of the TV set, the telephone, and the family car. The French are TV enthusiasts, and the conflict between watching TV and doing homework exists as it does in the United States. French students are expected to do all their homework before they may watch TV. There is great pressure to earn good grades and to pass the **baccalauréat**—the difficult examination that enables a person to go to the university or apply for a good job.

Telephones are much more difficult to obtain in France than in the United States. Children don't have their own phones, and even teenagers tend to keep their calls short so as not to monopolize the phone.

The use of the family automobile by a teenager poses less of a problem than in the U.S. because a French person cannot obtain an automobile driver's license (**permis de conduire**) before the age of eighteen.

les *parents terribles* de Jean Cocteau

2 Avoir + ans *to express age*

1 Compare the following sentences to see which verbs are used in French and English to express age.

> *J'ai 17 ans.*   I'm 17 years old.
> *Ma tante a 32 ans.*   My aunt is 32 years old.

a Which verb is used to express age in English—*to be* or *to have?* |
  to be

b Which verb is used to express age in French—*être* or *avoir?* |
  avoir

2 French uses *avoir + ans* (*years*) to express age: *Il a huit ans.* Does French also use the equivalent of *old*, as in *He is 8 years old?* |
  no

3 It may help you to remember *avoir + ans* if you think of age as accumulated experience in living. For example, *Roger a douze ans: Roger has 12 years (of experience in living)*. In the sentence *Marie a quatorze ans,* Marie has how many years of experience in living? |
  14

4 Here are the numbers 11 to 20 in French.

> 11 *onze*   13 *treize*   15 *quinze*   17 *dix-sept*   19 *dix-neuf*
> 12 *douze*   14 *quatorze*   16 *seize*   18 *dix-huit*   20 *vingt*

Look back at the bottom row of Henri Dupont's family tree. Tell how old each person is. Write out each number in full.

> Modèle: Monique Larue |
>   *Elle a vingt ans.*

a Henri Dupont |
      Il a dix-sept ans.

b Edouard Dupont |
      Il a douze ans.

c Jacqueline Dupont |
      Elle a quinze ans.

d Charles Larue |
      Il a dix-huit ans.

5 Suppose someone asks how old Jacqueline is. Read the question and answer.

> *–Jacqueline a seize ans?*
> *–Non, elle n'a pas seize ans, elle a quinze ans.*

Someone else asks how old Henri is. Complete the answer to the question.

> *–Henri a seize ans?*
> *–Non, ____, il a dix-sept ans.* |
>   *il n'a pas seize ans*

3 Practice with avoir

1 Write complete sentences with the following cues. Answers are in the answer key.

   a Mme Perrier / avoir / un grand bureau.   **c** M. et Mme Victor / avoir / deux enfants.

   b Je / avoir / des sœurs.   **d** Vous / avoir / quel âge?

2 Some students are trying to put off taking a test by telling the teacher they don't have any supplies. Use *ne...pas de* with the items below to write what they say. Answers are in the answer key.

      Modèle: des stylos ❙
             Mais nous n'avons pas de stylos!

  a des feuilles de papier   **c** une gomme

  b des crayons

3 The medical center put the wrong ages on the Desjardins family's records. The first number given below is the wrong age; the second number is the right age. Write what Mme Desjardins says in order to correct each error. Answers are in the answer key.

      Modèle: Je 13/33 ❙
           Je n'ai pas treize ans, j'ai trente-trois ans!

  a Le petit Jérôme 15/5   **b** Chantal 24/14

CHECK-UP	Tell how many of each relative you have. Use *ne...pas* if you have none.
Part 1	*la mère* *la fille* *le frère* *la cousine* *les grands-parents*
Part 2	Say how old you are.

VOCABULARY

un serpent snake

LE RECENSEMENT The Census
ma belle-mère my mother-in-law
ma femme my wife
un recenseur census-taker
ça fait that makes. . .
chez vous at your house

Vous avez quel âge? How old are you?

combien de...? how many. . . ?
personnes people
eh oui... (shows resigned acceptance) yeah. . .
en tout altogether
mais non! (shows strong disagreement) no! oh no!

1 The plural of adjectives of nationality

1 An adjective of nationality is one type of descriptive adjective. Compare the adjectives in the following sentences.

Jack is American.   Jack and Bob are American.
Lois is American.   Lois and Mary are American.

In English, does the sound or spelling of an adjective of nationality change when it refers to more than one person? **|**

no (It remains the same whether it refers to one male, one female, or to more than one male or female.)

2 The chart below illustrates what happens in French when an adjective of nationality refers to more than one male or female. Read the sentences in the chart aloud.

	SINGULAR	PLURAL
M	Jack est américain.	Jack et Bob sont américains.
F	Lois est américaine.	Lois et Mary sont américaines.

a In written French, what ending is added to *américain* and *américaine* to indicate plurality? **|**

s (The written plural of most adjectives is formed by adding -s to the singular form. This -s is not usually pronounced.)

b How many written forms of the adjective *américain* are there? **|**

four

c How many spoken forms of *américain* are there? **|**

two (*Américain, américains* sound alike, as do *américaine, américaines*.)

d Write the plural forms of *canadien* and *canadienne*. **|**

canadiens, canadiennes

3 Read this sentence: *Jack et Lois sont américains.*

a Does the adjective *américains* describe both Jack and Lois? **|**

yes (It is plural.)

b Is *américains* masculine or feminine? **|**

masculine (When an adjective describes nouns of both genders at once, it is always in the masculine form.)

4 Compare the following sentences. Pay special attention to the adjective *français.*

Il est français.   Ils sont français.

a If the masculine singular adjective already ends in *s,* does the masculine plural form change? **|**

no (The masculine singular and masculine plural forms are identical.)

b Rewrite this sentence with the information in parentheses.

Giles est anglais. (William et James) **|**

William et James sont anglais.

5 A sentence like *Il est américain* may be thought of as an equation. The subject is the left part of the equation. A form of *être* is the equals sign. The adjective is the right part of the equation.

> The initials MS stand for masculine singular.

> Il est américain.
> MS = MS

a Whatever is on one side of the equation must be balanced on the other side. When the subject is masculine singular, the adjective must also be ____. |

> masculine singular (MS = MS)

b Complete this sentence with the subject pronoun whose gender and number will balance the equation. ____ *est française.* |

> Elle (The subject must be feminine singular: FS = FS.)

6 Write the subject pronoun that balances this equation. ____ *sont canadiennes.* (FP = FP) |

> Elles

7 The people mentioned below are from various countries. Complete the statements about their nationalities by writing the correct form of *être* and the appropriate adjective.

> Modèle: Mes grands-parents sont d'Italie. Ils ____. |
> *sont italiens*

a M. et Mme Rocher sont de Belgique. Ils ____. |
> *sont belges*

b Les sœurs de mon ami Gilles sont de France. Elles ____. |
> *sont françaises*

c Mme Lamadrid est d'Espagne. Elle ____. |
> *est espagnole*

d Heinz et Werther sont d'Allemagne. Ils ____. |
> *sont allemands*

2 Pre-quiz practice: avoir

In your next class you will have a quiz to let you find out how well you have learned the present-tense forms of *avoir.* The exercise below will help you prepare for it. Write complete sentences with the correct forms of *avoir* and *ne...pas,* or *ne...pas de.* Answers are in the answer key. (Remember that *je* and *ne* before a vowel become *j'* and *n'.*)

> Modèle: elles / ne...pas / avoir / des tantes |
> *Elles n'ont pas de tantes.*

1 nous / avoir / des grands-parents
2 je / avoir / une tante qui / avoir / vingt ans
3 vous / ne...pas / avoir / trente ans
4 tu / avoir / un morceau de craie?

5 elles / avoir / un chien et un chat
6 il / avoir / dix-neuf ans / n'est-ce pas?
7 je / ne...pas / avoir / des frères
8 Guy et Henri / ne...pas / avoir / une sœur

Réunion de famille
à la campagne

3 Le Recensement *with variations*

In class you have been working with the dialogue **Le Recensement.** Try
your hand at rewriting it now. You may complete the dialogue below or
write your own based on a similar situation. You may use real or
imaginary statistics. Before you start, decide to whom the census-taker
is talking—a husband, wife, son or daughter, grandparent, etc. You will
probably have a chance to act out your dialogue in class.

Le Recensement

LE RECENSEUR	Alors, M __, il y a combien de personnes chez vous?
M __RAMBOUILLET	Eh bien, ___ et ___ enfants.
LE RECENSEUR	___ enfants? ___ fils? ___ filles?
M __RAMBOUILLET	___.
LE RECENSEUR	Bon, alors, ça fait ___ personnes en tout.
M __RAMBOUILLET	Mais non! Il y a aussi ___.
LE RECENSEUR	Alors, ça fait ___ personnes?
M __RAMBOUILLET	Oui, ___ personnes.
LE RECENSEUR	Très bien. Merci beaucoup, M __. Au revoir.
M __RAMBOUILLET	Au revoir, M __.

CHECK-UP
Part 1

Write the French equivalents for the following sentences.

1 This girl is Swiss.

2 My aunts are Canadian.

3 Mr. and Mrs. Schmidt are German.

4 Those men are French.

VOCABULARY

agent de police policeman
avocat, avocate lawyer
coiffeur, coiffeuse hairdresser
un chien dog

directeur, directrice principal; director
ingénieur engineer
mécanicien, mécanicienne mechanic
un chat cat

1 Plural forms of descriptive adjectives

1 In Preparation 30 you practiced with the plural form of adjectives of nationality. This part will give you practice with other descriptive adjectives. Look at the following sentences.

Il est grand.   *Ils sont grands.*
Elle est grande.   *Elles sont grandes.*

a In written French, what is added to **grand** and **grande** to indicate plurality? |

s (The plural of most adjectives is formed by adding -s to the singular form.)

b How many written forms of the adjective *grand* are there? |

four

c How many spoken forms are there? |

two (Remember that the -s ending is not usually pronounced.)

2 Complete the second sentence with the correct form of **grand. Nicolas est grand. Les sœurs de Nicolas sont ＿＿ aussi.** |

grandes

3 Now read the following sentences aloud.

Il est riche.   *Ils sont riches.*
Elle est riche.   *Elles sont riches.*

a In spoken French, do all the singular and plural forms of *riche* sound alike or different? |

alike

b In written French, what letter is added to **riche** to indicate plurality? |

s

4 Write the answers to the following questions. Use the correct plural form of the adjectives indicated and remember to use the correct form of *être.*

Modèle: Georges est riche. Et les sœurs de Georges? |

Elles sont riches aussi.

a Marie est maigre. Et les frères de Marie? |

Ils sont maigres aussi.

b Denise est petite. Et les frères de Denise? |

Ils sont petits aussi.

c Le fils des Dupont est intelligent. Et les filles? |

Elles sont intelligentes aussi.

d L'oncle de Charles est gentil. Et les cousins et les cousines de Charles? |

Ils sont gentils aussi.

5 Complete the second sentence. *Michel est français. Ses frères sont ___ aussi.* |

français

6 The adjective *français* does not add *-s* in the masculine plural. The same is true of the following adjectives: *gros, roux, jaloux, vieux.*

    a Finish this statement: An adjective ending in the letter ___ or ___ does not change form in the masculine plural. |

        s, x (The *x* here is an old French form of *s* that has been kept in some modern French words. As with a final *s*, a final *x* is not usually pronounced.)

    b Complete this description of the Rouquin family's hair color with the correct form of *roux*. (The feminine singular form is *rousse*.)

        M. et Mme Rouquin sont ___.

        Marc est ___.

        Sylvie est ___.

        Bernard et Pierre sont ___.

        Catherine et Patricia sont ___. |

        roux, roux, rousse, roux, rousses (Since the feminine singular form *rousse* ends in an *e*, you add *-s* to form the plural.)

    c Marianne sees her boyfriend Jean-Paul talking to another girl.

        Marianne est ___. |

        jalouse (For most adjectives in which the masculine form ends in *-x*, the feminine form ends in *-se*.)

7 Complete each sentence below according to the *modèle.* Answers are in the answer key.

        Modèle: Marie est grosse, mais les frères de Marie ___. |

        ne sont pas gros

    a La tante d'André est vieille, mais les oncles d'André ___.

    b Guy est jaloux, mais Yvette et Lise ___.

8 You have seen that when the letters *s* and *x* occur at the end of a masculine singular adjective, they occur at the end of the plural form also. Now compare the adjectives in the sentences below.

    Etienne et Paul sont grands et beaux.

    Barbara et Thérèse sont grandes et belles.

    a The masculine plural form of *beau* is ___. |

        beaux (All adjectives and nouns ending in *-eau* are made plural by adding *-x*.)

    b The feminine plural form of *belle* is ___. |

        belles (Since *belle* ends in an *e* in the singular, the ending *-s* is added to form the plural.)

9 Complete the following sentences with the correct form of *beau.* Answers are in the answer key.

    a Richard est très ___.

    b Christophe et Rémi sont très ___.

    c Sylvie est très ___.

    d Marie et Béatrice sont très ___.

2 The possessive markers mon, ma, ton, ta

You are familiar with several kinds of noun markers in French: definite (*le garçon*), indefinite (*un garçon*), and demonstrative (*ce garçon*). In this Preparation you will practice with a few of the possessive markers.

1 A possessive marker indicates possession of a thing, or close relationship to a person, thing, or idea. Read the following English sentences.

Mary is my sister.   This is my book.   That's my suggestion.

Write the marker that shows possession or relationship on your worksheet. ▮

my

2 In English, a speaker must use different possessive markers according to who the possessor is. Compare these sentences.

Charles: Is that your brother?
Paul: Yes, that's my brother.
Charles: And is that your sister?
Paul: Yes, that's my sister.

Write the two possessive markers on your worksheet. ▮

your, my

3 Read the French equivalent of the sentences in frame 2.

Charles: C'est ton frère?
Paul: Oui, c'est mon frère.
Charles: Et c'est ta sœur?
Paul: Oui, c'est ma sœur.

a Write the four possessive markers on your worksheet. ▮

ton, mon, ta, ma

b Which two forms mean *your?* ▮

ton, ta

c Which two forms mean *my?* ▮

mon, ma

d True or false? In French as in English, the possessive markers change according to who the owner is. ▮

true (*Mon* and *ma* mean *my;* *ton* and *ta* mean *your.*)

4 Look at the dialogue in frame 3 once more.

a Which two forms match *frère—mon* and *ton* or *ma* and *ta?* ▮

mon and ton

b Which two forms match *sœur—mon* and *ton* or *ma* and *ta?* ▮

ma and ta

c True or false? In French, the form of a possessive marker changes according to the gender of the noun it accompanies. ▮

true (*Mon* marks a masculine noun, *ma* marks a feminine noun.)

5 Write the French for *This is my sister* and *This is my brother.* ▮

C'est ma sœur. C'est mon frère.

6 Express the idea of *my* and *your* by rewriting these noun phrases with the appropriate possessive markers—***mon*** and ***ton*** or ***ma*** and ***ta.***

Modèle: cette cousine |
ma cousine, ta cousine

a un crayon |
mon crayon, ton crayon

b ce cousin |
mon cousin, ton cousin

c la boîte |
ma boîte, ta boîte

d cette cassette |
ma cassette, ta cassette

7 Compare the markers in these three groups of sentences.

C'est un cahier.   *C'est un écran.*   *C'est une affiche.*
C'est mon cahier.   *C'est mon écran.*   *C'est mon affiche.*

In the third group, ***mon*** is used with a feminine noun, ***affiche.*** Does ***affiche*** begin with a consonant sound or a vowel sound? |
with a vowel sound (*Mon* and *ton* are used before any singular noun beginning with a vowel sound, regardless of gender.)

8 Rewrite each noun phrase to express the idea of *my* and *your.* Use the correct possessive markers: ***mon*** and ***ton*** or ***ma*** and ***ta.***

Modèle: ce bureau |
mon bureau, ton bureau

a cette règle |
ma règle, ta règle

b cette étagère |
mon étagère, ton étagère

c un écran |
mon écran, ton écran

d une élève |
mon élève, ton élève

CHECK-UP **Part 1**	Write the correct form of the descriptive adjective for each sentence. **1** Les grands-parents de Georges sont ____. (*roux*) **2** Les sœurs de Georges sont ____. (*petit*) **3** Les frères de Georges ne sont pas ____. (*gros*)
Part 2	Write French equivalents for *my record, your record, my aunt, your aunt, my poster, your poster.*
VOCABULARY	MÉTIERS ET PROFESSIONS Trades and professions *chez Renault* at the Renault automobile factory *il/elle fait* he/she does *travailler* to work *à mi-temps* half-time *que fait ton père?* what does your father do?

A letter from France

This is a letter by a fifteen-year-old French girl who has studied English for four years. She wrote to an American girl who was coming to visit in an exchange program. The picture shows the shield of **Berry**, a typical rural house, and costumes worn for special celebrations.

You will probably feel as if you are reading English written with a French accent. An "accent" like this usually occurs when someone uses words from the new language in a sentence pattern from his or her own language.

Saturday, February 28th
Hello Carolyn!

I knew a few days ago that you'll come home during your staying in France and I am very glad of this. My teacher gave me your letters; I am also 15 years old but when you'll come, I'll be 16: my burthsday is on March 28th. I have a sister and a brother but both are older than me and the one lives in a study in Paris near her university and the other got married in December. So I live with my parents and we'll give you a hole bedroom when you'll come.

I went back home a week ago: I spent my holidays in the South-West of France: in the mountains of Pyrénées, where I can ski with friends. It's a pity that it was not longer than a week! I like this sport very much. In Paris I play a little tennis. At school we have only three ours of sport a week and it is not a lot! I learn English (you'd have guess it!), German, Latin, Mathematics, history et geography of France, Chimie and Physic. I like listening to music very much, but especially classic music and "chansons" (songs?). Do you like this? If you do you'll come with us to a concert. . . If you want to do absolutely something during your staying at home, you must write me what. It's the first time, I have a fireighner friend and I don't know exactly what I must do!

Saturday, February 28th.

Hello Carolyn!

I knew a few days ago that you'll come home during your staying in France and I am very glad of this. My teacher gave me your letters; I am also 15 years old but when you'll come, I'll be 16: my burthsday is on March 28th. I have a sister and a brother but both are older than me and the one lives in a study in Paris near her university and the other got married in December. So I live with my parents and we'll give you a hole bedroom when you'll come.

I went back home a week ago: I spent my holidays in the South-West of France: in the mountains of Pyrénées, where I can ski with friends. It's a pity that it was not longer than a week! I like this sport very much. In Paris I play a little tennis. At school we have only three ours of sport a week and it is not a lot! I learn English (you'd have guess it!), German, Latin, Mathematics, history et geography of France, chimie and Physic. I like listening to music very much but especially classic music and "chansons" (songs?). Do you like this? If you do you'll come with us to a concert... If you want to do absolutly something during your staying at home, you must write me what. It's the first time, I have a fireighner friend and I don't know exactly what I must do!

I hope to receive soon a letter from you

Best wishes.

Marianne

1 The possessive markers son and sa

In Preparation 31, you practiced using the possessive markers *mon* and *ma* (*my*) and *ton* and *ta* (*your*). In this section, you will practice using the possessive markers *son* (*his/her*) and *sa* (*his/her*).

1 Suppose you and your friend Paul see a tape recorder and a guitar on a table. You want to know if they belong to Robert, so you ask:

> You: Is that his tape recorder?
> Paul: Yes, it is.
> You: And is that his guitar?
> Paul: Yes, that's his guitar, too.

Write the possessive marker used with *tape recorder* and *guitar*. |

> his

2 Suppose you ask Paul if the things belong to Monique.

> You: Is that her tape recorder?
> Paul: Yes, it is.
> You: And is that her guitar?
> Paul: Yes, that's her guitar, too.

Write the possessive marker used with *tape recorder* and *guitar*. |

> her

3 Now read the French equivalent of the English exchange in frame 1. Remember, you are asking if the items belong to Robert.

> *Vous: C'est son magnétophone?*
> *Paul: Oui.*
> *Vous: Et c'est sa guitare?*
> *Paul: Oui, c'est sa guitare aussi.*

a Write on your worksheet the possessive markers used with *magnétophone* and *guitare.* |

> son (*magnétophone*), sa (*guitare*)

b Is the owner of the items male or female? |

> male (Robert)

c What is the English equivalent of *son* and *sa* when the owner is male? |

> his

4 Here is what the conversation would be if the items belonged to Monique:

> *Vous: C'est son magnétophone?*
> *Paul: Oui.*
> *Vous: Et c'est sa guitare?*
> *Paul: Oui, c'est sa guitare aussi.*

a Write on your worksheet the possessive markers used with *magnétophone* and *guitare.* |

> son (*magnétophone*), sa (*guitare*)

b Is the owner of the items male or female? |

female (Monique)

c What is the English equivalent of **son** or **sa** when the owner is female? |

her

5 Compare the use of **son** and **sa** in frames 3 and 4.

a Does the choice of **son** or **sa** depend on whether the *owner* is male or female? |

no

b Does the choice of **son** or **sa** depend on whether the *item owned* is masculine or feminine? |

yes

c **Son** and **sa** each have two English equivalents, depending on whether the owner is male or female. They both can mean ——— or ———. |

his, her

6 The next few frames will use some of the new nouns you learned in the last class. Spend a couple of minutes now with the vocabulary list on p. 139. Try the following technique. Look at the French marker and noun. Then look up from the page, say the phrase aloud, and think of the thing it represents.

Rewrite the following sentences, using the correct possessive marker **son** or **sa.** Remember that the marker must match the gender of the object possessed, not the possessor.

Modèle: C'est le piano de Paul. |

C'est son piano.

a C'est la clarinette de Paul. |

C'est sa clarinette.

b C'est la clarinette de Monique. |

C'est sa clarinette.

c C'est le vélo de Monique. |

C'est son vélo.

d C'est le vélo de Paul. |

C'est son vélo.

7 a What are the two English equivalents for **son vélo?** |

her bicycle, his bicycle

b Write the French for *his clarinet* and *her clarinet.* |

sa clarinette

8 You have learned that **mon** and **ton** are used instead of **ma** and **ta** before a feminine noun beginning with a vowel sound.

C'est mon affiche.   *C'est ton affiche.*

Which possessive marker is used before a feminine noun beginning with a vowel sound: **son** or **sa?** |

son (C'est son affiche.)

9 Answer the following questions in the affirmative, using a possessive marker.

> Modèle: C'est la guitare de Philippe? |
>
> > *Oui, c'est sa guitare.*

a C'est le téléphone de Véronique? |

> *Oui, c'est son téléphone.*

b C'est l'électrophone de Christophe? |

> *Oui, c'est son électrophone.*

c C'est la moto de M. Dujol? |

> *Oui, c'est sa moto.*

La moto pour le plaisir

2 Il y a *and numbers 30–69*

Write the answers to the arithmetic problems in frames 1–3. Refer to the list below to help you with the spelling of numbers. Answers are in the answer key.

20 *vingt*	30 *trente*	40 *quarante*
21 *vingt et un*	31 *trente et un*	41 *quarante et un*
50 *cinquante*	60 *soixante*	
51 *cinquante et un*	61 *soixante et un*	

> Modèle: Il y a quinze livres sur le bureau et vingt livres sur la table. Il y a combien de livres en tout (*altogether*)? |
>
> > *Il y a trente-cinq livres en tout.*

1 Il y a treize chiens devant la porte, dix-sept chiens derrière la porte, dix chiens dans une boîte, et quinze chiens sur les tables et les chaises. Il y a combien de chiens en tout?

2 Il y a vingt-cinq petits lions et onze grands lions dans le zoo. Il y a combien de lions en tout?

3 Il y a trente-sept hommes et trente-deux femmes dans le train. Il y a combien de personnes en tout?

CHECK-UP
Part 2

Write French equivalents for the following sentences.

1 That's her piano.
2 That's his clarinette.

3 Is it her clarinette?
4 Is it his piano, too?

VOCABULARY

un appareil-photo   camera
une auto   car
une clarinette   clarinet
un électrophone   record-player
une guitare   guitar
un magnétophone   tape recorder
une moto   motorcycle
un piano   piano
un saxophone   saxophone

un téléphone   telephone
un vélo   bicycle
un vélomoteur   motorized bicycle,
   moped
un ami, une amie   friend
un copain, une copine   close friend,
   buddy
sympathique   nice

1   The plural demonstrative marker ces

In Preparation 19, you learned about the singular demonstrative markers
ce, cet, and *cette.* Frames 1–4 will give you practice with these markers.

1 In English, you use *this* or *that* before any singular noun. You say *this
boy, this girl, this motorcycle; that boy, that girl, that motorcycle.* In
French, however, the singular demonstrative marker must match its
noun in gender. Read the following noun phrases, then answer items
a–c.

ce transistor   cet appareil-photo   cette moto
ce garçon   cet homme   cette fille

a If a noun is masculine singular and begins with a consonant sound,
you use the marker ____. I

ce (garçon)

b If a noun is masculine singular and begins with a vowel sound, you
use the marker ____. I

cet (homme) (There is a linking /t/ sound between this marker and the noun that
follows.)

c If a noun is feminine singular, you use the marker ____. I

cette (moto)

2 How would you say in French *this woman? this boy?* I

cette femme, ce garçon

3 How would you say in French *that boy? that child (male)?* I

ce garçon, cet enfant

Acceptez ces 5 disques ³³ ᵀ/₃₀ cm ou cassettes...stéréo pour 49ᶠ

4 Suppose you want to point out several people or several items to a friend. Compare the following English and French noun phrases.

ces garçons	ces filles	ces enfants
these boys	these girls	these children
those boys	those girls	those children

a In English, when you point out several things, you use the plural marker ____ or ____. |

these, those

b In French, when you point out several things that are either close or far away, you use the plural marker ____. |

ces (*Ces* is the French equivalent for both *these* and *those*.)

5 When *ces* occurs before a noun beginning with a vowel sound, there is liaison, just as with the markers *les* and *des*.

a What linking sound occurs in *ces affiches*—/s/ or /z/? |

/z/

b Say the following noun phrases aloud. Copy those in which a linking /z/ sound should occur, and put a link mark ‿ between *ces* and the noun.

   ces étudiants   ces guitares   ces élèves   ces hommes |

ces‿étudiants, ces‿élèves, ces‿hommes

6 How would you say in French *these bicycles? these guitars?* |

ces vélos, ces guitares

7 How would you say in French *those friends? those university students?* |

ces amis/amies, ces étudiants/étudiantes

8 You are in a department store with a friend, looking at expensive merchandise. Your friend finds something to criticize about every item. Write what your friend says when looking at each item. Answers are in the answer key.

   Modèle: guitare |

Je n'aime pas ces guitares.

a magnétophone

b électrophone

2 Practice with -er verbs

1 Here is a list of some of the *-er* verbs that you have been using up to now. Write the English equivalent of each one.

habiter   travailler   manger
nager   patiner   regarder
détester   tricoter   écouter ▌

to live (in)   to work   to eat
to swim   to skate   to look at, watch
to hate   to knit   to listen (to)

2 Write the forms of *travailler* that match the subjects given. Answers are in the answer key.

a je; tu; Michèle
b Dany et Monique
c toi et moi, nous
d Annick et toi, vous

3 Here are four *-er* verbs that you don't know. The items in this frame will help you think about their meanings.

a *Aider* is a cognate. One English equivalent is *to help*. What is the cognate equivalent? ▌

to aid

b The English meaning of *trouver* is the opposite of *to lose*. *Trouver* means ——. ▌

to find

c *Porter* is related to the English noun *porter*. What does a porter in a train station do for you if you have a very heavy suitcase? ▌

puts it on a cart to carry it for you (One meaning of *porter* is *to carry*.)

d You have heard *fermer* in class in the command *Fermez le livre*. *Fermer* means ——. ▌

to close

e The present-tense stem of *travailler* is *travaill-*. What are the present-tense stems of *aider, trouver, porter,* and *fermer?* ▌

aid-, trouv-, port-, ferm-

4 Rewrite the sentences below, using the pronouns or names in parentheses. After you have written your sentences, think of an English equivalent for each one. Answers are in the answer key.

Modèle: Pierre cherche un disque. (Jeanne et Henri) ▌
      Jeanne et Henri cherchent un disque.

a Vous trouvez le magnétophone? (tu)
b Jacques et Alice portent une grosse boîte. (je)
c Paul aide M. et Mme Peyre, qui sont très vieux. (nous)
d Gérard ferme la porte. (Hélène et Lucie)
e Vous fermez la fenêtre? (tu)
f Jacques ne trouve pas son cahier. (je)

3 Practice making sentences plural

1 Read this sentence: *La sœur de Jérémie aime beaucoup New York.* If you changed *sœur* to the plural *sœurs,* you would have to make other changes for this sentence to be correct.

    a You would have to change the marker *la* to ____. ▌

                 les (It must match the plural *sœurs.*)

    b You would have to change the verb *aime* to the plural form ____. ▌

                 aiment (It must match the subject *sœurs.*)

    c Now rewrite the sentence, replacing *sœur* with *sœurs.* ▌

              Les sœurs de Jérémie aiment beaucoup New York.

2 Now read this sentence: *Ce garçon est très gentil.*

    a If you replaced *garçon* with *filles,* what three other changes would you have to make in the sentence? ▌

              ce to *ces* (because *filles* is plural); *est* to *sont* (because the verb must match the subject); *gentil* to *gentilles* (remember the equation: FP = FP.)

    b Rewrite *Ce garçon est très gentil,* using *filles.* ▌

             Ces filles sont très gentilles.

3 This frame will give you further practice with making sentences plural. Use the word in parentheses to write a new sentence, and make any other changes that are necessary. Answers are in the answer key.

        Modèle: Cet homme est grand. (grands) ▌

              Ces hommes sont grands.

    a Cet élève a des crayons et des cahiers. (élèves)

    b Cette vieille femme est très sympathique. (vieilles)

    c Le fils de M. Poirier est beau. (beaux)

    d Je ne suis pas riche. (nous)

    e Elle n'est pas grande. (grandes)

CHECK-UP	
Part 1	Write the French equivalents: **1** He doesn't listen to these records. **2** Those two women are Spanish.
Part 2	Write the French equivalents: **1** Do you (*tu*) help your grandmother? **2** That woman is carrying a snake in a box.

Visages de France...

Monument mystérieux et solitaire

Océan tumultueux, campagne douce et riante

Harmonie, simplicité,

Intimité

1 *The present tense of* connaître

1 You have seen a form of the verb *connaître* in the dialogue *Conversation de lycéennes.* *Connaître* means *to know, to be acquainted with,* or *to be familiar with* a person, a place, or an idea. The following exchange illustrates the use of *connaître* with a person.

–*Tu connais ce garçon qui parle avec Paul?*
–*Oui, c'est mon cousin.*

Write an English equivalent for *Tu connais ce garçon?* |

Do you know that boy? (Are you acquainted with that boy?)

2 Now read the following question and answer.

–*Tu connais Paris?*
–*Oui, très bien.*

What is a good English equivalent of *Tu connais Paris?* |

Do you know Paris? (Are you familiar with Paris?)

3 Here is a chart for the present-tense forms of *connaître.* Refer to it as you answer items **a–d.**

je	connai s
tu	connai s
il / elle	connaî t
ils / elles	connaiss ent
nous	connaiss ons
vous	connaiss ez

a What are the two stems of *connaître?* |

connai- (spelled *connaî-* in the *il/elle*-form) and *connaiss-*

b Does the stem *connaiss-* appear in the singular or plural forms of *connaître?* |

plural

c What are the written endings of *connaître?* |

-s, -s, -t, -ent, -ons, -ez

d You have not seen the endings *-s, -s, -t* before. Have you seen the endings *-ent, -ons, -ez* before? |

yes (All regular *-er* verbs have the endings *-ent, -ons,* and *-ez* in the present tense, and most other French verbs do, too.)

4 Write the three verb forms in which the letter combination *ss* appears. |

connaissent, connaissons, connaissez

5 Spend a few minutes studying the forms of *connaître* in the chart. Then test yourself by writing the following subject pronouns and the matching forms of *connaître.* Check your answers against the chart.

a je, tu   **d** nous
b il, elle   **e** vous
c ils, elles

6 Rewrite each sentence with the correct form of *connaître,* as in the *modèle.* Say that the persons indicated are well acquainted with the city in which they live.

> Modèle: J'habite à Paris. ▌
> *Je connais bien Paris.*

a Tu habites à Bruxelles. ▌
> *Tu connais bien Bruxelles.*

b Il habite à Montréal. ▌
> *Il connaît bien Montréal.*

c Mon ami Birago et moi, nous habitons à Dakar. ▌
> *Nous connaissons bien Dakar.*

d Vous habitez à Port-au-Prince. ▌
> *Vous connaissez bien Port-au-Prince.*

e Marie-Hélène et Véronique habitent à Baton Rouge. ▌
> *Elles connaissent bien Baton Rouge.*

f J'habite à Toulouse. ▌
> *Je connais bien Toulouse.*

7 Write English equivalents of these sentences.

a Vous ne connaissez pas les Etats-Unis? ▌
> You don't know (You aren't familiar with) the United States?

b Ils connaissent cet homme qui parle avec Jeanne. ▌
> They know that man who is talking with Jeanne.

8 Write the French equivalent of *I know the United States well.* ▌
> *Je connais bien les Etats-Unis.*

2 *The possessive markers* mes, tes, ses

1 Compare the possessive markers in the chart below.

SINGULAR		PLURAL	
mon cousin	ma cousine	mes cousins	mes cousines
ton frère	ta sœur	tes frères	tes sœurs
son oncle	sa tante	ses oncles	ses tantes

a The markers *mon, ma, ton, ta, son, sa* are used with singular nouns. The markers *mes, tes,* and *ses* are used with what kind of nouns? ▌
> plural

b True or false? The possessive markers *mes, tes,* and *ses* may be used with plural masculine or plural feminine nouns. ▌
> true

c As in the case of *les, des,* and *ces,* there is a linking /z/ sound when *mes, tes,* and *ses* occur before nouns beginning with a ____ sound. ▌
> vowel

2 Write French equivalents for the following noun phrases. Use the correct plural marker: *mes, tes,* or *ses*.

a my brothers, your photos │

mes frères, tes photos

b his (male) friends, his (female) friends │

ses amis, ses amies (Remember that there is an *-e* at the end of *amie* when it refers to a female friend.)

3 Rewrite the sentences below so that each noun phrase is plural. Use the plural form of the possessive marker. In some cases you will also have to change the form of the verb.

Modèle: Où est mon cahier? │

Où sont mes cahiers?

a Où est ma cassette? │

Où sont mes cassettes?

b Tu as ton crayon? │

Tu as tes crayons?

c Voilà sa copine. │

Voilà ses copines.

4 Continue as in frame 3. Look at the printed answers for items **a–d** after you have written your own.

a Est-ce qu'il a mon disque?   **c** Ta boîte est sur la table.
b Vous connaissez son fils?   **d** Ce n'est pas ton cousin? │

a *Est-ce qu'il a mes disques?* b *Vous connaissez ses fils?* c *Tes boîtes sont sur la table.* d *Ce ne sont pas tes cousins?*

3 A dialogue with variations

Here is a recent dialogue adapted to meet a new situation. Copy the dialogue on your worksheet and fill in the missing letters. Answers are in the answer key.

Conversation de lycéens

ROGER   Tu c__nn___s ces d__ux fil____ qui parl___t avec t__ sœ___?

PAUL   Oui, bien s___, ce so___ mes c___sine__.

ROGER   T__s c___sine__! Oh là là, elles sont b___n!

PAUL   Oui, p___ mal. Et très g___til____.

ROGER   E___es sont ét__d___nt__s?

PAUL   Non, elles s___t m__sic__en____.

CHECK-UP	Write the French equivalents:
Part 1	**1** You know those writers, don't you?
	2 Is he familiar with Rouen?
	3 They don't know that man who's singing.

Part 2   Rewrite each noun phrase in the plural form: *mon magnétophone, ton oncle, sa moto.*

VOCABULARY   CONVERSATION DE LYCÉENNES   Conversation between high-school girls
une banque   bank
un lycéen, une lycéenne   high-school student
il est bien   he's good-looking
oh là là   wow!
pas mal   not bad
sans blague!   no kidding!

NOTE ✻

Friends

French-speaking people generally make more of a distinction between friends and acquaintances than most Americans do. A friend (**un ami** or **une amie**) is someone that you know well and for whom you have real affection. A **camarade** is someone you know well because you go to school together or work together, but who does not inspire the same warmth that a friend does. The French refer to a person they know only slightly as **une connaissance** (an acquaintance).

1 Pre-quiz practice: possessive markers

1 Here is a table showing the possessive markers *son, sa,* and *ses* in noun phrases. Refer to it as you complete the sentences below.

SINGULAR	PLURAL
son frère	ses frères
sa sœur	ses sœurs
son ami	ses amis
son amie	ses amies

a The marker ____ matches a masculine singular noun or a feminine singular noun beginning with a vowel sound. **I**

son

b The marker ____ matches a feminine singular noun that begins with a consonant sound. **I**

sa

c The marker ____ matches a masculine or feminine plural noun. **I**

ses

2 Compare the meanings of the markers in these two sentences.

Paul cherche son oncle, sa tante et ses cousins.
Monique cherche son oncle, sa tante et ses cousins.

a When the possessor is a male, what is the English meaning of *son, sa,* and *ses?* **I**

his

b When the possessor is a female, the English meaning of *son, sa,* and *ses* is ____. **I**

her

3 Answer the following questions in the affirmative. Use the marker *son, sa,* or *ses* in each response.

Modèle: Ce sont les cahiers d'Henri? **I**

Oui, ce sont ses cahiers.

a C'est le transistor d'Alice? **I**

Oui, c'est son transistor.

b C'est la moto d'Henri? **I**

Oui, c'est sa moto.

c Ce sont les disques d'Henri? **I**

Oui, ce sont ses disques.

d C'est l'amie d'Alice? **I**

Oui, c'est son amie.

4 Answer these two questions in the negative and use the possessive marker in your responses.

a C'est l'appareil-photo de Mlle Perrier? **I**

Non, ce n'est pas son appareil-photo.

b Ce sont les enfants de M. Duroc? |
Non, ce ne sont pas ses enfants.

5 Write French equivalents for the following dialogues.

a –Is that Paul's guitar?   –Yes, it's his guitar. |
–C'est la guitare de Paul?   –Oui, c'est sa guitare.

b –Is that Marie's bicycle?   –Yes, it's her bicycle. |
–C'est le vélo de Marie?   –Oui, c'est son vélo.

6 In your next class you will have a quiz on the possessive markers *mon/ma/mes, ton/ta/tes,* and *son/sa/ses.* The items below are similar to those in the quiz. For each item you will see a pair of sentences. You are to complete the second sentence in each pair with the appropriate possessive marker. The first letter of the marker is indicated. Answers are in the answer key.

Modèle: C'est l'amie de Jacques. C'est s __ amie. |
son

a J'ai un transistor. C'est m __ transistor.
b Tu as une clarinette. C'est t __ clarinette.
c Marie a un oncle qui habite à Baton Rouge. C'est s __ oncle.
d J'ai des disques de jazz. Ce sont m __ disques de jazz.
e Ce sont les cousins de Jacqueline. Ce sont s __ cousins.
f Tu as un vélomoteur. C'est t __ vélomoteur.
g Marc a une auto. C'est s __ auto.
h Tu as trois frères. Ce sont t __ frères.
i J'ai une voiture. C'est m __ voiture.

2 *Practice with* connaître

1 Two friends are looking at their class photograph and discussing some of the people they see. Complete each sentence with the correct form of *connaître.* To review the forms of *connaître,* refer to the chart on p. 146.

a –Tu ____ cette fille, n'est-ce pas? |
connais

b –Pas très bien. Mais je ____ sa sœur, Martine. |
connais

c –Tes parents ____ la directrice du lycée? |
connaissent (Remember that the plural stem ends in *ss.*)

d –Non, mais ma mère ____ sa sœur. |
connaît (Did you remember the *accent circonflexe?*)

e –Pierre et moi, nous ____ ce garçon. |
connaissons

f –Ah oui? Et vous ____ sa cousine aussi? |
connaissez

2 Write complete sentences, using the cues below and the correct form of *connaître.* Be sure to use the correct form of the demonstrative or possessive marker also. Answers are in the answer key.

> Modèle: Paulette / c __ journaliste **❙**
> *Paulette connaît ce journaliste.*

a Angélique et Jeanne / c __ avocat. **c** Paul / ne...pas / m __ tante
b Tu / c __ ville? **d** Je / c __ mécanicienne

3 Write French equivalents for *Do you (tu) know my buddy Sara?* and *They (ils) don't know Sara.* Answers are in the answer key.

3 *Practice asking* oui-non *questions*

You already know two ways to ask questions that can be answered by *oui* or *non.* This section introduces a third way.

1 One way of asking *oui-non* questions is to use rising intonation. Which question below would you ask with rising intonation?

> *Ton grand-père est français?*   *Il a quel âge?* **❙**
> *Ton grand-père est français?*

2 Another way is to use the tag phrase *n'est-ce pas.* Change the following statement to a question, using *n'est-ce pas,* and give the English equivalent: *Elle connaît M. Monet.* **❙**

> *Elle connaît M. Monet, n'est-ce pas?* She knows Mr. Monet, doesn't she?
> (*N'est-ce pas* is usually used when the speaker expects the listener to agree.)

3 A third way of asking *oui-non* questions in French is to use a special expression at the beginning of the sentence.

> *Est-ce que Pierre a une guitare?*   Does Pierre have a guitar?

What is the expression that is used at the beginning of a sentence to signal a *oui-non* question in French? **❙**

> *est-ce que*

4 Change the following statements into questions by using *est-ce que.*
  a Tu aimes le cours de français. **❙**

> *Est-ce que tu aimes le cours de français?*

  b Vous avez vingt ans. **❙**

> *Est-ce que vous avez vingt ans?*

5 Look at these two sentences.

> *Est-ce qu'il est architecte?*
> *Est-ce qu'Hélène aime Charles?*

How do you write *est-ce que* when it is used before a subject that begins with a vowel sound? **❙**

> *est-ce qu'*

6 Write questions with *est-ce que* that would bring about the following answers.

   a Oui, il parle espagnol. |

      Est-ce qu'il parle espagnol?

   b Non, elle ne connaît pas ce village. |

      Est-ce qu'elle connaît ce village?

CHECK-UP
Part 3

Use *est-ce que* to ask:
1 Is Mme Cardin knitting?
2 Are those boys Swiss?

Use *n'est-ce pas* to ask:
3 You (*tu*) like to skate, don't you?
4 They (*ils*) are German, aren't they?

PREPARATION 36

1 *The present tense of* voir

1 Read the following short dialogue. It is similar to one you have had in class.

    –Tu connais cette fille?
    –Oui, je la vois souvent à la cantine.

What does *je vois* mean in the context above? |

    | see

2 Compare the present-tense endings of *voir* and *connaître.*

je	voi	s		je	connai	s
tu	voi	s		tu	connai	s
il/elle	voi	t		il/elle	connaî	t
ils/elles	voi	ent		ils/elles	connaiss	ent
nous	voy	ons		nous	connaiss	ons
vous	voy	ez		vous	connaiss	ez

In written French, are the present-tense endings for *voir* the same as for *connaître?* |

      yes

3 In written French, the present tense of *voir* has two stems.

   a What are they? |

     voi-, voy-

   b Which subject pronouns are used with the stem *voy-?* |

     nous, vous

4 Take a few minutes to study the present-tense forms of *voir.* Then test yourself by writing the following subject pronouns and the matching forms of *voir.* Check your answers against the chart.

a nous

b vous

c ils

d tu

e je

f elle

g elles

5 Tell how many objects the following people see. The vocabulary list below may help you. Answers are in the answer key.

un vélo   un piano   une souris
une voiture un serpent   un saxophone

Modèle: Robert...

Robert voit deux éléphants.

a Je...

b Marc et Robert...

c Georges et moi, nous...

d Ils...

e M. Lafayette...

f Les enfants...

2 *The possessive markers* notre, votre, leur

1 Read the two-line dialogues below.

–*Monsieur Dufour, où est votre fille?*
–*Voilà ma fille.*

–*Madame Dufour, où est votre fils?*
–*Voilà mon fils.*

a What is the English equivalent of *votre?*
   your

b Do you use *votre* when you're talking to someone you would address with *tu,* or someone you would address with *vous?*
   someone you would address with *vous*

c Can *votre* be used with both masculine and feminine nouns?
   yes (*votre fils, votre fille*)

2 Ask Mme Dufour where the following people or items are. Use *votre* in your questions.

Modèle: la fille
         Où est votre fille?

a la famille
   Où est votre famille?

b l'auto |

Où est votre auto?

3 Now read this exchange.

   –*Monsieur et Madame Dufour, où est votre fille?*
   –*Elle est là-bas.*

   a Can *votre* be used when talking to two people? |

   yes (In line 1, the speaker is addressing Mr. *and* Mrs. Dufour.)

   b Does *votre* accompany a singular or a plural noun? |

   a singular noun (*fille*)

4 The possessive marker ***notre*** functions exactly like ***votre***. Read the following dialogue. Marie is talking to the twins, Jean and Jeanne.

   Marie: *C'est votre frère là-bas?*
   Jean: *Oui, c'est notre frère.*
   Marie: *Il est avec votre sœur?*
   Jeanne: *Non, ce n'est pas notre sœur; c'est notre cousine.*

Notre frère, notre sœur, and ***notre cousine*** mean ____. |

   our brother, our sister, our cousin

5 Use the cues to say whether the following items belong to your whole family.

   a C'est votre voiture, n'est-ce pas? (oui) |

   Oui, c'est notre voiture.

   b C'est votre télévision? (non) |

   Non, ce n'est pas notre télévision.

6 Now read this short exchange.

   –*Est-ce que c'est le chien de Sylvie et Michel là-bas?*
   –*Oui, c'est leur chien.*

   a What is the English equivalent of ***leur chien?*** |

   their dog

   b Is *leur* used when there's one possessor or more than one? |

   more than one (*leur* refers to Sylvie and Michel)

7 Like ***notre*** and ***votre, leur*** is used before either a masculine singular or a feminine singular noun. Complete the following answers, using ***leur.***

   a C'est la voiture de M. et Mme Rousseau? Oui, ____. |

   Oui, c'est leur voiture.

   b C'est le garage de M. et Mme Coste? Non, ____. |

   Non, ce n'est pas leur garage.

8 Complete each of the following sentences according to the ***modèle.***

   Modèle: M. et Mme Pasquier ont une belle caméra. |

   C'est leur caméra.

   a Mireille et moi, nous avons un appareil-photo. |

   C'est notre appareil-photo.

   b Madame Marmont, vous avez une moto. |

   C'est votre moto.

   c Etienne et Patrick ont un électrophone. |

   C'est leur électrophone.

3 Describing someone you know

In a few days you will be asked to write, for a grade, at least ten sentences describing someone. First, think of a male friend, relative, or acquaintance whom you know well enough to describe. Then answer the questions below.

Some nouns and adjectives are suggested, but use any you know. If you need help remembering additional words, refer to the lists at the ends of these Preparations: 4, 5, 32 (possessions); 8, 9, 20, 22 (adjectives); 15 (school subjects); 18, 21, 30 (occupations). Your teacher will collect your worksheet in class. You will have another chance to practice before you write in class for a grade.

1 Qui est-ce? (C'est votre ami Robert? votre cousin?)

2 Quel âge a-t-il?

3 Il est américain?

4 Où est-ce qu'il habite? (Quelle ville?)

5 Il a combien de frères et de sœurs?

6 Il est blond? brun?

7 Est-ce qu'il est grand ou petit? gros ou maigre? pas tellement gros?

8 À votre avis, est-ce qu'il est intelligent ou stupide? Vous le trouvez beau? pas très beau? gentil? très gentil? sympathique?

9 Que fait son père? Il est ouvrier? Est-ce que sa mère travaille? Qu'est-ce qu'elle fait?

10 Qu'est-ce qu'il voudrait être? acteur? mécanicien?

11 Est-ce qu'il a une radio? un vélo? une girafe? un chien? un piano? une voiture? Qu'est-ce qu'il voudrait avoir? une moto? une caméra?

12 Qu'est-ce qu'il aime? les maths? les voitures? Il aime danser? chanter? manger? patiner? écouter la radio?

CHECK-UP	Write the French equivalents:
Part 1	**1** They (*ils*) see two mice. **2** We see three snakes.
Part 2	Write French equivalents for *their dog, our dog, your dog*.
VOCABULARY	*un voisin, une voisine* neighbor

DIFFÉRENCE D'OPINION Difference of opinion
la cantine cafeteria
je la trouve... I think she is...
fou, folle crazy, mad
joli, jolie pretty
là-bas over there
moche ugly
souvent often
vrai true

NOTE ✻ *Dating patterns*

During weekends and vacations, French teen-agers like to spend time together in groups. Dating is less prevalent than in the United States, and the "blind date" does not exist at all. When young people go to the theater or movies, each person usually pays his or her own way. If a group of friends meets at a local café, however, one person may pay for a round of beverages.

PREPARATION 37

1 *Direct-object pronouns:* **le, la, les**

This section will explain what a direct object is and show you how to use some direct-object pronouns.

1 Read this sentence: ***Robert aide Marie.***
   a Who is doing the helping? Robert or Marie? |
         Robert (Robert is the subject of the verb. He is the doer of the action.)
   b Who is being helped? Robert or Marie? |
         Marie (Marie is the direct object of the verb. She is the one directly affected by the
         process of helping.)

2 Find the direct object in each of the following sentences and write it on your worksheet. Write the complete noun phrase.
   a Ma cousine aime l'algèbre. |
         l'algèbre
   b Mlle Duval a une grande voiture et aussi un vélomoteur. |
         une grande voiture, un vélomoteur
   c Jean-Pierre déteste son cousin. |
         son cousin
   d Tu aimes ces disques? |
         ces disques

3 Read the following exchange.

    –Tu connais ce garçon?

    –Oui, je le connais.

a What is the direct object of ***connais*** in ***Tu connais ce garçon?*** |

    ce garçon

b What word replaces ***ce garçon*** in the answer ***Oui, je le connais?*** |

    le (*Le* is a direct-object pronoun. It replaces a masculine singular noun or noun phrase.)

4 Compare the word order in the French sentence and its English equivalent.

    Je le connais.   I know him.

a In the English sentence, does the direct-object pronoun *him* precede the verb or follow the verb? |

    it follows the verb

b In the French sentence, does the direct-object pronoun ***le*** precede the verb or follow the verb? |

    it precedes the verb

5 Now read the following exchange concerning a girl.

    –Tu connais cette fille?

    –Oui, je la connais.

a Which direct-object pronoun replaces ***cette fille?*** |

    la (The direct-object pronoun *la* replaces a feminine singular noun phrase.)

b What is the English equivalent of ***Je la connais?*** |

    I know her.

6 Read the following dialogue to find another meaning for ***le*** and ***la.***

    –Véronique cherche son crayon. Est-ce que tu le vois?

    –Oui, je le vois. Il est sur la chaise.

    –Et sa gomme? Tu la vois aussi?

    –Oui, elle est sous son bureau.

What is the meaning of ***le*** or ***la*** when the pronoun refers to a thing instead of a person? |

    it

7 Read the following dialogue to see what happens when there is a plural direct object.

    Richard: Tu connais ces hommes là-bas?

    Jeanine: Oui, je les connais.

    Richard: Et ces femmes?

    Jeanine: Je les connais aussi.

a The direct-object pronoun ____ replaces both masculine and feminine plural direct objects. |

    les

b What is the meaning of ***les*** in ***Je les connais?*** |

    them

8 Write the French equivalents of *I see him* and *I know him.* |

    Je le vois. Je le connais.

9 Replace the direct-object phrases in the following sentences with the direct-object pronouns *le, la,* or *les.* Write the complete sentences, and give the English equivalents of your answers to frames **a** and **b**.

> Modèle: Je vois mon copain David. ❘
>> *Je le vois.* (I see him.)

a Je ferme les fenêtres. ❘
>> *Je les ferme.* (I'm closing them./I close them.)

b Je connais ces écrivains. ❘
>> *Je les connais.* (I know them.)

c Je cherche ma règle. ❘
>> *Je la cherche.*

10 Read the following sentences.

> *J'écoute mon professeur. Je l'écoute.*
> *J'écoute ma grand-mère. Je l'écoute.*
> *J'écoute mes parents. Je les écoute.*

a When *le* or *la* precedes a verb beginning with a vowel sound, it becomes ____. ❘
>> *l'*

b When *les* precedes a verb beginning with a vowel sound, what linking sound occurs? ❘
>> /z/

11 The direct-object pronouns are identical in form to another grammatical structure. Compare the sentences below.

> *Je vois le tableau. Je le vois.*　　　　*J'écoute l'acteur. Je l'écoute.*
> *Je vois la guitare. Je la vois.*　　　　*J'aime les films français. Je les aime.*

a When *le, la, l',* and *les* occur before a noun, they are definite ____. ❘
>> markers

b When *le, la, l',* and *les* occur before a verb, they are ____. ❘
>> direct-object pronouns

2　*Practice with singular possessive markers*

1 Here are the possessive markers you have been working with that are used with *singular nouns.*

mon		ma		notre	
ton	cahier	ta	règle	votre	cahier, règle
son		sa		leur	

a *Mon* and *ma* are equivalent to English ____. ❘
>> my

b *Ton, ta,* and *votre* are equivalent to English ____. ❘
>> your (*Ton* and *ta* are used for a person whom you address as *tu; votre* is used for a person whom you address as *vous* or for more than one person.)

c *Notre* is equivalent to English ____. |

our

d *Son* and *sa* are equivalent to English ____ or ____. |

his, her

e *Leur* is equivalent to English ____. |

their

2 Complete the second sentence in each pair with *son, sa,* or *leur.* Answers are in the answer key.

a Anne trouve une guitare. C'est la guitare de ____ camarade Guy.

b Michel trouve un cahier. C'est le cahier de ____ sœur.

c Nous connaissons la tante de Marcel et de Denise. Nous connaissons ____ tante.

3 Complete the French equivalents of the sentences below with *notre, votre,* or *leur.* Answers are in the answer key.

a Is your dentist nice? *Est-ce que ____ est gentil?*

b Our doctor is French. *____ est français.*

c Their teacher is intelligent. *____ est intelligent.*

3 *The possessive markers* leurs, nos, vos

1 Compare the possessive markers in the chart below.

	SINGULAR		PLURAL
notre cousin	notre cousine	nos cousins	nos cousines
votre frère	votre sœur	vos frères	vos sœurs
leur oncle	leur tante	leurs oncles	leurs tantes

a The possessive markers *notre, votre,* and *leur* are used with singular nouns. The corresponding plural markers ____, ____, and ____ are used with plural nouns. |

nos, vos, leurs

b Can *nos, vos,* and *leurs* be used with both masculine and feminine nouns? |

yes

2 When *nos, vos,* and *leurs* occur before a noun that begins with a vowel (like *oncles*), is there a linking /z/ sound? |

yes

3 Write the noun phrase that completes each sentence below to say what the people are looking for. Use the markers *nos, vos,* and *leurs.*

Modèle: Vous cherchez ____? (crayons) |

vos crayons

a Elles cherchent ____. (livres) |

leurs livres

b Nous cherchons ____. (cahiers) |

nos cahiers

c Jean-Pierre et toi, vous cherchez ____? (disques) |

vos disques

d Les Daumur cherchent ____. (enfants) |

leurs enfants

4 Write the French equivalent of the sentences below.

a We are looking for our records. |

Nous cherchons nos disques.

b They (**ils**) are looking for their camera. |

Ils cherchent leur appareil-photo.

c They (**elles**) are looking for their cassettes. |

Elles cherchent leurs cassettes.

CHECK-UP | Answer the questions below in the affirmative. Use the direct-object pronouns
Part 1 | *le, la,* and *les* in your responses.

1 Est-ce que tu connais M. Perrault? **3** Vous voyez ces affiches?

2 Vous voyez cette caméra?

Part 3 | Write the French equivalents of *our uncles, your parents, their pens, their pen.*

PREPARATION 38

1 *Round-up of possessive markers*

You now know all the French possessive markers. This part will help you review them.

1 On your worksheet, write the possessive markers that are in each of the following sentences. Then write the English equivalent of each sentence.

a Voilà ta mère avec son amie. |

ta, son There's your mother with her friend.

b Où est notre voiture? |

notre Where is our car?

c Ces jeunes filles aiment beaucoup leurs disques de rock. |

leurs Those girls like their rock records a lot.

The chart on the right may be a useful reference for the following frames.

THE OWNER	POSSESSIVE MARKERS		
je	mon	ma	mes
tu	ton	ta	tes
il/elle	son	sa	ses
ils/elles	leur	leur	leurs
nous	notre	notre	nos
vous	votre	votre	vos

2 A possessive marker gives you information about who owns an item. Which subject pronouns represent the owners of the following items?

   a ton magnétophone   **d** ses bandes
   b votre saxophone   **e** nos cassettes
   c sa guitare   **f** leur clarinette **l**

          a *tu*   b *vous*   c *il* or *elle*   d *il* or *elle*   e *nous*   f *ils* or *elles*

3 Complete the second sentence in each pair, using the appropriate possessive marker.

     Modèle: J'ai un grand-père. C'est ___ grand-père. **l**
                      mon

   a Tu as des cousins. Ce sont ___ cousins.
   b Ils ont une tante. C'est ___ tante.
   c Il a une tante. C'est ___ tante.
   d Elles ont des oncles. Ce sont ___ oncles. **l**
                a *tes*   b *leur*   c *sa*   d *leurs*

4 Write the French equivalents for each sentence below, using *est-ce que*. Answers are in the answer key.

     Modèle: Do you know his mother? **l**
              Est-ce que tu connais sa mère?

   a Do they (*elles*) know her brother?   **c** Do we know their uncles?
   b Does he know our aunts?

2 Practice with direct-object pronouns

Preparation 37 introduced the direct-object pronouns *le, la, l',* and *les.* This part will give you further practice with them.

1 Read this sentence: ***Béatrice cherche sa gomme.***

   a What is the direct object? **l**
           sa gomme

   b What object pronoun could replace ***sa gomme?*** **l**
           la

   c Rewrite the sentence, using the direct-object pronoun. **l**
           Béatrice la cherche.

2 Write an affirmative answer to this question, using a direct-object pronoun. ***Est-ce que tu as ton livre de français?*** |

Oui, je l'ai. (Did you remember to use *l'* instead of *le*?)

3 Answer the following questions with the information in parentheses. Use a direct-object pronoun in the answer.

Modèle: Où est-ce que Marc trouve son crayon? (sous la table) |
Il le trouve sous la table.

a Où est-ce que Nicolas trouve son stylo? (derrière la télé) |
Il le trouve derrière la télé.

b Vous deux, vous connaissez cette chanson? (oui, bien) |
Oui, nous la connaissons bien.

c Tu as ton cahier de physique, n'est-ce pas? (oui) |
Oui, je l'ai.

d Est-ce que Catherine aime ce disque de jazz? (oui, beaucoup) |
Oui, elle l'aime beaucoup.

e Votre famille et vous, vous voyez souvent vos amis canadiens? (oui, assez souvent) |
Oui, nous les voyons assez souvent.

NOTE ✳ **Formules de politesse (*Expressions of courtesy*)**

When two French-speaking people are introduced to each other, they shake hands and say **bonjour** with **monsieur, madame,** or **mademoiselle.**

The most common expression for "please" is **s'il vous plaît. Merci, merci bien,** and **merci beaucoup** are common ways to say "thank you."

When someone says **merci,** the proper equivalent for "you're welcome" is usually **de rien** (literally, "it's nothing") or the slightly more formal phrase **je vous en prie** (literally, "I beg of you").

To say "excuse me," a French speaker often uses **pardon, excusez-moi,** or **excuse-moi.** When someone sneezes, one can say jokingly **à vos amours** or **à tes amours** (to your loves). The normal response, however, is **à vos souhaits** or **à tes souhaits** (best wishes).

3 *The irregular verb* **faire**

1 In the dialogue *Métiers et professions,* you saw one form of the verb *faire* in this question: *Que fait ton père?* Complete the English equivalent: What does your father ____? |

do

2 Here is a chart of the present-tense forms of *faire* (to do, to make). Study it for a few moments, then test yourself by completing the phrases below. Write both subject and verb. Check your answers carefully against the chart.

je	fais
tu	fais
il/elle	fait
ils/elles	font
nous	faisons
vous	faites

    a tu ____   **d** je ____

    b elle ____   **e** ils ____

    c nous ____   **f** vous ____

3 M. Pince-Nez, a strict and proper *professeur d'anglais* at *Lycée Louis-le-Bête,* dreams one night that he can fly. He flies to the homes of his students, and inquires about what his students are doing. Each time, his unbelieving ears hear that they are doing their homework. Write the answers to M. Pince-Nez's questions.

    Modèle: Madame, que font vos fils? |

            Ils font leurs devoirs, Monsieur.

  a Madame, que font votre fils et votre fille? |

          Ils font leurs devoirs, Monsieur.

  b Monsieur, que fait votre fille? |

          Elle fait ses devoirs, Monsieur.

  c Marcel et Madeleine Morbleu, qu'est-ce que vous faites? |

          Nous faisons nos devoirs, Monsieur.

  d Charles Champignon, qu'est-ce que vous faites? |

          Je fais mes devoirs, Monsieur.

VOCABULARY   *les devoirs* homework

                 les exercices de français French homework

1 Practice describing someone you know

In the next class you will be asked to write, for a grade, at least ten sentences describing a person you know. In Preparation 36, you answered a series of questions about a male friend, relative, or acquaintance. Now write a description of a female friend, relative, or acquaintance. You can use the questions on p. 156 as a guide. Be as complete as possible in your description, and use as many adjectives as you can. Remember that adjectives match the nouns they accompany and that verbs match their subjects. Check your description against the sample description in the answer key to see if you have been complete enough.

2 Practice with markers in negative sentences

1 Read the following sentence: *Je n'ai pas de vélomoteur.* You remember that in a negative sentence, the indefinite markers *un, une,* and *des* usually become ____. |

> de

2 Now read this statement: *Je n'ai pas le livre de Patricia.* Do the definite markers *le, la, les* change form in a negative sentence? |

> no

3 Answer the following questions in the negative.
  a Est-ce que Marc a une moto? |

> Non, il n'a pas de moto.

  b Est-ce que tu as des sœurs? |

> Non, je n'ai pas de sœurs.

  c Est-ce que ces deux jeunes filles ont quatorze ans? |

> Non, elles n'ont pas quatorze ans.

  d Vous et Laure, vous avez les disques de Rémi? |

> Non, nous n'avons pas les disques de Rémi.

3 Voilà *with direct-object pronouns*

1 You and Monique are walking along a street in Paris. Suddenly you spot a famous face in the crowd. You turn to Monique and say:
> *Voilà l'actrice Brigitte Labelle!*

Monique replies:
> *Ah oui, la voilà!*

a What does the expression *la voilà* mean? |

there she is

b In the phrase *la voilà,* is *la* a definite marker or a direct-object pronoun? |

direct-object pronoun (Direct-object pronouns precede *voilà,* just as they do verbs. This is because the word *voilà* is a verbal expression. It comes from the expression *vois là,* meaning *see there.*)

c If you said to Monique *Voilà l'acteur Bernard Lebeau!,* Monique could reply *Ah oui, ___ voilà.* |

le

d Suppose you saw a group of circus performers: *Voilà les acrobates!* Monique could reply *Ah oui, ___ voilà.* |

les

2 Your friend Charles is amusing the guests at a party with a mind-reading act. You are his assistant. The two of you have hidden pictures of people and objects around the room. When he announces the location of an item, you "find" it.

Modèle: Charles: Il y a trois zèbres derrière la porte.
Vous: C'est vrai! ___ |

Les voilà.

a Charles: Il y a une vieille femme dans le tiroir.
Vous: C'est vrai! ___ |

La voilà.

b Charles: Il y a trois pianos sous le bureau.
Vous: C'est vrai! ___ |

Les voilà.

c Charles: Il y a un tigre derrière la porte.
Vous: C'est vrai! ___ |

Le voilà.

d Charles: Il y a deux souris dans cette boîte.
Vous: C'est vrai! ___ |

Les voilà.

VOCABULARY

In a few days you will have a progress test. As part of your preparation, it would be a good idea to spend a few minutes each day reviewing the vocabulary lists at the ends of the Preparations in this Phase.

Life in rural Haiti

Haiti is a predominantly rural country—fewer than 15% of the people live in cities. Agriculture is the primary industry, although much of the land is either too steep or too dry for successful farming. Therefore, most of the **paysans** (farmers or rural inhabitants) are quite poor. Of necessity, people are very ingenious at making small amounts of material go far.

Children assume household responsibilities at an early age. They carry water from local springs, tend animals or cooking fires, and take care of younger brothers and sisters while their parents work. As soon as they are old enough, the boys join their fathers at work in the fields and the girls accompany their mothers to market, often travelling many miles over mountain paths with heavy loads balanced on their heads.

Importance of the family

Family ties and interdependence are very strong in Haiti. Children may remain in the same house with their parents until their early thirties before striking out on their own. When a man marries, he usually builds his home in the immediate vicinity of his parents' home. The resulting clusters of houses (called **lacours**), occupied by several generations of one family, can be seen throughout Haiti. When parents become too old to provide for themselves, the family members living in the **lacours** take care of them. They spend their last years surrounded by their children and grandchildren. Many of these traditions survive among the middle class in the urban areas of Haiti.

Social gatherings

Work, amusement, and religion are combined with formal and informal song and dance in rural Haiti. Haitian song and dance traditions evolved almost entirely from African origins.

In fact, despite 175 years of isolation from Africa, some Haitian dance forms are identical to those in West Africa today.

At work in the fields, men often sing in chorus or in response to a caller, striking the ground with their hoes in time with the song; they may be accompanied by a conch shell or tin trumpet and a drum. Nighttime social gatherings are centered around dancing accompanied by drums and singing. Songs may be traditional, or they may be improvised during the evening's festivities. These gatherings, called **bamboches** in Haitian Creole, take place outdoors and are lit by gas lamps or small fires. Vendors supply the dancers with freshly-made peanut and coconut candy, bits of fried sweet potato and spiced meat, and other refreshments.

1 Pre-test practice: direct-object pronouns

In a few days you will have your third progress test. Take a few moments now to look at the Phase objectives and see if there is anything you feel unsure about. This Preparation and the two that follow should give you sufficient practice with the structures presented in Phase 3 to enable you to succeed on the test. However, you may also want to study the Summary (p. 176) and go over a few earlier Preparations. Keep in mind that a little practice every day will give far better results than a lot of practice in one day.

This part gives practice with direct-object pronouns. They were presented in Preparations 37, 38, and 39. All answers for this Preparation are in the answer key.

1 For each of the pictures below write the French equivalent of *I see him, her, it,* or *them.* Use the correct direct-object pronoun *le, la,* or *les.*

Modèle: |

Je la vois.

a

b

c

d

2 Look at each picture below and the cues that go with it. Write a complete sentence, using the correct direct-object pronoun: *le, la, l',* or *les.* Check the Summary if you need to review new verb forms.

Modèle: Michèle et Georges / regarder |

Ils la regardent.

a nous / connaître

b M. et Mme Vincent / chercher

c Madeleine / voir

d son père / aimer

e vous / écouter

2 Pre-test practice: writing practice

1 Below is a short dialogue made up of words you know, but with no punctuation or accent marks. Read the entire dialogue first. Then copy each sentence, using the appropriate capitalization, punctuation and accent marks.

HÉLÈNE	tu connais ce garcon la bas
RENÉ	bien sur c'est mon cousin jean pierre
HÉLÈNE	il est medecin n'est ce pas
RENÉ	mais non il est ingenieur
HÉLÈNE	ah oui ou est ce qu'il travaille
RENÉ	chez Renault

2 In this Phase you have learned how to describe people. You have also learned what details to consider when writing complete sentences. For example, adjectives and possessive markers must agree in gender and number with the nouns or pronouns they accompany. Keep this in mind as you write complete sentences, using the cues provided below. Remember punctuation and capitalization. Then check your answers for matching verb forms, adjectives and markers.

Modèle: vous / voir / m __ fils ▌

Vous voyez mon fils?

a il / connaître / New York et Paris / n'est-ce pas
b l __ infirmier / écouter / d __ médecins / célèbre
c c __ danseuses / être / grand / maigre / et joli
d est-ce que l __ père / chercher / s __ enfants
e l __ architecte / qui / travailler / dans m __ bureau / être / espagnol

3 Pre-test practice: possessive markers

1 There are many more forms for possessive markers in French than in English, and it takes practice to use them correctly. Below are some pairs of sentences. Complete the second sentence in each pair with the appropriate possessive marker. If you make mistakes, review the markers in Preparations 31, 32, 34, 35, and 36.

Modèle: J'ai une cousine. Voilà _____ cousine. ▌

ma

a Ma sœur et moi, nous avons quarante disques. Le dimanche nous écoutons _____ disques.

Nicole CROISILLE

CHEZ TOUS LES DISQUAIRES

Son premier coffret avec ses plus grands succès.

DP 37600/1/2 3 × ©

SON NOUVEL ALBUM

"La Femme et l'Enfant" DP 37503 Ⓐ

disques SONOPRESSE

b M. Voinchet, vous avez une caméra. C'est ＿＿ caméra?

c J'ai un saxophone. Voilà ＿＿ saxophone.

d Christine et Jean ont des sœurs? Est-ce que ＿＿ sœurs sont gentilles?

e Les parents de Charlotte ont une belle voiture. ＿＿ voiture est anglaise.

f J'ai une moto. J'aime ＿＿ moto.

g Mon frère a une moto aussi. Il préfère ＿＿ moto.

h Tu as un transistor? Tu écoutes souvent ＿＿ transistor?

4 *Practice with* voilà *and* il y a

Voilà was presented in Preparations 28 and 39. *Il y a* was presented in Preparations 28 and 32.

1 Each of the English sentences below either reports the existence of something or points out something. Read each sentence and write the French expression (*il y a* or *voilà*) that correctly expresses *there is* (*there's*) or *there are*.

    Modèle: There's a thief in my bathtub. |
                      il y a

        There's the thief, taking a shower! |
                      voilà

a Waiter, there's a fly in my soup.

b There's the fly now, doing the backstroke.

c Look! There's another fly, diving into my coffee!

d There are too many flies in here!

1 *Pre-test practice: demonstrative markers;* **connaître**

This Preparation will give you further review with the structures introduced in this Phase. Do a complete part before checking your answers with those in the answer key.

Agreement of demonstrative markers was presented in Preparation 33. **Connaître** was presented in Preparations 34 and 35.

1 Complete each sentence with the correct form of the demonstrative marker: *ce, cet, cette,* or *ces.*

 a ____ appareil-photo est beau.
 b ____ vélo est petit.
 c ____ étagère est grande.
 d ____ boîtes sont petites.

2 Use *connaître* and the demonstrative marker to say whom or what the people below are acquainted with.

   Modèle: je / village ▮
       Je connais ce village.

 a je / homme
 b nous / garçons
 c ils / professeur
 d elle / ville

2 *Pre-test practice:* **voir** *and* **travailler**

Voir was presented in Preparation 36.

1 The following people are in a museum that has all kinds of old things. Say what each person sees, using the appropriate form of *voir.*

 a Tu ____ un vieux téléphone.
 b Vous ____ une vieille moto.
 c Jean-Paul ____ une vieille chaise.
 d Nous ____ une vieille voiture.
 e Mes parents ____ un vieux piano.
 f Je ____ un vieux vélo.

2 Tell where the following people work by completing each sentence with the correct form of *travailler.* Remember that *travailler* is a regular *-er* verb. Its endings are the same as those of *chercher.*

 a Moi, je ____ dans une banque.
 b Toi, tu ____ chez un médecin.
 c Mon père ____ chez Renault.
 d Vous ____ dans un petit village.
 e Mes cousines ____ dans une grande ville.
 f Toi et moi, nous ____ à Marseille.

3 Pre-test practice: singular to plural

This part will give you further practice forming sentences with plural nouns, markers, adjectives, and verbs. Write new sentences with the following cues. Remember that when you change one word in a sentence it often affects other words.

Modèle: C'est un vélo. (vélos)

Ce sont des vélos. (*C'* becomes *ce*, *est* becomes *sont*, and *un* becomes *des*.)

1 Elle n'est pas américaine. (américains)
2 Ce garçon est blond. (filles)
3 Mon oncle habite à Québec. (oncles)

4 Il voit Mme Lautrec. (ils)
5 Sa sœur est gentille. (gentilles)

NOTE ❋

Modern agriculture in France

For much of its history, France was primarily an agricultural nation, and agriculture continues to play an important role in the economy. The varied geography and climate of France make possible the production of a wealth of food products—from raw materials like beef, dairy products, and grains to refined products such as aged cheeses and wines.

Transition to modern methods
Since the end of the last century, there has been—mostly for the young—a steady flow of people away from farms to the cities. In spite of this rural exodus, land reforms and modern technology have brought about a remarkable increase in farm production. The days of subsistence farming, with each family's tiny patches of land scattered at random outside the village, are nearly over. Now special agricultural schools teach the skills needed for modern agronomy, and it is estimated that today's farmer serves five times as many consumers as the farmer of a century ago. The **paysan** (rural inhabitant), working in the fields with oxen and uninformed about the world's happenings, is rarely seen today. Today's **cultivateur** (farmer-businessman) drives a tractor, uses scientific methods of crop and stock management, and depends on **la télé** for news and entertainment.

Getting ready for a test

This Preparation will help you prepare for your next progress test. Go through it frame by frame. If you make mistakes or discover items you want to review, turn to the Summary on p. 176 or go over the Preparations once again.

Parts A, B, and C will test your understanding of spoken French.

1 In Part A, you will hear a sentence twice. You will see the letters S and P. You should circle S if the subject is singular and P if the subject is plural. For the frames below, read the sentences aloud and write the correct letter—S or P—on your worksheet.

    a Mes parents sont français.   S   P
    b Tu es italienne.   S   P

2 In Part B, you will hear a pair of sentences in French. They will be read twice. At the same time, you will see three English sentences on your answer sheet. You are to circle the letter of the English sentence that best describes the pair of French sentences. For the example below, write the correct letter—A, B, or C—on your worksheet.

    Ma sœur Anne a une moto. C'est une vieille moto.

    My sister Anne . . .

    A has a beautiful new bicycle.
    B loves to ride her old bicycle.
    C has an old motorcycle.

3 In Part C, you will hear a question and three possible responses, all in French. Each will be read twice. On your answer sheet, you will see the letters A, B, C. You are to circle the letter corresponding to the best response. For now, write the correct letter on your worksheet.

    a Tu es italienne?   **b** Vous avez une voiture, Madame?
      A Non, je suis brune.   A Oui, j'ai une moto.
      B Non, j'ai quinze ans.   B Non, je n'ai pas de voiture.
      C Non, je suis espagnole.   C Non, je n'ai pas de moto.

4 In Part D, you are to change some sentences from singular to plural. You are to substitute the plural words in parentheses for the italicized words, and make all other necessary changes.

    Modèle: Cet *enfant* est très petit. (enfants) |

            Ces enfants sont très petits. (The marker *cet* changes to *ces*, the verb form *est* changes to *sont*, and the adjective *petit* changes to *petits*.)

    a Cette *fille* a dix-sept ans. (filles)
    b C'est un *écran*. (écrans)

5 In Part E, you will be tested on your ability to use direct-object pronouns correctly. On your answer sheet you will see a drawing of a person or an item. For the first group, you are to write the French equivalent of: *I see him, I see her, I see them,* or *I see it,* depending on the person or item shown.

Modèle:  |

Je le vois.

a    **b**

    For the second group, you are to write the French equivalent of *I'm listening to him, I'm listening to her, I'm listening to them,* or *I'm listening to it.*

Modèle: |

Je l'écoute.

c    **d**

6 In Part F, you will see some sentences with blanks. In each blank you are to write the demonstrative marker that matches the noun in the sentence. For now, write the marker on your worksheet.

  a ____ éléphant est grand.   **b** Tu vois ____ chien?

7 In Part G, you are to complete sentences with the correct form of *travailler.*

Modèle: Catherine ____ ici. |

travaille

  a Paul ____ ici.   **b** Vous et moi, nous ____ ici.

8 In Part H, you are to complete sentences with the correct form of *connaître.*

  a Vous ____ mes grands-parents?
  b Nous ____ ce journaliste.
  c Moi, je ne ____ pas ces hommes.

9 In Part I, you are to form questions with *est-ce que* and questions with *n'est-ce pas.*

  a Change the following statement into a question with *est-ce que: Il aime la géographie.*
  b Change the following statement into a question with *n'est-ce pas: Ils sont anglais.*

10 In part J, you are to complete sentences with the form of *avoir* that correctly matches each subject pronoun.

  a M. Beauregard ____ vingt-trois ans.   **b** Suzette et moi, nous ____ un frère aîné.

11 In Part K, you are to answer questions by stating that you don't have certain things or relatives.

    a Vous avez une clarinette?   **b** Vous avez des cousins?

12 In Part L, you are to complete sentences by writing the correct form of *voir*.

    a Je ___ deux livres sur la télé.   **b** Paul et toi, vous ___ cette affiche?

13 In Part M, you will be asked to use the correct form of the possessive markers with nouns.

First, you will see some nouns preceded by blanks. You are to write the correct possessive marker—*mon, ma,* or *mes*—in each blank space. For now, write the correct marker for each of these nouns: *tante, sœurs, enfant.*

Next, you will see some pairs of sentences. You are to complete the second sentence in each pair with an appropriate possessive marker.

    Modèle: Tu as des sœurs? ___ sœurs sont ici? |

                     Tes

    a Raoul a un électrophone. Voilà ___ électrophone.

    b Vous avez des cousines? ___ cousines travaillent dans cette ville?

14 In Part N, you will see a set of cues. You are to write complete sentences, using those cues. Be sure you make all necessary changes and use appropriate punctuation marks.

    Modèle: il y a / u ___ cassette / sur / l ___ bureau |

               Il y a une cassette sur le bureau.

    a est-ce que / elles / habiter / chez Louise

    b il / ne...pas / être / jeune

The last item in the test will be a dialogue that you can complete for extra credit. ***Bonne chance!*** (Good luck!)

EXTRAIT DE L'ACTE DE MARIAGE N° 1

Le *vingt - trois Avril*   mil neuf cent   *soixante treize*   à *seize*   heures *45*
devant Nous, ont comparu publiquement en la maison commune

MENTIONS MARGINALES (a)

ÉPOUX
NOM et prénoms *Le Pendeven*   *Pierre*
Né à *Vars (Charente)*   Le *quinze Janvier*   mil neuf cent *cinquante*

Fils de (1) *Jean-Marie Le Pendeven*
Et de (1) *Délia Gilberte Morrigat*

ÉPOUSE
NOM et prénoms *Prévot* *(Bernadette Charlotte Virginie*
Née à *Chaumont (Haute-Marne)*   Le *huit Janvier*   mil neuf cent *quarante-neuf*

Fille de (1) *Pierre Victor Prévot*
Et de (1) *Paulette Marie Rose Peltier*

Summary

1 The present tense of avoir (Preparation 27, 29, 30)

a. The present-tense forms of *avoir* are irregular. They do not consist of an infinitive stem followed by regular present-tense endings.

AFFIRMATIVE			NEGATIVE	
j'	ai	je	n' ai	pas
tu	as	tu	n' as	pas
il/elle	a	il/elle	n' a	pas
ils/elles	ont	ils/elles	n' ont	pas
nous	avons	nous	n' avons	pas
vous	avez	vous	n' avez	pas

b. *Avoir* is one of the most frequently used verbs in French. Its usual English equivalent is *to have*. It is also used with the meaning *to be* in telling age.

J'ai un transistor.   I have a transistor radio.
J'ai quinze ans.   I'm fifteen years old.

2 The present tense of connaître and voir (Preparation 34, 35, 38)

The present-tense forms of *connaître* (to know) and *voir* (to see) differ from those of regular *-er* verbs in two ways: there are two present-tense stems instead of one, and endings for the singular forms are *-s, -s, -t* instead of *-e, -es, -e.*

je	connai s	voi s
tu	connai s	voi s
il/elle	connaî t	voi t
ils/elles	connaiss ent	voi ent
nous	connaiss ons	voy ons
vous	connaiss ez	voy ez

3 The plural of nouns (Preparation 27)

a. For most French nouns, the plural is formed by adding *-s* to the singular. For nouns ending in *-eau*, the plural is formed by adding *-x.*

la voiture	un enfant	cet élève	le bureau
les voitures	des enfants	ces élèves	les bureaux

b. The plural ending *-s* or *-x* is usually silent in spoken French. The sound of the marker (*les, des, ces,* etc.) tells the listener that the noun is plural.

4 Plural markers (Preparation 27, 28, 33)

a. *Les* is the plural form of *le, la,* and *l'*. *Des* is the plural form of *un* and *une*, and *ces* is the plural form of *ce, cet,* and *cette.*

les garçons	des garçons	ces garçons
les filles	des filles	ces filles

b. The indefinite marker *des* must be used in French, in contrast to the English indefinite marker *some*, which is often omitted.

J'ai des crayons et des stylos.   I have (some) pencils and pens.

c. The demonstrative marker *ces* is equivalent to English *these* or *those*, depending on the situation or the context of a sentence.

Ces enfants sont grands.   **These** children (near the speaker) are tall.
                                  Those children (playing in the distance) are tall.

5 Ne...pas de + *noun* (Preparation 27)

In a negative sentence, the indefinite markers **un, une,** and **des** usually become **de** (or **d'** before a noun beginning with a vowel sound).

J'ai un frère, mais je n'ai pas de sœur.   I have a brother, but I don't have a sister.

Ils n'ont pas d'enfants.   They don't have any children.
Nous n'écoutons pas de disques.   We're not listening to records.

6 *Plural forms of descriptive adjectives* (Preparation 30, 31)

a. The plural of most masculine adjectives and all feminine adjectives is formed by adding *-s* to the singular form.

*Cet enfant est **petit.***   *Ces enfants sont **petits.***
*Cette voiture est **petite.***   *Ces voitures sont **petites.***

b. The plural of a singular masculine adjective ending in **-eau** is formed by adding *-x*.
*Ce garçon est **beau.***   *Ces garçons sont **beaux.***

c. The plural form of a masculine singular adjective ending in *-s* or *-x* is the same as the singular form. No change is made.

*Il est **français.***   *Ils sont **français.***
*Il est **jaloux.***   *Ils sont **jaloux.***

7 *Possessive markers* (Preparation 31, 32, 34, 36, 37, 38)

Possessive markers establish ownership (*my car, your guitar*) or show close relationship (*his aunt, our parents*). In contrast to English markers, French markers must match *the nouns they mark* in number and gender.

	ONE ITEM	MORE THAN ONE ITEM
One Owner	**mon, ma** my	**mes** my
	ton, ta, votre your	**tes, vos** your
	son, sa his/her	**ses** his/her
More than One Owner	**notre** our	**nos** our
	votre your	**vos** your
	leur their	**leurs** their

a. The possessive markers *mon, ton,* and *son* are used with masculine singular nouns.

mon bureau   ton père   son cahier

Mon, ton, and **son** are also used with a feminine singular noun beginning with a vowel sound: **mon amie Sylvie.**

b. The possessive markers *ma, ta,* and *sa* are used with feminine singular nouns except those beginning with a vowel sound.

ma tante   ta cousine   sa guitare

c. *Mes, tes,* and *ses* are used with both masculine and feminine plural nouns.

mes frères   tes sœurs   ses parents

There is a linking /z/ sound when *mes, tes,* or *ses* precedes a plural noun beginning with a vowel sound: **mes‿amis, tes‿enfants, ses‿électrophones.**

d. *Notre, votre,* and *leur* are used with masculine and feminine singular nouns. *Nos, vos,* and *leurs* are used with masculine and feminine plural nouns.

notre cousin   votre cousine   leur frère
nos cousins   vos cousines   leurs frères

There is a linking /z/ sound when *nos, vos,* or *leurs* precedes a plural noun beginning with a vowel sound: **nos‿oncles, vos‿affiches, leurs‿amis.**

8   *The direct-object pronouns* le, la, l' *and* les   (*Preparation 37, 38*)

a. A direct-object pronoun replaces a direct-object noun or noun phrase. The pronoun must match the noun it replaces in number and gender.

Je connais Pierre.	*Je **le** connais.*	I know him.
Je connais Marie.	*Je **la** connais.*	I know her.
J'aime Chantal.	*Je **l'** aime.*	I like her.
Je vois l'affiche.	*Je **la** vois.*	I see it.
Je vois les vélos.	*Je **les** vois.*	I see them.

b. In French, a direct-object pronoun usually precedes the verb form with which it is used. When *les* precedes a verb beginning with a vowel sound, there is a linking /z/ sound.

c. When direct-object pronouns are used with the expression *voilà,* they always precede it.

Les voilà.   Here they are.

9   Voilà *and* il y a   (*Preparation 28, 32*)

a. *Voilà* is used to point out something visible. *Il y a* is used to report the existence of something.

Voilà *une souris!*   Here's a mouse! There's a mouse!
Voilà *deux souris!*   Here're two mice! There're two mice!

Il y a une souris sous la table.	There's a mouse under the table.
Il y a deux souris sous la table.	There're two mice under the table.

b. The negative of *il y a* is *il n'y a pas* (de).

Il n'y a pas de souris sous la table.	There isn't any mouse (There aren't any mice) under the table.

10   *Three ways of asking* oui-non *questions*   (*Preparation 35*)

Three common ways of asking *oui-non* questions in French are:

a. to use rising intonation at the end of a statement.

Vous êtes française?	You're French?

b. to use the tag phrase *n'est-ce pas* at the end of a statement.

Tu as quinze ans, n'est-ce pas?	You're fifteen years old, aren't you?

c. to use the interrogative expression *est-ce que* at the beginning of a statement. Before a vowel sound, *que* changes to *qu'*.

Est-ce que tu habites ici?	Do you live here?
Est-ce qu'elle habite ici?	Does she live here?

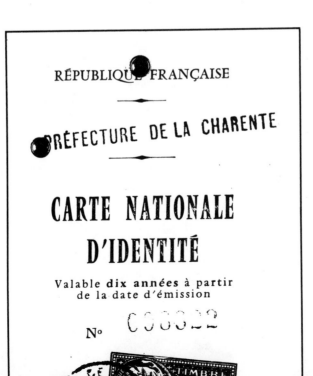

Required document for every French citizen

Famille et amis

On n'est jamais content!

Simone and Mathieu are looking at Simone's photograph album.

MATHIEU	Qui est ce garçon? C'est ton frère?
SIMONE	Non, c'est mon cousin, malheureusement.
MATHIEU	Malheureusement? Pourquoi?
SIMONE	Bof! J'ai une grande sœur, j'ai deux petites sœurs, mais je n'ai pas de frères.
MATHIEU	Moi, j'ai quatre frères, mais pas de sœurs.
SIMONE	Oh là là! Quatre frères! Tu es l'aîné?
MATHIEU	Oui. C'est bien, hein?
SIMONE	Oh, oui, alors! Mais quatre petits frères...C'est beaucoup!

Le Recensement

A census-taker, who is a little hard of hearing, interviews M. Moraud about his family.

LE RECENSEUR	Il y a combien de personnes chez vous, Monsieur?
M. MORAUD	Eh bien, ma femme et moi et deux enfants.
LE RECENSEUR	Douze enfants. Bon.
M. MORAUD	Non, non, pas *douze*, deux! Une fille et un fils.
LE RECENSEUR	Ah, bon! Alors, ça fait...quatre personnes en tout.
M. MORAUD	Mais non! Il y a aussi ma belle-mère.
LE RECENSEUR	Alors, ça fait cinq personnes?
M. MORAUD	Eh oui... Ça fait cinq.

Métiers et professions

*Solange asks Yvette, a newcomer to the **lycée,** what her parents do.*

SOLANGE	Que fait ton père?
YVETTE	Il est ingénieur chez Renault.
SOLANGE	Et ta mère, elle travaille?
YVETTE	Oui, à mi-temps.
SOLANGE	Qu'est-ce qu'elle fait?
YVETTE	Elle est infirmière.

Conversation de lycéennes

Hélène asks Brigitte about a good-looking boy who is talking with a friend of theirs named Paul.

HÉLÈNE   Tu connais ce garçon qui parle avec Paul?
BRIGITTE   Oui, bien sûr. C'est un de mes copains.
HÉLÈNE   Sans blague! Dis donc, il est bien!
BRIGITTE   Oui, pas mal. Et très gentil.
HÉLÈNE   Il est étudiant?
BRIGITTE   Non, il travaille dans une banque.

Différence d'opinion

Jean-Pierre and Marcel are talking together in the school corridor.

JEAN-PIERRE   C'est vrai? C'est ta cousine, cette fille là-bas?
MARCEL   Oui, c'est ma cousine Yvette. Pourquoi?
JEAN-PIERRE   Je la vois souvent à la cantine.
MARCEL   Ah oui? Elle est moche, hein?
JEAN-PIERRE   Ah non! Moi, je la trouve très jolie.
MARCEL   Tu la trouves jolie? Tu es fou!

EXERCICES

1   Pronunciation practice: numbers + nouns

	Devant une consonne	*Devant une voyelle*
un	un père	un écrivain
deux	deux crocodiles	deux actrices
trois	trois morceaux de craie	trois éléphants
quatre	quatre pilotes	quatre ouvriers
cinq	cinq personnes	cinq acteurs
six	six filles	six antilopes
sept	sept lions	sept activités
huit	huit garçons	huit appartements
neuf	neuf secrétaires	neuf élèves
dix	dix comptables	dix étagères

2 Voilà *and* il y a

3 *Visual-graphic drill: demonstrative markers*

	1 garçon		1 jeune(s)
ce	2 écrivain	est	2 riche(s)
cet	3 femme	sont	3 sympathique(s)
cette	4 architectes		4 petit(e)(s)
ces	5 filles		5 canadien(ne)(s)
	6 étudiante		6 français(e)(s)

4 *Visual-lingual drill:* son, sa, ses

	1 magnétophone		1 sur la table
son	2 cassette	est	2 sous la chaise
sa	3 disques	sont	3 devant le bureau
ses	4 électrophone		4 là
	5 règles		5 dans la boîte
	6 guitare		

5 *Possessive markers: visual-lingual drill*

1 je		1 amie
2 la voisine	chercher	2 vélos
3 Robert		3 cousines
4 vous		4 voiture
5 ma mère		5 magnétophone
6 nous		6 enfants
7 M. et Mme Belcourt		7 secrétaire
8 tu		

ALLEZ, LES SPORTIFS!

PHASE FOUR OBJECTIVES

In this Phase you will talk about sports, musical instruments, weather and seasons. You will learn to say what you want to do, what you can do, and where you want to go. By the end of this Phase you will be able to:

1 Say what you want to do by using the verb **vouloir,** and what you are able to do by using the verb **pouvoir.**

2 Say what you know, and what you know how to do, using **savoir.**

3 Say where you are going and what you are going to do, with the verb **aller.**

4 Use the French equivalents of the object pronouns **me, you, us (me, te, vous, nous).**

5 Give emphasis to the subject of a sentence with stressed pronouns like **moi.**

6 Talk about playing a sport **(jouer à)** or a musical instrument **(jouer de).**

7 Talk about taking a walk, a trip, making plans, going skiing or camping, and having a party, with expressions using **faire.**

8 Count from 70–100.

�֍ The cultural notes discuss French holidays and customs, vacations in France, seashore recreation in France, and some favorite French sports: **le football, les boules,** and **le ski.**

1 *Expressions with* faire

1 In Phase 3 you had practice with the verb *faire,* meaning *to do.* You used it in two types of situations.

a One situation is shown in the question *Tu fais des devoirs de maths ce soir?* Write the English equivalent. |

Are you doing math homework tonight?

b You also used *faire* when talking about occupations. Give the English equivalent of *Que fait ton père?* |

What does your father do? (for a living)

2 Compare the English and French verb forms in the sentences below.

Do you *like* jazz?　　　*Tu **aimes** le jazz?*

What *does* your mother *do?*　　*Que **fait** ta mère?*

In English, the verb forms *do* and *does* are often used to signal the beginning of a question. Does French use an equivalent of *do* or *does* for beginning a question? |

no

3 Write French equivalents of these sentences.

a Do you like to skate? |

Tu aimes patiner?

b What does your father do? |

Que fait ton père?

4 The verb *faire* is used frequently in French and it has many English meanings besides *to do.*

a See if you can write the English equivalent of this sentence: *Ces ouvriers font des chaises.* |

These workers are making chairs.

b *Faire* can mean *to do* or ____. |

to make

5 A form of *faire* is often used with other words to make a fixed expression. In these expressions, *faire* may mean something other than *to do* or *to make.* The following sentences give two examples.

Je fais une promenade à la campagne.　　*Nous faisons du ski dans les Alpes.*

a What are the English cognates in the expressions *faire une promenade* and *faire du ski?* |

promenade (this is the term used in square dancing to mean *to walk*); ski

b *Je fais une promenade à la campagne* means ____. |

I'm taking a walk in the country.

c Now write an English equivalent of *Nous faisons du ski dans les Alpes.* |

We're skiing in the Alps./We ski in the Alps.

6 You probably remember all the present-tense forms of *faire.* However, if you're not sure, look at the chart in the Summary on page 176 for a minute or two. Complete the sentences below with the correct form of *faire,* and write the English equivalents.

  a Qu'est-ce qu'ils ___? |
  > *font (What are they doing?/What are they making?)*

  b Tu ___ tes exercices de français? |
  > *fais (Are you doing your French exercises/homework?)*

  c Nous ___ une promenade cet après-midi. |
  > *faisons (We are taking a walk this afternoon.)*

  d Alain et Michèle, qu'est-ce que vous ___ après les cours? |
  > *faites (Alain and Michèle, what are you doing after school?)*

  e Est-ce que Christine ___ du ski? |
  > *fait (Does Christine ski?)*

7 Use the cues below to write a French equivalent of each English sentence.

  a Are you taking a walk today? *Tu ___ aujourd'hui?* |
  > *Tu fais une promenade aujourd'hui?*

  b Are we skiing on Sunday? *Est-ce que nous ___ dimanche?* |
  > *Est-ce que nous faisons du ski dimanche?*

  c Those workmen are making tables. *Ces ouvriers ___ des tables.* |
  > *Ces ouvriers font des tables.*

2 The present tense of vouloir

Vouloir (to want) is a very useful verb that helps you discuss what you and others want to have or want to do. You have already used *je voudrais,* which is a special polite form of *vouloir* meaning *I would like.* This section will give you practice with the present-tense forms.

1 Study the chart for a few minutes. Notice that the present-tense stem of *vouloir* has three forms.

je	veu	x
tu	veu	x
il/elle	veu	t
ils/elles	veul	ent
nous	voul	ons
vous	voul	ez

  a Which form of the stem matches *je, tu, il,* and *elle?* |
  > *veu*

  b Which form of the stem matches *ils* and *elles?* |
  > *veul*

  c Which form of the stem matches *nous* and *vous?* |
  > *voul*

PROMENADES SUR LA SEINE A TRAVERS PARIS
Square du Vert-Galant - Ile de la Cité
VEDETTES DU PONT-NEUF - T.l.j. - Tél. : 633-98-38

d In the present tense, the *nous*- and *vous*-forms of *vouloir* have endings that are pronounced. Write those forms. |

nous voulons, vous voulez

e What are the endings of the *je*- and *tu*-forms? |

x, x (The *x* is an old form of the *s* that appears in the *je*- and *tu*-forms of many verbs, such as *je vois, tu vois*.)

2 Give the English equivalent of this sentence: ***Je veux un disque de jazz.*** |

I want a jazz record.

3 To see if you have learned the forms of ***vouloir,*** complete the sentences below to say what each person wants. Correct your answers by checking them against the chart.

a Paul et moi, nous ____ une affiche de Notre-Dame.
b Yvonne et André ____ une motocyclette.
c Moi, je ____ un appareil-photo.
d Vous ____ une guitare.
e Jacqueline ____ un disque de musique classique.

4 So far you have practiced using ***vouloir*** with a noun, as in ***Je veux un disque. Vouloir*** can also be followed by an infinitive verb phrase. This is the same as for the English verb *to want.*

> *Je veux un vélo français.*   I want a French bicycle.
> *Je veux jouer au basket.*   I want to play basketball.

a In which sentence above is ***vouloir*** followed by an infinitive verb phrase? |

Je veux jouer au basket.

b Which verb form matches the subject—the first verb, sometimes called the conjugated verb—or the second verb (the infinitive)? |

the first verb (the conjugated verb)

c What is the French equivalent of *He wants to play basketball?* |

Il veut jouer au basket. (The form of *vouloir* that you use must match the subject *il*.)

5 When ***vouloir*** is followed by an infinitive, the infinitive does not change in form.

See if you can write the French equivalent of *We want to watch television.* |

Nous voulons regarder la télévision.

6 What do the following people want or want to do? Answer each question, using the cue in parentheses. Say the English equivalent of the sentence you've written before you check your answer against the book.

Modèle: Qu'est-ce que tu veux faire? (regarder la télé) |
Je veux regarder la télé. (I want to watch TV.)

Qu'est-ce qu'il veut? (un magnétophone) |
Il veut un magnétophone. (He wants a tape recorder.)

a Qu'est-ce que tu veux faire? (écouter des disques) |
Je veux écouter des disques. (I want to listen to records.)

b Qu'est-ce qu'ils veulent? (une photo de leurs amis) |
Ils veulent une photo de leurs amis. (They want a photograph of their friends.)

c Qu'est-ce qu'il veut faire? (une promenade) |
Il veut faire une promenade. (He wants to go for a walk.)

d Qu'est-ce que vous voulez faire, Caroline et vous? (patiner) |
Nous voulons patiner. (We want to ice skate.)

CHECK-UP
Part 1

Write in French what the following people are doing.
1 Marc is skiing.   **3** The workers are making a table.
2 I am taking a walk.

Part 2

Write the French equivalents.
1 They want to dance.   **2** Do you want a jazz record?

VOCABULARY

septembre September
octobre October
novembre November
décembre December
janvier January
février February
le printemps spring

l'été (m.) summer
l'automne (m.) fall, autumn
l'hiver (m.) winter
faire une promenade to go for a walk
faire une promenade à vélo to take a bike ride
faire du ski to ski

UN COUP DE TÉLÉPHONE A telephone call
l'après-midi (m. or f.) afternoon
le basket-ball basketball
jouer au basket to play basketball
répond (he, she) answers
sonner to ring
téléphoner to call, to make a telephone call
le téléphone telephone
à quelle heure? when? at what time?
à deux heures at two o'clock
à tout à l'heure see you later
d'accord O.K.
on we, you, people
si tu veux if you want

1 À + *definite markers*

1 Theater critic Charles Duchamp is writing about the great conductor, Mimi Fontinelle. Below are some notes he took at a party on opening night. As you read the notes he took, notice the phrases at the end that begin with a form of the preposition *à.*

> *Le photographe Albert Matignon arrive. Mimi parle au photographe.*
> *La chanteuse américaine Barbara Sellers arrive. Mimi parle à la chanteuse.*
> *L'écrivain Paul Poirot arrive. Mimi parle à l'écrivain.*

a Write an English equivalent of the first note. |

> The photographer Albert Matignon arrives. Mimi talks with the photographer.

b Look again at the first note, then complete this statement. The preposition *à* contracts (combines) with *le* and forms the word ___. |

> au

c Look at the note about Barbara Sellers. Does *à* contract with *la?* |

> no (The preposition *à* never contracts with *la.*)

d And in the last note, does *à* contract with *l'?* |

> no

2 Here are some more of Charles Duchamp's notes.

> *Voilà les musiciens. Mimi parle aux musiciens.*
> *Et voilà les danseuses italiennes. Mimi parle aux danseuses italiennes.*

The preposition *à* contracts with *les* and forms the word ___. |

> aux

Below is a summary of the ways in which *à* combines with definite markers.

> *à + la = à la*   *à + le = au*
> *à + l' = à l'*   *à + les = aux*

3 In spoken French there is a linking sound between *aux* and a noun beginning with a vowel sound, just as there is with *les* and *des.* Say the following phrases aloud. In which of the phrases is there a linking /z/?

> *aux écrivains*   *aux danseuses*   *aux hommes* |

> *aux écrivains, aux hommes* (Remember that the first sound in *hommes* is a vowel
> sound because the *h* is not pronounced.)

4 Write the French equivalent of *Mimi is talking to the reporters.* |

> *Mimi parle aux journalistes.*

5 After taking notes, the critic decides to stop working and talk to people. Using the cues provided, write sentences to tell whom he talks to.

> Modèle: le journaliste |

> > *Il parle au journaliste.*

a l'actrice anglaise |

> > *Il parle à l'actrice anglaise.*

b les chanteurs français |

Il parle aux chanteurs français.

c les danseuses américaines |

Il parle aux danseuses américaines.

d le musicien italien |

Il parle au musicien italien.

e la coiffeuse |

Il parle à la coiffeuse.

6 *À* is also used with the verb *jouer* to talk about playing games and sports. Write the English equivalent of *Philippe joue au tennis.* |

Philippe is playing tennis. (The English equivalent has no preposition.)

7 In class you have used the names of several sports and games. Take a moment to review this new vocabulary on p. 194. Then continue this frame.

a Write the French equivalent of *I play cards.* |

Je joue aux cartes.

b Write the French equivalent of *I play chess.* |

Je joue aux échecs.

8 Rewrite the following sentences, replacing the indicated words with the phrase in parentheses. Make all necessary changes.

Modèle: J'aime jouer *au tennis.* (les cartes) |

J'aime jouer aux cartes.

a Tu veux jouer *aux boules* cet après-midi?   (le volley-ball) |

Tu veux jouer au volley-ball cet après-midi?

b Renée et Raoul jouent *aux échecs.*   (le hockey) |

Renée et Raoul jouent au hockey. (Remember that *le hockey* is one of the few words beginning with *h* that take the marker *le* instead of *l'.*)

c Patrick veut jouer *au basket.* (le ping-pong) |

Patrick veut jouer au ping-pong.

d Nous jouons *au tennis.* (les boules) |

Nous jouons aux boules.

Cards commemorating the French Revolution: **le roi** (king) **et la dame** (queen).

2 Telling time

1 Phillippe has forgotten to turn his clock ahead to daylight-saving time. His watch says it is eight o'clock. But as he glances at the hall clock, he stops short, and says: *Zut! Il est neuf heures!*

   a What is the English equivalent of *Il est neuf heures?* |

        It's nine o'clock. (Literally, "It is nine hours.")

   b Does *il* in *Il est neuf heures* mean *he* or *it?* |

        it

   c *Il est* is a fixed expression that is used in telling time. Complete this statement to say that it's four o'clock. _____*quatre heures.* |

        Il est

2 See if you can complete this question to ask what time it is in French:
Quelle heure _____-il? |

        est (When a question begins with a form of the question word *quel?*, the verb precedes the subject.)

3 **a** In spoken French, does *heure* begin with a consonant sound or a vowel sound? |

        a vowel sound (An initial *h* never represents a sound.)

   b Is there a linking /z/ sound in both of these phrases: *deux heures, dix heures?* |

        yes (deux heures, dix heures)

4 For each of the clocks below write in French *What time is it?* and then write the correct time.

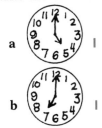

   a |

        Quelle heure est-il? Il est cinq heures. (Did you remember to put a hyphen between *est* and *il* in the questions? Did you make *heures* plural in the answer?)

   b |

        Quelle heure est-il? Il est sept heures.

5 Write a complete sentence to tell what the following people are doing at a certain time.

     Modèle: Qu'est-ce que tu fais à une heure? (manger à la cantine) |

        À une heure, je mange à la cantine.

   a Qu'est-ce qu'elle fait à deux heures? (une promenade avec son grand-père) |

        À deux heures, elle fait une promenade avec son grand-père.

   b Qu'est-ce qu'ils font à six heures? (leurs devoirs de maths) |

        À six heures ils font leurs devoirs de maths.

6 If you saw that a train was leaving on a schedule at *3h,* you could guess that the *h* stands for ____. |

        heures (This abbreviation is used on most timetables and listings of public events.)

Les Boules

Les boules (or **la pétanque**) is a game played mostly in smaller towns **dans le Midi** (in southern France). The rules are simple, but the opportunities for heated discussion are endless. One player tosses **le cochonnet** (a small wooden ball that serves as the target). Each player then tries to toss a heavy metal ball to get close to the target or knock away the ball of the closest competitor. The game of **boules** is played by men and women, young and old. You may be familiar with the Italian version of the game, which is called **bocci**.

CHECK-UP
Part 1

Complete these sentences to say what Françoise is doing.

1 Elle parle ____ docteur.

2 Elle parle ____ architecte.

3 Elle joue ____ boules.

4 Elle parle ____ mécanicienne.

Part 2

Say what time it is according to these cues: *6h; 2h.*

VOCABULARY

les boules	French game
les cartes	playing cards
les échecs	chess
le football	soccer
le hockey	hockey

le ping-pong	table tennis
le tennis	tennis
le volley-ball	volleyball
faire des projets	to make plans
quelle heure est-il?	what time is it?

1 *The direct-object pronouns* me, te, nous, vous

You have practiced using **le, la,** and **les** as equivalents for the direct-object pronouns *him, her, it,* and *them.* This section presents the equivalents for *me, you,* and *us.*

1 The following exchange takes place during a hide-and-seek game.
>—*Est-ce que tu vois Guy?*
>—*Oui, je le vois. Il est sous le bureau.*

  a Give the English equivalent of **Oui, je le vois.** |
>Yes, I see him.

  b What kind of pronoun is **le**—subject or direct-object? |
>direct-object

  c Does the direct-object pronoun precede or follow the verb? |
>It precedes the verb.

2 Later in the game, Guy is "it." Since he doesn't like to be "it," he has given up without looking very hard. One of his friends calls out to say where he is.
>—*Guy, tu me vois? Je suis ici.*   —Guy, do you see me? I'm here.

  a What is the subject in the phrase **tu me vois?** |
>tu

  b There is also a direct-object pronoun in **tu me vois.** Write it and give the English equivalent. |
>me; me (Although the French and English words are spelled the same way, they are pronounced differently. *Me* in French rhymes with *le.*)

3 Here is the complete conversation between Guy and his friends.
>Jérome: *Guy! Tu me vois?*
>Guy: *Ah oui, je te vois. Tu es derrière la porte.*
>Lucie et Nanette: *Hé, Guy! Tu nous vois?*
>Guy: *Mais oui, je vous vois. Vous êtes sous la table.*

The phrases below come from the dialogue you just read. For each phrase write the direct-object pronoun and its English equivalent. Refer to the dialogue if necessary.

  a Je te vois. |
>te; you (I see you.)

  b Tu nous vois. |
>nous; us (If you hesitated, remember that *nous* can't be the subject here: the verb *vois* matches *tu,* not *nous.*)

  c Je vous vois. |
>vous; you (*Vous* couldn't be the subject here because *vois* matches *je.*)

  d Tu me vois. |
>me; me

4 Complete the French equivalents of the following sentences, using *me, te, nous,* or *vous.*

    a Marc is looking for you, Peter. *Marc ____ cherche, Pierre.* |
           te

    b Now, Catherine and Michel, you speak and we listen to you.
    Maintenant, Catherine et Michel, vous parlez et nous ____ écoutons. |
            vous

    c That man knows me. *Cet homme ____ connaît.* |
            me

    d Patricia is looking at us. *Patricia ____ regarde.* |
            nous

5 Write the English equivalents of these sentences.

    a Nous vous aimons beaucoup. |
            We like you very much. (*Nous* must be the subject of *aimons.*)

    b Elles te connaissent, n'est-ce pas? |
            They know you, don't they?

    c Vous nous écoutez? |
            Are you listening to us? (*Vous* must be the subject of *écoutez.*)

2   *Practice with* à + *definite markers*

1 In Preparation 44 you learned how to use *à* with definite markers. Complete the equations below. Remember that *à* contracts with two of the definite markers.

    à + la = ____   à + l' = ____   à + le = ____   à + les = ____ |
    à la; à l'; au; aux

2 You already know two types of expressions in which *à* is used.

    a To talk about playing a game or a sport, you use the expression ____. |
            jouer à

    b To say that someone is talking to somebody else, you can use the expression ____. |
            parler à

3 Write sentences to say what the following people are doing. Answers occur after **d.**

    a Colette/jouer/le tennis   **c** Laurent/parler/l'agent de police
    b Marc et Delphine/jouer/les échecs   **d** Chantal/parler/la directrice |

        a *Colette joue au tennis.* b *Marc et Delphine jouent aux échecs.* c *Laurent parle à l'agent de police.* d *Chantal parle à la directrice.*

4 The preposition *à* is also used in the expression *être à,* meaning *to be someplace.*

    a Jeanne is going to be late getting home, so she telephones her parents to let them know where she is. She says: *Je suis à la bibliothèque.* Write the English equivalent. |
            I'm at the library.

b An hour later, Jeanne calls to say that she's with some friends at the café (*le café*). Complete her sentence. *Je ___ café.* ▮

           suis au (Remember that *à + le = au*.)

5 It's another typical day in the lives of the people below. Say that they are in their usual places of work or play. Write the English equivalent of where they are. (You can refer to the vocabulary on p. 199.)

    Modèle: Mark Lepied: le stade ▮

           Mark Lepied est au stade. At the stadium.

a Le médecin: l'hôpital ▮

           Le médecin est à l'hôpital. At the hospital. (Did you remember the *accent circonflexe*?)

b L'ouvrière et l'ouvrier: l'usine ▮

           L'ouvrière et l'ouvrier sont à l'usine. At the factory.

c Le professeur et moi, nous: la bibliothèque ▮

           Le professeur et moi, nous sommes à la bibliothèque. At the library.

d Tu: le cinéma ▮

           Tu es au cinéma. At the movies.

3 *The subject pronoun* on

1 In class you have been reading the dialogue *Un Coup de téléphone.* At one point, Pierre asks his friend the following question: *On joue au basket cet après-midi, n'est-ce pas?*

a Write the English equivalent. ▮

           We're playing basketball this afternoon, aren't we?

b Here, *on* is the equivalent of the English pronoun ___. ▮

           we (*On* is often used in French instead of *nous*.)

c Is the verb *jouer* in the *il/elle*-form or in the *ils/elles*-form? ▮

           il/elle-form (Even though *on* has a plural meaning in the sentence above, it combines with a singular form of the verb. It's like the formal expression in English, "One goes to school every weekday.")

2 Camille and François have just finished playing a game of chess on a rainy Saturday. Camille doesn't know what to do next. Write the English equivalent of her question: *Qu'est-ce qu'on fait maintenant?* ▮

           What do we do now?

3 In frames 1 and 2, *on* had the meaning of *we*. *On* can also have the meaning of *people in general.* What do you think is the English equivalent of *En France, on parle français?* ▮

           In France, people (they) speak French. (Here, *on* is similar to the pronoun *one*, as in *In Germany, one speaks German.*)

4 Complete this sentence to say that in Canada, people play hockey. *Au Canada, ___ au hockey.* ▮

           on joue

5 Suppose you are a camp counselor, and one of your campers wants to know what the group is doing today. Answer the questions using **on** and the cues given in parentheses. Write the English equivalent of your answer to **a**.

> Modèle: Qu'est-ce qu'on fait cet après-midi? (jouer aux cartes) |
>> *Cet après-midi, on joue aux cartes.* (This afternoon, we're playing cards.)

a Qu'est-ce qu'on fait à quatre heures? (nager) |
>> *À quatre heures, on nage.* (At four o'clock, we swim.)

b Qu'est-ce qu'on fait à huit heures? (jouer au ping-pong) |
>> *À huit heures, on joue au ping-pong.*

c Qu'est-ce qu'on fait à neuf heures? (regarder la télévision) |
>> *À neuf heures, on regarde la télévision.*

4 *Pre-quiz practice:* vouloir

In your next class, you will be given a written quiz on *vouloir.* If necessary, review the forms of the verb on p. 188 before doing the following exercises. Answers are in the answer key so that you can test yourself.

1 Write the correct form of *vouloir* for each sentence below.
  a Tu ____ jouer aux cartes avec nous?
  b Je ne ____ pas manger maintenant.
  c Qu'est-ce que vous ____ faire maintenant?
  d On ____ écouter des disques de jazz.
2 Write complete sentences with the cues below.
  a Qui / vouloir / faire une promenade?
  b On / ne...pas / vouloir / jouer aux échecs
  c Est-ce que / Paul et Marie / vouloir / jouer au volley-ball demain?
  d Nous / ne...pas / vouloir / habiter à New York

CHECK-UP
Part 1

Write the French equivalents.

1 He sees me. **2** They know us.

Part 3

Write complete sentences with the cues provided.

1 On / jouer / le pingpong **2** On / vouloir / les photos

VOCABULARY

un aéroport airport
une bibliothèque library
un café coffee house, restaurant, or bar
un cinéma movie theater
un hôpital hospital

une maison house, home
une plage beach
un stade stadium
une usine factory
le matin morning; in the morning
le soir evening; in the evening

PREPARATION 46

1 *The verb* aller

The verb *to go* is used to say where you are going (*I'm going to the movies*) or what you will do in the near future (*I'm going to watch TV tonight*). The French equivalent **aller** is also used in these ways.

je	vais
tu	vas
on/il/elle	va
ils/elles	vont
nous	allons
vous	allez

1 What is the infinitive ending of **aller?** |
 -er

2 Look at the chart for a moment. Is **aller** a regular **-er** verb? |
 no (*Aller* is the only irregular *-er* verb. All other *-er* verbs have the same present-tense endings as *chercher.*)

3 Some forms of **aller** can be predicted from the infinitive and others cannot. Which two forms use the stem of the infinitive? |
 nous allons, vous allez

4 The form of **aller** that matches **ils** and **elles** is ____ . |
 vont

5 What form of **aller** matches **je?** |
 vais

6 What form of **aller** matches **tu?** |
 vas

7 What form of **aller** matches **on, il, elle?** |
 va

8 The verb **aller** may be followed by a noun phrase or by an infinitive. The same is true of the verb *to go* in English.

   Je vais au stade.   Nous allons jouer au tennis demain.

   a Copy the first sentence and write the English equivalent. ❘

   Je vais au stade. I'm going to the stadium.

   b To say that someone is going somewhere, is **aller** followed by a noun phrase or by an infinitive phrase? ❘

   noun phrase

   c Copy the sentence *Nous allons jouer au tennis demain,* and write the English equivalent. ❘

   Nous allons jouer au tennis demain. We're going to play tennis tomorrow.

   d To say that someone is going to do something in the near future, **aller** is followed by an ___ phrase. ❘

   infinitive verb (In French, this use of *aller* is called *futur proche*—near future.)

9 Take a few moments to read aloud to yourself the forms of **aller,** then complete the sentences below that say what various members of your imaginary family are doing today. Write English equivalents of **a–c.**

   a Mon frère ___ au zoo. ❘

   va (My brother is going to the zoo.)

   b Mes sœurs ___ au cinéma. ❘

   vont (My sisters are going to the movies.)

   c Je ___ à la bibliothèque. ❘

   vais (I'm going to the library.)

   d À six heures, nous ___ au café. ❘

   allons

   e Jean-Claude et papa, vous ___ à l'aéroport? ❘

   allez

   f Et toi, maman, tu ___ à la plage, n'est-ce pas? ❘

   vas

10 Complete the sentences below to say where people are going. If you can't remember the gender of a word, look at the vocabulary list. Answers follow **d.**

   Modèle: Louis / plage ❘

   Louis va à la plage.

   a nous / café   **c** les ouvriers / usine
   b le docteur / hôpital   **d** je / cinéma ❘

   a *Nous allons au café.* b *Le docteur va à l'hôpital.* c *Les ouvriers vont à l'usine.* d *Je vais au cinéma.*

11 How would you say in French *We're going to the library?* ❘

   Nous allons à la bibliothèque.

12 What is the French equivalent for *She's going to the zoo?* ❘

   Elle va au zoo.

13 Say in French *That worker (**ouvrière**) is going to the factory.* ❘

   Cette ouvrière va à l'usine.

2 Practice with direct-object pronouns

1 In Preparation 45 you learned how to use the direct-object pronouns *me, te, nous, vous.* To see if you remember them, complete the French equivalents of the sentences below.

a They know me. *Ils ——— connaissent.* ▮
me

b She likes us. *Elle ——— aime.* ▮
nous

c He's looking for you, Mrs. Moreau. *Il ——— cherche, Madame.* ▮
vous

d I see you, Frank. *Je ——— vois, Frank.* ▮
te / vous

2 Like other words you've learned, certain object pronouns change form when they occur before a word beginning with a vowel sound.

a Before a vowel, *le* and *la* are written ———. ▮
l'

b Before a vowel, *me* and *te* are written ——— and ———. ▮
m', t'

3 Write the French equivalent of these sentences.

a Paul is listening to me. ▮
Paul m'écoute.

b Does Laurent like you? ▮
(Est-ce que) Laurent t'aime?

Here is a chart of the direct-object pronouns. You can refer to it when doing the following exercises.

> me, m'
> te, t'
> le, la, l'
> les
> nous
> vous

4 Answer the following questions with the correct direct-object pronoun form—*le, la, l',* or *les.*

> Modèle: Est-ce que vous connaissez les sœurs de Paul? ▮
> *Oui, je les connais.*

a Est-ce que Mme Charpentier connaît ton père? ▮
Oui, elle le connaît.

b Vous invitez l'amie de Paul au match de football? ▮
Oui, je l'invite. (Did you remember the *élision* before the verb, since it begins with a vowel?)

c Tu vois ces garçons qui jouent au basket? ▮
Oui, je les vois.

5 Pretend that you and some friends are hiding from Christian. Another friend walks up to you and you ask her how Christian is doing in his search. Write your friend's answers to your questions. (Start all answers with **oui**.)

> Modèle: Est-ce que tu vois Christian? |
> *Oui, je le vois.*

a Est ce que Christian voit Marc et Sylvie? |
> *Oui, il les voit.*

b Est-ce que Christian nous cherche, Béatrice et moi? |
> *Oui, il vous cherche.*

c Est-ce qu'il te voit? |
> *Oui, il me voit.*

d Est-ce qu'il me voit maintenant? |
> *Oui, il te voit.*

3 Spelling practice

In class you will be writing some sentences from the dialogue **Un Coup de téléphone.** This exercise will help you practice with the spelling.

Read each sentence to yourself and decide what letters belong in the blanks. Then write the complete sentence. Answers are in the answer key.

1 All __, Andr __? __'est Pi __ __re.
2 O.__ j __ue a __ basket ce __ apr __s-m __d __, n'es __-c __ pas?
3 À d __ux h __ __re __, s __ tu v __ __x.
4 B __ n, d' __ cco __ d. À to __ t à __'h __ __re.

CHECK-UP	Write sentences to say where these people are going.
Part 1	**1** Tu / aller / l'aéroport **3** Je / aller / la plage
	2 Ils / aller / bibliothèque
Part 2	Comment dit-on en français?
	1 We're looking at them. **3** She knows you.
	2 Are you listening to me?

VOCABULARY

inviter to invite

QUEL SALE TEMPS! What awful weather!

la science–fiction	science fiction	*on peut*	we can
un film	movie	*tu sais*	you know
arriver	to arrive	*je crois*	I think
il pleut	it's raining	*allons-y*	let's go

1 Weather and seasons

The success of our favorite pastimes may depend on the weather conditions. Below are some of the French expressions used to talk about the weather. **Quel temps fait-il?**

Il fait beau.

Il fait chaud.

Il pleut.

Il fait du vent.

Il fait mauvais.

Il fait froid.

Il neige.

Il fait frais; il ne fait pas chaud, et il ne fait pas très froid.

1 You should be able to guess the English meaning of **Quel temps fait-il?** |

> What's the weather like?

2 Compare the verbs in these French and English sentences:

  Quel temps fait-il?   What's (What is) the weather like?
  Il fait beau.   It's (It is) nice.

a Which verb is generally used in English to talk about the weather—a form of *to do* or a form of *to be?* |

> to be

b Which is generally used in French—a form of **faire** or **être?** |

> faire

c Some weather expressions don't use the verb **faire.** How would you say *It's snowing* in French? |

> Il neige.

3 Here is a quick review of the names of the seasons in French.

    a Which is the equivalent of *summer—l'automne* or *l'été?* |
        l'été

    b Which is the equivalent of *spring—le printemps* or *l'automne?* |
        le printemps (from the Latin for *first season*)

    c Which is the equivalent of *winter—l'été* or *l'hiver?* |
        l'hiver (It's related to English *hibernate.*)

    d And how do you say *fall* in French? It's a cognate of *autumn.* |
        l'automne (The *m* in *automne* is not pronounced, but the *n* is.)

4 Answer the questions in **a–c.**

    a Quand fait-il froid? En été ou en hiver? |
        En hiver.

    b Quand il pleut, est-ce qu'on préfère jouer au baseball ou aux échecs? |
        Aux échecs.

    c On fait du ski quand il pleut ou quand il neige? |
        Quand il neige.

Frames 5–10 are based on a weather map of the U.S. and Canada. Pretend that you are interpreting the map for a visitor from France. Answers are in the answer key.

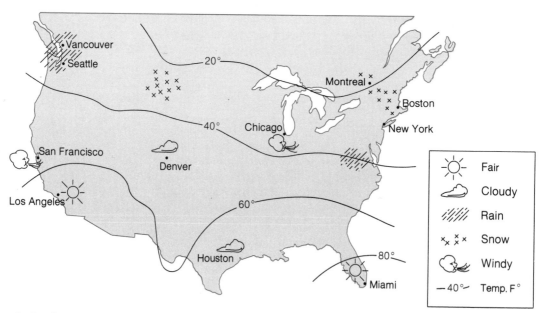

5 Quel temps fait-il à Montréal? Il pleut ou il neige?
6 Quel temps fait-il à Miami? Il fait beau ou mauvais?
7 Et à Chicago? Il fait chaud ou il fait du vent?
8 Quel temps fait-il à Vancouver? Il pleut ou il neige?
9 Il fait beau ou mauvais à Denver?
10 Il fait frais ou chaud à San Francisco?

NOTE **Le Football**

Le football (soccer) is a very popular sport in France. Two teams of eleven players try to score a goal **(marquer un but).** They can touch the ball only with their heads or feet: no hands allowed!

Although girls are beginning to play, **le football** has traditionally been a sport for boys and men. They play after school or work, and on weekends. There are informal neighborhood games and organized competitions between **clubs sportifs** and between towns. The fans **(les supporters)** are very loyal to their home teams and turn out in great numbers for games. At the national and international level, **le football** is the focus of as much talent, interest, and money as American football.

2 Practice with direct-object pronouns

1 To answer the questions below, begin with *Oui,* and use a direct-object pronoun. Make sure the subject pronoun you begin your answer with makes sense in relation to the question. If necessary, refer to the chart of direct-object pronouns on p. 201.

a Vos grands-parents vous invitent souvent au théâtre? ▮
     Oui, ils nous invitent (ils m'invitent) souvent au théâtre.

b Ton professeur d'anglais te connaît bien, n'est-ce pas? ▮
     Oui, il me connaît bien.

c Catherine et Jean, est-ce que vous connaissez Martin Pasquier? ▮
     Oui, nous le connaissons.

d Toi et moi, nous invitons Martine et Vincent au théâtre? ▮
     Oui, nous les invitons au théâtre.

e Georges! Tu m'écoutes? ▮
     Oui, je t'écoute. / Oui, je vous écoute.

f Claude et Nathalie, vous m'invitez au restaurant demain? ▮
     Oui, nous t'invitons (nous vous invitons) au restaurant demain.

2 Imagine that you are thinking about some of your friends. Say what it is that you like especially about each one. Make sure the form of the adjective matches the gender of the direct-object pronoun.

    Modèle: Chantal / gentil ▮
       Je la trouve gentille.

a Henri / beau ▮
     Je le trouve beau.

b Jean-Yves et ses parents / sympathique ▮
     Je les trouve sympathiques. (Remember to add *-s* to *sympathiques.*)

c Marguerite / joli ▮
     Je la trouve jolie. (Add *-e* to *joli* to make it match *la.*)

3 Write an English equivalent for *Je les trouve sympathiques.* ▮
     I think they're nice. / I find them nice.

3 Vocabulary practice: sound and spelling

This section will give you a little practice with new vocabulary and will also give you tips on how to pronounce words properly. When you do each frame, pronounce all the French words aloud.

1 In French, when an *s* occurs between two vowels in a word, it is pronounced /z/, as in **chaise,** for example. Read the words below and copy those in which the *s* is pronounced /z/.

      le magasin   *le stade*   *la discothèque*
      le restaurant   *la maison*   *l'usine* |

le magasin, la maison, l'usine

2 In French, an /s/ sound, as in *sa,* can be spelled in different ways. See what letters can represent the sound /s/ by writing the letters that are missing from these words.

      __upermarché, __inéma, fran __ais, gro __ __ e |

s, c, ç, ss (The letter c is pronounced /s/ when followed by i or e, or written with a cedilla.)

3 In French, the /k/ sound (as in the English *cat*) has two spellings. Fill in the missing letters: __*afé, bibliothè* __ __ *e.* |

c, qu (The letter c is pronounced /k/ when followed by a, o, or u. The letters qu are always pronounced /k/.)

4 Practice with aller *in the negative*

You have had practice saying where people are going. This section will give you practice saying where people are *not* going.

1 Say in French that you are going to the airport. |

Je vais à l'aéroport.

2 How do you think you would say that you are *not* going to the airport? **Je ____ à l'aéroport.** |

ne vais pas (Ne precedes the verb, pas follows it.)

3 The people below have had to cancel their plans. Use **aller** to tell where they are *not* going. Refer to the vocabulary if you need to review the markers that go with each noun.

      Modèle: Pascal et moi / stade |

Pascal et moi, nous n'allons pas au stade.

a Colette / usine |

Colette ne va pas à l'usine.

b Je / librairie |

Je ne vais pas à la librairie.

c Mes copains / discothèque ▌

Mes copains ne vont pas à la discothèque.

d Vous / parc ▌

Vous n'allez pas au parc.

CHECK-UP
Part 1

Write the following in French.

1 The weather's bad.   **2** It's raining.

Part 3

From the fragments below, write a complete word for each item.

1 éche __ __   **2** __ in __ ma   **3** m __ g __ __ in

VOCABULARY

un appartement apartment	*un match* athletic contest
une banque bank	*un western* a Western
un bureau desk; office	*quel temps fait-il?* what's the weather?
une discothèque discotheque	*il fait beau* it's nice
un garage garage	*il fait chaud* it's warm, hot
une librairie bookstore	*il fait frais* it's cool
un magasin store	*il fait froid* it's cold
un parc park	*il fait mauvais* the weather's bad
un restaurant restaurant	*il fait du vent* it's windy
une station-service gas station	*il neige* it's snowing
un supermarché supermarket	*il pleut* it's raining
un théâtre theater	

NOTE ❊

Les Français et le ski

In France an active winter vacation consists of skiing—usually in the **Alpes** or **Pyrénées.** School children by the thousands go with their teachers for a month of **classes de neige,** with schoolwork in the morning and skiing in the afternoon. Some French people who don't ski themselves enjoy following the progress of French competitors in the international ski trials and in the Olympics. Skiing is one of the events in which French competitors often rank at the top.

**Skiez
nous gardons
vos enfants.**

1 The present tense of pouvoir

In Preparation 43, you learned how to say *want to* with the present-tense forms of ***vouloir.*** You won't succeed at something you *want* to do unless you *can* do it. This Preparation will teach you to use the forms of ***pouvoir*** to say *can, be able.*

1 Compare the forms of ***pouvoir*** with those of ***vouloir.***

je	veu	x		je	peu	x
tu	veu	x		tu	peu	x
on/il/elle	veu	t		on/il/elle	peu	t
ils/elles	veul	ent		ils/elles	peuv	ent
nous	voul	ons		nous	pouv	ons
vous	voul	ez		vous	pouv	ez

a Are the endings of ***vouloir*** and ***pouvoir*** the same? |
    yes
b What are the three forms of the stem of ***vouloir?*** |
    veu–, veul–, voul–
c What are the three forms of the stem of ***pouvoir?*** |
    peu–, peuv–, pouv–

2 Say the forms of ***pouvoir*** to yourself for a few moments. Then write the forms that match the subject pronouns below. Check your answers carefully against the chart.

  a nous   **d** je
  b vous   **e** on/il/elle
  c ils/elles   **f** tu

3 Read these two sentences.

>   *On peut jouer au tennis aujourd'hui.*
>   *Est-ce que je peux aller au cinéma, s'il te plaît?*

  a Write the English equivalent of the first sentence. |
       We can play tennis today.
  b Write the English equivalent of the second sentence. |
       Can (May) I go to the movies, please? (Here, *pouvoir* is used to ask permission.

4 Nicolas keeps asking friends to do things with him. Everyone wants to, but nobody can. Write the answers to all his questions. Write the English equivalent for frame **a.**

   Modèle: Marc, tu veux jouer au basket? |
            Oui, mais je ne peux pas. (Yes, but I can't.)

  a Catherine, tu veux aller au concert? |
            Oui, mais je ne peux pas. (Yes, but I can't.)

b Jean-Paul et Solange, vous voulez aller au cinéma? |

Oui, mais nous ne pouvons pas.

c Est-ce que Sara et Eric veulent aller au café avec moi? |

Oui, mais ils ne peuvent pas.

d Est-ce que Christine veut jouer aux cartes avec moi? |

Oui, mais elle ne peut pas.

5 Write the French equivalents of the following sentences. Answers are in the answer key.

Modèle: I want to play tennis today, but I can't. |

Je veux jouer au tennis aujourd'hui, mais je ne peux pas.

a You (*tu*) want to listen to the radio now, but you can't.

b You (*vous*) want to go to the movies, but you can't.

6 Here is a French proverb that uses both ***vouloir*** and ***pouvoir***. Can you guess the equivalent English proverb? ***Vouloir, c'est pouvoir.*** |

Where there's a will, there's a way. (To want to is to be able to.)

2   *Vocabulary practice: sound and spelling*

1 The letter *g* represents two different sounds in French. Look at the words below.

magasin	*Guy*	*photographe*
plage	*gymnastique*	*biologie*

a Copy the words in which *g* sounds like *g* in ***gomme.*** |

magasin, Guy, photographe (The letter *g* is pronounced like *g* in ***gomme*** when it is followed by *a, o, u,* or a consonant.

b Copy the words in which *g* sounds like *g* in ***gentil.*** |

plage, gymnastique, biologie (The letter *g* sounds like *g* in ***gentil*** when it is followed by *e, i,* or *y.*)

2 An accent may be important to the meaning of a word, or its sound, or both. Write the following words, and supply all missing accents: ***ou, supermarche, aeroport, theatre, cafe, hopital.*** |

où, supermarché, aéroport, théâtre, café, hôpital

3   *Practice with possessive markers*

You haven't had practice with possessive markers for quite a while. This section will give you a quick review. First, answer frames 1 and 2. If you miss either one, look back at the Summary of Phase 3, p. 176. Then do frames 3–6. Those answers are in the answer key.

1 How would you say *his book* in French? |

son livre

2 How would you say *her book* in French? |

son livre

3 In French, can you tell whether the owner is male or female by looking at the possessive marker?

4 French possessive markers match in ___ and ___ the nouns they accompany.

5 Write the singular and plural equivalents for each marker.

    a my: *m ___, m ___, m ___*

    b your: *t ___, t ___, t ___*

    c his or her: *s ___, s ___, s ___*

    d our: *n ___, n ___*

    e your: *v ___, v ___*

    f their: *l ___, l ___*

6 Write French equivalents for the missing markers below.

    a my cards: ___ *cartes*

    b her motorbike: ___ *vélomoteur*

    c their factory: ___ *usine*

    d our school: ___ *école*

    e their buddies: ___ *copains*

    f his cameras: ___ *appareils-photos*

4 Vocabulary practice: logical responses

In English there are phrases that express emotions and attitudes: among others, *You're kidding!* (skepticism), *Darn it!* (annoyance), and *Well . . .* (to fill time while you are putting your thoughts together). There are many expressions of this sort in French, too. Below are some of the ones you have seen in the dialogues so far. Spend a few minutes looking at them now to make sure you know when they are used.

SURPRISE, ASTONISHMENT
Oh là là!
Pas possible!
Ça alors!
Tiens!
Sans blague!
Dis donc!
C'est vrai!
Tu plaisantes!

AGREEMENT
Bien sûr!
D'accord!
Mais oui!
Oh oui, alors!

DISAGREEMENT
Mais non!
Ah non, alors!

INDIFFERENCE
Bof...

SKEPTICISM
Tu plaisantes!
C'est vrai?
Pas possible!
Sans blague?

ANNOYANCE
Zut!
Ça alors!
Oh ça va, ça va!

STALLING FOR TIME
Alors...

CHECK-UP
Part 1

Comment dit-on en français?

1 We can speak French.

2 I can play tennis today.

Part 4

Give a French equivalent for each exclamation below.

1 You're kidding!

2 Absolutely not!

3 Of course!

4 Darn it!

VOCABULARY

mars March
avril April

mai May
juin June

juillet July
août August

NOTE ✳

Customs and holidays in France (1)

Le premier avril
April Fool's day originated when King Charles IX changed the calendar and moved the first day of the year from April to January. It is a day for practical jokes. In France, school children may try to sneak up behind a classmate and fasten a **poisson d'avril** (paper fish) to the person's back.

Le premier mai
This is the French equivalent of Valentine's Day. Traditionally, people give little bouquets of **muguet** (lily of the valley) to those they love. **Le premier mai** is also called **la fête du Travail** (Labor Day), and is a legal holiday.

Le 14 juillet
La Fête Nationale (Bastille Day) marks the day the Bastille prison was stormed in 1789 to set off the French Revolution. There are military parades, fireworks, and dancing in the streets in all towns, big and small. The dancing and other festivities often continue into the wee hours of the morning.

— PRISE DE LA BASTILLE —
14 JUILLET 1789

PREPARATION 49

1 Practice with direct-object pronouns

1 You are showing a French exchange student a photograph of a huge family picnic you had last year. She asks you to point out some of your relatives. Answer her questions, using *voilà* and the appropriate direct-object pronoun *le, la,* or *les.*

Modèle: Où est ta sœur? |
La voilà.

a Où est ton père? |
Le voilà.

b Où sont tes grands-parents? |
Les voilà.

2 If you called up a friend and he wanted to know where you were calling from, he might ask *Où es-tu?* What is the English equivalent of *Où es-tu?* |

> Where are you? (In both the French and the English question, the word order is the same: question word + verb + subject.)

3 Some friends are showing you photographs of a trip they took to Canada with the French Club. Occasionally, you can't find someone on the photograph. Complete your friends' answers to your questions, using the appropriate direct-object pronoun.

> Modèle: –Richard, où es-tu?
> –____, derrière Nicole. |
>
> *Me voilà*

a –Jean-Paul et David, où êtes-vous?
–____, derrière la statue. |

> *Nous voilà*

b –Où est Christophe?
–____, devant la porte du musée. |

> *Le voilà*

c –Pierre, où es-tu?
–____, devant Michel. |

> *Me voilà*

d –Où sont Etienne et Bernard?
–____, dans le café. |

> *Les voilà*

4 At a family reunion, everyone is gossiping. Use direct-object pronouns to complete what is being said about the people whose names are in parentheses. Write the English equivalent of **a** and **b**.

> Modèle: Sa tante ____ trouve bête. (Pierre) |
>
> *le* (His aunt thinks he's stupid. / His aunt finds him stupid.)

a Ses grands-parents ne ____ invitent pas souvent au restaurant. (Nathalie) |

> *l'* (Her grandparents don't invite her often to the restaurant.)

b Les filles Poirier ____ détestent. (leurs cousins) |

> *les* (The Poirier daughters hate them.)

c Ma grand-mère ____ écoute toujours quand je joue du piano. (moi) |

> *m'*

d Notre petite sœur ____ adore. (Olivier et moi) |

> *nous*

e Votre cousine ____ trouve gentils. (Vous, Jacques et Andrée) |

> *vous*

f Je ne ____ trouve pas très gentille. (Angélique) |

> *la*

g Tu ____ écoutes jouer de l'accordéon? (ton oncle Maurice) |

> *l'*

2 Aller + *infinitive* (futur proche)

1 In Preparation 43 *aller* + infinitive was presented as a way to talk about something that's going to happen in the future. Write the English equivalent of *Je vais voir un film.* |

I'm going to see a movie.

2 Say what the people below are going to do on Saturday. Answers are in the answer key. If you need to review *aller* first, study the chart on p. 199.

a Paul et moi, nous / voir un film

b Tu / tricoter

c Tante Geneviève / faire une promenade

3 Here is Jean Roty's appointment schedule for the week of August 1–7. Refer to the chart to answer items **a–d** below.

L	1	2h. écouter des disques chez Paul
M	2	8h / voir Sophie / hôpital / avec Gilles
M	3	8h - voir Les Enfants Terribles avec Paul
J	4	
V	5	8h - jouer aux échecs chez Jeanne
S	6	3h - voir match de football avec Suzanne
D	7	4h - promenade - plage avec Denise

Write a complete sentence to indicate what Jean is going to do, where he is going to do it, and with whom, if anybody.

Modèle: Lundi à deux heures. |

Il va écouter des disques chez Paul.

a Mardi à huit heures. |

Il va voir Sophie à l'hôpital avec Gilles.

b Mercredi à huit heures. |

Il va voir **Les Enfants Terribles** avec Paul.

c Vendredi à huit heures. |

Il va jouer aux échecs chez Jeanne.

d Samedi à trois heures. |

Il va voir le match de football avec Suzanne.

e Dimanche à quatre heures. |

Il va faire une promenade à la plage avec Denise.

4 The verb *aller* has another common use in French. In the expression *aller chez* it means *to visit someone*.

> *Je vais aller chez Annick ce soir.*   I'm going to visit Annick this evening.

The cognate *visiter* means *to visit a monument or a place*.

> *Ils veulent visiter New York.*   They want to visit New York.
> *Je veux visiter le musée des Beaux-Arts.*   I want to visit the Fine Arts Museum.

Write the verb form that correctly completes each sentence below.

  a Tu (vas chez / visites) Marc ce soir? |
     vas chez

  b Mon professeur veut (aller chez / visiter) le musée Rodin. |
     visiter

NOTE ✵   *Customs and holidays in France* (2)

La Toussaint
Le premier novembre is, in France, a somber holiday when families visit the cemetery to pay respect to the dead and leave flowers on the graves and tombs.

L'Armistice
Le 11 novembre commemorates the end of World War I, in which France lost nearly one quarter of its population. There are military parades, and **les monuments aux morts de la guerre** (monuments to the war dead) in every city and town are decorated with wreaths and flowers. In Paris, the torch that burns on the tomb of the unknown soldier **(le tombeau du Soldat inconnu)** is rekindled with great ceremony.

3   *Vocabulary round-up: locatives*

Words that refer to a place or location are called *locatives*. This section will give you practice with the spelling and gender of locatives you have learned recently. Answers are in the answer key.

1 Write the complete word with its indefinite marker, **un** or **une**.

  a h _ pi _ al
  b a _ _ art _ m _ nt
  c sup _ _ mar _ h _
  d s _ a _ ion-ser _ i _ e

2 Use the definition, hint, or riddle with each item below to help you figure out the locative noun. The first and last letter are given as clues. Write the word with its indefinite marker.

  a The U.S. president lives in a white one: *m _ _ _ _ n*
  b A place to buy something: *m _ _ _ _ _ n*
  c During a big soccer game, it's full of spectators: *s _ _ _ e* ,
  d When is a desk not a desk? When it's an office: *b _ _ _ _ u*
  e You can buy the latest novel here: *l _ _ _ _ _ _ _ e*

Loisirs...

Même avec des amis, on aime gagner!

Santé, vigueur, camaraderie

De la neige, du soleil, des copains . . .

La vie est Belle!

1 *How to use* de + *the definite markers*

1 You have had quite a bit of practice recently talking about playing games and sports.

    a the verb *jouer* by itself means ____. |

         to play

    b To talk about playing a sport or game in French, you use the expression *jouer* ____. |

         à

2 When *jouer* is used to talk about playing a musical instrument, however, a different preposition is used. Find that preposition in this sentence: *J'aime jouer de la guitare.* |

         de

3 Compare the forms of *à* and *de* when they are used with definite markers. Note that both prepositions contract with *le* and *les.*

à + la	= à la	de + la	= de la
à + l'	= à l'	de + l'	= de l'
à + le	= au	de + le	= du
à + les	= aux	de + les	= des

Refer to the right-hand chart to complete the sentences below, and write the English equivalents for **a** and **b.**

    a Vous jouez ____? (le violon) |

         du violon (Do you play the violin?)

    b Ma mère aime jouer ____. (la trompette) |

         de la trompette (My mother likes to play the trumpet.)

    c Tu connais M. Ferrier, qui joue ____? (les cymbales) |

         des cymbales

    d Tu sais qui va jouer ____ ce soir? (l'accordéon) |

         de l'accordéon

4 Pretend that you are introducing your fellow musicians to a friend. Say what instrument each person plays.

    a Chantal: le piano |

         Chantal joue du piano.

    b Jean-Claude: la flûte |

         Jean-Claude joue de la flûte.

    c Bernadette: la batterie |

         Bernadette joue de la batterie.

    d Moi: le saxophone |

         Je joue du saxophone.

5 The preposition *de* also shows possession or close relationship.

    a Write the English equivalent of *C'est le chien de Robert.* |

         It's Robert's dog.

b Instead of saying *It's Robert's dog,* you might say *It's the boy's dog.*
Complete the French equivalent of that sentence. (Remember about
contraction.) ***C'est le chien ___ garçon.*** ▎

> *du (de + le = du)*

c Now complete the French equivalent of *It's the children's dog.* ***C'est***
le chien ___ enfants. ▎

> *des (de + les = des)*

6 Write the English equivalent of each phrase below.
  a le stylo du médecin ▎

> the doctor's pen

  b l'enfant de la femme ▎

> the woman's child

7 Now write French equivalents for the phrases below. The words for
the instruments are in the Vocabulary of this Preparation.
  a the student's cymbals ▎

> *les cymbales de l'élève*

  b the (female) musician's flute ▎

> *la flûte de la musicienne*

  c the (male) musician's trumpet ▎

> *la trompette du musicien*

2 *More on telling time*

1 In French, time is expressed by ***il est*** + number + ***heure/s.***
  Il est une heure.   Il est quatre heures.   Il est dix heures.
The English equivalent of ***Il est dix heures*** is ___. ▎

> It's ten o'clock.

2 Tell what time it is by the following clocks.

a   **b** ▎

> a *Il est sept heures.* b *Il est onze heures.*

3 Now look at this clock and the French sentence.

  Il est dix heures et demie.
  a In English, what time is it by the clock above? ▎

> It's half past ten./It's ten-thirty.

  b In ***Il est dix heures et demie,*** what two words express the half-
hour? ▎

> *et demie* (***Demie*** means *half.*)

4 Write in French what time it is by the following clocks.

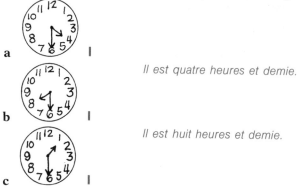

a |

Il est quatre heures et demie.

b |

Il est huit heures et demie.

c |

Il est une heure et demie.

3 The numbers 70–100

Use the numbers below to answer the questions in this part.

60 *soixante*	79 *soixante-dix-neuf*	91 *quatre-vingt-onze*
61 *soixante et un*	80 *quatre-vingts*	99 *quatre-vingt-dix-neuf*
69 *soixante-neuf*	81 *quatre-vingt-un*	100 *cent*
70 *soixante-dix*	89 *quatre-vingt-neuf*	
71 *soixante et onze*	90 *quatre-vingt-dix*	

1 From 20 to 69 the pattern of counting in French is the same: *vingt, vingt et un, vingt-deux...; trente, trente et un, trente-deux... .* After 69, the pattern changes.

69 = 60 + 9, or *soixante-neuf*   70 = 60 + 10, or *soixante-dix*

Thus, 71 = 60 + ___ , or ___ . |

11, soixante et onze (Whenever *et* is used, there are no hyphens.)

2 Using what you know already about counting in French, write out the names of the numbers 72, 75, and 77. |

soixante-douze, soixante-quinze, soixante-dix-sept

3 *Eighty* in French is expressed as four 20s: ***quatre-vingts.*** Write out the French name for 81 after you have looked at the chart. |

quatre-vingt-un (Except for ***quatre-vingts***, the numbers in the eighties have no *s* at the end of *vingt*. *Quatre-vingt-un* uses hyphens instead of *et.*)

4 Ninety in French is expressed as four 20s + 10. Write the French name for 91. |

quatre-vingt-onze (*Et* is not used here either.)

5 Write the entire word for each number below.

a 64 *soixante-___*   74 *soixante-___* |

soixante-quatre; soixante-quatorze

b 82 quatre-vingt-___   92 quatre-vingt-___ |

quatre-vingt-deux; quatre-vingt-douze

CHECK-UP
Part 1

1 Say in French that you play the piano and the accordion.
2 Say that you have the teacher's book.

Part 2

Give the French equivalent of *It's five-thirty.*

Part 3

Write out these numbers in French: 98, 76.

VOCABULARY

la batterie drums
un accordéon accordion
les cymbales (f.) cymbals

une flûte flute
une trompette trumpet
un violon violin

PROJETS D'ANNIVERSAIRE Birthday plans
une diapo slide (abbreviation of *une diapositive*)
être d'accord to agree, to think something is all right
faire une petite fête to have a small party
avec animation excitedly
bientôt soon
où ça? where? (informal)
formidable! great!
bonne idée! good idea!

PREPARATION 5**1**

1 Savoir *vs.* connaître

You have had practice using the verb *connaître* (to know). This Preparation introduces the verb *savoir,* which also has the meaning of *to know* but is used in different situations.

1 To see if you remember the forms of *connaître,* complete these sentences.

a Tu ____ ma cousine Sophie, n'est-ce pas? |
  connais

b Sophie est française. Elle ____ la France, bien sûr! |
  connaît

c Sophie et moi, nous ____ bien la plage de Cannes. |
  connaissons

d True or False: You can use *connaître* to say either that you are acquainted with a person or that you are familiar with a place. |
  true

2 In French, to say that you know factual information, you use the verb *savoir.* Compare the meanings of these sentences.

    Je connais Patrick.   I know Patrick.

    Je sais que Patrick est français.   I know that Patrick is French.

  a Does the first sentence indicate that you know Patrick personally, or that you have particular information about him? |
      know him personally

  b The second sentence indicates that you know something factual about Patrick, although you may never have met him. What is it that you know about him? |
      that he is French

3 Decide which verb you would use for each of the sentences below, and write the infinitive—*savoir* or *connaître.* Remember that *savoir* means to know factual information. *Connaître* means to be acquainted with a person, place, or thing.

  a Does he know the people next door? |
      connaître

  b Do you know when the next train arrives? |
      savoir

  c I know what time it is. |
      savoir

  d They don't know Quebec very well. |
      connaître

  e We know where the best apples are sold. |
      savoir

4 Another meaning of *savoir* is *to know how to do something.* Look at this sentence: *Je sais patiner.*

  a What do you think the English equivalent is? |
      I know how to ice-skate.

  b There are two verb forms in the sentence: *sais* and *patiner.* Which verb is in its infinitive form? |
      patiner (As in other cases where two verbs are used together, the first verb changes form to agree with a new subject. The second verb remains in the infinitive form.)

5 Here is a chart of the present-tense forms of *savoir.* Study them for a few moments, noting the stems and endings.

je	sai	s
tu	sai	s
on/il/elle	sai	t
ils/elles	sav	ent
nous	sav	ons
vous	sav	ez

  a Are the present-tense endings of *savoir* the same as those of regular *-er* verbs or those of *connaître?* |
      those of *connaître*

  b What is the stem for the singular forms? |
      sai-

c What is the stem for the plural forms? |

sav-

6 Complete the sentences below with the correct form of *savoir*. Check your answers carefully against the chart.

    a Tu ____ si tu peux venir demain?
    b Ces enfants ____ toujours leurs leçons.
    c Vous ____ faire du ski.
    d Nous ____ quelle heure il est.
    e Je ____ jouer de la batterie.

7 In the following sentences, you have to decide two things: which verb to use, and which form of the verb matches the subject. Complete the sentences by writing the correct forms of *savoir* or *connaître*.

    a Je ____ le médecin qui habite dans ton village. Je ____ qu'il n'est pas à l'hôpital aujourd'hui. |

connais, sais

    b Ah, tu ____ cette jeune fille! Est-ce que tu ____ si elle joue au tennis? |

connais, sais

2 More expressions with faire

1 The following French expressions all contain the verb *faire*. Some you already know. Others you should be able to guess. Write the English equivalents for each.

    a faire une promenade
    b faire des projets
    c faire du ski
    d faire une petite fête
    e faire du camping
    f faire beau |

a to take a walk   b to make plans   c to ski/to go skiing   d to have a small party   e to go camping/to camp   f to be nice (weather)

2 The English sentences in this frame all contain equivalents of French expressions with *faire*. Complete the French equivalents.

    Modèle: We go skiing in March.   ____ *en Mars.* |
                  Nous faisons du ski.

    a You go camping in the springtime, don't you?   ____ *au printemps, n'est-ce pas?* |

Tu fais du camping/Vous faites du camping

    b She's going to have a small party for her sister.   ____ *pour sa sœur.* |

Elle va faire une petite fête

    c They're making plans for next week.   ____ *pour la semaine prochaine.* |

Ils font des projets

    d Do you want to take a walk in the park this afternoon?   ____ *dans le parc cet après-midi?* |

Tu veux faire une promenade

Customs and holidays in France (3)

Noël

Christmas is a time of great festivity in France, with the same hustle and bustle of preparation as in the U.S. Children write letters to **le Père Noël** (Santa Claus), and people shop in gaily-decorated stores. French families may decorate a tree or set up a **crèche** (nativity scene). Some **crèches** are peopled with **santons,** painted terra cotta figures that are made in **Provence** in the South of France. They include the people one would see in an old-fashioned village—the mayor, the baker, a lady with a basket of eggs, and so forth. Some French people also send cards saying **Joyeux Noël!** (Merry Christmas) and **Meilleurs Voeux!** (Best wishes).

un Père Noël pour tous les enfants

For practicing Catholics, the high point of Christmas is the midnight mass **(la messe de minuit).** All the churches are decorated and have a **crèche** on display. Following the mass, **on réveillonne:** everyone sits down to a feast. Delicacies may often include oysters, turkey or goose, suckling pig, and champagne. A special dessert is **la bûche de Noël,** a rich cake roll in the shape of a Yule log. In some families, the feast and the exchange of gifts may occur on Christmas Day.

Le 31 décembre

French people may celebrate **le réveillon du jour de l'An** (New Year's Eve) with parties and dances at home or in a night club, and they may have a feast similar to the Christmas **réveillon.**

Le Jour de l'An

New Year's Day may be celebrated with phone calls or visits to older members of the family. **Le premier janvier** is also the day when one may give **étrennes** (small money gifts) to the **gardien/gardienne d'immeuble** (custodian), **le facteur** (mail carrier), and other household help and municipal employees. The equivalent for "Happy New Year" is **Bonne année.**

La Fête des rois

This holiday, also known as **la fête de l'Épiphanie,** is named for the three wise men who brought gifts to the infant Jesus. On **le six janvier** the tradition is to share **la galette des rois,** a flat round cake with a flaky crust and the texture and mild sweetness of a breakfast pastry. Hidden inside is a dried bean or a tiny plaster figurine. The person who receives the piece with the hidden object becomes king or queen, wins a paper crown, and is toasted by everyone.

3 Practice with à and de + definite markers

1 Compare *Je joue du violon* and *Je joue au base-ball.* The expression *jouer de* conveys the idea of playing a ____. The expression *jouer à* is used to talk about playing a ____. |

    musical instrument; sport

2 Write sentences to say that those who like a certain game want to play it. Don't forget that *vouloir* must match the subject.

        Modèle: Hélène et Robert aiment le base-ball. |
                Hélène et Robert veulent jouer au base-ball.

  a J'aime les échecs. |
         Je veux jouer aux échecs. (Did you remember to keep *jouer* in the infinitive?)

  b Elles aiment le hockey. |
         Elles veulent jouer au hockey.

3 Write sentences to say that those who like a certain musical instrument want to play it.

  a Tu aimes le violon.   **b** Nous aimons la flûte. |
        a Tu veux jouer du violon. *b Nous voulons jouer de la flûte.*

4 If you're not sure that you remember the names of instruments or games, review the vocabulary on pages 194 and 220 before doing this frame. Answers are in the answer key.

  a Tell a friend that you like to play the piano.
  b Tell a friend that you like to play soccer.
  c Ask a friend if he or she likes to play the drums.
  d Ask a friend if he or she likes to play cards.

5 Another use of the preposition *de* is to express possession or a close relationship. Rewrite these statements of ownership using *de* according to the model. Say that the items these people have, actually do belong to them. (Remember that *de* contracts only with *le* and *les.*)

        Modèle: L'élève a un vélomoteur. |
                C'est le vélomoteur de l'élève.

  a Les frères Grandet ont une moto. |
         C'est la moto des frères Grandet.

  b Le garçon a un piano. |
         C'est le piano du garçon.

  c Mme Grandet a une caméra. |
         C'est la caméra de Mme Grandet.

  d La directrice du lycée a un magnétophone. |
         C'est le magnétophone de la directrice du lycée.

CHECK-UP   Complete these sentences with the correct form of *savoir* or *connaître.*
Part 1
         1 Je ____ jouer du saxophone.   **3** Vous ____ quelle heure il est?
         2 Nous ____ ce musicien.   **4** Elles ____ Paris.

1 Direct-object pronouns in negative sentences

1 So far you have practiced using direct-object pronouns only in affirmative sentences. Complete the answer to this question, and underline the direct-object pronoun.

—Hé, les copains, vous avez les cadeaux pour Michèle? —Oui, ___. ▯

> —Oui, nous <u>les</u> avons.

2 Now compare the affirmative response with a negative response to the same question.

> Oui, nous les avons.   Non, nous **ne** les avons **pas.**

a In the affirmative sentence, does the direct-object pronoun precede the verb or follow it? ▯

> it precedes

b In the negative sentence, does the direct-object pronoun precede the verb or follow it? ▯

> it precedes (The position of the direct-object pronoun is the same in affirmative and negative statements like these.)

c Does the negative particle **ne** occur just before the object pronoun or just before the verb? ▯

> just before the object pronoun

d Where does **pas** occur? ▯

> just after the verb (The object pronoun and the verb make a unit that is surrounded by *ne...pas.*)

3 Rewrite the following sentences in the negative. Then read your answers aloud to help you get used to the word order.

a On la regarde. ▯

> On ne la regarde pas.

b Je l'invite. ▯

> Je ne l'invite pas.

c M. Pantin les cherche. ▯

> M. Pantin ne les cherche pas.

4 Write a complete negative answer to each question, and use the correct direct-object pronoun. After you have written your answers, read them aloud.

a Vous aimez ce musicien, Madame? Non, je ___. ▯

> Non, je ne l'aime pas.

b L'agent de police cherche le directeur de la banque? Non, l'agent ___. ▯

> Non, l'agent de police ne le cherche pas.

c Tes frères regardent la télévision maintenant? Non, ils ___. ▯

> Non, ils ne la regardent pas.

d Vous voulez ces vieux disques? Non, nous ____. |

Non, nous ne les voulons pas.

e Est-ce que tu as mon vélo? Non, je ____. |

Non, je ne l'ai pas.

2 Vocabulary practice: sports, music, weather

All answers for this part are in the answer key.

1 All the words but one in this frame are cognates. Each cue below will list some of the features of a particular sport. Write the name of the sport with its definite marker.

    a L__ t_____, le p___—_____ : two or four players and a net.

    b L__ v_____-_____ : two teams, a big ball, and a net.

    c L__ f_____ : two teams, two goals, no hands allowed.

    d L__ h_____ : sticks and goalies.

2 Write the name of each game and its definite marker.

    a L___ c_____ : pictures of kings and queens.

    b L___ é_____ : pieces that look like towers and pieces that look like horses' heads.

    c L___ b_____ : a game that French people play outdoors with metal balls.

3 Write the names of the musical instruments shown below. Write the definite marker also.

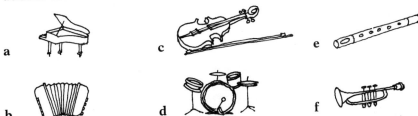

4 Write a French sentence to describe the weather in the situations below. Answers are in the answer key.

    Modèle: The sky is dark, the wind is howling, and sleet is falling. |

        Il fait mauvais.

    a You are perspiring all over. You could drink a gallon of iced tea.

    b The sky is clear, the sun is shining, and the temperature is just right.

    c Papers and leaves are flying everywhere and a man is chasing his hat down the street.

    d There's snow on the ground and people are skating on a pond.

    e There is a flash of lightning, a crack of thunder, the heavens open, and suddenly you're all wet.

3 Pre-quiz practice: à and de

In class, you will be given a written quiz on the use of *à* and *de* with definite markers. This part will help you practice for it.

1 Where would you go to buy the items mentioned below? Write the location in French using *à* + the definite marker.

a a can of peas and some sardines ▮

au supermarché

b some books ▮

à la librairie

c gasoline and oil for your car ▮

à la station-service

2 Write in French where you would go to do each of the following. Use the correct form of *à* + the definite marker.

a to see a car being made ▮

à l'usine

b to see a play ▮

au théâtre

c to borrow some books ▮

à la bibliothèque

3 Jeanne has an old bicycle that has had several owners. Use *c'était* (it was) and the correct form of *de* to tell who owned the bike before Jeanne.

Modèle: le vélo / sœur / Jeanne ▮

C'était le vélo de la sœur de Jeanne.

a le vélo / voisin / Jeanne ▮

C'était le vélo du voisin de Jeanne.

b le vélo / frères / voisin / Jeanne ▮

C'était le vélo des frères du voisin de Jeanne. (It was the bicycle of the brothers of the neighbor of Jeanne.)

4 This frame is similar to the quiz you'll have in class. You are to complete each sentence with the correct form of *à* or *de* + definite marker. Answers are in the answer key.

a –Danielle, tu vas jouer ＿＿ piano maintenant?
–Non, je préfère jouer ＿＿ échecs ou ＿＿ ping-pong.

b –Jacques et toi, vous allez jouer ＿＿ hockey aujourd'hui?
–Non, nous allons chez Max; il va jouer ＿＿ accordéon.

CHECK-UP

Part 1

Rewrite these affirmative sentences as negative ones.

a Je l'ai.

b Nous le voyons.

c Vous la regardez.

d Elles les écoutent.

VOCABULARY

faire du bateau (à voile) to go boating (sailing)
faire du camping to go camping
faire des commissions to do errands
faire du patin to go skating
faire les vendanges to harvest grapes

NOTE

Seashore recreation

The seacoast, which makes up at least two-thirds of France's boundaries, is a focal point for many leisure activities. The character of the French coast is quite varied. **La Bretagne,** in the north, has a coast of rugged granite, with few sandy beaches. **La Normandie** in the north and **la Côte d'Azur** on the Mediterranean have a mix of beaches covered with sand, and beaches covered with **galets** (large flat pebbles). Camping, picknicking, fishing, sailing, and swimming are all popular seaside activities.

In France, sailing is a professional competitive sport as well as a hobby. Those who design and sail a ship that can weather the dangers of a trans-Atlantic crossing quickly become popular heroes.

PREPARATION 53

1 *Stressed pronouns*

1 Consider the sentence *Moi, j'ai quatre frères.* What word in the sentence has the same meaning as the subject *je?*

> *moi* (*Moi* is called a stressed pronoun. Here it is used to add emphasis to the subject pronoun *je*. In English you would probably simply stress the word *I* to say that *you*—nobody else—have four brothers.

2 The stressed pronoun can be used in another way. Look at this exchange: *–Qui est là? –Moi.*

  a Give the English equivalent.

> –Who's there? –Me.

  b Does *moi* need a verb in order to make sense?

> no (*Moi* and other stressed pronouns can stand alone.)

3 The stressed pronoun is also used in a third way. In the sentence **Paul est derrière moi,** the word that precedes **moi** is not a noun or a verb, but a ___. ▮

preposition

4 There are stressed pronoun forms for all subject pronouns. Use the chart to compare them.

SUBJECT PRONOUNS	STRESSED PRONOUNS
je	moi
tu	toi
il/elle	lui/elle
ils/elles	eux/elles
nous	nous
vous	vous

a The subject pronoun **elle** and the stressed pronoun **elle** are identical in form. Which other stressed pronouns are the same as their subject pronouns? ▮

nous, vous, elles

b The stressed pronoun form of **je** is **moi.** The stressed form of **tu** is ___. ▮

toi

5 To practice using stressed pronouns for emphasis, write the correct stressed pronoun for the subject pronoun in each sentence below.

a ___, tu vas au café? ▮

Toi

b ___, je vais téléphoner à mes cousins en Suisse. ▮

Moi

c ___, ils vont faire du bateau. ▮

Eux

d ___, il va faire un voyage à Rome. ▮

Lui

e ___, elles font des camping en été. ▮

Elles

6 Véronique is planning a party for some friends. She asks who can do various things for it. Use the information in parentheses to answer the questions with stressed pronouns.

Modèle: Qui a un électrophone et des disques? *(Robert indicates Marc.)* ▮
Lui.

a Qui peut jouer de la guitare pour nous? *(Robert indicates Alice.)* ▮
Elle.

b Qui va faire les crêpes pour la fête? *(Robert indicates Danielle and Jérôme.)* ▮
Eux.

c Qui veut faire des commissions avec moi? *(Yvette and Robert volunteer.)* ▮
Nous.

7 To practice using a stressed pronoun after a preposition, say that the following people are going home. Answers are in the answer key.

> Modèle: Paul va chez _____. |
> *lui*

a Christine, Eric et Jean vont chez _____.
b Nous allons chez _____.
c Patricia va chez _____.
d Le médecin va chez _____.
e Ces trois jeunes filles vont chez _____.

2   *Direct-object pronouns in negative sentences*

1 Answer this question in the negative, using the correct direct-object pronoun. ***Est-ce que tu cherches ces disques?*** |

> *Non, je ne les cherche pas.* (Remember that the direct-object pronoun *les* and the verb *cherche* form a verb phrase that is surrounded by *ne...pas.*)

2 The same rule of placement exists for the pronouns *me, te, nous,* and *vous.* Rewrite the sentences below, making them negative. Then read them aloud.

a Robert me connaît bien. |

> *Robert ne me connaît pas bien.*

b Nos professeurs nous aiment. |

> *Nos professeurs ne nous aiment pas.*

c Annie et moi, nous vous invitons au concert. |

> *Nous ne vous invitons pas au concert.*

d Stéphanie te connaît? |

> *Stéphanie ne te connaît pas?*

3 Complete each sentence to show that the actions and feelings of the people below are not mutual.

> Modèle: Tu aimes Michèle Daumier, mais elle... |
> *...elle ne t'aime pas.*

a J'écoute mes parents, mais ils... |

> *...ils ne m'écoutent pas.*

b Nous vous écoutons toujours, mais vous... |

> *...vous ne nous écoutez pas toujours.*

c Tu aimes Alain, mais il... |

> *...il ne t'aime pas.*

d Vous détestez les frères de Lucie, mais ils... |

> *...ils ne vous détestent pas.*

CHECK-UP   Complete these sentences to say that the following people are going home.
Part 1   **1** Marc va chez _____.   **2** Les Durand vont chez _____.

1 Stressed pronouns after c'est and ce sont

You already know that stressed pronouns can be used alone, for emphasis, or after a preposition such as *chez.* They can also be used after the verb *être.*

1 Mme Thévenard hasn't seen her cousin's children for years. On a visit she points to one teenager and asks if that's Pierre.

–*Qui est-ce? C'est Pierre?*
–*Oui, c'est lui.*

Write the English equivalent of the answer. |

Yes, it's he/him.

2 A stressed pronoun can follow *c'est* or *ce sont.*

SINGULAR	PLURAL
C'est moi.	C'est nous.
C'est toi.	C'est vous.
C'est lui.	Ce sont eux.
C'est elle.	Ce sont elles.

a *C'est* is used with what singular stressed pronouns? |

all (*moi, toi, lui, elle*)

b *C'est* is used with two plural stressed pronouns, ___ and ___. |

nous, vous

c *Ce sont* is used with the plural pronouns ___ and ___. |

eux, elles

3 Mme Thévenard continues asking her friend who's who. Write all the answers using *c'est* or *ce sont.*

Modèle: C'est Martine? |

Oui, c'est elle.

a Ce sont Christophe et Rémi? |

Oui, ce sont eux.

b Ce sont Béatrice et Catherine? |

Oui, ce sont elles.

c C'est Jean-Claude? |

Oui, c'est lui.

d Jean et Jeanne, c'est vous? (*She's talking to the twins.*) |

Oui, c'est nous.

4 Write the French equivalent for this question and answer.

–Who is it?
–It's us, Luc and Thérèse. |

–Qui est-ce? –C'est nous, Luc et Thérèse.

2 Pre-quiz preparation: aller

1 You already know how to use *aller* in two different ways.

a To say where people are going, you use a form of *aller* + the preposition ___ + a locative noun. |

à

b To say what people are going to do, you can use a form of *aller* + a verb in the ___ form. |

infinitive

Answers to the remainder of the frames are in the answer key. If necessary, look at the forms of *aller* in the Summary.

2 Complete each sentence with the correct forms of *aller.*

  a Demain, je ___ téléphoner à mon ami Eric.
  b Il ___ travailler dans le restaurant de mon père.
  c Eric et sa famille ___ habiter dans notre village.
  d Ils ___ arriver la semaine prochaine.
  e Nous ___ chercher un appartement pour eux.

3 The people mentioned below are doing something today. Write complete sentences to say what they will be doing tomorrow.

    Modèle: Aujourd'hui, mon père regarde un match de football. (tennis) |
            Demain, il va regarder un match de tennis.

  a Aujourd'hui, je travaille avec Claude. (Michèle)
  b Aujourd'hui, les ouvriers font des tables. (chaises)
  c Aujourd'hui, vous allez au cinéma. (plage)

4 Write complete sentences to tell where the following people are going.

    Modèle: nous / plage en juillet |
            Nous allons à la plage en juillet.

  a M. Belcourt / station-service dans sa voiture
  b les élèves / zoo avec leurs amis
  c le docteur Pasquier et l'infirmier / hôpital

château
de
THOIRY EN YVELINES
parc , zoo
réserve africaine

3 Preparation for an oral test

Below are lists of questions on sports and leisure activities, weather, and music. In a few days your teacher will test your ability to communicate in French by asking you questions like these. Choose five questions from *Sports, loisirs, projets,* two from *Musique,* and three from *Temps* and write answers to them. You will have time to correct them in the next class.

Sports, loisirs, projets
1 Quels sports est-ce que vous aimez regarder à la télévision?
2 Vous aimez jouer au football ou vous préférez regarder le football à la télévision?
3 Quel est votre sport préféré (*favorite*)?
4 Qui est votre joueur/joueuse préféré(e)?
5 Vous faites du ski? Où est-ce que vous faites du ski?
6 Vous faites du camping? En quelle saison? Avec qui? Où est-ce qu'on peut faire du camping?
7 Vous aimez jouer aux cartes? aux échecs? au ping-pong? Avec qui est-ce que vous jouez?
8 Qu'est-ce que vous voudriez savoir faire? Jouer à.../jouer de... .
9 Est-ce que vous avez souvent des amis chez vous? Quand? Pour des petites fêtes? Pour des anniversaires?
10 Qui est-ce que vous invitez à ces fêtes et anniversaires? Qu'est-ce que vous faites? Est-ce que vous jouez de la musique, vos amis et vous? Quel(s) instrument(s)?
11 Est-ce que vous faites des projets pour ce dimanche? Quels projets?
12 Qu'est-ce que vous allez faire ce week-end? la semaine prochaine?
13 Est-ce qu'il y a un jour de la semaine que vous préférez? Quel jour? Pourquoi? Qu'est-ce que vous faites?
14 Où est-ce que vous aimez aller avec vos amis? Au cinéma? au restaurant?

Musique
1 Vous faites de la musique? Vous jouez de la flûte? Quels instruments avez-vous?
2 Vous jouez avec un groupe de musiciens?
3 Vous aimez la musique classique?
4 Vous préférez la musique classique, le rock, ou le jazz?
5 Est-ce qu'il y a des musiciens chez vous? Qui?
6 Vous avez un copain ou une copine qui joue de la batterie? de la guitare? du violon?

Temps
1 Quel temps fait-il aujourd'hui?
2 Quel temps fait-il ici en été? en automne?

3 Qu'est-ce que vous aimez faire en hiver? au printemps?

4 Quelle saison est-ce que vous préférez? Qu'est-ce que vous aimez faire dans cette saison?

5 Qu'est-ce que vous aimez faire quand il pleut? quand il neige? quand il fait beau?

1 Pre-quiz practice: direct-object pronouns

You will be having a quiz on direct-object pronouns in class. Test yourself on the items below. The answers follow **d.** If you miss any items, review Preparations 45 and 52.

1 Answer with a direct-object pronoun.

  a Vous voyez cette belle voiture là-bas? Oui...

  b Tu m'aimes, n'est-ce pas? Oui...

  c Alain et Marie, vous nous cherchez? Oui...

  d Tu invites tes amis au concert? Oui... ▌

        a *Oui, je la vois.* b *Oui, je t'aime.* c *Oui, nous vous cherchons.* d *Oui, je les invite.*

2 Answer these questions, beginning each with *Non.* Remember where *ne* and *pas* go.

  a Est-ce que vos élèves vous écoutent, M. Colbert?

  b Tu regardes la télévision ce soir?

  c Marc et Eric, est-ce que Catherine vous invite au théâtre? ▌

        a *Non, ils ne m'écoutent pas.* b *Non, je ne la regarde pas.* c *Non, elle ne nous invite pas.*

2 False cognates

By now you have probably realized that many French words look like familiar English words. Some, however, have different meanings. These words are called false cognates or *faux amis* (false friends). *Faux amis* are tricky; they seem to be helpful but they'll let you down. If you see a French word that looks like an English word, but the English meaning doesn't seem to make sense, you may have *un faux ami*. Check a French-English dictionary for the meaning of the word.

1 You are familiar with all of the false cognates below. Write the correct English equivalents. Answers follow **d.**

a anniversaire

b librairie

c football

d commissions |

a birthday   b bookstore   c soccer   d errands

2 Each sentence below has a cognate you've never seen in this book. Write what you think the English equivalent of the cognate is. Then write *faux ami* if you think it's a false cognate.

a Je suis en retard. Mon père va être *furieux*. |

furious

b Pour jouer au football, il faut un *ballon*. |

ball—*faux ami* (*Ballon* designates an inflatable ball. It may also mean *balloon*.)

c Jouer aux échecs, c'est un bon *passe-temps*. |

pastime

3 Pre-test practice: reading comprehension

In Progress Test 4, you will be asked to read a dialogue and answer some true-false questions on it. The following reading passage will give you practice. Read it carefully before answering the questions.

Que faire aujourd'hui?

C'est samedi. Marc et Henri parlent.

MARC	Tu vas travailler cet après-midi?
HENRI	Non, je vais jouer au tennis.
MARC	Et ce soir, qu'est-ce que tu fais?
HENRI	Je ne sais pas.
MARC	Tu veux aller au cinéma?
HENRI	Ça dépend°. À quelle heure?
MARC	À huit heures.
HENRI	D'accord. À tout à l'heure.

That depends

For each statement below, write *vrai* or *faux* on your worksheet. Answers are in the answer key.

1 Henri va travailler cet après-midi.

2 Henri joue au tennis cet après-midi.

3 Henri veut aller au match de tennis ce soir.

4 Henri déteste aller au cinéma.

5 Henri et Marc vont au cinéma à huit heures.

NOTE ✳ *Customs and holidays in France (4)*

Mardi Gras, Pâques et Pentecôte

Mardi Gras means "fat Tuesday" and signifies the last great feast before Lent **(le carême).** This period of fasting is ushered in with costume parades, dances, and parties.

The name **Pâques** (Easter) comes from **la Pâque** (Passover), the Jewish holiday which is also celebrated at this time of year. **Le lundi de Pâques** is a national holiday and, weather permitting, people go for picnics and walks in the woods. Depending on whether **Pâques** is early or late, **les vacances de printemps,** a two-week break from school, may occur at this time.

La Pentecôte occurs in May or early June, on the seventh Sunday after **Pâques.** The Thursday before **la Pentecôte** begins the last long holiday weekend before summer, and people usually go to the country.

PREPARATION 56

1 *Pre-test practice:* aller, faire, savoir

By now you should be comfortable with the forms of *aller, faire,* and *savoir.* This part will give you a chance to test yourself. All answers are in the answer key. If you make mistakes, take some time to review. Remember, this is to help you do well on the test; copying answers won't help.

Aller was presented in Preparations 46, 47, 49, and 54. *Faire* was presented in Preparations 43 and 51. *Savoir* was presented in Preparation 51.

1 Write the correct form of *aller* to say what the following people are going to do soon.

a Gilles ___ travailler chez lui.

b Jules et moi, nous ___ voir un film.

c Mes sœurs ___ faire du patin.

d Je vais ___ à la campagne.

2 Now write the correct form of ***aller*** to ask or tell where these people are going.

    a À 10h, je ____ chez ma grand-mère.   **c** Vous ____ à la bibliothèque?

    b Tu ____ à la plage demain?   **d** Ils ____ au parc avec leurs enfants.

3 To practice the various uses of the verb ***faire,*** write a French equivalent for each sentence below with one of the following expressions.

    faire des projets   *faire du camping*   *faire des crêpes*   *faire*

    a Are you making plans?   **c** We're making crêpes today.

    b What's he doing?   **d** Do they go camping in September?

4 Complete each sentence below by writing the correct form of ***savoir.*** Remember that ***savoir*** is used with these meanings: to know factual information; to know how to do something.

    a Vous ____ où cet homme habite?

    b Albert veut ____ si tu as un cadeau pour lui.

    c Je ____ qu'il ne neige pas à la Martinique.

    d Tu ____ quelle heure il est?

    e Ma tante et ma mère ____ patiner.

2 *Pre-test practice:* à + *definite marker*

À + definite marker was presented in Preparations 44, 45, 51, and 52. You have learned to use this structure to say where you are, to say where you are going, and to say what sport or game you play.

    For practice, complete each infinitive phrase below with the correct form of *à* + definite marker.

    1 jouer ____ cartes   **4** être ____ usine

    2 aller ____ café   **5** être ____ campagne

    3 aller ____ hôpital   **6** jouer ____ échecs

3 *Pre-test practice: answering questions*

Write a complete sentence to answer each question below. Only sample answers are given for this part, since answers will vary. (The sample is in the answer key.) However, you will be able to give your answers in class. After you have completed the part, check your sentences carefully. Does the verb match the subject? Did you spell words correctly?

1 Quel est votre sport préféré? Mon sport préféré est...

2 Qu'est-ce que vous faites le samedi? Le samedi je... (*List at least three things.*)

3 Qu'est-ce que vous aimez faire au printemps? Au printemps, j'aime...

1 Pre-test practice: pouvoir and vouloir

The present-tense forms of **pouvoir** and **vouloir** are very similar: the changes in the stem follow a similar pattern; the endings are identical. If you think you've forgotten the forms of either verb, review them before doing this part. **Pouvoir** was presented in Preparation 48. **Vouloir** was presented in Preparations 43 and 45. Answers are in the answer key.

1 Write complete sentences to say that the second person or group of people mentioned can't do what the first person or group is doing.

> Modèle: Le journaliste parle avec le président. Je... |
>> Je ne peux pas parler avec le président. (Remember that the second verb is always in the infinitive.)

    a Cette danseuse va à Bruxelles en juin. Ce musicien...
    b Vous faites du ski en Suisse. Thierry et Mathieu...
    c Je regarde le match de basket à la télé. Tu...
    d Nous faisons des crêpes ce soir. Nos voisins...

2 Write sentences with **vouloir** to say that the second person or group of people wants to do something different from what the first person or group is doing.

> Modèle: Etienne va au concert. (Sylvie/au zoo) |
>> Sylvie veut aller au zoo.

    a Ils chantent en français. (Elles / en allemand)
    b Louise et Marie jouent aux boules. (Je / au ping-pong)
    c Mes parents font une promenade. (Mon frère et moi, nous / du bateau)

2 Pre-test practice: savoir vs. connaître

Savoir and **connaître** both mean to know, but they are used in different situations. If necessary, review them in the Summary.

1 Look at each English sentence below. Decide whether **savoir** or **connaître** would be the correct verb to use if you were writing the sentences in French, then write the infinitive of the verb. Answers are in the answer key.
    a Do you know how far it is from Orléans to Rouen?
    b Are you acquainted with the city of Rouen?
    c Do you know where the cathedral is?

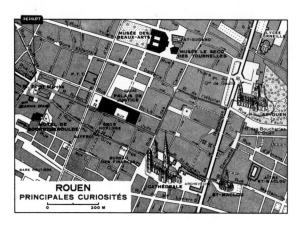

Ville historique et industrielle en Normandie

d My friend Emile Monnier lives near the cathedral. Do you know him?

e The *Musée des Beaux Arts* in Rouen has some early Monet paintings I want to see. Do you know what days it's open?

f We always drive from Rouen to Paris. Do you know how to drive?

2 For each sentence below, decide first whether to use *savoir* or *connaître.* Then write the correct form of the verb.

    a Qui est cette jeune fille blonde? Tu la ____?

    b Ces enfants ____ bien patiner.

    c Bill Jones ne ____ pas bien Paris.

    d Je cherche mes parents. Je ne ____ pas où ils sont.

3 Pre-test practice: writing practice

This section will give you practice both in spelling and in writing complete sentences. Answers are in the answer key.

1 Rewrite the sentences below so that they are correctly punctuated. Remember to include capital letters and accents or cedillas.

    a cet apres midi je vais a l aeroport avec ma mere et ma sœur

    b est ce que tu travailles a l usine

2 Nicolas is talking to René when a third boy approaches them. Read their English conversation and rewrite it with French equivalents. Check your punctuation, and be sure that verb forms match their subjects, and that markers match their nouns. (The French dialogue is in the answer key.)

NICOLAS	There's Alain. Hi, Alain.
RENÉ	Hi, Alain. Do you want to play soccer with us this afternoon?
ALAIN	Oh darn! I can't.
NICOLAS	Why?
ALAIN	I'm going to my sister's. It's her birthday.

1 *Pre-test practice: direct-object pronouns*

Here's another chance for you to check yourself on the forms and use of direct-object pronouns. If you think you will need it, do a little review first by referring to the Summary or to Preparations 37, 38, 45, 46, 47, 49, 52, 53, and 55. Answers are in the answer key.

1 Answer the questions below with *Oui...* . Use direct-object pronouns, and write complete, logical sentences.

> Modèle: Tu connais M. Delisle? |
> > *Oui, je le connais.*

a Tu regardes mon livre d'anglais?
b Le petit garçon écoute sa mère?
c Nous invitons les Meunier à la fête?
d Est-ce que les chats aiment les souris?

2 Answer the questions below with *Non...,* using a direct-object pronoun in each answer.

a Robert te connaît bien?
b Dis donc, tu m'écoutes?
c Est-ce que tes sœurs te cherchent?
d Tu regardes la télévision le matin?

2 *Pre-test practice:* de + *definite marker*

De + definite marker was presented in Preparations 50 and 51. Answers are in the answer key.

1 You and some of your friends have formed an orchestra. Tell what instrument each person plays.

> Modèle: Gaston / flûte. |
> > *Il joue de la flûte.*

a Nicole et Martine / piano
b Je / accordéon
c Tu / cymbales / et / batterie
d Le petit Maurice / violon
e Vous / trompette
f Françoise / saxophone

2 Rewrite each sentence below with *de* + definite marker.

> Modèle: La jeune fille a des disques de rock. |
> > *Ce sont les disques de rock de la jeune fille.*

a Cette femme a trois chiens.
b Le médecin a une voiture.
c Les sœurs Bourget ont un restaurant.
d Cet enfant a un vélo.

3 Pre-test practice: writing practice

1 Write complete sentences using the words provided. Make all necessary changes. Answers are in the answer key.

> Modèle: tu / vouloir / aller / cinéma ce soir? I
> *Tu veux aller au cinéma ce soir?*

a est-ce que / tu / faire des commissions / c ___ après-midi?
b elles / aller / match de football
c je / ne...pas / pouvoir / trouver m ___ livres

2 Rewrite the sentences below with the correct capital letters, punctuation marks, and accents or cedillas.

a marie jeanne connait yvonne une jeune musicienne qui joue de la flute
b on aime etre a la plage en aout n est ce pas

NOTE ❋   *Les Grandes Vacances*

Traditionally, people have taken their summer vacation **(les grandes vacances)** in July or August. Most people are entitled to a four-week vacation with pay called **les congés payés.**

At the beginning of July and August, railroad stations are mobbed with travelers, and huge traffic jams develop as people take to the roads. For the many French people who drive to Spain, there is a wait of many hours at the border.

During August, Paris seems to be peopled only by tourists from other countries. Most Parisians have abandoned the city for the beaches and countryside, or for travels to Spain, England, Germany and other lands. Most theaters and some museums close for a time. Neighborhood bakeries, butcher shops, grocery stores, and drug stores, as well as many restaurants and cafés, close on a rotating basis for the **fermerture annuelle** (yearly closing). Life returns to normal as people come home in September in time for **la rentrée** (the beginning of the school year).

Cabourg

Deauville

Boulogne - Sur - Mer

Getting ready for a test

In your next class, you will have a test. This Preparation will give you very useful practice for it. If you make any mistakes, review the Summary on pp. 245–247. All the answers for this Preparation are in the answer key.

Parts A, B, and C will check your understanding of spoken French.

1 In Part A, you will hear a French sentence twice. On your test paper, you will see three English sentences. You are to circle the letter of the correct English equivalent. For the example below write the correct letter (A, B, or C) on your worksheet.

a *You hear:* Pierre ne peut pas aller au match de football.
You see: A Pierre doesn't want to go to the soccer game.
     B Pierre can't go to the soccer game.
     C Pierre isn't going to go to the soccer game.

b *You hear:* Elle va danser ce soir.
You see: A She wants to dance tonight.
     B He is going to dance tonight.
     C She is going to dance tonight.

2 In Part B, you will see some pictures on your answer sheet. You will hear a series of statements in French. Each one will be said twice. You are to write the letter of the picture that each statement describes.

A   B   C   D

 a *You hear:* Il fait froid.   **b** *You hear:* Il est trois heures.

3 In Part C, you will read a dialogue similar to the one below. Then you are to indicate whether statements based on it are true or false.

Read the following telephone conversation.

SUZANNE	Allô, Pierre? Tu veux aller au cinéma avec nous?
PIERRE	Je ne peux pas.
SUZANNE	Pourquoi?
PIERRE	Je fais mes devoirs pour demain.

Now look at the statements below. In the test, you will see the words *vrai* and *faux,* and will circle the correct word. For now, write it on your worksheet.

 a Suzanne veut aller au match de football. **c** Pierre regarde la télévision.
 b Pierre ne va pas au cinéma avec Suzanne.

4 In Part D, you will be checked on your knowledge of the present tense of the irregular verbs *faire, vouloir, pouvoir, savoir,* and *aller.*

You will complete sentences by writing the correct form of the verb shown in parentheses.

a (faire) Qu'est-ce que vous ___ demain?
b (vouloir) Jeanne et Lise ___ aller danser samedi.
c (aller) Tu ___ jouer au basket maintenant?

5 In Part E, you will need to decide whether sentences should be completed with *savoir* or *connaître* and then to write their forms. For each sentence below, write the correct form of the verb you have chosen.

a Est-ce que ses parents ___ où elle est?   **b** Tu ___ ce film?

6 In Part F, you are to complete sentences with the appropriate direct-object pronoun. In some cases, you have to add *ne...pas.*

a Est-ce qu'ils connaissent Mme Berthot? Oui, ils ___.
b Tu aimes ce film? Non, je ___.

7 In Part G, you are to complete sentences with a form of *à* + the definite marker. For now, write the answer on your worksheet.

a Ma mère va ___ usine.
b Nous allons jouer ___ tennis cet après-midi.

8 In part H, you are to complete sentences with a form of *de* + the definite marker.

a Jacques joue très bien ___ guitare.
b La voiture ___ professeur est petite.

9 In Part I, you are to write sentences using a set of cues, making all the necessary changes. In some cases you have to add the correct combination of *à* or *de* + the definite marker.

a Thérèse et moi, nous / aller / jouer / tennis
b Tu / ne...pas / aller / supermarché avec nous?

10 In Part J, you are to answer questions by writing complete sentences that make sense.

a Qu'est-ce que vous faites samedi après-midi?
b Quel temps fait-il aujourd'hui?

Summary

1 The subject pronoun on (*Preparation 45*)

The subject pronoun **on** can mean *we, you,* or *they,* depending on the context. **On** is used with the **il/elle**-form of the verb.

On va au cinéma?	Shall we go to the movies?
On parle français en France.	They (*people*) speak French in France.
*Comment dit-on **book** en français?*	How do you say *book* in French?

2 The present tense of faire *and* aller (*Preparation 43, 46, 47, 48, 51*)

je	fais	vais
tu	fais	vas
on/il/elle	fait	va
ils/elles	font	vont
nous	faisons	allons
vous	faites	allez

a. The verb *faire* often means *to do* or *to make.* It is also used in many idiomatic expressions; for example, *faire une promenade* (to take a walk); *faire des projets* (to make plans). It is also used in most weather expressions.

b. When *aller* is followed by an infinitive, it indicates that something will occur in the near future. In French, this use is called the *futur proche.*

Demain, je vais jouer au tennis.   Tomorrow I'm going to play tennis.

c. When *aller* is used with *à* + a locative, it means *to go somewhere.*

Elle va à la plage.   She's going to the beach.

3 The present tense of vouloir *and* pouvoir (*Preparation 43, 48*)

je	veu	x	peu	x
tu	veu	x	peu	x
on/il/elle	veu	t	peu	t
ils/elles	veul	ent	peuv	ent
nous	voul	ons	pouv	ons
vous	voul	ez	pouv	ez

a. *Vouloir* (to want) can be followed by a noun or by an infinitive phrase.

Je veux un appareil-photo.	I want a camera.
Je veux être photographe.	I want to be a photographer.

b. *Pouvoir* (can, to be able) is usually followed by an infinitive phrase. However, it can be used alone.

–Tu peux aller au cinéma ce soir?	–Can you go to the movies tonight?
–Oui, je peux.	–Yes, I can.

4 The present tense of savoir *(Preparation 51)*

je	sai	s
tu	sai	s
on/il/elle	sai	t
ils/elles	sav	ent
nous	sav	ons
vous	sav	ez

a. One meaning of **savoir** is *to know factual information.* When a form of **savoir** is followed by an infinitive, **savoir** means *to know how to.*

Je sais la date de ton anniversaire. I know the date of your birthday.
Je sais nager. I know how to swim.

b. The verb **connaître** also means to know, but in the sense of *to be acquainted with someone* or *to be familiar with a place or thing.*

Je connais ce garçon, mais je I know that boy, but I don't
ne sais pas son nom. know his name.

5 À + definite marker *(Preparation 45, 51)*

a. When the preposition **à** is used with the definite marker **la** or **l'**, there is no contraction. When **à** is used with **le** or **les,** there is a contraction.

à + la = à la   *à + le = au*
à + l' = à l'   *à + les = aux*

b. The preposition **à** + definite marker is often used in these verb phrases.

être à + locative   *Je suis à la maison.*   I'm at home.
aller à + locative   *Je vais à l'aéroport.*   I'm going to the airport.
jouer à + sport or game   *Je joue au hockey.*   I play hockey.
     Je joue aux cartes.   I play cards.

c. In spoken French, a linking /z/ occurs between **aux** and a noun that begins with a vowel sound: **Je joue aux échecs.**

6 De + definite marker *(Preparation 50, 51)*

a. When **de** is used with the definite marker *la* or *l'*, there is no contraction. When **de** is used with **le** or **les,** there is a contraction.

de + la = de la   *de + le = du*
de + l' = de l'   *de + les = des*

b. The preposition **de** + definite marker is used with the verb **jouer** to talk about playing an instrument. It is also used with a noun to show possession or a close relationship.

Je joue de la trompette. I play the trumpet.
C'est le livre de l'élève. It's the student's book.
C'est la fille de M. Barrault. It's M. Barrault's daughter.

7 Direct-object pronouns *(Preparation 45, 46, 47, 49, 52)*

SINGULAR	me, m'
	te, t'
	le, la, l'
PLURAL	les
	nous
	vous

a. Direct-object pronouns usually come directly before the verb.

–Tu nous vois? –Do you see us?
–Oui, je vous vois très bien. –Yes, I see you very well.

b. The pronouns *m', t', l',* are used with a verb that begins with a vowel sound. In spoken French, when *les, nous,* or *vous* precedes a verb form beginning with a vowel sound, there is a linking /z/.

c. When a direct-object pronoun precedes a verb, the particle *ne* precedes the pronoun; the particle *pas* follows the verb.

*Je **ne** l'aime **pas**.* I don't like him/her.
*Tu **ne** les regardes **pas**.* You aren't looking at them.

8 Weather expressions *(Preparation 47)*

a. The verb *faire* is used in most weather expressions.

Quel temps fait-il? What's the weather like?
Il fait beau et chaud. It's nice weather and it's warm.

b. The French equivalents for *It's snowing* and *It's raining* are ***Il neige*** and ***Il pleut.***

9 Telling time *(Preparation 50)*

a. The phrase *il est...heure(s)* is used to tell time in French. Instead of AM and PM, the expressions *du matin, de l'après-midi, du soir* are used in spoken French.

Il est une heure du matin. It's one AM.
Il est trois heures de l'après-midi. It's 3 PM.
Il est dix heures du soir. It's 10 PM.

b. The phrase ***et demie*** is used to give the half-hour.

Il est trois heures et demie. It's half past three.

DIALOGUES ET LECTURES

Sports et loisirs

Un Coup de téléphone

Pierre téléphone à son ami André. Le téléphone sonne. André répond.

ANDRÉ   Allô?
PIERRE   Allô, André? C'est Pierre.
ANDRÉ   Ah bonjour, Pierre. Ça va?
PIERRE   Oui, ça va. On joue au basket cet après-midi, n'est-ce pas?
ANDRÉ   Oui, bien sûr! À quelle heure?
PIERRE   À deux heures si tu veux.
ANDRÉ   Bon, d'accord. À tout à l'heure.

Quel sale temps!

C'est samedi. Il pleut. Bernard arrive chez Suzanne.

BERNARD   Dis donc, quel sale temps!
SUZANNE   Oui, on ne peut pas jouer au tennis aujourd'hui.
BERNARD   Non, bien sûr... On peut aller au cinéma si tu veux.
SUZANNE   Tu sais quel film on joue au Palace?
BERNARD   Un film de science-fiction, je crois.
SUZANNE   Oh, très bien. Allons-y.
BERNARD   D'accord.

Projets d'anniversaire

À la cantine du lycée. Gabrielle et Marc parlent avec animation. Florence arrive.

GABRIELLE   Tu sais, Florence, c'est bientôt l'anniversaire de Jean-Paul!
MARC   On va faire une petite fête!
FLORENCE   Ah oui? Où ça?
MARC   Chez moi. Mes parents sont d'accord.
5 FLORENCE   Formidable! Quel jour?
GABRIELLE   Dimanche après-midi, à quatre heures.
FLORENCE   Et qu'est-ce qu'on va faire?
GABRIELLE   On peut écouter des disques, danser, jouer de la guitare...
MARC   On peut aussi regarder des diapos.
10 FLORENCE   Oui, bonne idée!

Chien et chat

Un soir chez les Mallet... Yvette (14 ans), Pascal (16 ans), Maman.

YVETTE Oh là là! Il est presque° six heures! La télé, vite°!

MAMAN Pourquoi? Il y a quelque chose de° spécial?

YVETTE Bien sûr! Il y a des gymnastes sur la première chaîne°.

PASCAL Ah non! Moi, je veux regarder le concert sur la deuxième chaine°.

YVETTE Toi et ta musique! Toujours° la musique!

PASCAL Et toi! Tu regardes seulement° les programmes de sport!

MAMAN Ça suffit°, vous deux! Taisez-vous°, ou pas de télévision toute la semaine°!

PASCAL Oh, ça va, ça va°. Regarde tes gymnastes. Maman, je vais chez Christian. Il regarde toujours les concerts, lui.

almost
quick
something
Channel 1
Channel 2
always
only
That's enough / Be quiet
all week
OK! OK!

EXERCICES

1 Pronunciation practice: cognates ending in **-tion**

1. conversation
2. circulation
3. direction
4. éducation
5. situation
6. information
7. imagination
8. distinction

2 Variations on **Projets d'anniversaire**

With your partner, write a dialogue in which you make plans for a party. Below are partial dialogue lines you can use as a beginning.

For the third line, choose a place for the party; for the fifth line, choose a day and time. For the seventh line, choose a few things to do; for the eighth line, think of one more thing to do.

ÉLÈVE 1 On va faire une petite fête avec la classe.
ÉLÈVE 2 Ah oui? Où ça?
ÉLÈVE 1 (chez, à)
ÉLÈVE 2 Formidable! Quel jour?
ÉLÈVE 1 (jour, heure)
ÉLÈVE 2 Et qu'est-ce qu'on va faire?
ÉLÈVE 1 On peut...(jouer à, jouer de, aller à, faire)
ÉLÈVE 2 Et on peut ________ aussi?
ÉLÈVE 1 Oh oui, bonne idée.

3 Pronunciation practice: /u/ vs. /y/

tout/tu	loup/lu	sous/su	pou/pu
doux/du	nous/nu	mou/mu	roue/rue
bout/bu	vous/vu	fou/fut	joue/jus

1. Salut, Louise!
2. Bonjour, Suzanne!
3. Je vous trouve fou.
4. Tu joues beaucoup aux boules en août?
5. Lulu écoute de la musique classique.
6. Zut! La voiture est sur ma flûte.
7. L'homme roux n'est pas du tout jaloux.
8. J'écoute le turlututu de la flûte.

4 Irregular verbs

Complete each sentence by writing the correct form of the verb in parentheses.

1. Qu'est-ce qu'on _____ ce soir?   (faire)
2. Ils _____ un voyage en Italie.   (faire)
3. Qu'est-ce que vous _____ voir au cinéma?   (aller)
4. Mes parents _____ chez les voisins pour jouer aux cartes.   (aller)
5. Je ne _____ pas faire ces devoirs en une heure.   (pouvoir)
6. Est-ce que vous _____ jouer au tennis aujourd'hui?   (pouvoir)
7. Est-ce que vous _____ la date de son anniversaire?   (savoir)
8. Elle ne _____ pas où j'habite.   (savoir)
9. Paul et moi, nous _____ faire du camping dans les montagnes. (vouloir)
10. Tu _____ danser?   (vouloir)

5 Time and weather

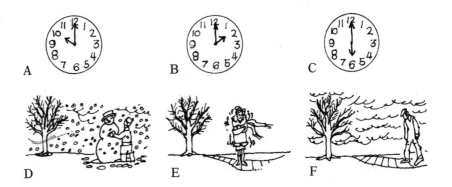

A   B   C

D   E   F

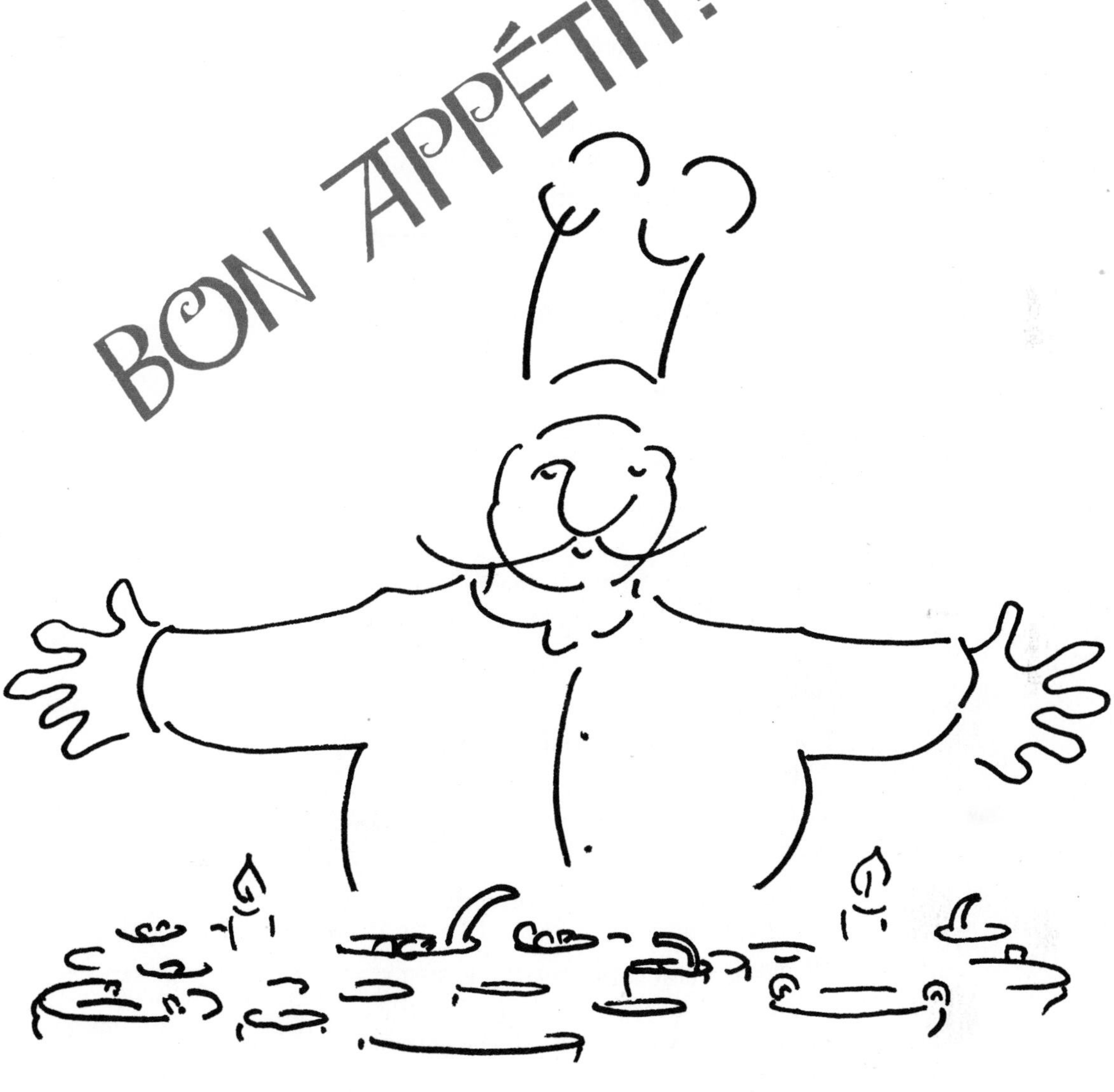
BON APPÉTIT!

PHASE FIVE OBJECTIVES

The theme of this Phase is food. You will talk about what you eat and what your likes and dislikes are concerning food. You will also listen to and read longer passages of French in a story called **Les Résolutions de Marie-Jeanne.** By the end of this Phase, you should be able to:

1 Identify various foods by using food vocabulary with the appropriate markers (definite, indefinite, and partitive).

2 Talk about food, using the verb **prendre** (to take, to have).

3 Tell time in minutes, quarter hours, and half hours.

4 Say when people are coming or where they are coming from, using the present tense of **venir** (to come).

5 Say what people must do, using the phrase **il faut** + infinitive.

6 Say if you are cold, hot, thirsty, hungry, or if you are right, by using expressions with **avoir.**

7 Ask questions using inversion with certain verbs and expressions.

8 Ask questions and make exclamations, using all forms of **quel.**

9 Use the verbs **être, avoir, aller,** and **faire** as equivalents of the English verb "to be."

10 Use **si** instead of **oui** in response to a negative statement.

❇ The cultural notes describe typical French meals, eating out in a restaurant, French bread and cheese, and some special regional and holiday foods.

1 Count nouns and measure nouns

In both English and French, there are certain items that are usually counted and others that are usually measured. You'll need to know the difference between them in order to talk about food in French.

1 Apples are easy to count. So are oranges. Things that can be counted are called *count nouns*. Which of the following are count nouns?

      sugar   salt   tomatoes   pickles ❙

          tomatoes, pickles

2 Sugar and salt are more easily measured than counted: *a spoonful of sugar, a dash of salt.* They are called *measure nouns*. Which of the following nouns would you be more likely to measure than count?

      peaches   cherries   water   tea   onions ❙

          water, tea

3 Count nouns may occur in the singular or in the plural: *one pickle, ten pickles.* Measure nouns usually occur only in the singular. Which of the following nouns usually occur only in the singular?

      potato   banana   milk   bean   juice ❙

          milk, juice (You don't normally say ''three milks'' or ''three juices'' unless perhaps you're a server in a restaurant.)

4 Match the names of the foods below with the drawings in **a–e**, and say whether each item is a count noun or a measure noun. Check your spelling carefully.

      café   *pomme*   *haricot vert*   *eau*   *lait*

a   **b**   **c**   **d**   **e**   ❙

      a *eau:* measure noun b *haricot vert:* count noun c *café:* measure noun
      d *lait:* measure noun e *pomme:* count noun

2 The metric system

1 In France, as in most European countries, people's height is measured in meters and centimeters. The French word for *centimeter* is **centimètre.** What do you think is the French word for *meter?* ❙

        mètre (Check your spelling for the accent and the last two letters.)

2 The abbreviation *cm* stands for **centimètre.** What do you think is the abbreviation for *mètre?* ❙

        m (There is no period after *cm* and *m*, unless they come at the end of a sentence.)

3 In class, you heard the beginning of a story about a girl named Marie-Jeanne, who is *1,52 m* tall (about five feet tall). Notice that a comma is used instead of a decimal point.

    a Copy her height, then say it aloud: *un mètre cinquante-deux.* |

             1,52 m (Notice that you don't have to use the word centimètre.*)*

    b Complete this statement to say that you are one meter and seventy-five centimeters tall. (Use abbreviations.) *Je mesure ____.* |

             1,75 m (Un mètre soixante-quinze.)

4 You also heard in class that Marie-Jeanne weighs fifty-two kilograms. In France, weight is measured in kilograms and grams.

    a The French equivalent for *kilogram* is *kilogramme.* What is the French equivalent for *gram?* |

             gramme (Did you write two m*'s?)*

    b The abbreviation for *kilogramme* (or *kilo*) is *kg.* What do you think is the abbreviation for *gramme?* |

             g (There is no period after kg *or* g *unless they come at the end of a sentence.)*

    c Write Marie-Jeanne's weight using numbers and abbreviations, then read it aloud. |

             52 kg (Cinquante-deux kilogrammes or *cinquante-deux kilos.)*

5 Use numbers and abbreviations to say that you weigh fifty-eight kilos. *Je pèse ____.* |

             58 kg

6 Imagine that you are in a contest in which you must give the size and weight of various objects and people. Write the measurements for the items below, using numbers and abbreviations.

    a A banana: *dix-huit centimètres* in length; *deux cents grammes* in weight. |

             18 cm; 200 g

    b Marc: *un mètre quatre-vingts* in height; *soixante-douze kilos* in weight. |

             1,80 m; 72 kg

    c A pumpkin: *quatre-vingt-cinq centimètres* in circumference; *quatre kilos* in weight. |

             85 cm; 4 kg

CHECK-UP
Part 1

    1 Which of these nouns are count nouns?
        tomato   orange juice   orange   soup
    2 Which of these nouns are measure nouns?
        bean   milk   leaf   onion

Part 2

    Rewrite the following using numbers and abbreviations.
    1 forty-six grams
    2 ten kilograms
    3 two meters and ten centimeters
    4 twenty-seven centimeters

une boisson beverage	*une poire* pear
le café coffee	*le poisson* fish
l'eau (f.) water	*une pomme* apple
une fraise strawberry	*le poulet* chicken
le fromage cheese	*la viande* meat
un fruit fruit	*un centimètre* centimeter
un haricot vert green bean	*un gramme* gram
le lait milk	*un kilogramme* kilogram
une laitue head of lettuce	*un kilomètre* kilometer
un légume vegetable	*un mètre* meter
le pain bread	

LES RÉSOLUTIONS DE MARIE-JEANNE Marie-Jeanne's Resolutions

une lycéenne, un lycéen high school student	*penser* to think
mesurer to be ... tall; to measure	*peser* to weigh

NOTE

French breakfasts and French bread

For breakfast **(le petit déjeuner)** a French family usually has **café au lait** (hot coffee with hot milk) or **chocolat au lait** (hot chocolate), toast or fresh bread with butter and jam. Often, people like to replace the bread with **une biscotte,** something similar to a thick Melba toast. Some American dry cereals are also sold in France, but they have not yet become part of the traditional French breakfast. They are sometimes eaten as snacks or light supper dishes. The **croissants** mentioned in **Les Résolutions de Marie-Jeanne** are usually reserved for Sundays or festive occasions. Fresh **croissants** or **brioches** (very light, round, buttery rolls) are bought at the **boulangerie-pâtisserie** (bakery-pastry shop).

Bread is an essential part of any French meal. "French" bread with a crunchy crust and a chewy center is bought fresh every day. It is sold, unsliced, in a variety of shapes and sizes, ranging from long and thin **(une baguette)** to round, thick, and often a foot in diameter **(une miche).** Rye bread **(pain de seigle)** and whole wheat bread **(pain complet)** are also available.

1 Markers used with count and measure nouns

In Preparation 60, you learned how to distinguish between count and measure nouns. This part will explain which markers to use with the different kinds of nouns.

1 Look at these nouns: *pomme, lait, fraise, confiture, croissant.*
  a Which nouns are count nouns? |
    pomme, fraise, croissant
  b Can count nouns be used in both the singular or plural form? |
    yes

2 Read this sentence: *Je voudrais une pomme, un croissant et des fraises.*
  a What type of marker is used? |
    an indefinite marker (Count nouns can be used with singular and plural indefinite markers.)
  b Give the English equivalent of the sentence. |
    I would like an apple, a croissant, and (some) strawberries.

3 Say that you would like the items below. Use *je voudrais* and *un, une,* or *des.* Write the English equivalent of **a** and **b**.

a |

    . *Je voudrais une pomme de terre.* I would like a potato.

b  |

    Je voudrais des poires. I would like some pears.

c |

    Je voudrais une pomme.

d  |

    Je voudrais des haricots verts.

4 Now look at these nouns: *poire, chocolat au lait, fraise, soupe, viande.*
  a Which nouns are measure nouns? |
    chocolat au lait, soupe, viande
  b Are measure nouns usually used in the singular or plural form? |
    singular

5 Which of these sentences are you more likely to say: *I would like a meat* or *I would like some meat?* |

> I would like some meat. (In English, the word *some* is often used with a measure noun: I would like some soup, some milk, some coffee...)

6 Compare the French and English sentences below.

> *Il y a de la soupe pour le déjeuner.*   There's some soup for lunch.

a Is an indefinite marker used in the French sentence? |

> no

b In the sentence above, what two French words are the equivalent of *some?* |

> *de la* (*De la* is a partitive marker. Partitive markers are used with measure nouns in French to mean *some.*)

7 Read the sentence below, then write the three partitive markers that are used with measure nouns.

> *Je voudrais de la viande, du fromage et de l'eau.* |

> *de la, du, de l'* (Partitive markers are forms of *de* + definite markers.)

8 Instead of saying *There's some soup for lunch,* could you say *There's soup for lunch?* |

> yes (In English, you don't have to use the word *some.* In French, however, you must always use the partitive marker.)

9 Complete the sentences below with partitive markers and write an English equivalent for each sentence. If you don't remember the gender of the noun, check the Vocabulary.

a Je voudrais _____ confiture. |

> *de la;* I would like (some) jam.

b Il y a _____ lait sur la table. |

> *du;* There's (some) milk on the table.

c Elle veut _____ poisson. |

> *du;* She wants (some) fish.

d Vous voulez _____ eau? |

> *de l';* Do you want (some) water?

10 Identify the drawings below, using *c'est* or *ce sont* and the appropriate marker. Remember to use indefinite markers with count nouns, and partitive markers with measure nouns. Answers follow **f.**

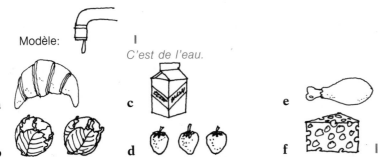

Modèle: |

C'est de l'eau.

a

b

c

d

e

f |

> **a** *C'est un croissant.* **b** *Ce sont des laitues.* **c** *C'est du lait.* **d** *Ce sont des fraises.* **e** *C'est du poulet.* **f** *C'est du fromage.*

11 Read this little dialogue carefully to remind yourself of what happens to indefinite markers in negative sentences.

> –Est-ce que tu veux des bananes?
> –Non, je ne veux pas de bananes, merci.

In negative sentences, indefinite markers usually become ____. ❙

de (or d')

12 In negative sentences, partitive markers also become **de** or **d'**. Complete the answer to the question below.

> –Est-ce que tu veux du poisson?
> –Non, je ne veux pas ____. ❙

de poisson

13 Answer the questions below to say that Jean-Paul doesn't want any of the food he's offered.

a Est-ce que Jean-Paul veut des légumes? ❙

Non, il ne veut pas de légumes.

b Est-ce qu'il veut du poisson? ❙

Non, il ne veut pas de poisson.

c Est-ce qu'il veut un fruit? ❙

Non, il ne veut pas de fruit.

d Est-ce qu'il veut de l'eau? ❙

Non, il ne veut pas d'eau. (Remember that *de* becomes *d'* when it precedes a vowel sound.)

Le Champignon de Paris.
Un légume tout rond, tout bon.

2   More about telling time

In Phase 4 you learned how to tell time on the hour and on the half hour. Now you'll learn how to tell time "in between."

1 Look at the clock and its caption.

Il est cinq heures et quart.

a Write in English the time shown. ❙

It's (a) quarter past five.

b Which two French words correspond to *quarter past*? ❙

et quart

c What is the French equivalent of *It's (a) quarter past six*? ❙

Il est six heures et quart.

2 A radio announcer is likely to give the time with the exact number of minutes after the hour. Say this time aloud in English: *It's 10:22.* |

It's ten twenty-two.

3 French speakers write *10:22* nearly the way they say it. It is written **10h22.** Copy it on your worksheet. |

10h22 (Notice that there's no period after *h.*)

4 A French speaker reads **10h22** aloud as **dix heures vingt-deux.** Read aloud **10h25.** |

dix heures vingt-cinq

5 Give the times shown below in French. Write a complete sentence, and then write the time along with numbers and abbreviations.

Modèle: |

Il est trois heures cinq.   3h05.

a |

Il est une heure vingt.   1h20.

b |

Il est quatre heures dix.   4h10.

c |

Il est neuf heures cinq.   9h05.

6 Now look at this clock and its caption.

Il est cinq heures moins le quart.

a The clock shows quarter to five. Which three French words correspond to *quarter to?* |

moins le quart (This is the only time phrase in French that uses a definite marker.)

b Write the French equivalent of *It's quarter to six.* |

Il est six heures moins le quart.

7 As you saw in **6**, French uses **moins** to express time *before* the hour. Now look at the clock below.

Il est deux heures moins dix.

a Is a definite marker used in the French sentence? |

no (A definite marker is only used in the expression *moins le quart.*)

b Complete this sentence to say that it's five minutes to two: **Il est deux heures _____.** |

moins cinq

8 Say what time it is according to the clocks. Write complete sentences.

a

Il est une heure moins vingt.

b

Il est six heures moins le quart. (Did you remember to use *le*?)

c

Il est quatre heures quarante-huit (cinq heures moins douze).

9 Say that you are going to the zoo at quarter past two. |

Je vais au zoo à deux heures et quart.

10 Say that you are going to the movies at ten to eight. |

Je vais au cinéma à huit heures moins dix.

CHECK-UP Part 1	Write the French equivalent of these sentences. **1** I would like some hot chocolate. **2** There's jam on the table.
Part 2	Write complete sentences to tell the times shown below. **1** 4:15 **2** 8:05 **3** 3:45 **4** 6:40

VOCABULARY

et quart quarter past (the hour)
moins le quart quarter to (the hour)

LE RÉVEIL Waking up
la chambre room
le chocolat au lait hot chocolate
la confiture jam, preserves
un croissant crescent roll
le matin morning; in the morning
midi noon
le petit déjeuner breakfast
le régime diet
prêt, -e ready
arrêter to stop
avoir faim to be hungry
dormir to sleep
écoute! listen!
être au régime to be on a diet
il faut it is necessary
réveiller to wake (someone) up

debout up; get up!
encore un peu a little more
mais si! (contradictory) yes it is!
   yes I can!
parce que because
sans without
sans faute without fail
vraiment really

1 *The present tense of* prendre

1 The verb *prendre* (to take) is often used
with foods and beverages to mean *to have, to
eat* or *to drink*. Study the present-tense forms
in the chart by saying the subjects and verb
forms aloud a few times.

je	prend	s
tu	prend	s
on/il/elle	prend	
ils/elles	prenn	ent
nous	pren	ons
vous	pren	ez

a The present-tense stem of *prendre* has three written forms. Write
the three forms on your worksheet. |

prend-, prenn-, pren-

b Write the ending that matches the *je-* and *tu*-forms. |

-s

c Which form has no present-tense ending? |

the *il/elle*-form

d Which endings are the same as those of regular *-er* verbs? |

-ent, -ons, -ez (These three endings are used with the plural present-tense forms of
almost all French verbs.)

2 Complete the sentences below with the appropriate forms of *prendre.*
Write both the subject and the verb on your worksheet.

a Marc ____ du poulet. |

Marc prend

b Moi, je ____ du poisson. |

je prends

c Est-ce que tu ____ du café pour le petit déjeuner? |

tu prends

d Ces jeunes filles ____ des fraises. |

Ces jeunes filles prennent

e Nous ____ du fromage. |

Nous prenons

f Est-ce que vous ____ une pomme? |

vous prenez

3 Write an English equivalent for *Ces jeunes filles prennent des fraises*
and *Moi, je prends du poisson.* |

These girls are having (some) strawberries. I'm having (some) fish.

4 Look back at the phrases referring to food in the sentence in frame 2.

a Which nouns are count nouns? |

fraises, pomme

b What type of marker was used with those nouns: definite (*le, la,
les*), indefinite (*un, une, des*), or partitive (*du, de la, de l'*)? |

indefinite

c Which nouns are measure nouns? |

poulet, poisson, café, fromage

d Which type of marker was used with those nouns? |

partitive markers

5 Say what the following people are having for lunch or dinner. Use the appropriate indefinite or partitive marker.

Modèle: Philippe: soupe, fromage |

Philippe prend de la soupe et du fromage.

a Nathalie: poisson, pommes de terre |

Nathalie prend du poisson et des pommes de terre.

b Je: viande, haricots verts, lait |

Je prends de la viande, des haricots verts et du lait.

c Vous: poisson, légumes, poire, café |

Vous prenez du poisson, des légumes, une poire et du café.

6 In a negative sentence, which word is used instead of **un, une, des** or **du, de la, de l'**? **Je ne prends pas ___ lait.** |

de (or d')

7 Say that these people aren't having any of what is offered.

a Vous prenez de la viande? (Non, je...) |

Non, je ne prends pas de viande.

b Les enfants prennent des légumes? |

Non, ils ne prennent pas de légumes.

c Bertrand prend du fromage? |

Non, il ne prend pas de fromage.

2 *More practice with* vouloir *and* pouvoir

In Phase 4 you learned how to say what people *can* do and *want* to do.
This part will help you review the forms of *pouvoir* and *vouloir*.

1 Read this sentence: *Véronique veut regarder la télévision, mais elle ne peut pas.*
  a What is the English equivalent? |
> Véronique wants to watch television, but she can't.

  b Is the verb that directly follows *veut* in a present-tense form or in the infinitive form? |
> in the infinitive (When verbs like *vouloir*, *pouvoir*, etc. are followed by another verb, the second verb is in the infinitive form.)

  c Is *ne peut pas* followed by another verb? |
> no (Forms of *pouvoir* and *vouloir* may be used without another verb.)

2 Give the French equivalent of this sentence: *We want to go to the beach, but we can't.* |
> *Nous voulons aller à la plage, mais nous ne pouvons pas.*

3 Say that these people want to do the activity indicated, but that they can't.

  Modèle: Sylvie: écouter des disques |
> *Sylvie veut écouter des disques, mais elle ne peut pas.*

  a Jacques: faire une promenade |
> *Jacques veut faire une promenade, mais il ne peut pas.*

  b Nous: dormir |
> *Nous voulons dormir, mais nous ne pouvons pas.*

  c Elles: travailler |
> *Elles veulent travailler, mais elles ne peuvent pas.*

4 If you made any mistakes in frame 3, study *vouloir* and *pouvoir* in the Phase 4 Summary before doing this frame.
  Write the subject and the appropriate form of *vouloir* and *pouvoir*. Answers are in the answer key.

  Modèle: Je ____ téléphoner à mon copain. |
> *Je veux, Je peux*

  a Nous ____ commencer un régime.
  b Tu ____ dormir.

  c Elles ____ parler français.
  d Il ____ manger maintenant.

CHECK-UP

Part 1

1 Write the English equivalent of *Ce matin, je vais prendre du café au lait avec du pain et de la confiture.*

2 Say what these people are having to eat or drink.
  a Eric: croissant
  b Elles: lait

VOCABULARY

minuit midnight

1 More on talking about food: all vs. some

This section will explain which markers to use in order to talk about a whole category of food or just a portion of it.

1 Read this sentence: *Je veux une poire et des pommes.*
  a Give the English equivalent. ▮
> I want a pear and some apples.

  b Does the speaker want *all* pears and apples or *some portion* of these fruits? ▮
> some portion

  c Are *poire* and *pomme* count or measure nouns? ▮
> count

  d What type of marker is used—definite or indefinite? ▮
> indefinite

2 Now read this sentence: *Je veux du pain et de la confiture.*
  a Write the English equivalent. ▮
> I want (some) bread and (some) jam.

  b Does the speaker want *all* the bread and jam that exist or just *some portion* of these things? ▮
> some portion (a part)

  c Are *pain* and *confiture* count or measure nouns? ▮
> measure

  d What type of marker is used—definite or partitive? ▮
> partitive

3 To make a statement about some portion or part of a category, the indefinite markers ___, ___, ___ are used with count nouns, and the partitive markers ___, ___, ___ are used with measure nouns. ▮
> un, une, des; du, de la, de l'

4 For each sentence below, write the appropriate marker to tell what Caroline is having for lunch, and give the English equivalent for the food.

> Modèle: Caroline prend ___ riz. ▮
> *du;* (some) rice

  a Caroline prend ___ viande. ▮
> *de la;* (some) meat

  b Caroline prend ___ légumes. ▮
> *des;* (some) vegetables

  c Caroline prend ___ pêche. ▮
> *une;* a peach

  d Caroline prend ___ eau minérale. ▮
> *de l';* (some) mineral water

5 Now read this French sentence and its English equivalent.

J'aime les pêches.   I like peaches.

a Does the speaker like the whole category *peaches*, or just some portion of the category? |

the whole category (The speaker likes all peaches in general.)

b Is *pêches* a count noun or a measure noun? |

a count noun

c Which marker is used—definite or indefinite? |

definite

6 And now read these French and English sentences.

J'aime le fromage.   I like cheese.
J'adore la viande.   I love meat.
Je déteste l'eau.   I hate water.

a Are the statements about *all* cheese, meat, and water, or about *some portion* of those foods? |

about all cheese, meat, and water (The speaker likes cheese in general, loves meat, and hates water.)

b Are the nouns above count or measure nouns? |

measure

c Which kind of marker is used—definite or partitive? |

definite (Notice that no marker is used in the English sentences.)

7 To make a statement about all of a category of food, the definite markers ____, ____, ____ are used with both count nouns and measure nouns. | ·

le (l'), la (l'), les

8 Write the French equivalent for each sentence. Use a definite marker.

a I love strawberries. |

J'adore les fraises.

b I like jam. |

J'aime la confiture.

c I hate coffee. |

Je déteste le café.

d I don't like fish. |

Je n'aime pas le poisson.

9 Complete the sentences below to say that you like each food and that you're going to have some. Remember to use *le, la, l'* or *les* when referring to a whole category, and *un, une, des* or *du, de la, de l'* to refer to some portion of a category.

Modèle: J'aime ____riz. Je vais prendre ____riz. |

le; du

a J'aime ____ viande. Je vais prendre ____ viande. |

la; de la

b J'aime ____ haricots verts. Je vais prendre ____ haricots verts avec ____ sel. |

les; des, du

c J'aime ＿＿ thé. Je vais prendre ＿＿ thé. **I**
  le; du

d J'aime ＿＿ eau minérale. Je vais prendre ＿＿ eau minérale. **I**
  l'; de l'

e J'aime ＿＿ poires. Je vais prendre ＿＿ poire. **I**
  les; une

f J'aime ＿＿ fruits. Je vais prendre ＿＿ fruit. **I**
  les; un (For speakers of French, *fruit* is a count noun.)

NOTE ✱ ## *Eating out in a French restaurant*

The excellence of French **cuisine** (cooking) is famous the world over. Even small restaurants can usually provide a typical example of good French cooking. Most of the time you can consult the menu outside the restaurant, on the door or the window, and compare the various choices and prices. If you choose a **menu à prix fixe,** you can have a complete meal for a set price. You might be served an **hors d'œuvre** (like cold cuts or sliced tomatoes), **l'entrée** (usually a hot dish), then the main course—for example, **une grillade** (grilled steak) with French fries, or **un sauté d'agneau** (lamb stewed with tomatoes and green peppers in a wine sauce). After the main course you would be offered a salad to "refresh" the appetite. You would finish with **un plateau de fromages** (cheese platter) and a dessert or a pastry. Sometimes a beverage **(du vin, de l'eau minérale)** is included in the price, too **(boisson comprise).**

If you prefer, you can eat **à la carte** and choose only one or two dishes.

Most menus say **service compris,** meaning that a tip of 10% to 15% has already been included in the price of the meal. When you wish to pay the bill, say **s'il vous plaît** to the **serveur** or **serveuse** and ask for **l'addition.** If you liked the meal and the service, remember the name and address of that restaurant and share it with your friends. French people like to recommend a good place to eat!

2 *The present tense of* manger *and* commencer

1 Look at these words: *girafe, magasin, gentil, gomme, gymnastique.*
 a Which words have a *g* sound like the *g* in *garçon?* |
      magasin, gomme (These are ''hard'' *g* sounds.)
 b Which vowels follow *g* in *magasin* and *gomme?* |
      a, o
 c Copy the words that have a *g* sound like the *g* in *ingénieur.* |
      girafe, gentil, gymnastique (These are ''soft'' *g* sounds.)
 d Which vowels follow the *g* in *girafe, gentil, gymnastique?* |
      i, e, y

2 When *g* is followed by the vowels *e, i,* or *y,* it is pronounced like the *g* in *ingénieur.* When *g* is followed by any other letter, it is pronounced as in *garçon.* Which of these words have a ''hard'' *g* as in *garçon?* *angle, ange, grave, langue, Gilbert.* |
      angle, grave, langue

3 Here are the present-tense forms of *manger* (to eat). The endings are regular *-er* endings. The stem has one irregular form.

je	mang	e
tu	mang	es
on/il/elle	mang	e
ils/elles	mang	ent
nous	mange	ons
vous	mang	ez

 a The written present-tense stem is the same as the infinitive stem *mang-* except for one form. What form is that? |
      the *nous*-form (In the *nous*-form, an *e* is added to the stem *mang-*.)
 b Is the *g* in *mangeons* ''soft'' or ''hard''? |
      soft (The *e* is added in the *nous*-form so that the written *g* represents the same sound as in the other present-tense forms.)

4 Complete the sentences below, using the verb *manger.* Check your answers against the chart above.
 a J'aime ___ des pommes.
 b Nous ___ de la salade à midi.
 c Tu ___ vite.
 d Christine et moi, nous ___ beaucoup.
 e Mon grand-père ___ beaucoup de pain.

5 You have just seen that the letter *g* can be pronounced in two different ways, depending on which letter follows it. The same is true of the letter *c.* Say these words out loud: *célèbre, caméra, comment, cinq, cuisine.*
 a Which words have a *c* that sounds like the *c* in *cadeau?* |
      caméra, comment, cuisine (These are ''hard'' *c* sounds.)
 b Which vowels follow the *c* in *caméra, comment,* and *cuisine?* |
      a, o, u
 c Which words have a *c* that sounds like the *c* in *cinéma?* |
      célèbre, cinq (These are ''soft'' *c* sounds.)
 d What letters follow the *c* in *célèbre* and *cinq?* |
      é, i

6 Now say these words aloud: *garçon, cousin.*

a In both words the letter that follows the *c* is an *o*. Which word has a soft *c* sound? |

> *garçon* (The cedilla under the *c* indicates a soft *c* sound.)

b Complete this word and say whether it has a hard or soft *c* sound: *fran __ ais.* |

> *ç*; soft sound (Without the cedilla, the *c* would represent a hard sound.)

7 Now look at the present-tense forms of *commencer* (to begin). The endings are regular. The stem, however, has one irregular form.

je	commenc e
tu	commenc es
on/il/elle	commenc e
ils/elles	commenc ent
nous	commenç ons
vous	commenc ez

a How does the stem of the *nous*-form differ from the other present-tense stems? |

> There is a cedilla under the *c*.

b Without the cedilla, would the *c* be pronounced like the *c* in the other forms? |

> no (A *c* followed by an *o* would be hard. In all the other present-tense forms the *c* is followed by an *e* and is therefore soft.)

8 Complete the sentences below with a form of *commencer.* Check your answers carefully against the chart.

a Ils ___ un régime parce qu'ils sont très gros.
b Le garçon ___ ses devoirs à six heures du soir.
c Nous ___ nos devoirs après le dîner.
d Le cours de français ___ à onze heures.

CHECK-UP
Part 1

Say that Marc likes each of these items and that he wants some: *poires, eau minérale, sucre.*

Part 2

Complete these sentences with the correct form of the verb in parentheses.
1 Nous ___ souvent du poulet. (manger)
2 Nous ___ les cours en septembre. (commencer)

VOCABULARY

le sel salt
le poivre pepper
le sucre sugar
le beurre butter
un sandwich sandwich
le jambon ham
le riz rice
les petits pois peas
un œuf egg
une pêche peach

une cerise cherry
la glace ice cream
une tarte pie
le jus (de fruit) (fruit) juice
le thé tea

1 *Expressions with* avoir

1 You already know one French expression that uses the verb *avoir.* Give the French equivalent of *I'm fifteen years old.* ▮

J'ai quinze ans.

2 All the responses below contain expressions with the verb *avoir.* Read the exchanges carefully.

–Il fait beau, n'est-ce pas?   *–Oui, mais j'ai chaud.*
–Oh là là, il neige beaucoup!   *–Oui, et j'ai très froid.*
–Tu veux de l'eau?   *–Oh oui, j'ai soif.*
–Tu veux du pain et du beurre?   *–Non, merci, je n'ai pas faim.*
–Tu vois, il fait beau.   *–Ah oui, tu as raison.*

Complete the English equivalents below. You should know the first two expressions. Try to guess the meaning of the other expressions from their contexts. Write the complete English equivalent on your answer sheet.

a *J'ai chaud.* I'm ____. ▮

I'm hot.

b *J'ai très froid.* I'm very ____. ▮

I'm very cold.

c *J'ai soif.* I'm ____. ▮

I'm thirsty.

d *Je n'ai pas faim.* I'm not ____. ▮

I'm not hungry.

e *Tu as raison.* You're ____. ▮

You're right.

3 *Je n'ai pas faim* means *I'm not hungry.* How would you say *I'm not thirsty?* ▮

Je n'ai pas soif.

4 *J'ai très froid* means *I'm very cold.* How would you say *I'm very hot?* ▮

J'ai très chaud. (While *très* is not usually used after forms of *avoir,* it is used to give emphasis to *avoir faim/soif/chaud/froid* and a few other *avoir* expressions.)

5 Write the French equivalent of the following sentences. Use the expressions *avoir faim, avoir soif, avoir chaud, avoir froid, avoir...ans,* and *avoir raison.*

a Are you thirsty? (Use *vous.*) ▮

Vous avez soif?/Est-ce que vous avez soif?

b I'm very hot. ▮

J'ai très chaud.

c They (*elles*) aren't hungry. ▮

Elles n'ont pas faim.

d He is eighty-five years old. ❙

       Il a quatre-vingt-cinq ans.

e We're not cold. ❙

       Nous n'avons pas froid.

f Of course, he's right. ❙

       Bien sûr, il a raison.

g I'm not thirteen, I'm fourteen. ❙

       Je n'ai pas treize ans, j'ai quatorze ans.

6 Complete each answer below with a logical response. Use an expression with ***avoir***.

  a –Tu veux de l'eau? –Oui,...

  b –Tu veux du lait? –Non,...

  c –Elles ferment les fenêtres? –Oui,... ❙

        a Oui, j'ai soif.   *b Non, je n'ai pas soif.*   *c Oui, elles ont froid.*

2   *More practice with food*

In Preparation 63 you learned which markers to use when talking about some or all of a category. This section will help you practice what you learned and will also prepare you for a quiz in class.

1 For each frame below, write *all* if the English sentence refers to a whole category, and *some* if it refers to a portion of a category. Then write the definite marker that completes the French equivalent.

  a I like apples. ***J'aime ____ pommes.*** ❙

      all; les

  b I hate meat. ***Je déteste ____ viande.*** ❙

      all; la

  c It's milk. ***C'est ____ lait.*** ❙

      some; du (The English sentence could have been: *It's some milk.*)

  d I'm having vegetables. ***Je prends ____ légumes.*** ❙

      some; des (The English sentence could have been *I'm having some vegetables.*)

  e He's having tea for breakfast. ***Il prend ____ thé pour le petit déjeuner.*** ❙

      some; du (The English sentence could have been *He's having some tea for breakfast.*)

2 Refer to the answers for frame 1 if necessary.

  a To talk about a whole category of food, French uses the definite markers *l __ , l __ , l __ .* ❙

      le (l'), la (l'), les

  b To talk about some portion of a category, you use either the indefinite markers *u __ , u __ , d __ ,* or the partitive markers *d __ , d __ , d __ .* ❙

      un, une, des; du, de la, de l'

Viennoiserie St Honoré

3 Say that you love the first category of food but don't like the second
one.

    a beurre / confiture
             b légumes / viande |

a J'aime le beurre mais je n'aime pas la confiture. *b J'aime les légumes mais je
n'aime pas la viande.*

4 Three friends are in the cafeteria discussing what they're going to
have. Complete the sentences with the appropriate markers. Keep in
mind whether the statement refers to a whole category or only to some
portion, and whether the nouns are count or measure.

      Modèle: Moi, j'aime ＿＿ pain. Je vais prendre ＿＿ pain. |

          le, du

  a Tu aimes ＿＿ pommes de terre, n'est-ce pas? Tu vas prendre ＿＿
pommes de terre? |

          les, des

  b Tiens, tu prends ＿＿ haricots! Tu aimes ＿＿ haricots, toi aussi. |

          des, les

  c Je vais prendre ＿＿ poisson. Et toi, tu aimes ＿＿ poisson? |

          du, le

5 Read the exchanges below, and pay attention to the markers used in
the answers.

    –Tu veux des cerises?   *–Non, je ne veux pas de cerises.*
    –Tu prends de la glace?   *–Non, je ne prends pas de glace.*
    –Tu aimes les légumes?   *–Non, je n'aime pas les légumes.*

a In negative sentences, the indefinite markers **des** and **de la** are
replaced by ＿＿. |

    *de (In most negative sentences, the markers un, une, des and du, de la, de l' are
replaced by de or d'.)*

b In the last negative sentence above, the definite marker
les ＿＿. |

    stays the same (In negative sentences, definite markers do not change.)

6 Nicolas is a very finicky eater. Say that he doesn't want any of the foods he is offered because he doesn't like them.

> Modèle: petits pois **|**
>
> *Il ne veut pas de petits pois. Il n'aime pas les petits pois.*

a poulet **|**

Il ne veut pas de poulet. Il n'aime pas le poulet.

b œufs **|**

Il ne veut pas d'œufs. Il n'aime pas les œufs.

c fromage **|**

Il ne veut pas de fromage. Il n'aime pas le fromage.

NOTE **Le Fromage**

There is a saying that illustrates the important role of cheese in a French meal: **Un repas sans fromage n'est pas un repas** ("A meal without cheese is not a meal."). More than three hundred types of cheese are produced and eaten in France. A few of the more common ones are **camembert** (a round, semi-soft cheese with a crust), **gruyère** (a Swiss cheese), **fromage de chèvre** (sharp-flavored, made from goat's milk), and **Roquefort** (a sharp, blue-veined cheese).

Le roi des fromages.

3   The expression il faut + infinitive

1 In *Les Résolutions de Marie-Jeanne,* Maman says to Marie-Jeanne: *Il faut manger le matin.* What must Marie-Jeanne do in the morning, according to her mother? **|**

eat

2 Copy the sentence *Il faut manger le matin* and underline the words that express the meaning *you must.* **|**

Il faut manger le matin.

3 In the sentence *Il faut manger le matin,* what verb form follows *il faut*—a present-tense form or an infinitive form? **|**

an infinitive form (*manger*)

4 In the expression *il faut,* does *il* refer to a male? **|**

no (*Il faut* is an *impersonal expression.* It never changes form, and *il* does not refer to a specific person. The meaning of *il* is determined by the context.)

5 The meaning of *Il faut manger le matin* may be expressed in English in several ways.

You have to eat in the morning.   You must eat in the morning.
We have to eat in the morning.   We must eat in the morning.
It is necessary to eat in the   One must eat in the morning.
morning.

Give two English equivalents of *Il faut dormir.* |

You must sleep. / We have to sleep. / It is necessary to sleep. / One must sleep.

6 Following the *modèle* below, write complete sentences with the expression *il faut.* Give an English equivalent of each French sentence (no need to write it). Your English equivalents may differ slightly from those listed.

Modèle: Pour aller à la montagne, ____ avoir une voiture. |

Pour aller à la montagne, il faut avoir une voiture. In order to go to the mountains, it's necessary to have a car.

a Si vous voulez voir la Tour Eiffel, ____ aller à Paris. |

Si vous voulez voir la Tour Eiffel, il faut aller à Paris. If you want to see the Eiffel Tower, you must go to Paris.

b Si on veut être riche, ____ travailler. |

Si on veut être riche, il faut travailler. If one wants to be rich, one must work.

7 Pretend you are a parent whose children sometimes refuse to do certain things. Each time one of your children refuses to do something, tell him or her that it's necessary to do it.

Modèle: Je ne veux pas aller chez le dentiste. |

Il faut aller chez le dentiste.

a Je n'aime pas aller à l'école.
b Je ne vais pas manger à midi.
c Je ne veux pas jouer du piano. |

a *Il faut aller à l'école.*   b *Il faut manger à midi.*   c *Il faut jouer du piano.*

CHECK-UP Part 1	Write French equivalents. **1** I'm thirsty. **2** You're right.
Part 3	Complete each sentence below with the French equivalent of the phrase in parentheses. **1** En France, ____. (*you must speak French*) **2** Si tu as faim, ____. (*it's necessary to eat*)
VOCABULARY	*avoir faim* to be hungry *avoir chaud* to be hot *avoir froid* to be cold *avoir raison* to be right *avoir soif* to be thirsty

1 More practice with food

1 To see if you remember which markers to use with food, complete the sentences below. The markers may be **un, une, des** or **le, la, les,** or **du, de la, de l'.** If you make any mistakes, review Preparation 64. Then continue with frame 2.

a Il y a ___ soupe pour ce soir? |
de la

b Nous prenons ___ fruits. |
des

c Elle déteste ___ eau minérale. |
l'

d C'est ___ jambon? |
du

2 Poor Nathalie. Her father's telling her what's for dinner, and it sounds as if she isn't going to enjoy it much. Complete the sentences with the appropriate marker.

a –Pour le dîner, il y a ___ soupe.
–Oh, je déteste ___ soupe. |
de la; la

b –Il y a aussi ___ poulet, ___ haricots verts et ___ pommes de terre.
–Tu sais que je n'aime pas ___ poulet, et je déteste ___ haricots verts et ___ pommes de terre. |
du, des, des; le, les, les

c –Comme dessert, il y a ___ fromage, ___ glace aux fraises et ___ fruits.
–Alors, je vais prendre ___ fruits. Je déteste ___ glace aux fraises et ___ fromage. |
du, de la, des; des, la, le

3 Jean-Pierre seems to be quite a finicky eater also. Complete this description of what he is or isn't going to have. Answers are in the answer key.

a Je ne prends pas ___ légumes: je déteste ___ légumes.

b Je ne veux pas ___ viande et je ne veux pas ___ poisson: je n'aime pas ___ viande et je déteste ___ poisson.

c Je vais prendre ___ pain, ___ fraises, ___ pêches et ___ jus de fruit.

d J'adore ___ pain, ___ fraises, ___ pêches et ___ jus de fruit.

2 *Reading comprehension:* **Un croque-monsieur**

This is an illustrated, step-by-step recipe. It contains some new vocabulary, but with the aid of the pictures you should be able to figure out most of the steps. Try to understand the French by using the pictures. There is a glossary after frame 9. After finishing this Preparation, you could try out the recipe.

> –*Comment fait-on un croque-monsieur?*
> –*C'est facile!*

1 Prenez une tranche de pain.
2 Mettez du beurre sur la tranche de pain.
3 Mettez une tranche de jambon et du fromage sur la tranche de pain.

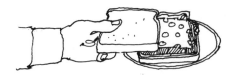

4 Prenez une seconde tranche de pain.
5 Mettez du beurre sur cette seconde tranche de pain.
6 Mettez la seconde tranche sur la première tranche. Vous avez un sandwich, n'est-ce pas?

7 Bon. Mettez du beurre sur les deux côtés du sandwich.
8 Mettez ce sandwich dans le four chaud.
9 Après huit ou dix minutes, ouvrez le four. Le sandwich est grillé. C'est un croque-monsieur! Bon appétit!

GLOSSARY

une tranche	slice	*facile*	easy
le jambon	ham	*grillé*	grilled
le four	oven	*première*	first
le côté	side	*seconde*	second
mettez	put		

Bon appétit! means much more than simply *good appetite!* It is a wish that the whole occasion be enjoyable: the food, the people, the atmosphere, and the conversation.

10 What is the nearest English equivalent of ***un croque-monsieur?*** **a** a peanut-butter-and-jelly sandwich **b** a grilled ham-and-cheese sandwich **c** a crocodile sandwich ▌

a grilled ham-and-cheese sandwich

Regional specialties

If you travel through France, you will soon discover that each region has its own special foods. Here are just a few.

In Bourgogne, you might try the **escargots** (snails); Alsace is well-known for its **choucroute garnie** (sauerkraut simmered in wine, garnished with sausages, smoked ham, bacon, and potatoes). Visitors like to sample all the different kinds of **crêpes** (thin pancakes with fillings) served in Brittany **(la Bretagne).** Near Toulouse, there is a good **cassoulet** (a baked bean and sausage casserole), and in the South of France around Marseille, the specialty is **bouillabaisse,** a flavorful stew with several kinds of fish and shellfish.

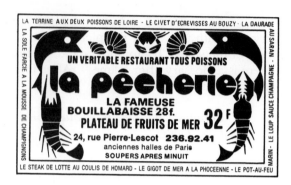

3 *Practice with stressed pronouns*

1 To see if you remember the forms of the stressed pronouns, complete the sentences below to say that the people mentioned are going home.

> Modèle: Tu vas chez ____. ▮
> *toi*

a Marc va chez ____.
b Nous allons chez ____.
c Sylvie va chez ____.

d Ils vont chez ____.
e Vous allez chez ____.
f Je vais chez ____. ▮

a *lui* b *nous* c *elle* d *eux* e *vous* f *moi*

2 If you made any mistakes in frame 1, take a few minutes to practice the forms again (see the Summary, p. 313). Then write complete sentences to say what the people below are doing right now. Answers are in the answer key.

> Modèle: Jacques: manger ▮
> *Lui, il mange.*

a Marie-Jeanne: manger
b Nous: commencer nos devoirs
c Marc et Eric: faire une promenade

d Tu: aller au café
e Vous: manger
f Je: aller au cinéma

Abondance des produits de la terre . . .

Pain *frais et croustillant*

Fromages riches et délectables

P̂êche *scintillante au soleil*

Raisins *mûrs et parfumés*

1 *Equivalents of* to be: être, avoir, faire

1 Read the sentences below, and notice the verbs that are used.

 Elle est très grande. Je vais bien.
 Il a dix-neuf ans. Il fait froid.

a Give the infinitive form of *est, a, vais,* and *fait.* ▮

 être, avoir, aller, faire

b Think of the English equivalents for the sentences. What verb is used in English? ▮

 to be (She's very tall. He's nineteen. I'm well. It's cold.)

2 The English verb *to be* has three French equivalents other than *être.* The context tells you which verb to use. The verb ____ is used to talk about age; the verb ____ is used to talk about health; the verb ____ is used to talk about the weather. ▮

 avoir, aller, faire

3 Complete the short dialogues below using the appropriate equivalents of *to be.*

a –Bonjour, Christophe, tu ____ bien?
 –Oui, merci, ça ____ très bien. ▮

 vas, va

b –Marie-Christine ____ dix-huit ans aujourd'hui.
 –Elle ____ contente? ▮

 a, est

c –J' ____ très froid ce matin.
 –Oui, il ____ froid dehors (*outside*). ▮

 ai, fait

4 For a quick vocabulary review, write the French equivalents of the sentences below. Answers are in the answer key.

a The weather's nice.
b It's cold.
c The weather isn't bad today.
d It's not hot.

5 Certain French expressions use the verb *avoir* where English uses the verb *to be.* Give the French equivalents of the sentences below. Answers are in the answer key.

a We're hungry.
b I'm not thirsty.
c Patricia's right.
d They're very cold.
e Thierry is fifteen years old.

2 More on possessive markers

1 This section will give you a quick review of how to say *his, her,* and *their* in French. Read these two sentences.

> *Robert aime son frère, sa sœur et ses amis.*
> *Marie-Jeanne aime son frère, sa sœur et ses amis.*

a Copy the possessive markers in the first sentence and give the English equivalent. |

son, sa, ses; his

b Now copy the possessive markers in the second sentence and give the English equivalent. |

son, sa, ses; her (The meaning of *son, sa,* and *ses* depends on whether the owner is male or female.)

c In French, does the possessive marker agree in gender and number with the item possessed or with the possessor? |

with the item possessed

d Are *son, sa, ses* used with one possessor or with more than one? |

one

2 Complete the answers below with the appropriate possessive marker. Write the English equivalent of each marker.

a –C'est la photo de Pierre?   –Oui, c'est ____ photo.
b –Tu as les livres d'Annick?   –Oui, j'ai ____ livres.
c –Je peux prendre le vélo de Patricia?   –Oui, tu peux prendre ____ vélo. |

a *sa;* his   **b** *ses;* her   **c** *son;* her

3 Read the sentences below.

> *Voilà leur frère.*   *Voilà leurs frères.*   *Voilà ses frères.*

a Which sentences indicate that there is more than one possessor? |

Voilà leur frère. Voilà leurs frères.

b Which sentences indicate that there is more than one brother? Write the English equivalents. |

Voilà ses frères. There are his brothers. *Voilà leurs frères.* There are their brothers.

c The two French equivalents for *their* are ____ and ____. |

leur, leurs

d The English equivalent of the marker *ses* is ____. |

his or *her*

4 Complete the French equivalents of these sentences.

a They love their dog. *Ils aiment ____ chien.* |

leur

b They also love their cats. *Ils aiment aussi ____ chats.* |

leurs

c They always have their animals with them. *Ils ont toujours ____ animaux avec eux.* |

leurs

5 English-speaking people sometimes need extra practice in distinguishing between *son, sa, ses* and ***leur, leurs.*** Use these markers to complete the second sentence in each pair below. Answers are in the answer key.

> Modèle: Christine et Gérard ont une voiture. C'est ＿＿. |
> *leur voiture*

a Monique a une maison. C'est ＿＿.
b Marie-Jeanne a un vélomoteur. C'est ＿＿.
c Monsieur et Madame Dupont ont des enfants. Ce sont ＿＿.
d Michel a une guitare. C'est ＿＿.
e Mon ami Vincent a des disques. Ce sont ＿＿.
f Le petit garçon a une trompette. C'est ＿＿.
g Mon père et mon oncle ont un restaurant. C'est ＿＿.

VOCABULARY

affreux, affreuse terrible
bon, bonne good
heureux, heureuse happy
malheureux, malheureuse unhappy
mauvais, -e bad

merveilleux, merveilleuse wonderful
avant before
lentement slowly
vite quickly
terminer to finish

UN MESSAGE PUBLICITAIRE A commercial

le dessert dessert
les jeunes gens young people
la météo weather report
les informations news
diététique dietetic
distraitement inattentively
élégant elegant
mince slender

nourrissant nourishing
raffiné refined
solitaire lonely
attirer l'attention to attract attention
soudain suddenly
vite quick
avec plaisir with pleasure
en même temps at the same time

1 Focusing attention on food items

In Phase 2, you learned how to identify an item using the markers *un, une, des.* To refer to the same item later, you used the markers *le, la, les.* This section will give you more practice using definite, indefinite, and partitive markers in conversational situations.

1 Imagine the following scene. You're walking down the street with a friend when suddenly he says:

Look, there's a dog driving that car!

But it's all right—the dog is wearing glasses.

a Look at the markers that are used with *dog.* Which marker is used to focus the listener's attention on the kind of thing being talked about: the definite marker *the* or the indefinite marker *a?* |

the indefinite marker *a* (The indefinite markers are used to focus a listener's attention on the person or thing being discussed.)

b Which marker is used with *dog* after the listener already knows what is being talked about: the indefinite marker *a* or the definite marker *the?* |

the definite marker *the* (Definite markers are used after attention has been focused on the topic of conversation.)

2 Now imagine you're in France. Your neighbor Bernard bursts in while you're having dinner. Complete each sentence with the appropriate marker: *la* or *une.*

a Il y a ＿＿ girafe dans mon garage! |

une (Bernard uses the indefinite marker to focus your attention on what's in his garage: a giraffe.)

b ＿＿ girafe joue aux cartes! |

La (When Bernard refers to the giraffe a second time, he uses the definite marker *la.*)

3 Sylvie's father is telling her what's available for dessert. Read this exchange between them.

–Il y a une pomme, une pêche et des cerises. Qu'est-ce que tu veux?

–Je veux la pêche, papa.

a Is *pêche* a count noun or a measure noun? |

a count noun

b Which French marker is used to focus attention on the peach? |

une (an indefinite marker)

c Which French marker is used once the focus has been established? |

la (a definite marker)

4 Mathieu's cousin Louis is looking in the refrigerator to find them something to eat. He discovers a plain yogurt and a strawberry yogurt. Write what the boys say to each other, using the cues below and the appropriate markers, **un** or **le.**

> Louis: Il y a (*yaourt nature*) et (*yaourt aux fraises*).
> Qu'est-ce que tu prends?
>
> Mathieu: Je vais prendre (*yaourt aux fraises*). ▌

–Il y a un yaourt nature et un yaourt aux fraises. Qu'est-ce que tu prends?
–Je vais prendre le yaourt aux fraises.

5 Now compare these French and English sentences.

> *Il y a du jus d'orange sur la table.* There's some orange juice on the table.
> *Passe-moi le jus d'orange, s'il te plaît.* Pass me the orange juice, please.

a Is **jus d'orange** a count noun or a measure noun? ▌

a measure noun

b Which French marker is used to focus attention on the juice? ▌

the partitive marker du

c Which French marker is used to refer to the juice after attention has been focused on it? ▌

the definite marker

6 Give the English equivalent of these sentences.

a Il y a du poulet sur la table. ▌

There's (some) chicken on the table.

b Passez-moi le poulet, s'il vous plaît. ▌

Pass me the chicken, please.

7 Marie-Jeanne has just sat down at the table. As soon as she spots something she wants, she asks someone to pass it to her. Complete the sentences below.

> Modèle: Il y a ____ fromage! Passez-moi ____ fromage, s'il vous plaît. ▌
> *du, le*

a Il y a ____ poisson! Passez-moi ____ poisson, s'il vous plaît. ▌
du, le

b Il y a ____ beurre! Passez-moi ____ beurre, s'il vous plaît. ▌
du, le

c Il y a ____ jambon! Passez-moi ____ jambon, s'il vous plaît. ▌
du, le

d Il y a ____ glace! Passez-moi ____ glace, s'il vous plaît. ▌
de la, la

8 To summarize what you have just learned about markers, complete these statements.

a The markers ____, ____, ____ or ____, ____, ____ are used to focus attention on a kind of food. ▌

un, une, des; du, de la, de l'

b The markers ____, ____, ____ may be used after attention has been focused on a particular item of food. ▌

le (l'), la (l'), les

2 *Reading comprehension:* **Les grandes vacances**

Here's a dialogue about some friends' plans for their summer vacation
(*les grandes vacances*). Read it carefully, then answer the frames that
follow. Try to understand new words from the context. (New vocabulary is listed on the side.)

Les grandes vacances

LUCIE	Aujourd'hui, c'est le premier juin°—bientôt°, les vacances!	June first / soon
MICHÈLE	Où vas-tu pour tes vacances, Lucie?	
LUCIE	Ma sœur et moi, nous allons à Londres: nous voulons voir les théâtres, les discothèques, le Palais° de Buckingham... Et vous, où est-ce que vous allez?	palace
MICHÈLE	Moi, je vais à la montagne° avec ma cousine. Nous allons faire du camping en Suisse. C'est si° beau!	to the mountains so
PHILIPPE	Mon cousin et moi, on va à Quimper°. On va aller à la plage, faire de la voile°, et aller à la pêche°. J'adore la Bretagne!	in Brittany go sailing go fishing
MICHÈLE	Et toi, André? Où vas-tu?	
ANDRÉ	Moi, je vais passer mes vacances° dans le désert.	spend my vacation
LUCIE	Tu vas dans le désert? Tu es fou!	
ANDRÉ	Pas du tout°. Je vais à Las Vegas!	Not at all
PHILIPPE	À Las Vegas? En Amérique? Oh là là, tu vas revenir° très riche!	come back
MICHÈLE	Ou très pauvre!	

1 Now try to answer each of the following questions about *Les grandes
vacances.* Write complete sentences. Your answers may vary slightly
from those given.

  a Où va Lucie pour ses vacances? |
        Elle va à Londres.

  b Michèle et sa cousine, où est-ce qu'elles vont? |
        Elles vont à la montagne.

  c Qu'est-ce que Philippe va faire à Quimper? |
        Il va aller à la plage, faire de la voile et aller à la pêche.

  d Où va André? |
        Il va dans le désert, à Las Vegas.

CHECK-UP
Part 1

Write the French equivalents of these sentences.

Pass me the jam.   Pass me the butter.   Pass me the pie.

1 Asking questions with inverted word order

1 You already know three ways of asking questions in French.
a Say the French equivalent of *Do you like French bread?* first with intonation, then using *est-ce que.* Use *tu.* |

Tu aimes le pain français? Est-ce que tu aimes le pain français?

b Say the French equivalent of *You like French bread, don't you?* Use *n'est-ce pas.* |

Tu aimes le pain français, n'est-ce pas?

c In each of the questions above, which comes first: the subject *tu* or the verb *aimes?* |

the subject *tu*

2 You also know a fourth way to ask a question in French. Look at this exchange:

–*Quelle heure est-il?*
–*Il est huit heures et demie.*

a In *Il est huit heures et demie,* which comes first: the subject *il* or the verb *est?* |

the subject *il*

b In *Quelle heure est-il?* which comes first: the subject *il* or the verb *est?* |

the verb *est* (Reversing the positions of the subject and the verb is called *inversion.*)

c When *il* and *est* are inverted (reversed), what punctuation mark comes between them? |

a hyphen (A hyphen is used every time a subject pronoun and a verb are inverted.)

d The English equivalents of these two French sentences are *What time is it?* and *It is eight-thirty.* In the English question, are the positions of the subject and the verb inverted? |

yes (Inversion takes place in English as well as in French.)

3 Practice writing the following phrases with inverted word order.
a il est
b vous êtes
c elle fait
d ils vont |

a *est-il* b *êtes-vous* c *fait-elle* d *vont-ils*

4 The word *quel* is called a question word since it is used to ask questions. Sentences that begin with question words usually have inverted word order. Complete this question: *Quel temps ____ ?*

fait-il (Did you remember the hyphen?)

5 Below are some answers. Using the cues provided, write the questions you would ask to get those answers. Use inverted word order.

Modèle: C'est ma cousine Marie-Louise. (Qui...)

Qui est-ce?

a Il est midi. (Quelle...)

Quelle heure est-il? (Did you remember the hyphen?)

b Il fait beau. (Quel...)

Quel temps fait-il?

c Nous allons au cinéma. (Où...)

Où allez-vous? / Où allons-nous?

6 You can use inversion alone to ask a question, without using a question word. Write the English equivalent of *Aimez-vous le jazz?*

Do you like jazz?

7 Rewrite the questions below, using inversion. Remember the hyphen.

a Vous prenez du chocolat au lait?

Prenez-vous du chocolat au lait?

b Nous allons à la campagne ce week-end?

Allons-nous à la campagne ce week-end?

8 Now read this question with inverted word order: *Quel âge a-t-elle?*

a What is added between the verb *a* and the subject *elle?*

-t-

b Does the *-t-* occur between two consonants or two vowels?

two vowels

9 The *-t-* is used with the *on/il/elle-* form of *avoir, aller,* and all regular *-er* verbs because these forms end with a written vowel. The /t/ sound was present in the old Latin forms and was kept in the language as modern French developed.

a Write the inverted form of *elle habite.*

habite-t-elle

b Give the French equivalent of *Where does she live?*

Où habite-t-elle? (Did you remember the hyphens?)

c Give the French equivalent of *Where are we going?* Use *on.*

Où va-t-on?

10 Rewrite these questions, using inversion.

a Il nage en été?

Nage-t-il en été?

b Tu vas à la montagne cet hiver?

Vas-tu à la montagne cet hiver?

c Où est-ce que tu habites?

Où habites-tu? (The phrase est-ce que is not used in an inverted question.)

2 The present tense of venir

You already know how to use **aller** to mean *to go*. In this part you will learn to use **venir** (*to come*). Look at the chart to see which stem and ending match each subject pronoun.

je	vien s
tu	vien s
on/il/elle	vien t
ils/elles	vienn ent
nous	ven ons
vous	ven ez

1 The present-tense stem of **venir** has three forms. What are they? |
    vien-, vienn-, ven-

2 Which forms have the same endings as regular *-er* verbs? |
    ils/elles-, nous-, vous- forms

3 Study the present-tense forms of **venir** for a few moments, then for frames **a** and **b** write the subject pronouns and the corresponding verb forms. Check your answers carefully against the chart.

   a on, elles, vous   **b** nous, tu, je

4 The preposition *de* can mean *of* or *from*. Give the English equivalent of this sentence: **Jean vient de la bibliothèque.** |
    Jean is coming from the library.

5 Complete these sentences to say where people are coming from. Remember that *de* contracts with *le* and *les*.

   Modèle: Caroline / la librairie |
            Caroline vient de la librairie.

   a Nous / la cantine   **c** Je / l'aéroport
   b Elles / le théâtre   **d** Marc / le lycée |
            a *Nous venons de la cantine.* b *Elles viennent du théâtre.* c *Je viens de l'aéroport.* d *Marc vient du lycée.*

6 *Venir* can be followed by other prepositions. Read this sentence:
Patrick vient chez moi.
   a Here **venir** is followed by the preposition ____. |
            chez
   b Give the English equivalent of the sentence. |
            Patrick is coming to my house.
   c What is the English for **Marie vient à l'aéroport avec nous?** |
            Marie is coming to the airport with us.

7 Now look at this sentence: **Il vient écouter des disques.**
   a Here, **venir** is followed by ____. |
            écouter (Remember that the second verb is in the infinitive.)
   b Write the English equivalent of the sentence. |
            He's coming to listen to some records.

8 Write complete sentences to say what these people are doing. Answers are in the answer key.
   a Tu / venir / jouer aux cartes   **b** Vous / venir / chez nous

NOTE ✳ ***Les Boissons***

Most French people drink wine with **le déjeuner** and **le dîner.** In some regions, beer or hard cider replaces wine. Mineral water or tap water is always present on the table. Mineral water, which may or may not be carbonated, is considered to be good for the digestion and one's general health.

   Children often drink water and may sometimes add a little wine to their glasses. Traditionally, milk has only been used for cooking and with breakfast coffee or hot chocolate, but it is gaining in popularity as a beverage. After **le déjeuner** and sometimes after **le dîner,** adults may have a small cup of strong coffee with sugar.

3 *Some nouns can be counted and measured*

You have learned that nouns are usually either count nouns or measure nouns. Certain nouns, however, can be count nouns in one context, and measure nouns in another.

1 *Chicken* can be either a count noun or a measure noun, depending on the situation.

   a Someone goes to the store and says to the butcher *Je veux un poulet.* Is *poulet* a count noun or a measure noun here? ▌
                a count noun (In English also you could say *I'd like a chicken.*)

   b If someone asks you what you want for dinner, however, you would say *Je veux ___ poulet.* ▌
                du (Here *poulet* is a measure noun. You don't want a whole chicken, only a portion of a chicken.)

2 *Fish* can also be either count or measure.

   a If Nathalie says in French *I've caught some fish: a bass and a perch,* will she say *du poisson* or *des poissons?* ▌
                des poissons (Here fish are whole animals that can be counted.)

   b Nathalie then cooks the fish for dinner. If she asks a dinner guest in French *Would you like some fish?*, does she say *du poisson* or *des poissons?* ▌
                du poisson (She's referring to a portion of food. Fish is a measure noun here.)

3 Mme Dufour is at the poultry stand of her local outdoor market. She wants to buy a chicken. Write her reply to the salesperson's question.

    –Oui, Madame, vous voulez...?

    –___, s'il vous plaît. ▮

Un poulet

4 There's another situation in which nouns that usually represent measurable things can become count nouns.

    a You are at a *café* with some friends. The server comes over to take your order and you say ***Nous voulons un thé et un jus d'orange.*** Are *tea* and *orange juice* treated as count nouns or measure nouns? ▮

count nouns (In orders, food is often a count noun.)

    b Tell the server you also want one ice cream, two coffees, and one *tarte* (small pie). ▮

Nous voulons aussi une glace, deux cafés et une tarte.

CHECK-UP

Part 1

Rewrite these questions using inversion.

1 Il habite à Québec?   **2** Vous voulez danser?

Part 2

Complete these sentences with the appropriate form of *venir*.

1 Ils ___ chez moi ce soir.   **3** Je ___ du restaurant.

2 Vous ___ aussi?   **4** Elle ___ au cinéma avec moi.

VOCABULARY

une banane banana
le bœuf beef
un bonbon piece of candy
une carotte carrot
un gâteau cake
un hamburger hamburger
un hot dog hot dog
le pain grillé toast
un pamplemousse grapefruit
un petit pain roll
le porc pork
une tomate tomato

À LA CANTINE SCOLAIRE
  At the school cafeteria
la cantine scolaire school cafeteria
la cour courtyard
le déjeuner lunch
les frites French fries
le steak haché ground beef
déjeuner to eat lunch
depuis since
quel dommage! what a pity!

1 Practice asking questions

1 In Preparation 68 you practiced using inversion after question words such as *quel.* Compare the forms of *quel* in these two questions.

> *Quel temps fait-il?*   *Quelle heure est-il?*

a Write the form of *quel* that goes with the masculine word *temps.* |

> *quel* (This is the masculine singular form.)

b Write the form of *quel* that goes with the feminine word *heure.* |

> *quelle* (This is the feminine singular form.)

2 From your practice with adjectives, you should be able to give the plural forms of *quel* and *quelle.* Complete the questions below.

a ___ légumes aimez-vous? |

> *Quels* (To form the masculine plural, add an *-s* to the masculine singular.)

b ___ chansons aimez-vous? |

> *Quelles* (To form the feminine plural, add an *-s* to the feminine singular.)

3 Complete each of the following questions with the correct form of *quel.* Write the English equivalent of frames **a** and **b.**

a ___ sports faites-vous en hiver?   **c** ___ chanteurs aimez-vous?

b ___ boissons aimez-vous?   **d** ___ actrices préférez-vous? |

> **a** *Quels;* Which sports do you do in the winter?   **b** *Quelles;* Which beverages do you like?   **c** *Quels*   **d** *Quelles*

4 Béatrice has just run into her friend Philippe, who's holding a child by the hand. Below are Philippe's answers to her questions. Write Béatrice's questions, using inversion and the appropriate question word: *qui, quel, quelle, comment,* or *où.*

a –___?
–Je vais bien, merci. |

> *Comment vas-tu?* (Did you remember the hyphen between the verb and subject pronoun?)

b –___?
–C'est ma cousine Paulette. |

> *Qui est-ce?*

c –___?
–Elle a trois ans. |

> *Quel âge a-t-elle?* (Did you remember to insert *-t-* between the verb and pronoun?)

d –___?
–Nous allons au parc. |

> *Où allez-vous?*

e –___?
–Il est trois heures et demie. |

> *Quelle heure est-il?*

2 *Practice with* aller, venir, *telling time*

This part will give you some practice with the verbs **aller** and **venir,** and with telling time. Since you haven't practiced writing the time recently, you may wish to review Preparation 61 quickly.

1 Write complete sentences to say what time each clock shows.

 a   b   c   d

a *Il est quatre heures trois.*   **b** *Il est une heure et quart / une heure quinze.*   **c** *Il est neuf heures et demie / neuf heures trente.*   **d** *Il est sept heures moins le quart / six heures quarante-cinq.*

2 Write complete sentences to say where the following people are going, and at what time. Answers are in the answer key.

Modèle: le pilote
5:30

Le pilote va à l'aéroport à cinq heures et demie / cinq heures trente.

a nous
8:15

c les ouvrières
5:45

b le médecin
10:55

d le comptable
8:20

3 Write the French equivalent of *Where are you going?* (Use **tu** and inversion.)

Où vas-tu?

4 What do you think this means: **D'où viens-tu?**

From where are you coming? / Where are you coming from? (*De* becomes *D'* because it precedes a vowel sound.)

5 Write the French equivalent of *Where is she coming from?*

D'où vient-elle?

6 For each frame below, ask where the person is coming from, then give the person's answer, using the cue provided. Use the appropriate subject pronouns in your answers.

Modèle: Marc / café

–D'où vient Marc?   –Il vient du café.

a tu / station-service

–D'où viens-tu?   –Je viens de la station-service.

b Nathalie / banque **|**

–D'où vient Nathalie? –Elle vient de la banque.

c vous / supermarché **|**

–D'où venez-vous? –Nous venons du supermarché.

3 Practice with possessive markers

1 This part will give you further practice with **son, sa, ses, leur, leurs.**
  a Which markers are the French equivalent of *their?* **|**

leur, leurs

  b Which markers are equivalent to *her* and *his?* **|**

son, sa, ses

  c Which markers are used in plural noun phrases? **|**

ses, leurs

2 Use a possessive marker to say that each item below belongs to the
person or people mentioned. Answers are in the answer key.

Modèle: Marie a une moto. **|**

C'est sa moto.

a Pierre a un vélo.
b Eric et Jean ont une voiture.
c Corinne a une flûte.
d Nicolas a une guitare.

e Thierry et Jean ont une caméra.
f Elles ont des chiens.
g Etienne a des singes.
h Alice a un poisson.

PREPARATION *70*

1 Getting ready for a dictée

In class you will be having a *dictée.* The following frames will help you
connect the way a word looks with the way it sounds. Be sure to say all
the French sentences aloud.

1 In Preparation 63 you learned that the letter *g* may have a hard sound
as in *gomme* or a soft sound as in *manger.*
  a Is the *g* soft or hard if it precedes an *o* or an *a?* **|**

hard

  b Write the *nous*-form of *manger.* **|**

nous mangeons (You need an *e* between the *g* and *o* so that the stem of the
nous-form sounds the same as the stem of the other forms.)

2 Write the subject and corresponding form of *manger* for the following sentences.

    a Ils ____ du gâteau au chocolat.
    b Je ____ une tarte aux fraises.
    c Nous ____ de la glace à la vanille. |

a Ils mangent b Je mange c Nous mangeons

3 The letter *c* can have a hard sound or a soft sound.

    a Which of these words have a hard *c: cette, camping, curieux, cinéma, comment, célèbre?* |

camping, curieux, comment

    b A *c* can be soft even when it precedes an *a* or an *o* if it has a special mark. What mark is that? |

a cedilla (français, garçon)

4 Write the subject and corresponding form of *commencer* for each sentence. Both of the present-tense stems sound alike.

    a Tu ____ tes devoirs à 6 heures.   **b** Nous ____ nos devoirs à 8 heures. |

a Tu commences b Nous commençons

5 Several forms of *venir* sound alike, but are spelled differently. The subject pronoun tells you how to spell the verb. Write both the subject pronoun and the verb form for each sentence below.

    a Il ____ du bureau à 6 heures.
    b Tu ____ chez moi.
    c Ils ____ souvent chez nous. |

a Il vient b Tu viens c Ils viennent

6 Often the sound of the verb form will tell you which subject pronoun to use. Write the subject pronoun that completes each sentence below.

    a ____ prennent du café. (il, ils)
    b ____ prend une pomme. (elle, elles) |

a ils b elle

7 Many words may sound alike, but be spelled differently. The verb forms *manger* and *mangez* sound alike. Only the context will tell you how to spell them.

    Complete these sentences with the correct form of *manger.*

    a Est-ce que vous ____ avec moi?   **b** Non, je vais ____ avec ma copine. |

a vous mangez b je vais manger

8 The word *ses* and the phrase *c'est* also sound alike. Complete these sentences with the appropriate word or phrase.

    a ____ très beau.   **b** ____ cousins sont très beaux. |

a C'est b Ses

9 The plural and singular forms of many nouns sound identical. Markers and verbs will tell you whether the nouns are singular or plural. For items **a–c** insert the correct noun.

    a C'est son ____. (frères, frère)
    b Voilà ses ____. (sœurs, sœur)
    c Sa ____ a un beau chien. (cousines, cousine) |

a frère b sœurs c cousine

2 Practice with food

This part will give you a quick review of which markers to use when talking about food. Remember that markers change with the context.

1 Say that Paul is having a portion of each food listed. Use the verb *prendre.*

   a carottes   **c** bœuf
   b salade   **d** banane

> a *Paul prend des carottes.*   b *Paul prend de la salade.*   c *Paul prend du bœuf.*   d *Paul prend une banane.*

2 All these items are on the dinner table. Ask your neighbors to pass them to you. Use ***Passez-moi..., s'il vous plaît.***

   a eau   **c** tomates
   b poulet   **d** beurre

> a *Passez-moi l'eau, s'il vous plaît.*   b *Passez-moi le poulet, s'il vous plaît.*   c *Passez-moi les tomates, s'il vous plaît.*   d *Passez-moi le beurre, s'il vous plaît.*

3 Say that Jacques hates all these kinds of foods.

   a légumes   **c** salade
   b viande   **d** fruits

> a *Jacques déteste les légumes.*   b *Jacques déteste la viande.*   c *Jacques déteste la salade.*   d *Jacques déteste les fruits.*

4 You and some friends are at a café. To make things easier, you do all the ordering. Write what you would say to the waiter.

      Modèle: 1 thé

>   *Nous voulons un thé.*

   a 2 cafés   **c** 1 tarte aux fraises
   b 1 jus d'orange   **d** 3 glaces

> *Nous voulons deux cafés, un jus d'orange, une tarte aux fraises et trois glaces.*

NOTE

Le Goûter

For an after-school snack **(goûter),** French children like **une tartine,** a slice of bread with either a piece of chocolate or some **confiture** or honey **(miel).** Sometimes on the way home from school they buy **un pain au chocolat** (a soft roll with a piece of chocolate baked in its center). Water or perhaps **du jus de fruit** is the usual beverage, although during cold weather **du chocolat chaud** or **du café au lait** may accompany the snack.

Sirops de fruits Teisseire

1 *Making up a menu*

In this part you will make up three sample meals: breakfast, lunch, and dinner.

The following frames will help you remember the French for certain words. Write the complete noun phrase in each answer.

1 The French word for *lunch* is *le* ___. ❙

> *le déjeuner*

2 In French, the phrase for *breakfast* is the equivalent of *little lunch*. It is *le* ___. ❙

> *le petit déjeuner*

3 The French word for *dinner* is a cognate, but the spelling is different. Write the complete word: *le __î__er.* ❙

> *le dîner*

4 *Un sandwich au jambon* is *a ham* ___. ❙

> *a ham sandwich*

5 What is *a cheese sandwich* in French? ❙

> *un sandwich au fromage*

6 *An apple pie* is ___ *aux pommes.* ❙

> *une tarte aux pommes*

7 *A strawberry pie* is ___ *aux* ___. ❙

> *une tarte aux fraises*

8 *Some vanilla ice cream* is ___ *à la vanille.* ❙

> *de la glace à la vanille*

9 *Some chocolate ice cream* is ___ *au* ___. ❙

> *de la glace au chocolat*

SOUPE, VIANDE, ETC.	ŒUFS ET PRODUITS LAITIERS	FRUITS ET LÉGUMES	DESSERTS
le bœuf	le beurre	la banane	le fromage
le poisson	le fromage	la fraise	le gâteau (au chocolat)
le porc	la glace	l'orange (f.)	la glace
le poulet	le lait	le pamplemousse	la tarte (aux pommes)
le sandwich (au jambon)	l'œuf (m.)	la poire	le yaourt
la saucisse	le yaourt	la pomme	
la soupe		la carotte	PAIN, ETC.
le steak	BOISSONS	les frites	le croissant
le steak haché	le café	les haricots verts	le pain
	le chocolat au lait	la laitue	le petit pain
	l'eau (f.) minérale	les pommes de terre	le pain grillé
	le jus d'orange	la salade	la confiture
	le lait	la tomate	
	le thé		

Now write the French headings for breakfast, lunch, and dinner. Then write your menu for each of these meals. You may want to refer to the list of foods on p. 298 (***produits laitiers*** means *dairy products*). List at least 4 items for breakfast, 4 items for lunch, and 6 items for dinner. Use a partitive marker, an indefinite marker, or a number (for example, ***deux œufs***). You'll have a chance to compare menus with your classmates.

2 Getting ready to talk about food

In the next few class meetings you will be talking and writing about food. This section of the Preparation will help you prepare to talk about the foods you like and dislike.

1 Say that you like these foods in general: ***viande, haricots verts, jambon.*** ❙

> *J'aime la viande, les haricots verts et le jambon.*

2 Say that you want some of the following foods and beverages: ***salade, eau minérale, tomates, bonbons.*** ❙

> *Je veux de la salade, de l'eau minérale, des tomates et des bonbons.*

3 Say that you don't like the foods listed below.

> Modèle: porc ❙
>
> *Je n'aime pas le porc.*

a riz
b carottes
c pamplemousses ❙

> a *Je n'aime pas le riz.*   b *Je n'aime pas les carottes.*   c *Je n'aime pas les pamplemousses.*

4 Say that you aren't going to have any of the foods listed below.

> Modèle: frites ❙
>
> *Je ne vais pas prendre de frites.*

a café
b croissants
c bœuf
d fruits ❙

> a *Je ne vais pas prendre de café.*   b *Je ne vais pas prendre de croissants.*   c *Je ne vais pas prendre de bœuf.*   d *Je ne vais pas prendre de fruits.*

5 Write the English equivalent for ***Pour le dîner, je vais prendre de la soupe.*** ❙

> *For dinner, I'll have (some) soup.*

6 Write the French equivalent of *I'll have a ham sandwich for lunch.* ❙

> *Pour le déjeuner, je vais prendre un sandwich au jambon.*

7 Write a complete sentence telling two of the things you will have for breakfast. ❙

> *Pour le petit déjeuner, je vais prendre des croissants et du thé.*

1 *Reading comprehension:* **La Truite d'Or**

In class you will have an opportunity to play the part of a customer or a server in a restaurant skit. The following dialogue will give you an idea of what kinds of things you can say.

First, read the dialogue once straight through. Keep the words in the margin covered and use them only after you've tried to guess the general meaning of the new words in context. As you read, look for the answers to the following questions.

Does M. Grandet order chicken, meat or fish? What does he have to drink with his meal? He is offered ice cream, pastry, fruit, and cheese for dessert—what does he have?

After reading the dialogue, do frames 1–4. This will give you some practice with new expressions and vocabulary.

La Truite d'Or°

The Golden Trout

MAÎTRE D'HÔTEL°	Bonsoir, Monsieur.	headwaiter
M. GRANDET	Bonsoir, Pierre. Ça va?	
MAÎTRE D'HÔTEL	Très bien, merci, Monsieur. Vous voulez cette table, n'est-ce pas?	
5 M. GRANDET	Oui, comme d'habitude°. (*Il s'assied*°.)	as always / he sits down
MAÎTRE D'HÔTEL	Vous voulez regarder le menu, Monsieur?	
M. GRANDET	Oui, s'il vous plaît.	
MAÎTRE D'HÔTEL	(*Il lui donne*° *le menu.*) Voilà, Monsieur. Bon appétit!	gives him
10	(*M. Grandet regarde le menu, puis fait signe*° *à la serveuse*°.)	signals waitress
SERVEUSE	Bonsoir, Monsieur. Vous voulez commander°?	to order
M. GRANDET	Oui. Voyons°... (*Il regarde le menu.*) comme	let's see
15	hors-d'œuvre...du pâté°, du saucisson°....Non... Qu'est-ce que vous avez comme soupe?	meat spread / salami-like sausage
SERVEUSE	Ce soir, nous avons de la soupe à l'oignon°. Elle est très bonne.	onion soup
M. GRANDET	D'accord, je prends la soupe à l'oignon.	
20	Comme plat°... (*Il regarde le menu.*)	main dish
	Voyons...Poulet aux champignons°, gigot	mushrooms
	d'agneau°, truite°... Je vais prendre le gigot	leg of lamb / trout
	d'agneau.	

SERVEUSE	Bien, Monsieur. Qu'est-ce que vous voulez comme légumes? Nous avons des haricots verts, des carottes, des petits pois et des oignons à la crème°.	creamed onions
M. GRANDET	Je vais prendre les haricots verts. Vous avez des pommes de terre?	
SERVEUSE	Oui, Monsieur. Des pommes au gratin°, des frites...	with grated bread crumbs and cheese
M. GRANDET	Des pommes au gratin...	
SERVEUSE	Bien, Monsieur. Vous allez prendre une salade?	
M. GRANDET	Bien sûr! Maintenant, comme boisson...	
SERVEUSE	Du vin° rosé? rouge?	wine
M. GRANDET	Non, pas de vin aujourd'hui. Une demi-bouteille° d'eau minérale.	half-bottle
SERVEUSE	Bien, Monsieur.	
	(*Plus tard...*)	
SERVEUSE	C'est terminé° avec le gigot, Monsieur? On peut débarrasser°?	are you finished? / clear the table
M. GRANDET	Oui...Qu'est-ce que vous avez comme dessert?	
SERVEUSE	Nous avons de la glace, des fruits, des pâtisseries°...	pastries
M. GRANDET	Euh... Quels fruits avez-vous?	
SERVEUSE	Des poires et des pêches.	
M. GRANDET	Bon, alors je vais prendre une pêche.	
SERVEUSE	Du fromage avant le dessert, Monsieur?	
M. GRANDET	Non, pas de fromage, merci.	
SERVEUSE	Bien, Monsieur.	
M. GRANDET	Et donnez-moi° l'addition° avec le dessert, s'il vous plaît. Je suis un peu pressé ce soir.	give me / bill
SERVEUSE	Très bien, Monsieur.	

1 Now go back and read lines 1–13 again, then answer the following questions with a word or phrase.

a M. Grandet mange-t-il souvent au restaurant ***La Truite d'Or?*** |

oui (You can tell because he knows the Maître d'hôtel, and he says he'll sit at his usual table.)

b Comment dit-on *to order* en français? |

commander

c Qui est-ce qui commande? le maître d'hôtel? la serveuse? M. Grandet? |

M. Grandet

2 Now read lines 14–23.

a Qu'est-ce que M. Grandet prend comme soupe? |

de la soupe à l'oignon

b Est-ce que la truite est un dessert ou un poisson? ▮
un poisson

3 Answer these questions based on lines 24–35.
   a Qu'est-ce que M. Grandet prend avec le gigot d'agneau? ▮
des haricots verts, des pommes au gratin
   b M. Grandet prend de la salade? ▮
oui

4 Reread lines 35–54.
   a Qu'est-ce qu'il prend comme boisson? ▮
une demi-bouteille d'eau minérale
   b À *La Truite d'Or,* qu'est-ce qu'il y a comme dessert? ▮
de la glace, des fruits, des pâtisseries

NOTE

Crêpes

In the United States we serve pancakes for a hearty breakfast. The French serve **crêpes** for snacks or parties, lunch or dinner. **Crêpes** are very thin pancakes fried to a golden brown on the griddle. When served as **entrées,** the **crêpes** are filled with such delicacies as shrimp, lobster, or melted cheese. Dessert **crêpes** can be prepared in many ways. Sometimes they are sprinkled with sugar; sometimes they are covered with a butter sauce cooked and flavored with orange liqueur; sometimes they are topped with jelly, and then folded and served. Tourists in France can sample **crêpes** without splurging on **haute cuisine.** Vendors sell "dessert" **crêpes** on beaches and street corners for the price of an ice cream cone.

   La Chandeleur, a holiday on February 2, has traditionally been an occasion for families to get together and eat **crêpes.** Sometimes people will try to flip the **crêpe** with a **coup sec** (a quick flick of the wrist) while holding a gold coin in the other hand. According to custom, if they succeed in flipping the **crêpe** without dropping the coin, they will prosper in the coming year.

TO MAKE A DOZEN **CRÊPES—**

one egg	butter for the pan
one cup of flour	confectioners' sugar
one cup of milk	jam
one teaspoon oil	ice cream
a pinch of salt	

Combine the egg and the flour. Add the milk, the oil, and the salt. It is a good idea to put this through a blender. Let the **pâte** (the batter) sit, covered, for a few hours in the refrigerator. Heat a frying pan and melt a teaspoon of butter. Pour in a small amount of batter to cover the pan with a thin coating. (You may have to tilt and turn the pan to help spread the batter.) After a few moments, turn the **crêpe** to brown it on both sides. Slide it onto a plate. Add some sugar, perhaps ice cream, custard sauce, and/or marmalade. Fold it in four. **Voilà!**

---

2 Equivalents of "to be"

1 This frame will help you check whether you remember which verbs are used in certain French expressions.

a Which French verb is used to talk about the weather? *Il ___ beau.* (Write the infinitive form of the verb.) |

   faire

b Which French verb is used to talk about age? *Elle ___ 45 ans.* |

   avoir

c Which verb is used to talk about being cold, hot, hungry, thirsty? *Nous ___ très faim.* |

   avoir

d Which verb is used to talk about health? *Vous ___ bien?* |

   aller

2 Two neighbors have just met in the street. Complete their dialogue with the correct forms of the verbs *être, avoir, aller,* or *faire.* Answers are in the answer key.

–Bonjour, Monsieur, comment ___-vous?

–Bien merci. Quel beau temps, n'est-ce pas?

–Oui. Mais il ___ frais.

–Ah oui? Vous ___ froid?

–Oui, un peu.

–Venez prendre un café avec moi. Vous n' ___ pas pressé?

–Si, malheureusement. Je ___ en retard.

1 Pre-test practice: prendre

In a few days you will have a progress test. Before you begin the review exercises here, you may wish to look through the Summary beginning on p. 311. (All answers to pre-test practices are in the answer key.)

  Practice using *prendre* by writing the verb form that completes each of the following sentences. The present tense of *prendre* was presented in Preparation 62.

1 Est-ce que tu ___ du chocolat au lait?

2 Mes parents ___ du vin.

3 Nous ___ des cerises comme dessert.

4 Vont-ils ___ du café après le dessert?

5 Moi, je ne ___ pas de café.

6 Vous ne ___ pas de jus d'orange aujourd'hui?

2 Pre-test practice: markers with food

Write the markers that complete each sentence: definite (*le, la, les*), partitive (*du, de la, de l'*), or indefinite (*un, une, des*). Markers with food were practiced in Preparations 61, 62, 63, 64, 65, 67, 68, 70, 71.

1 Elle n'aime pas ____ chocolat au lait mais elle aime beaucoup ____ café au lait.

2 Ma sœur et moi, nous aimons ____ viande, mais nous ne prenons pas ____ viande aujourd'hui.

3 Je ne veux pas ____ petits pois, parce que je n'aime pas ____ légumes.

4 Aimez-vous ____ fraises? Voudriez-vous ____ fraises avec ____ sucre?

5 Chantal n'aime pas ____ cerises, mais elle veut prendre ____ banane.

6 Suzanne aime ____ jambon. Elle voudrait ____ jambon pour son déjeuner.

7 Paul aime bien ____ pommes. Il va avoir ____ pomme comme dessert.

8 Yvonne adore ____ chocolat. Mais elle est au régime; elle ne prend pas ____ chocolat.

9 J'aime beaucoup ____ eau minérale. Je vais prendre ____ eau minérale maintenant.

10 Le petit Jean veut ____ bonbons, mais sa mère n'a pas ____ bonbons.

Vendeur de glace au Sénégal

3 Pre-test practice: stressed pronouns

Stressed pronouns were presented in Preparation 53 and practiced in Preparation 65.

Say what these people are doing at four o'clock. Start each sentence with a stressed pronoun to refer to the person named.

Modèle: Catherine: jouer aux cartes. |

Elle, elle joue aux cartes.

1 Nicolas: faire des commissions
2 je: faire mes devoirs
3 vous: écouter la radio

4 tu: chanter
5 Pierre et Sophie: aller au cinéma
6 Marie et Nathalie: jouer aux échecs

4 Pre-test practice: rejoinders

For each item below choose the response that is most logical.

1 Vous aimez les fruits?
  a Oui, je les vois.
  b Oui, beaucoup, comme dessert.
  c Bon, ce soir, sans faute.
2 Voulez-vous voir ce film de science-fiction?
  a Formidable! C'est mon sport préféré.
  b Oui, mais je n'ai pas soif.
  c Non, merci. J'ai trop de devoirs.
3 Y a-t-il des sandwichs au jambon?
  a Mais si! Je mange bien à midi.
  b Non, mais il y a des croque-monsieurs.
  c Bonne idée! Nous allons au restaurant.
4 Je n'aime pas la viande.
  a Alors, il faut prendre du bœuf.
  b Alors, il faut prendre de la viande.
  c Alors, il faut prendre du poisson.
5 Est-ce qu'on fait du ski en été?
  a Mais oui! On fait du ski en hiver.
  b Mais non! On fait du ski en hiver.
  c Mais si! On fait du ski en hiver.
6 On va à la plage?
  a D'accord! Je vais avec toi!
  b Je vais bien, merci.
  c Bof! Je ne sais pas patiner.

1 *Pre-test practice:* **venir**

The present-tense forms of *venir* were presented in Preparations 68 and
69. For practice, write the verb forms that complete each of the following sentences.
1 Hé, Paul, tu ___ avec moi travailler à la bibliothèque cet après-midi?
2 Ma tante Sophie ___ toujours chez nous le vendredi soir.
3 Dites, vous voulez ___ jouer aux cartes?
4 Avril ___ après mars.
5 Vous ___ d'Italie, n'est-ce pas, Madame Gardini?
6 Le printemps ___ après l'hiver.
7 –Albert, où es-tu? –Je ___, maman!
8 Nous ___ toujours à ce café après les matchs de tennis.
9 Voilà nos parents qui ___ nous chercher!

2 *Pre-test practice: possessive markers*

You practiced using the possessive markers *son, sa, ses, leur, leurs* in
Preparations 66 and 69. Complete these sentences with the appropriate
possessive marker.

> Modèle: Les Vincent ont une jolie maison. C'est ___ maison. I
> *leur*

1 Annick a un bateau à voile. C'est ___ bateau à voile.
2 Bernard a une flûte. C'est ___ flûte.
3 Mes parents ont une télévision. C'est ___ télévision.
4 Le professeur a des livres sur la table. Ce sont ___ livres.
5 M. et Mme Martin n'habitent pas dans cette maison. Ce n'est pas ___
maison.

3 *Pre-test practice: reading comprehension*

This section will help you prepare for the reading comprehension
exercise in the test. Read the following passage carefully. Then answer
the multiple-choice questions by writing the correct word or phrase.

Nadine est une jolie lycéenne de 15 ans. Elle est gentille et intelligente,
mais elle a un problème: elle est trop maigre. Elle n'aime pas manger, et
elle ne prend pas de petit déjeuner.

Saucisse sèche d'Auvergne

pur porc · sans colorant

Calixte à Vernoux en Vivarais · Ardèche

Samedi matin, Nadine est chez elle. Elle monte (*climbs*) sur la bascule (*scale*) et...oh là là...elle pèse seulement 45 kilos (*99 lbs.*)! Elle est trop maigre! C'est décidé: elle n'a pas faim, mais elle va manger son petit déjeuner. Et à midi elle mange beaucoup: du steak haché, des frites, des haricots verts, de la salade, du fromage, du pain, une pomme et une poire. À 4 heures elle mange du pain et du chocolat, et elle prend du jus d'orange. Vite, elle monte sur la bascule: 46 kilos maintenant! Fantastique! Mais à 8 heures elle est très malheureuse: elle n'a pas faim, elle ne peut pas dîner!

1 Nadine est...
  a étudiante **b** écolière **c** lycéenne
2 Elle est...
  a moche **b** laide **c** jolie
3 Elle n'est pas...
  a intelligente **b** stupide **c** gentille
4 Mais elle a un problème. Elle est...
  a grande **b** maigre **c** grosse
5 Alors, samedi matin elle décide de...
  a manger son dîner **b** ne pas manger **c** manger son petit déjeuner
6 Elle déjeune à quelle heure?
  a à midi **b** à 4 heures **c** à une heure
7 Pour le déjeuner elle ne mange pas de...
  a viande **b** légumes **c** poisson
8 À quatre heures elle mange...
  a des croissants **b** du lait et du pain **c** du pain et du chocolat
9 L'après-midi, Nadine monte sur la bascule. Est-elle heureuse?
  a oui **b** non
10 À huit heures, elle...
  a a soif **b** a faim **c** n'a pas faim

Getting ready for a test

In your next class you will have a test. If you have been doing your homework regularly and participating actively in class, you will be ready for the test. This Preparation will give you practice with the kinds of questions you can expect. If you need extra practice, review the Summary and go over earlier Preparations. All answers are in the answer key.

1 In Part A, you will hear a series of short French conversations between two teenagers, Alain and Valérie. On your answer sheet you will see questions in English based on the conversations. You are to write the answers in English.

    a (Alain): Est-ce que je peux venir chez toi cet après-midi?
        (Valérie): Oui, bien sûr.
        What is Alain going to do this afternoon?
    b (Alain): Tu sais, je commence mon régime aujourd'hui.
        (Valérie): Pourquoi? Tu n'es pas gros!
        What is Alain doing today?

2 In Part B, you will see some pictures of foods, labeled A, B, C, etc. You will hear a series of statements in French. You are to write the letter of the food item or items that are mentioned in each statement.

    a You hear: *Est-ce que Renée va prendre une poire ou du fromage?*
        You write the letters ____ and ____.
    b You hear: *Tu veux de la viande ou du poisson?*
        You write the letters ____ and ____.

  3 In Part C, you will hear a question or statement. You are to circle the letter of the most logical response.

    a Les singes n'aiment pas les bananes.
      A Mais si, ils les aiment!
      B Oui, ils ont faim.
      C Oh, zut! Il n'y a pas de bananes.
    b Veux-tu aller au stade avec moi?
      A Oui, parce que j'aime bien le cinéma.
      B D'accord! Je veux bien.
      C Mais non! Je n'ai pas froid.

4 In Part D, you will see a series of paired sentences. You will be asked to complete the second sentence in each pair with the appropriate indefinite or partitive marker.

    a -J'aime beaucoup le thé.
       –Veux-tu prendre ____ thé maintenant?
    b Ma mère aime les légumes.
       Elle achète ____ petits pois.
    c –Il aime les fruits comme dessert?
       –Oui, il va prendre ____ pomme.
    d Noëlle aime le sucre, mais elle est au régime.
       Alors, elle ne prend pas ____ sucre avec son café.

5 In Part E, you are to complete some sentences by writing the correct form of *prendre.*

    a Vous ____ du fromage?
    b Elles ____ une glace comme dessert.
    c Tu vas ____ du poisson?
    d Je ____ souvent du thé.

6 In Part F, you are to complete some sentences by writing the correct form of *venir.*

    a Les petits enfants ____ du parc.
    b ____-vous de Marseille, Madame?
    c À quelle heure ____-il?
    d Je ____ chez toi à 4 heures.

7 In Part G, you are to complete some sentences by filling in the blanks with the correct form of *être, avoir, aller,* or *faire.*

    a Marie-Jeanne ____ très faim.
    b Il ____ du vent aujoud-hui.
    c Mais oui, je ____ américaine!
    d Salut! Comment ____-tu?

8 In Part H, you will read a series of pairs of sentences. You are to complete the second sentence of each pair with the correct marker: *son, sa, ses, leur,* or *leurs.*

       Modèle: Mes parents ont une maison. C'est ____ maison. |
                  leur

    a M. Leblanc a un restaurant. ____ restaurant est très joli.
    b Mon ami Georges a une station-service. ____ station-service est à Lyon.
    c On aime manger les croissants de Mme Filibert. ____ croissants sont très bons.

9 In Part I, you are to complete sentences to say that people are going home. Use the appropriate stressed pronoun.

    a Je vais chez ____.
    b Il va chez ____.
    c Elles vont chez ____.
    d Ils vont chez ____.

10 In Part J, you read a narrative. Then you see some multiple-choice questions. You are to circle the letter of the correct answer.

Les Guilbert vont toujours au supermarché le vendredi. Il faut acheter de la viande, des légumes et des fruits pour le week-end. Mais ce samedi, des amis viennent dîner. Alors, il faut trouver un dessert spécial—une bonne glace au chocolat, peut-être?

  a Les Guilbert vont toujours au supermarché...
    A quand il fait beau
    B le vendredi
    C le samedi
  b Ils veulent trouver une bonne glace au chocolat...
    A parce qu'ils aiment la glace.
    B parce que c'est vendredi.
    C parce que des amis viennent dîner chez eux.

11 In Part K, you answer questions with complete sentences.
  a Qu'est-ce que vous préférez comme petit déjeuner?
  b Qu'est-ce que vous allez manger ce soir pour le dîner?

SUMMARY

1 **Count nouns and measure nouns** (*Preparations 60, 61, 63, 68*)

    a. Nouns representing things that can be counted are called *count nouns*. They may occur in the singular or plural.

J'ai une pomme.	I have an apple.
Je veux dix oranges.	I want ten oranges.

    b. Nouns representing things that are usually measured, like milk or water, are called *measure nouns*. Measure nouns are almost always used in the singular.

Je veux du lait.	I want some milk.
Je prends de l'eau.	I'm having some water.

    c. Some nouns may be used as either count nouns or measure nouns.

Je veux un poulet.	I want a (whole) chicken.
Je veux du poulet.	I want some chicken.

2 **Some vs. all** (*Preparation 63*)

    a. The type of marker used with count and measure nouns varies with the context of the sentence.

	COUNT NOUNS	MEASURE NOUNS
All of a category	J'aime les légumes. J'adore les fruits. Je déteste les gâteaux.	J'aime le pain. J'adore la viande. Je déteste l'eau.
Some portion of a category	J'ai un pamplemousse. Je mange une carotte. Je veux des croissants.	J'ai du fromage. Je mange de la viande. Je veux de l'eau.

    b. The verbs *aimer, adorer, détester* usually refer to a whole category. Definite markers are generally used with nouns following these verbs.

    c. The verbs *avoir, manger, vouloir, prendre* usually refer to some portion of a category. The expressions *il y a, c'est,* and *ce sont* also usually refer to a portion. Indefinite and partitive markers are usually used with nouns following these verbs.

    d. In English, nouns are often used without markers. In French, however, nouns are almost always used with markers.

J'aime les fraises.	I like strawberries.
Il veut du café.	He wants (some) coffee.

3 Focusing attention (*Preparation 67*)

Indefinite and partitive markers are used to focus attention on the kind of food under discussion. Definite markers are used to refer again to the item mentioned.

–J'ai une pêche et une poire. Qu'est-ce que tu veux?
–Je prends la poire.

4 Markers in negative sentences (*Preparation 61*)

a. Definite markers do not change in negative sentences.

J'aime la glace.   *Je n'aime pas la glace.*

b. Indefinite and partitive markers change to *de (d')* in negative sentences with almost all verbs.

*Tu veux **des** cerises?*	*Non, je ne veux pas **de** cerises.*
*Vous prenez **de la** viande?*	*Non, je ne prends pas **de** viande.*
*Vous voulez **de l'**eau?*	*Non, je ne veux pas **d'**eau.*

The major exception is *être*. **Ce n'est pas une pomme, c'est une poire.**

c. In French, markers are always used with nouns in negative sentences. They do not always occur in English.

Je ne veux pas de yaourt.	I don't want (any) yogurt.
Je n'aime pas les cerises.	I don't like cherries.

5 The present tense of prendre *and* venir (*Preparations 62, 68*)

a. The present-tense endings of ***prendre*** (to take) and ***venir*** (to come) are identical except for the ***on/il/elle***-form. The stems are irregular.

je	prend	s	vien	s
tu	prend	s	vien	s
on/il/elle	prend		vien	t
ils/elles	prenn	ent	vienn	ent
nous	pren	ons	ven	ons
vous	pren	ez	ven	ez

b. When ***prendre*** is used with meals or with items of food, it often means *to have*, in the sense of *to eat* or *to drink*.

6 The present-tense forms of manger *and* commencer (*Preparation 63*)

In the present tense, ***manger*** and ***commencer*** are regular *-er* verbs, except for a spelling change in the ***nous***-form stem: ***nous mangeons, nous commençons.***

7 Il faut + *infinitive* (*Preparation 64*)

Il faut is an impersonal expression meaning *it is necessary, you must, one must.* It is often followed by an infinitive or an infinitive phrase.

Il faut travailler.   It's necessary (you must, one must) work.

8 Questions with inverted word order *(Preparation 68)*

    a. In speech, inversion of subject and verb is common in set phrases such as **Quelle heure est-il?** Inversion is often used in written French.

       Vous habitez à Paris?   *Habitez-vous à Paris?*   Do you live in Paris?

    b. With an **on/il/elle**-form that ends in a written vowel, a **-t-** is inserted between the verb and the subject. This occurs in the present-tense forms of **avoir, aller,** and all other **-er** verbs.

       Quel âge a-t-elle?   *Comment va-t-il?*   *Habite-t-elle à Paris?*

    c. Inversion almost never occurs with the **je**-form. Rising intonation, an **est-ce que** phrase, or a *tag phrase* is used instead.

9 The forms of quel *(Preparation 69)*

    a. The written form of **quel?** (what?, which?) matches the noun to which it refers. It has four written forms, but only one spoken form: **Quel garçon? Quelle fille? Quels garçons? Quelles filles?**

    b. **Quel** is also used in exclamations: **Quel bon film!** (What a good movie!)

10 Stressed pronouns *(Preparation 65)*

Stressed pronouns may be used to give emphasis. They can also be used after a preposition (such as **chez**), or alone.

*je / **moi***   *il / **lui***   *ils / **eux***   *nous / **nous***
*tu / **toi***   *elle / **elle***   *elles / **elles***   *vous / **vous***

Moi, j'aime faire du patin.   I like to skate.
Tu vas chez toi?   Are you going home?
–Qui est là? –Moi.   –Who's there? –Me.

11 More about telling time *(Preparation 61)*

In French, the hour is given first. The minutes or parts of an hour are then added or subtracted.

Il est huit heures vingt.

Il est huit heures moins vingt.

Il est huit heures et quart.

Il est huit heures moins le quart.

Il est midi.

Il est minuit.

Les Résolutions de Marie-Jeanne

Marie-Jeanne est une jolie lycéenne de 16 ans. Elle n'est pas très grande (elle mesure 1,52 m) et elle pense qu'elle est trop grosse (elle pèse 52 kilos). Son grand problème est qu'elle adore manger! Que faire?

SCÈNE 1   *Le réveil*

C'est le matin. Mme Bertrand entre dans la chambre de sa fille, Marie-Jeanne, et la réveille.

MÈRE	Debout, Marie-Jeanne! Il est sept heures moins le quart. Le petit déjeuner est prêt.
MARIE-JEANNE	Je peux dormir encore un peu. Je ne veux pas de petit déjeuner.
MÈRE	Ah? Pourquoi?
MARIE-JEANNE	Parce que je suis au régime.
MÈRE	Tu es folle! Tu ne peux pas aller en classe sans manger.
MARIE-JEANNE	Mais si, je peux... Je n'ai pas faim.
MÈRE	Vraiment? Il y a du chocolat au lait, des croissants chauds, de la confiture...
MARIE-JEANNE	Oh non, arrête, arrête...
MÈRE	Écoute, il faut manger le matin. Tu peux commencer ton régime à midi.
MARIE-JEANNE	Bon, d'accord. À midi, sans faute.

SCÈNE 2   *Un message publicitaire*

Marie-Jeanne mange son petit déjeuner avec grand plaisir. En même temps, elle écoute distraitement la radio: musique, informations, météo... Soudain un message publicitaire attire son attention.

«Êtes-vous jeune, jolie et solitaire? Vos amies vont au cinéma, à la plage, à la discothèque avec des jeunes gens beaux et élégants. Mais vous, on ne vous invite pas. Pourquoi? Vous savez la réponse... Vous n'êtes pas mince, vous n'êtes pas élégante. Vite, commencez votre régime—AU-JOURD'HUI—avec SILHOUETTE, le yaourt diététique et nourrissant. SIL-HOUETTE, le yaourt naturel! SILHOUETTE, le dessert idéal des personnes minces, élégantes et raffinées!»

Marie-Jeanne arrête la radio... C'est décidé: elle va manger du yaourt et seulement du yaourt...!

SCÈNE 3   *À la cantine scolaire*

Il est midi, l'heure du déjeuner à la cantine scolaire. Marie-Jeanne est avec son amie Yvonne dans la cour du lycée.

YVONNE   Tu viens déjeuner, Marie-Jeanne?
MARIE-JEANNE   Non, je ne déjeune pas aujourd'hui.
YVONNE   Pourquoi? Tu n'as pas faim?
MARIE-JEANNE   Si, j'ai faim. Mais je suis au régime.
YVONNE   Ah oui? Depuis quand?
MARIE-JEANNE   Depuis aujourd'hui.
YVONNE   Quel dommage! Et il y a du steak haché et des frites.
MARIE-JEANNE   Oh non...! J'adore les frites...
YVONNE   Alors viens. Tu peux commencer ton régime ce soir.
MARIE-JEANNE   Bon, ce soir, sans faute!

EXERCICES

1 French terms related to cooking and restaurants

café	à la carte	soufflé	parfait
restaurant	hors d'œuvre	filet mignon	à la mode
chef	soupe du jour	au gratin	flambé
maître	entrée	au jus	bon appétit
d'hôtel	dessert	roquefort	gourmet

2 Visual-lingual drill: stressed pronouns

1 Bertrand	1 dormir
2 je	2 manger chez mes grands-parents
3 Marie	3 aller au musée
4 Jean et Eric	4 faire une promenade
5 tu	5 jouer de la guitare
6 Sylvie et Marc	6 écouter des disques
7 nous	7 regarder la télévision
8 Béatrice et Diane	8 tricoter
9 vous	9 jouer aux boules

3 Pronunciation practice: g *and* c

/ʒ/	/g/	/s/	/k/
gentil	garçon	cinéma	caméra
girafe	magasin	cinq	cadeau
régime	guitare	célèbre	comptable
ingénieur	gomme	cymbale	comment
gymnastique	grand	garçon	parc

4 Paired words

avant - après	heureux - malheureux	bien - mal
ici - là-bas	merveilleux - affreux	commencer - terminer
vite - lentement	bon - mauvais	minuit - midi

5 Practice with food

6 Food vocabulary

1 une tomate	6 le porc	11 un bonbon
2 une carotte	7 un hot dog	12 un gâteau
3 une banane	8 un hamburger	13 un petit pain
4 une orange	9 un pamplemousse	14 le pain grillé
5 la salade	10 le bœuf	

7 Visual-lingual drill: possessive markers

1 Le frère	1 de Béatrice	1 faire du ski
2 La sœur	2 d'Alain et Chantal	2 faire une promenade
3 Le copain	3 de Thierry	3 faire du camping
4 Les copines	4 de Véronique et Sophie	4 faire du patin
5 Les copains	5 de Bernard	5 faire du bateau

8 Food

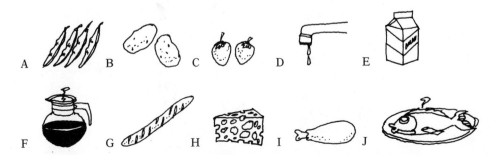

DES GOÛTS

ET DES COULEURS

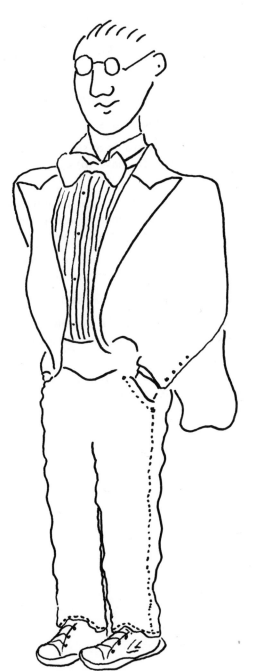

PHASE SIX OBJECTIVES

In this Phase you will talk about buying and wearing clothing for school, sports, and leisure activities. By the end of this Phase, you should be able to:

1 Identify various articles of clothing.

2 Tell what color something is.

3 Say what people have to do or should do, by using the verb **devoir** (to have to) or the expression **il faut.**

4 Talk about clothing with the verbs **acheter** (to buy), **préférer** (to prefer), **donner** (to give), **porter** (to wear), and **mettre** (to put on, to wear).

5 Refer to people or things you've already mentioned, using indirect object pronouns.

6 Report what someone else has said.

7 Use the French equivalents for **something** and **nothing, someone** and **no one, sometimes** and **never.**

8 Make a suggestion or tell someone what to do, using **nous-, vous-,** and **tu-**command forms of verbs.

❀ The cultural notes describe some French attitudes toward buying clothes, some regional costumes, and some of the background of the French Revolution.

1 *The present tense of* devoir

This section will show you how to say in French that you have to or you must do something, by using forms of the verb *devoir* with the infinitive form of another verb.

1 Victor can't play tennis today. Read the following conversation to find out why.

> Michel: *Dis, Victor, tu veux jouer au tennis?*
> Victor: *Non, je ne peux pas.*
> Michel: *Pourquoi pas?*
> Victor: *Je dois faire mes devoirs.*

a Why can't Victor play tennis? |

Because he has to do his homework.

b One English equivalent of *Je dois faire mes devoirs* is *I have to do my homework.* What are some other equivalents that mean just about the same thing as *I have to?* |

I must / I should / I'm supposed to / I've got to

2 In *Je dois faire mes devoirs,* what verb form follows *je dois?* |

infinitive

3 Complete each French equivalent below with *je dois* and the appropriate infinitive.

a I have to make a birthday cake. ____ *un gâteau d'anniversaire.* |

Je dois faire

b I must do some errands. ____ *des commissions.* |

Je dois faire

c I've got to work Saturday. ____ *samedi.* |

Je dois travailler

4 Here is a chart showing the present-tense forms of *devoir.* Use the chart to help you do items **a–d** below.

je	doi	s
tu	doi	s
on/il/elle	doi	t
ils/elles	doiv	ent
nous	dev	ons
vous	dev	ez

a The present tense of *devoir* has three stems. What are they? |

doi-, doiv-, dev-

b Which stem occurs in the *je-, tu-,* and *on/il/elle*-forms? |

doi-

c Which stem occurs in the *nous-* and *vous*-forms? |

dev-

d Which stem occurs in the *ils/elles*-form? |

doiv-

5 Now read aloud each subject pronoun and the corresponding verb from the chart. Then complete the sentences below without looking at the chart. Answers are given after item **f.** Tell what these people have to do. Write the appropriate forms of **devoir** on your worksheet.

a Les enfants Dulac ____ aller chez le dentiste.

b Vous ____ dîner à huit heures ce soir.

c Tu ____ trouver ton imperméable.

d Dans ce cours on ____ parler français.

e Mon père ____ aller chercher la voiture.

f Nous ____ faire nos devoirs ce soir. ❙

a *doivent*   b *devez*   c *dois*   d *doit*   e *doit*   f *devons*

2   *Practice with agreement of adjectives*

As you do this part, remember that in French the form of an adjective must match the number and gender of the noun it describes. Most feminine adjectives are formed by adding *-e* to the masculine. The plural of most adjectives is formed by adding *-s* to the singular.

1 Complete the second sentence in each pair with the appropriate form of the adjective used in the first sentence.

Modèle: Jean est un élève intelligent.
Jeanne est une élève ____ . ❙
intelligente

a Paul est un touriste américain.
Ces femmes sont des touristes ____ . ❙
américaines

b Annette est petite.
Louis et Jean-Paul sont ____ . ❙
petits

c Alain est absent aujourd'hui.
Nicole est ____ aujourd'hui. ❙
absente

d David est intelligent.
Sara et Madeleine sont ____ . ❙
intelligentes

2 You know a number of adjectives like *jeune* and *pauvre* that end in *-e* in both the masculine and feminine singular. See if you can complete these adjectives with the correct letters: *s __ iss __, célè __ __ e, r __ ch __, st __ p __ d __, bê __ e.* |

suisse, célèbre, riche, stupide, bête

3 A few adjectives in French double their final letter before adding *-e* to form the feminine. Complete each exchange below with the correct form of the adjective in parentheses.

    a –Jean-Pierre est très ____, n'est-ce pas? (gentil)
    –Oui, et ses sœurs sont très ____ aussi. |

gentil, gentilles

    b –Mme Renart a une fille qui est ____. (gros)
    –Elle a aussi un fils qui est ____. |

grosse, gros

    c –Ces fraises sont ____! (bon)
    –Ce gâteau est ____ aussi! |

bonnes, bon

4 Compare the adjectives in these pairs of sentences.

    Paul n'est pas un garçon jaloux.   *Quel film merveilleux!*
    Lise n'est pas une fille jalouse.   *Quelle chanson merveilleuse!*

Now complete this statement: The feminine singular forms of *jaloux, merveilleux, affreux, heureux,* and *malheureux* (and many other masculine adjectives ending in *x*) end in the letters ____. |

-se

5 Complete the second sentence in each pair with the appropriate form of the adjective used in the first sentence.

    a Je n'aime pas tellement les filles jalouses.
    Je n'aime pas tellement les garçons ____.
    b Je déteste ce pantalon! Il est affreux!
    Je déteste cette robe! Elle est ____.
    c Ils ont un examen de maths aujourd'hui. Qu'ils sont malheureux!
    Elles ont un examen de maths aujourd'hui. Qu'elles sont ____! |

a jaloux b affreuse c malheureuses

6 The adjectives *beau* and *vieux* are irregular.

    a The feminine of *beau* is ____; the feminine of *vieux* is ____. |

belle, vieille

    b Adjectives that end in *-x* in the masculine singular do not change for the plural. Thus, the masculine plural of *vieux* is ____. |

vieux

    c The plural of *beau,* like the plural of *vieux,* ends in ____. |

-x

7 Complete these sentences with the correct form of *vieux* or *beau.*

    a Cet homme a cent ans. Il est très ____. Ses enfants sont ____ aussi!
    b Moi, je trouve cette robe affreuse, mais ma mère la trouve ____.
    c J'adore ces monuments. Ils sont très ____. |

a vieux, vieux b belle c beaux

3 Practice with demonstrative markers

You've been using demonstrative markers since Phase 2, so this section should be easy for you. If you make an error, review by looking at the Summary on p. 106.

1 The demonstrative marker *ce* is used with a masculine singular noun that begins with a consonant sound.

   a Which form of the marker is used with a masculine singular noun beginning with a vowel sound? |

            cet

   b The form ____ is used with any feminine singular noun. |

            cette

   c The plural form of *ce, cet,* and *cette* is ____. |

            ces

2 *Ce, cet,* and *cette* may mean *this* or ____. *Ces* may mean *these* or ____. |

            that; those

3 Complete each sentence below according to what you see in the picture. Use a noun phrase containing a demonstrative marker. Answers occur after **d.**

      Modèle: Je vais donner ____ à mon frère. |

              cette règle

   a Y a-t-il une chaise devant ____?

   b Tout le monde a chaud. Malheureusement, on ne peut pas ouvrir ____.

   c Asseyez-vous sur ____, s'il vous plaît.

   d On va montrer le film sur ____. |

          a *ce bureau* **b** *cette fenêtre* **c** *ces chaises* **d** *cet écran*

CHECK-UP   Write French equivalents for these sentences.

Part 1   **1** I have to work today.

               2 He's supposed to come at two o'clock.

Part 2   Write French equivalents for *Mme Leroi is very old and famous* and *Those apples are very good.*

VOCABULARY

un *cardigan* cardigan sweater
un *chapeau* hat
des *chaussettes* (f.) socks
des *chaussures* (f.) shoes
une *chemise* man's shirt
un *chemisier* woman's blouse or shirt
un *collant* pantyhose
un *imperméable* raincoat
une *jupe* skirt
un *manteau* coat
un *pantalon* pants
devoir ought to, must, should;
    to have to

HISTOIRE DE CHAUSSURES A question of shoes
la *scène* scene
se *passer* to happen
un *grand magasin* department store
parisien Parisian
le *rayon* department of a store
une *cliente*, un *client* customer
une *vendeuse*, un *vendeur* salesperson
content, -e happy

1 *Position of adjectives with nouns*

You know that adjectives must match the gender and number of the noun they describe. In this section, you will practice using some adjectives in French that follow the noun.

1 Notice the position of the adjectives in these sentences.

Je voudrais acheter une chemise **bleue.**   *Vous connaissez cette dame* **italienne?**
Ma sœur a une jupe **rouge.**   *Roger est un étudiant* **américain.**

a Do adjectives of color, like **bleu** and **rouge,** precede or follow the noun? |

follow

b Adjectives of nationality, like **italien** and **américain,** also ___ the noun. |

follow

2 Because English adjectives usually precede the noun, the French word order will seem strange to you at first. The next couple of frames will give you some practice.

Write French equivalents for the sentences below. Use the appropriate form of *canadien, martiniquais,* and *belge.*

> Modèle: Roger is an American university student. |
>> *Roger est un étudiant américain.*

a Marie-France is a Canadian university student. |
>> *Marie-France est une étudiante canadienne.*

b Jean-Pierre is a university student from Martinique. |
>> *Jean-Pierre est un étudiant martiniquais.*

c Marianne is a Belgian university student. |
>> *Marianne est une étudiante belge.*

3 Write the French equivalent for each phrase below.
a a red skirt, a white blouse |
>> *une jupe rouge, un chemisier blanc*

b black shoes, gray socks |
>> *des chaussures noires, des chaussettes grises* (Did you remember that *des* is the plural of *un/une* and that it need not be said in English?)

4 Here are some other adjectives you know that usually follow the noun: *affreux, célèbre, intelligent, maigre.* Use them with the following nouns to write French equivalents for the phrases below: *un film, une secrétaire, un acteur, un chien.* Answers occur after **d.**

a an awful film
b an intelligent secretary
c some famous actors
d two thin dogs |

>> a *un film affreux* b *une secrétaire intelligente* c *des acteurs célèbres* d *deux chiens maigres*

5 Although the majority of French adjectives usually follow the noun they describe, there are a few that usually precede the noun. They tend to be adjectives that are used very frequently. Here is a list of the ones you have learned so far.

> beau, belle   gros, grosse   joli, jolie   petit, petite
> bon, bonne   jeune   mauvais, mauvaise   vieux, vieille

In items **a–c,** add the correct form of the adjective to each sentence.

> Modèle: (gros) C'est un éléphant. |
>> *C'est un gros éléphant.*

a (bon) C'est une idée. |
>> *C'est une bonne idée.*

b (vieux) J'ai un pantalon. |
>> *J'ai un vieux pantalon.*

c (joli) Il n'y a pas de manteaux dans ce magasin. |
>> *Il n'y a pas de jolis manteaux dans ce magasin.*

NOTE ## *French clothing and shoe sizes*

If you went to a French department store, you might at first have some difficulty finding clothes in your size. French **tailles** (clothing sizes) and **pointures** (shoe sizes) differ considerably from American sizes. However, airlines and some large department stores try to help American tourists by publishing conversion charts for sizes. Some of the ranges are given here.

Of course, the size you take will depend on the cut of the dress or suit, and may vary from store to store, just as it often does in the United States.

		FRENCH	AMERICAN
MEN	Suits:	34–52	34–46
	Sweaters:	46–59	36–46
	Shoes:	41–46	9–13
WOMEN	Dresses:	40–48	10–16
	Sweaters:	40–48	32–40
	Shoes:	36–43	6–10

2 **Il faut** *and* devoir *to express obligation*

Both *il faut* and *devoir* are commonly used to express obligation in French. An obligation is a duty that a person is expected to carry out.

The impersonal expression *il faut* is usually used to make a general statement. *Devoir* is usually used to make a statement concerning a specific person. Both *devoir* and *il faut* can express many shades of obligation, depending on the context and the speaker's tone of voice.

1 Here are examples of *il faut* and *devoir* put to use.
a A soccer coach is talking to several members of the soccer team. He says: *Pour bien jouer au football, il faut jouer souvent.* What is the English equivalent? I

> To play soccer well, it's necessary to (you must, should) play often.

b The next day the coach says to one of the team members: *Pour bien jouer au football, tu dois jouer souvent.* What is the English equivalent? I

> To play soccer well, you must (you have to, you've got to) play often.

2 In expressing obligation, the forms of *devoir* and the expression *il faut* are followed by a verb in the ___ form. I

> infinitive

3 When you use the verb *devoir,* you must use the form of the verb that matches the ___. I

> subject (For example, you use *dois* to match *tu.*)

4 When you use *il faut,* does *il* refer to a person? I

> no (*Il faut* is an impersonal expression. It never changes form and it never refers to a specific person.)

5 Use *il faut* to write a sentence saying that it's necessary to go to the dentist. |

Il faut aller chez le dentiste.

6 Use *devoir* to write a sentence saying that Marc and Alain have to go to the dentist tomorrow. |

Marc et Alain doivent aller chez le dentiste demain.

3 Practice with paired words

1 Look at each pair of opposites below, and try to say the English equivalents. Go through the whole list once before you check the equivalents shown in the answer.

   a *pourquoi–parce que*   **d** *merveilleux–affreux*   **g** *bien–mal*
   b *heureux–malheureux*   **e** *vite–lentement*   **h** *avant–après*
   c *commencer–terminer*   **f** *bon–mauvais*   **i** *minuit–midi* |

a why-because b happy-unhappy c begin-end d marvelous-awful
e quickly-slowly f good-bad g well-badly h before-after i midnight-noon

2 Answer each question below by using a word that is opposite in meaning to the italicized word. Keep your answer short.

       Modèle: Ils vont arriver à *midi?* |

       Non, à minuit.

a Tu *termines* tes devoirs? |

       Non, je les commence.

b Tu vas jouer au football *après* le déjeuner? |

       Non, avant le déjeuner.

c *Pourquoi* est-ce que tu ne veux pas faire du bateau avec nous? |

       Parce que.

d Ces musiciens jouent *mal*, n'est-ce pas? |

       Mais non, ils jouent bien!

3 Which of the following do *not* belong in each group? Answers follow **d.**

   a maison, appartement, manteau, hôtel
   b croissant, viande, poisson, soir
   c jouer des cymbales, jouer au football, jouer du violon, jouer de la guitare
   d petits pois, pêches, pommes de terre, carottes |

a *manteau* b *soir* c *jouer au football* d *pêches*

CHECK-UP
Part 1

Write French equivalents for:
1 Those are Italian shoes.
2 I want to buy a red hat.
3 That's a beautiful house.

VOCABULARY

HISTOIRE DE CHAUSSURES

je vous dis I tell you
la pointure shoe size
environ about, approximately
jamais de la vie! not on your life!
au maximum at most
vous entendez you hear
donner to give
donnez-moi give me
le pied droit right foot
aïe! ouch!

voyons (impatience) oh, come on!
  look here!
au moins at least
c'est trop fort! that's going too far!
gardez-les! keep them!
je regrette I'm sorry
en sortant while leaving
à mi-voix softly, under one's breath
j'en ai marre! I'm fed up!

PREPARATION 78

1 Vous- *and* nous-*commands*

In school, teachers often tell students to do things like *Take out a sheet of paper* and *Pass in your homework.* In this part you will learn how to give commands in French, using the **vous**-form and the **nous**-form of verbs.

1 Here's a command addressed to **vous: *Prenez une feuille de papier.***
  a Which word expresses the action of the command? |

    Prenez

  b Is a subject pronoun used with the command form? |

    no

2 Even though no subject pronoun appears in ***Prenez une feuille de papier,*** a subject is implied or understood.
  a Which subject pronoun could be added? |

    vous

  b Compare ***Prenez une feuille de papier*** and ***Vous prenez une feuille de papier.*** Is the command form of the verb the same as, or different from the form that is used with **vous?** |

    the same as (The *vous*-command form of most verbs is identical to the present-tense *vous*-form.

3 Complete each sentence below with the **vous**-command of the verb in parentheses.
  a (donner) _____ vingt francs à la vendeuse. |

    Donnez

  b (téléphoner) _____ à vos parents à huit heures. |

    Téléphonez

4 The **vous**-command of most French verbs is identical to the present-tense **vous**-form. Write the **vous**-command that completes each sentence below.

a (venir) ____ chez moi demain soir. |
       Venez

b (prendre) ____ vos affaires, s'il vous plaît. |
       Prenez

c (faire) ____ une bonne soupe pour ce soir. |
       Faites (The *vous*-form of *faire* and the command form are identical.)

5 The command form of a verb is also called the imperative form. As in English, it may be used more as a suggestion than as a command. Read this ad for a resort on the **Côte d'Azur,** on the Mediterranean sea.

> ### *Pour des vacances parfaites°...*
>
> Vous êtes fatigué°? Vous voulez prendre des vacances? Alors, pour des vacances parfaites, venez à l'Auberge° de la Couronne d'Or°. Laissez° vos problèmes chez vous! Passez° vos journées à la plage, jouez au tennis, au golf, aux boules. Faites de la voile° ou allez à la pêche°. Le soir, prenez votre dîner dans notre restaurant quatre étoiles°. La Couronne d'Or, c'est le paradis sur terre°!

perfect

tired

Inn / Golden Crown
leave / spend

go sailing
go fishing
four stars (very high quality)
paradise on earth

a Write English equivalents for **Venez à l'Auberge de la Couronne d'Or!** and **Laissez vos problèmes chez vous!** |
       Come to the Golden Crown Inn! Leave your problems at home!

b Write the French equivalent of *Play tennis* and *Go sailing*. |
       Jouez au tennis. Faites de la voile.

6 In the conversation below, someone makes a suggestion by using the **nous**-command form of a verb. See if you can find it.

    Georges: *Allons au cinéma. Il y a un bon film ce soir.*
    Marianne: *D'accord, je veux bien.*

a The command form in the conversation above is ____. |
       allons

b Does **allons** above have a subject pronoun? |
       no

c **Allons** is a **nous**-command. Is the command form of the verb different from the **nous**-form of the present tense? |
       no (The *nous*-commands of most French verbs are identical to the *nous*-forms of the present tense.)

7 What is the English equivalent of **Allons au cinéma?** |
       Let's go to the movies. (The English equivalent of a *nous*-command begins with *Let's*. The speaker includes himself or herself in the group.)

8 Write the French equivalent of *Let's go to the soccer game.* |

> *Allons au match de football.*

9 Say that you want to do the things suggested below. Write a **nous**-command to express the idea of *Let's.*

> Modèle: Tu veux aller au cinéma? |
>
> > *Bon, allons au cinéma.*

a Vous voulez jouer au ping-pong? |

> *Bon, jouons au ping-pong.*

b Je voudrais faire de la voile. |

> *Bon, faisons de la voile.*

c Tu voudrais faire une promenade? |

> *Bon, faisons une promenade.*

2   *The present tense of* acheter *and* préférer

1 Here are the present-tense forms of *acheter* (to buy) and *préférer* (to prefer).

j'	achèt	e	préfèr	e
tu	achèt	es	préfèr	es
on/il/elle	achèt	e	préfèr	e
ils/elles	achèt	ent	préfèr	ent
nous	achet	ons	préfér	ons
vous	achet	ez	préfér	ez

a Are the endings of *acheter* and *préférer* like those of regular *-er* verbs? |

> yes

b Which subject pronouns match the stems *achet-* and *préfér-?* |

> *nous, vous*

c Do the stems *achet-* and *préfér-* occur with endings that are pronounced or not pronounced? |

> pronounced

d Which subject pronouns match the stems *achèt-* and *préfèr-?* |

> *je (j'), tu, on, il, elle, ils, elles*

e Do the stems *achèt-* and *préfèr-* occur with endings that are pronounced or not pronounced? |

> not pronounced (The *è* (*e accent grave*) occurs in the last pronounced syllable of the verb form.)

2 Look at the charts above. Say each subject pronoun and its verb form aloud and notice which accents it has (if any).

Now write each of the following verb phrases with its missing accent marks; **j'achete, je prefere, ils achetent, nous preferons.** |

> *j'achète, je préfère, ils achètent, nous préférons*

3 Some friends happen to meet in the *rayon de disques* of a large department store. Complete the sentences below with the appropriate forms of *acheter.* To get used to the two sounds of the stem, read each sentence aloud.

    a Qu'est-ce que vous ____? |

        achetez

    b Nous ____ des disques pour Sylvie. |

        achetons

    c Jean-Luc! Nous devons ____ ce disque de Brahms pour Marc. |

        acheter

    d Est-ce que Pierre et son frère ____ souvent des disques? |

        achètent

    e Moi, je ne suis pas riche cette semaine. Je n' ____ pas de disques. |

        achète

4 Compare the use of *préférer* in the responses to each of the following questions:

      –Tu aimes les pommes?   *–Tu veux manger?*

      –Non, je préfère les poires.   *–Non, je préfère jouer.*

Préférer can be followed by either a noun or an ____. |

      infinitive verb form (as in English)

5 Complete each sentence with the proper form of *préférer.* Then read the sentence aloud.

    a Moi, je ____ regarder un film à la télé. |

        préfère

    b Vous ____ les films italiens, n'est-ce pas? |

        préférez

6 Write the English equivalents.

    a Vous préférez les films italiens, n'est-ce pas? |

        You prefer Italian films, don't you?

    b Nous devons acheter ce disque de Brahms pour Marc. |

        We have to buy this Brahms record for Marc.

3 *Practice with clothing vocabulary*

Choose the items of clothing that complete each situation below. Here, the verb *mettre* means *to put on* and *porter* means *to wear.*

    Modèle: Sur la tête (*head*) vous mettez un ____. (chapeau, collant, jupe) |

      un chapeau

1 Quand il pleut, on met un ____. (chemisier, gant, imperméable) |

    un imperméable

2 Si vous avez froid aux pieds, vous mettez d'abord des ____ et ensuite des ____. (chapeaux, chaussures, chaussettes) |

    des chaussettes, des chaussures

3 En général, les hommes portent des ___ et les femmes portent des ___. (chemisiers, chemises) |

des chemises, des chemisiers

4 Pour nager, il faut porter un ___. (maillot de bain, gilet, tailleur) |

un maillot de bain

5 En général, les hommes portent ___ quand il fait froid. (un sac, des gants, un chemisier) |

des gants

6 Thérèse ne peut pas trouver ___ de son tailleur. (la veste, le short, les chaussettes) |

la veste

CHECK-UP
Part 1

1 Complete the following *vous*-commands.
    a (Fermer) la porte, s'il vous plaît.
    b (Faire) vos devoirs ce soir.
2 Complete these *nous*-commands.
    a (Prendre) une glace.   **b** (Aller) à la plage.

Part 2

Complete the following sentences with the proper form of the verb in parentheses.
1 Nous (préférer) le poisson mais Jean-Louis (préférer) le poulet.
2 J' (acheter) du cidre.
3 Est-ce que vous (acheter) souvent de la viande?

VOCABULARY

un blue-jean blue jeans
un costume man's suit
des gants (m.) gloves
un gilet vest
un maillot de bain bathing suit
un pull sweater
une robe dress
un sac handbag
un short shorts
un tailleur woman's suit
une veste jacket

1 *More on placement of adjectives*

You learned in Preparation 77 that many French adjectives usually follow the noun they describe. This section will give you practice with some of those adjectives, and also with some adjectives that usually precede the noun.

1 Adjectives of nationality and hair color almost always follow the nouns they describe. Here is a list of other adjectives you have learned in earlier Phases. If there are any you don't remember, check the end vocabulary.

affreux, affreuse	*laid, laide*	*maigre*
intelligent, -e	*merveilleux, merveilleuse*	*moche*
heureux, heureuse	*malheureux, malheureuse*	*riche*
jaloux, jalouse	*célèbre*	*stupide*

Complete the following sentences with a noun phrase using an appropriate adjective from the list.

a Cet homme n'est pas intelligent, c'est ____. |
un homme stupide

b Cette chanson n'est pas merveilleuse, c'est ____. |
une chanson affreuse

c Cet enfant n'est pas heureux, c'est ____. |
un enfant malheureux

2 While having coffee at a café in Québec, Anne tells Guy who some of the people in the café are. Rewrite each sentence below, using the adjective provided. Then read each sentence aloud. Answers follow item **c**.

Modèle: Cet homme est musicien.   (roux) |
Cet homme roux est musicien.

a Cette femme est journaliste.   (maigre)
b Ces hommes sont architectes.   (italien)
c Cet homme est un écrivain célèbre.   (laid) |

a *Cette femme maigre est journaliste.*   b *Ces hommes italiens sont architectes.*   c *Cet homme laid est un écrivain célèbre.*

3 These frames review the adjectives of color.

blanc, blanche	*jaune*	*rose*
bleu, bleue	*marron*	*rouge*
brun, brune	*noir, noire*	*vert, verte*
gris, grise	*orange*	*violet, violette*

Marron and **orange** are two colors that do not change form in the feminine or in the plural. Clothing is usually described by **marron**, eye and hair color by **brun**. **Brun** is usually darker than **marron**.

Write the English equivalents of **Elle a des crayons bruns** and **Il a un pantalon marron.** ❘

She has some brown pencils. He has brown pants.

4 Tell what Anne-Marie is packing for her weekend trip. Write the noun phrases that complete each sentence below.

Modèle: Elle prend une jupe (marron). ❘
une jupe marron

a Elle prend sa robe (blanc) et sa veste (violet). ❘
sa robe blanche, sa veste violette

b Elle a un imperméable (vert) et des chaussettes (orange). ❘
un imperméable vert, des chaussettes orange

QUINZAINE DE L'IMPERMEABLE
style-30 ans-classique

5 Although most French adjectives follow the noun, the adjectives listed below usually precede the noun.

beau (*bel*), belle	jeune	mauvais, mauvaise
bon, bonne	joli, jolie	vieux (*vieil*), vieille
gros, grosse	petit, petite	

The adjectives **bel** and **vieil** are used with masculine nouns that begin with a vowel sound: **un bel enfant, un vieil homme.**
Now read these sentences:

C'est un film intéressant.   Ce sont des films intéressants.
C'est un bon film.   Ce sont de bons films.

In the sentences above, the marker **des** becomes ____ when it is used with an adjective that comes before the noun. ❘

de (This use of de before an adjective is changing. More and more, French speakers use des.)

6 Rewrite each sentence below to start with **C'est** or **Ce sont.** Then read each sentence aloud. Answers follow item **f.**

Modèle: Ce restaurant est petit. ❘
C'est un petit restaurant.

a Ce gâteau est bon.
b Ces tables sont vieilles.
c Cette fille est jolie.

d Ces musiciens sont mauvais.
e Cet éléphant est vieux.
f Cet appartement est beau. ❘

*a C'est un bon gâteau. b Ce sont de vieilles tables. c C'est une jolie fille.
d Ce sont de mauvais musiciens. e C'est un vieil éléphant. f C'est un bel appartement.*

2 Practice with direct-object pronouns

Remember that in French, direct-object pronouns usually come before the verb.

1 Rewrite each sentence below, replacing the italicized noun phrase with a direct-object pronoun.

> Modèle: J'aide *Michèle et toi.* |
> *Je vous aide.*

a Tu donnes *l'appareil-photo* à Guy? |
> *Tu le donnes à Guy?*

b Nous écoutons *les professeurs.* |
> *Nous les écoutons.*

c Ils invitent *Guy, Michèle et moi* chez eux. |
> *Ils nous invitent chez eux.*

2 Write a complete sentence to answer each question below. Follow the cues and use a direct-object pronoun in each answer.

> Modèle: Tu me vois? (non) |
> *Non, je ne te vois pas.*

a Il fait froid. Veux-tu mon cardigan rose? (oui) |
> *Oui, je le voudrais. / Oui, je le veux.*

b Donnes-tu ta guitare à Sophie? (oui) |
> *Oui, je la donne à Sophie*

c Est-ce qu'on nous invite, Thierry et moi? |
> *Oui, on vous invite.*

d Robert et Jean-Pierre, vous cherchez Michèle? (non) |
> *Non, nous ne la cherchons pas.*

3 Pre-quiz practice: devoir

Paul and some friends are going to make a strawberry tart. Say that the following people have to buy the following things, using the appropriate form of ***devoir***.

> Modèle: Paul: des œufs |
> *Paul doit acheter des œufs.*

1 Jeanne: du beurre |
> *Jeanne doit acheter du beurre.*

2 nous: des fraises |
> *Nous devons acheter des fraises.*

3 toi: du sucre |

Tu dois acheter du sucre.

4 vous: du lait |

Vous devez acheter du lait.

5 moi: de la farine (*flour*) |

Je dois acheter de la farine.

6 Raoul et Marc: de la confiture |

Raoul et Marc doivent acheter de la confiture.

CHECK-UP
Part 1

Write French equivalents. Begin each sentence with *C'est.*
1 She's a good actress.   **3** That's an old film.
2 He's an intelligent man.

VOCABULARY

bleu, -e blue
blanc, blanche white
brun, -e brown
gris, -e gray
jaune yellow
marron brown

noir, -e black
orange orange
rose pink
rouge red
vert, -e green
violet, -te purple

PREPARATION 80

1 *Practice with the relative pronoun* qui

1 This section gives you practice in joining ideas by using the relative pronoun *qui. Qui* is used to combine two related sentences into one. For example:

Je vois une femme.   ***Cette femme** téléphone.*
*Je vois une femme **qui** téléphone.*

Vous avez un livre.   ***Ce livre** est intéressant.*
*Vous avez un livre **qui** est intéressant.*

a Does *qui* come directly before or after the noun it refers to? |

after

b Is *qui* followed by a noun or a verb? |

verb

2 a Write English equivalents for the sentences with *qui* in frame 1. |

I see a woman who is telephoning. You have a book that's interesting.

b The English equivalent for *qui* is ___ or ___. |

who, that

3 An employment counselor had a waiting room full of clients, but they've all gone out for lunch. Write what she says as she asks the office secretary where each client is. Begin each sentence with *Où est* or *Où sont*.

> Modèle: le clown   (chanter) |
>
> *Où est le clown qui chante?*

a la secrétaire   (parler anglais) |
> *Où est la secrétaire qui parle anglais?*

b les musiciens   (jouer du jazz) |
> *Où sont les musiciens qui jouent du jazz?*

c la photographe   (prendre des photos en couleur) |
> *Où est la photographe qui prend des photos en couleur?*

d les danseuses   (faire de la danse classique) |
> *Où sont les danseuses qui font de la danse classique?*

e le journaliste   (venir de Marseille) |
> *Où est le journaliste qui vient de Marseille?*

f les vendeurs   (préférer travailler le week-end) |
> *Où sont les vendeurs qui préfèrent travailler le week-end?*

4 Write an English equivalent for *Où sont les vendeurs qui préfèrent travailler le week-end?* |
> Where are the salesmen who prefer to work on the weekend?

2   More about commands

1 Which of the sentences below are commands?
> *Nous invitons Georges.*   *Invitons aussi Philippe.*
> *Vous mangez du gâteau.*   *Mangez de la tarte!* |
>
> *Invitons aussi Philippe. Mangez de la tarte!*

a Are subject pronouns used in French commands? |
> no

b Are the *nous-* and *vous-* command forms the same as the present-tense forms of the verb? |
> yes (The command forms and the present-tense forms are the same for most verbs.)

2 Write **nous-** or **vous-**commands, using the cues below.

> Modèle: vous: écouter ce disque |
> *Écoutez ce disque!*

a nous: aller aux Galeries Lafayette |
> *Allons aux Galeries Lafayette!*

b vous: acheter une veste pour Louis |
> *Achetez une veste pour Louis!*

c vous: prendre le déjeuner maintenant |
> *Prenez le déjeuner maintenant!*

d nous: commencer les devoirs |
> *Commençons les devoirs!*

3 Now compare present-tense **tu-**forms of these verbs with their **tu-**command forms.

> *Tu viens?*   *Viens vite!*
> *Tu prends ton gros pull?*   *Prends ton gros pull!*

a What are the **tu-**command forms of **venir** and **prendre?** |
> *viens; prends*

b Are the **tu-**command forms of **venir** and **prendre** identical to the present-tense **tu-**forms? |
> yes (This is true for most verbs except for *-er verbs and a few irregular verbs.*)

4 Now read and compare the verb forms in these sentences:

> *Tu cherches ton pull.*   *Cherche ton pull!*
> *Tu vas chez Julie.*   *Va chez Julie!*

a What are the **tu-**command forms of **chercher** and **aller?** |
> *cherche; va*

b Is the **tu-**command of an **-er** verb the same as or different from its present-tense **tu-**form? |
> different from

c How is the **tu-**command of an **-er** verb different from the present-tense **tu-**form? |
> The *tu-*command form drops the final *-s: Tu cherches. Cherche! Tu vas. Va!*

5 Claire is having a dinner for two friends who have just returned from South America. Rewrite each sentence below, replacing the italicized word or phrase with the word or phrase in parentheses. Be sure to change the command form and make any other necessary changes.

> Modèle: Prenez du fromage, *si vous voulez.* (si tu veux) |
> *Prends du fromage, si tu veux.*

a Passez le pain, s'il *vous* plaît. (te) |
> *Passe le pain, s'il te plaît.*

b Parlez de *votre* voyage. (ton) |
> *Parle de ton voyage.*

c Montrez *vos* photos. (tes) |
> *Montre tes photos.*

d Si *vous* savez jouer de la guitare, prenez cette guitare. (tu) ▮

Si tu sais jouer de la guitare, prends cette guitare.

e Si *vous* voulez, chantez une chanson brésilienne! (tu) ▮

Si tu veux, chante une chanson brésilienne.

6 Thérèse wants Pierre and Marie to go to the soccer game with her. Complete these sentences with the command form that corresponds to the verb and pronoun in parentheses.

Modèle: Marie et Pierre, (vous/venir) au match de football avec moi! ▮

venez

a D'accord! (tu/porter) ton manteau, Marie; il fait froid. ▮

Porte

b J'ai faim. (nous/prendre) quelque chose avant d'aller au stade. ▮

Prenons

c Mais non, Pierre, il est tard. (tu/faire) un sandwich. Tu peux le manger au stade. ▮

Fais

NOTE ✳

Regional costumes

In the United States, people occasionally dress up in colonial costumes for a festival or an historic holiday. In France, especially in small towns and **dans les provinces** (regions outside of Paris), people may wear traditional folk costumes for patriotic holidays, folk festivals, and weddings.

Each region has its distinctive costumes—some ornate, and some plain. Women usually wear a long dress, or skirt and full-sleeved blouse, with a lace head-dress called a **coiffe.** The dark skirts are often embroidered with bright colors. In some regions, such as **Bretagne,** the tall, round, starched **coiffes** are intricate works of art that have cost the **dentellière** (lacemaker) weeks of work.

Men usually wear dark pants with an embroidered vest, and sometimes a round felt hat. In many regions, **sabots** (wooden shoes) accompany the costumes.

These costumes are usually handed down from one generation to the next. As the skills of lace-making and embroidery become more rare, the costumes become valuable heirlooms.

3 Practice with **devoir,** *clothing, and colors*

The Larose family is going to the wedding of a close friend. Write complete sentences to say what they have to get, using the verb *devoir.*

Modèle: Je / acheter / / vert ▮

Je dois acheter une robe verte.

1 Patrice et Marc / acheter / / noir ▮

Patrice et Marc doivent acheter des chaussures noires.

2 M. Larose / acheter / / gris ▮

M. Larose doit acheter une veste grise.

3 tu / acheter / / gris ▮

Tu dois acheter des chaussettes grises.

4 Mme Larose / acheter / / bleu ▮

Mme Larose doit acheter un chemisier bleu.

5 nous / acheter / / blanc ▮

Nous devons acheter des gants blancs.

CHECK-UP
Part 2

Tell a friend to do the following things. Then suggest that you do them together. Write a *tu*- and *nous*-command for each infinitive phrase.
1 prendre le train
2 inviter Marcel
3 aller chez Lucie

1 Practice with some irregular verbs

This section gives you practice expressing the ideas of *doing, wanting, being able to,* and *knowing* with **faire, vouloir, pouvoir, savoir** and **connaître.** If you've forgotten any of the forms, look back at the charts in the Summaries on pp. 176, 245 and 246.

1 Complete these sentences with the appropriate forms of *faire.* Answers occur after item **e.**

  a Tu ____ un gâteau au chocolat pour la fête samedi?
  b Nous ____ des commissions cet après-midi.
  c Qu'est-ce que vous ____ ce soir?
  d Mes cousins ____ du camping en Suisse.
  e Je ____ mes devoirs après le dîner.
  f Il ____ beau aujourd'hui, n'est-ce pas? |

a fais   b faisons   c faites   d font   e fais   f fait

2 Madeleine and Barbara decide to go shopping. Say what they want to do and can do. Complete the sentences with the appropriate forms of **vouloir** and **pouvoir.**

      Modèle: –Barbara, tu p ____ venir au Printemps avec moi?
               Je v ____ acheter une jupe. |
               peux, veux

  a –Bon, d'accord! Ma cousine v ____ un livre comme cadeau d'anniversaire. Je p ____ l'acheter là-bas. |
               veut, peux

  b –Je v ____ aussi aller au rayon de disques. On p ____ toujours trouver de bons disques de jazz dans ce magasin. |
               veux, peut

  c –Et ensuite nous p ____ aller au café pour prendre quelque chose, n'est-ce pas? |
               pouvons

3 Read these sentences and compare the meanings of the verbs.
    *Je **sais** que Lyon est une jolie ville, mais je ne la **connais** pas.*
    *Je voudrais tricoter un pull pour ma mère, mais je ne **sais** pas tricoter!*
  a Which verb form above means *know* in the sense of knowing something or knowing factual information? |
               sais (from *savoir*)
  b Which verb form means *know* in the sense of being acquainted with a person or being familiar with a place? |
               connaît (from *connaître*)

4 Complete these sentences with forms of *connaître* or *savoir*.

      Modèle: Vous ___ Paris? Vous ___ où est l'Opéra? |

               connaissez, savez

a Vous ___ les Fournier? Ma mère les ___ bien. |

        connaissez, connaît

b Nous ___ bien l'Italie et nous ___ parler italien. |

        connaissons, savons

c Ils ___ que Paris est la capitale de la France, mais ils ne ___ pas la France. |

              savent, connaissent

2 Negative expressions

You have learned to make any statement negative with *ne...pas.* This section will show you some other negative expressions.

1 Transport yourself back to the time of the French Revolution in 1789. Imagine that you are a revolutionary leader in Paris. You wish to stir up the people against the ruling class. So, in a speech you cry out:

      Eux, ils ont du pain! Et nous, nous n'avons pas de pain.
      Eux, ils ont du vin! Et nous, nous n'avons pas de vin.
      Eux, ils ont de la viande! Et nous, nous n'avons pas de viande.
      Eux, ils ont tout! **Et nous, nous n'avons rien!**

a What does the last line of your speech mean in English? |

      They have everything! And *we* have nothing!

b In the negative expression *ne...rien, ne* precedes the verb and ___ follows it. |

      rien

2 Answer the questions below, using *ne...rien.*

      Modèle: Est-ce qu'il y a quelque chose sur la table? |

        Non, il n'y a rien sur la table.

a Est-ce que tu manges quelque chose à midi? |

        Non, je ne mange rien à midi.

b Est-ce que Philippe cherche quelque chose? |

        Non, il ne cherche rien.

3 The negative expression *ne...personne* is used when you are talking about people. For example:

      Où sont les élèves et le professeur? Je ne vois personne.

a Write an English equivalent of *Je ne vois personne.* |

      I don't see anyone./I see no one.

b Does *ne* precede the verb and *personne* follow the verb, as in the case of *ne...pas* and *ne...rien?* |

      yes

4 Contradict each statement below with either *ne...personne* or *ne...rien,* according to the context.

      Modèle: Ce matin il y a beaucoup de monde sur la plage. ▌
               Ce matin il n'y a personne sur la plage.

  a Paul connaît quelqu'un ici. ▌
               Paul ne connaît personne ici.

  b Ce soir Guy danse avec Sophie. ▌
               Ce soir Guy ne danse avec personne.

  c Je vois un bateau à l'horizon. ▌
               Je ne vois rien à l'horizon.

  d Ils parlent à leurs amis. ▌
               Ils ne parlent à personne.

5 Write an English equivalent for ***Ils ne parlent à personne*** and for ***Je ne vois rien à l'horizon.*** ▌

         They aren't talking (don't talk) to anyone (anybody).   I don't see anything (I see nothing) on the horizon.

6 Now compare the ideas of *sometimes* and *never* in these sentences.
    –*Tu vas quelquefois au cinéma?*
    –*Non, je ne vais jamais au cinéma.*

  a Write an English equivalent for ***Non, je ne vais jamais au cinéma.*** ▌
         No, I never go to the movies./No, I don't ever go to the movies.

  b Write the French equivalent of *I never eat at that restaurant.* ▌
         Je ne mange jamais dans ce restaurant.

7 The Ledoux children have become very unruly. Use ***ne...jamais*** to say that they never do any of the things they are supposed to do.

      Modèle: Ils doivent téléphoner à leurs grands-parents. ▌
               Ils ne téléphonent jamais à leurs grands-parents.

  a Robert doit aider sa petite sœur. ▌
               Robert n'aide jamais sa petite sœur.

  b Julie doit préparer la salade. ▌
               Julie ne prépare jamais la salade.

  c Ils doivent faire leurs devoirs. ▌
               Ils ne font jamais leurs devoirs.

8 *Jamais* can be used with *de* + a noun to mean *never . . . any.* Compare the use of *jamais de* and *pas de* in these sentences.
    Cet homme est végétarien. Il ne mange pas de viande.
    Il n'achète jamais de viande.
Write an English equivalent for ***Il n'achète jamais de viande.*** ▌

         He never buys any meat. (Like *pas de,* the expression *jamais de* may be used with either count or measure nouns in a negative sentence.)

9 Use ***prendre*** and ***ne...jamais de*** to answer these questions about what people are having to eat and drink.
  a Tu vas prendre du thé? ▌
         Non, je ne prends jamais de thé.

b Est-ce que Marc veut un dessert? |
Non, il ne prend jamais de dessert.

c Est-ce que Lise va prendre de l'eau minérale? |
Non, elle ne prend jamais d'eau minérale.

CHECK-UP
Part 2

1 Express in English:
  a Je ne veux rien.
  b Tu ne m'aides jamais.
  c Nous ne voyons personne.

2 Express in French:
  a He doesn't eat anything.
  b You never listen to me.
  c They don't telephone anyone.

VOCABULARY

encore again, still
rarement rarely
toute l'année all year

toute la journée all day
tout de suite right away

TÊTU COMME UNE MULE Stubborn as a mule

les vêtements (m.) clothing
le mari husband
au contraire on the contrary
à la mode fashionable
parfait perfect
porter to wear

achetons-lui let's buy (something) for him
l'anniversaire (m.) birthday
seulement only
changer to change
de temps en temps from time to time

Grand magasin à Genève

1 Practice with porter and clothing vocabulary

1 In the United States, clothing that is manufactured in large quantities and sold in department stores is often called *ready-to-wear*. In France, this type of clothing is called **prêt-à-porter.** If you know that the French equivalent of *ready* is **prêt,** then you can probably guess that the French equivalent of the verb *to wear* is ____. |

porter

2 Compare the meaning of **porter** in these sentences:

Guy porte une chemise blanche.   Guy is wearing a white shirt.
Sylvie porte deux valises.   Sylvie is carrying two suitcases.

a When **porter** is used with articles of clothing, it can mean ____. |

to wear

b When **porter** is used with objects other than clothing, it means ____. |

to carry

3 Tell what each person below is wearing to a costume party. Write sentences using the cues provided and the appropriate forms of **porter.** (**Porter** is a regular **-er** verb. If you don't remember the present-tense forms of **-er** verbs, look at the Summary on p. 106.)

Modèle: Albert: un gilet rose et noir |

Albert porte un gilet rose et noir.

a toi: un pantalon de velours
b Georges et Jules: des chapeaux jaunes
c nous: des costumes de clown et de grandes chaussures
d Sophie: un short orange, un pull vert et un collant rose |

a Tu portes un pantalon de velours. b Georges et Jules portent des chapeaux jaunes. c Nous portons des costumes de clown et de/des grandes chaussures. d Sophie porte un short orange, un pull vert et un collant rose.

2 The present tense of mettre

1 Compare the meaning of **mettre** in these sentences:

*Julie **met** son imperméable.*   Julie is putting on her raincoat.
*Qu'est-ce que vous **mettez** sur la table?*   What are you putting on the table?

a When **mettre** is used with articles of clothing, it usually means ____. |

to put on

b When *mettre* is used with objects other than clothing, it means
____ . |

to put something somewhere

2 Here are the present-tense forms of *mettre.*
Take a minute to look and see which stem and
ending go with each subject pronoun.

je	met	s
tu	met	s
on/il/elle	met	
ils/elles	mett	ent
nous	mett	ons
vous	mett	ez

a The present-tense stem of *mettre* has two forms. What are they? |

met-, mett-

b The plural stem *mett-* is the same as the infinitive stem *mett-.*
Which stem is used in the singular forms of the verb? |

met-

3 The following people decide to put on what they have just bought at
the *marché aux puces* (flea market). Complete the sentences below with
the appropriate forms of *mettre.*

Modèle: Philippe ____ sa cravate de soie (*silk*). |

met

a Nous ____ nos chapeaux rouges. |

mettons

b Tu ____ ton grand manteau noir. |

mets

c Anne et Nathalie ____ de vieux gants violets. |

mettent

d Jules ____ son pantalon de clown. |

met

e Je ____ un gros pull marron. |

mets

4 Write an English equivalent of *Je mets un gros pull marron.* The
answer is in the answer key.

5 Tell what clothing each person is putting on for the occasion stated.
Write a complete sentence, using *mettre* and the appropriate article of
clothing. Answers are in the answer key.

Modèle: Marianne va jouer au tennis. (un short, un manteau, un collant) |
Elle met un short.

a M. Legrand va au bureau. (maillot de bain, costume, blue-jean)
b Nous sommes à la plage. (des chaussettes, un maillot de bain, une
veste)
c Vous avez froid aux pieds. (des chaussettes, des gants, un chapeau)
d Rosalie et Charles voient qu'il pleut. (un imperméable, une jupe, un
gilet)
e Tu vas jouer au basket. (un sac, un gilet, un short et une chemise)

3 When do we do things? (Adverbs of time)

This section will give you practice with the meanings of some common adverbs of time. Most of them should be familiar already.

après	*quelquefois*	*tard*	*tout de suite*
avant	*rarement*	*tôt*	*toute l'année*
encore	*souvent*	*toujours*	*toute la journée*
jamais			

1 Choose the correct English equivalent for the French phrase in italics in each sentence below. Answers follow **g**.

> Modèle: Françoise travaille *toute la journée* dans une banque. (all day, right away) |
> all day

a *Quelquefois* je vais au café Fleur avec elle. (early, sometimes)
b Là, on trouve *toujours* des amis. (always, immediately)
c Nous jouons *souvent* aux échecs. (never, often)
d Françoise va passer *toute l'année* à Toulouse. (immediately, all year)
e Elle doit prendre le train très *tôt* demain. (early, always)
f Elle va arriver *tard* à Toulouse. (all day, late)
g Je dois lui téléphoner *tout de suite!* (early, right away) |

> a sometimes b always c often d all year e early f late g right away

2 Max is going to spend a year in the United States and has many questions about the climate in some parts of the country. Choose and write the word or phrase that best answers his questions.

a Est-ce qu'il neige à Miami en juillet?
oui, souvent / oui, quelquefois / non, jamais |
> non, jamais

b Est-ce qu'il pleut dans le Nevada en été?
oui, toujours / rarement / oui, souvent |
> rarement

c Est-ce qu'il neige dans le Vermont en mars?
oui, quelquefois / rarement / non, jamais |
> oui, quelquefois

CHECK-UP **Part 2**	Write French equivalents for these sentences. **1** He puts on a raincoat when it rains. **2** She is putting the record on the table.
Part 3	Write French equivalents. **1** We go to the beach often in summer. **2** She works all day long.
VOCABULARY	*quelque chose* something *quelquefois* sometimes *quelqu'un* someone

Jours de fête *et de détente. . .*

Danses traditionnelles,

Costumes folkloriques...

Allégresse populaire

1 *Telling what other people say*

When you see a statement like *Paul says, "I'm going to the movies.",* you are seeing a direct quotation of Paul's exact words. When you see the statement *Paul says that he's going to the movies,* you see a report from someone else of what Paul says. This is called an *indirect* quotation. In this section, you'll learn how to express indirect quotations in French.

1 Read the following conversation. Write what Edouard says about the film. Copy the sentence on your worksheet.

> Monique: *Tu veux aller au cinéma?*
> Edouard: *Non. Mon frère dit que le film n'est pas bon.* |
>
> *Mon frère dit que le film n'est pas bon.*

a Does Edouard report the exact words used by his brother? |

> not necessarily (His brother might have said *"Le film est affreux," "C'est un mauvais film,"* etc.)

b In *Mon frère dit que le film n'est pas bon,* which word links *Mon frère dit* with *le film n'est pas bon?* |

> que

c Write the English equivalent of *que: My brother says ___ the film isn't good.* |

> that

d Look at the English sentence in **c.** Is the linking word *that* necessary in order for the sentence to make sense? |

> no (It's correct to say *My brother says the film isn't good* or *My brother says that the film isn't good.*)

2 In French the linking word *que* is always necessary in indirect quotations. Rewrite the following statement to report what the speaker says. Be sure to use *que. Jeanne dit: Cette chemise est jolie.* |

> *Jeanne dit que cette chemise est jolie.*

3 Write English equivalents for these sentences: *Alain dit: J'ai faim. Alain dit qu'il a faim.* |

> Alain says: "I'm hungry." Alain says (that) he's hungry.

4 In frame 3 the direct quotation beginning with *j'ai* is reported as an indirect quotation beginning with *qu' ___.* |

> il (A direct quote beginning with *je* or *nous* is reported with the *il/elle* or *ils/elles* subject pronouns and verb forms, and corresponding changes in possessive markers.)

5 Rewrite this direct quote as an indirect quotation: *Jean-Luc dit: Je vais au stade avec Jean-Paul.* |

> *Jean-Luc dit qu'il va au stade avec Jean-Paul.*

6 Report what each person is saying by writing an indirect quotation.

   a Anne dit: Ma robe n'est pas jolie. |

       Anne dit que sa robe n'est pas jolie.

   b Olivier dit: Il fait beau. |

       Olivier dit qu'il fait beau. (Did you remember that *que* becomes *qu'* before a vowel?)

7 Rewrite the following sentences as indirect quotations. Answers are in the answer key.

   a Maryse dit: Ma voiture est belle.   **c** Jacques dit: Nous pouvons aller à la plage.

   b Marcel dit: Je dois travailler.

2 Practice with liaison

You have been practicing liaison (linking) since Phase One in phrases like **un̮homme, elles̮ont faim,** etc. In French, liaison is obligatory in some situations, and optional in others.

   This part of the Preparation will give you practice with cases of obligatory liaison. Each frame below describes a situation in which liaison occurs. Read the sample sentences and write those in which liaison occurs. Then draw a link mark ̮ to indicate the liaison.

1 Liaison between *c'est + un/une:*

     C'est une chemise.   *C'est la chemise de Louis.*   *C'est sa chemise.* |

       C'est̮une chemise.

2 Liaison between *nous, vous, ils, elles* + a verb form beginning with a vowel:

     Elles font du bateau.   *Elles ont un bateau.*   *Elles aiment faire du bateau.* |

       Elles̮ont un bateau. *Elles̮aiment faire du bateau.*

3 Liaison between a marker ending in *-s* (*les, des, ces, mes,* etc.) + a noun beginning with a vowel:

     Voilà mes amis.   *Voilà leurs parents.*   *Voilà ses sœurs.* |

       Voilà mes̮amis.

4 Liaison between numbers ending in *-n, -s* or *-x* + a noun beginning with a vowel:

   a un éléphant   deux girafes   deux éléphants   deux zèbres |

       un̮éléphant, deux̮éléphants

   b dix ans   dix jours   dix nuits |

       dix̮ans

5 Liaison between markers ending in *-n* (*mon, ton, son*) + a noun beginning with a vowel:

   a mon frère   mon oncle   mon grand-père |

       mon̮oncle

   b son cahier   son vélo   son électrophone |

       son̮électrophone

6 Liaison between an inverted verb form that ends in *-d* or *-t* + a subject pronoun that begins with a vowel:

a Prenez-vous du thé? Est-il intelligent? Ont-elles faim? |
Est-il intelligent? Ont-elles faim?

b As-tu des frères? Prennent-ils le train? Prend-elle du lait? |
Prennent-ils le train? Prend-elle du lait?

3 Pre-quiz practice: adjectives

In your next class there will be a quiz to check your skill in using the form of an adjective that matches the gender and number of the noun it describes.

1 See if you can remember the adjectives you have learned that often occur in front of a noun. Write the complete masculine singular form, using the cues provided.

a j __ n __ (*young*)
b b __ __ (*good*)
c gr __ __ (*fat, heavy*)
d j __ l __ (*pretty*)
e ma __ __ __ __ s (*bad*)

f p __ __ __ t (*small*)
g v __ __ __ x (*old*)
h be __ __ (*handsome*)
i gr __ __ __ (*big*) |

a *jeune* b *bon* c *gros* d *joli* e *mauvais* f *petit* g *vieux* h *beau*
i *grand*

2 You have learned three kinds of adjectives that always follow a noun: *roux* and other adjectives that describe ___; *vert* and other adjectives describing ___; and *français* and other adjectives describing ___. |
hair color; color; nationality

3 For practice with the forms of adjectives, rewrite each sentence, and place the correct form of the adjective before the noun it describes. Answers are in the answer key.

a C'est mon oncle Georges. (vieux)
b C'est une tomate. (beau)
c Il y a un parc là-bas. (joli)

d Ce sont deux poulets. (gros)
e C'est une idée. (bon)
f J'ai une moto. (vieux)

4 Now rewrite each sentence below, and place the correct form of the adjective after the noun it describes. Answers are in the answer key.

   a Ce sont mes grands-parents. (canadien)   **d** Renée est une jeune fille. (jaloux)
   b Je ne mange jamais de pommes. (vert)   **e** Je préfère les pulls. (blanc)
   c C'est un avocat. (célèbre)

If you wish to review the feminine forms of adjectives that often precede a noun, refer to the list on p. 326. For adjectives of color, see the vocabulary list on p. 337.

CHECK-UP   Write French equivalents for these sentences.
Part 1
                  1 My sister says it's nice out today.
                  2 Jacques says he doesn't like to swim.

VOCABULARY   *il/elle dit* he/she says   *que (qu')* that

1 *Reading comprehension:* la fête du Mardi Gras

In class you will soon begin a dialogue that takes place at the time of Mardi Gras. Here is a reading that gives you some background information about *le Mardi Gras.*

   Read the questions that precede each paragraph. They help to give you a context for understanding what you read. Read the paragraph, and then write brief answers in French to the questions. No answers are given in the book. Some words are glossed in the margin. Some cognates that you may be able to guess are not glossed.

1 À Nice et à Cannes fait-il beau ou mauvais en général?
2 Est-ce que le Carnaval d'aujourd'hui est une fête religieuse ou une fête folklorique?

Nice et Cannes sont deux villes sur la Côte d'Azur, dans le Midi de la France. La région est renommée° pour son climat tempéré°, ses fleurs° et ses parfums. Les deux villes sont célèbres aussi pour leurs fêtes du Carnaval. La fête du Carnaval dure° une semaine au début du printemps. C'est une grande fête d'origine religieuse mais qui est aujourd'hui une fête folklorique et populaire.

              famous / temperate / flowers

              lasts

Now that you've read the paragraph, look back at questions **1** and **2**, and write brief answers in French.

3 Que font les gens (*people*) pour le Mardi Gras?
4 Quelles sortes de personnages y a-t-il dans les chars (*floats*)?

Le Mardi Gras est le dernier° jour du Carnaval. L'atmosphère est gaie. Les gens sont joyeux°. Ils dansent, ils chantent, ils s'amusent° beaucoup! À Nice il y a des défilés° qui passent sur la Promenade des Anglais (la plus grande rue° de Nice). On voit des chars avec beaucoup de jolies fleurs. Dans les chars il y a des personnages en costume. Ce sont des personnages historiques, ou bien° des personnages de légende. Les spectateurs regardent le défilé. Ils sont là aussi pour les batailles° de fleurs et de confettis.

last
merry / enjoy themselves
parades
the longest street

or else

battles

Now write brief answers to questions **3** and **4**. Then continue reading.

5 Que portent les danseurs le soir du Mardi Gras? À votre avis, c'est amusant (*fun*) de porter un costume de Carnaval?
6 Aux Etats-Unis est-ce qu'on voit des feux d'artifice le 25 décembre ou le 4 juillet?

Le soir du Mardi Gras, il y a souvent des fêtes et des bals. On les appelle° des bals masqués parce que les danseurs portent des costumes et des masques. À Nice, ce soir-là, Sa Majesté° Carnaval (le mannequin° grotesque qui représente l'esprit° du Carnaval) est jetée° dans la mer°. Il y a des feux d'artifice° merveilleux.

they are called
King
giant doll or puppet / spirit / thrown
sea / fireworks

Answer questions **5** and **6** briefly. Then read the last section.

7 La fête du Carnaval est célébrée dans deux îles (*islands*) de notre hémisphère. Quelles sont ces îles?
8 Quelle est la ville américaine où on célèbre la fête du Mardi Gras?

Cette grande fête est célébrée également° à la Martinique et à la Guadeloupe, à la Nouvelle-Orléans, et dans d'autres pays° où cette tradition continue.

also
other countries

Write answers for questions **7** and **8**.

2 *Indirect-object pronouns* **lui** *and* leur

You've been using the direct-object pronouns *le, la, les* since Phase 3. In this Preparation, you'll contrast their use with the use of the indirect-object pronouns *lui* and **leur.**

1 See if you can guess the meaning of **lui** in this two-line conversation.
>   *–Tu parles à Henri?*
>   *–Oui, je lui parle.*

  a Which pronoun in the second line replaces the phrase *à Henri?* |
>   *lui*

  b Write an English equivalent for *Je lui parle.* |
>   I'm talking to him.

  c Does **lui** precede or follow the verb? |
>   precede

2 Now look carefully at this two-line conversation.
>   *–Tu parles à Marie?*
>   *–Oui, je lui parle.*

  a What pronoun replaces the phrase *à Marie?* |
>   *lui*

  b Write an English equivalent for *Je lui parle.* |
>   I'm talking to her.

3 True or false? The indirect-object pronoun *lui* can refer to either a male or a female. |
>   true

4 Here is still another two-line conversational exchange.
>   *–Tu parles à Henri et à Marie?*
>   *–Oui, je leur parle.*

The English equivalent of *Je leur parle* is *I'm talking to* ____. |
>   them

5 A direct-object noun usually answers the question *what?* An indirect-object noun usually answers the question *to whom?* or *for whom?* Read this sentence, which contains both a direct-object noun and an indirect-object noun: *Je donne un livre à Paul.*

  a *What* is the speaker giving? |
>   *un livre*

  b *To whom* is the speaker giving the book? |
>   *à Paul*

  c The direct-object noun phrase is ____. |
>   *un livre*

  d The indirect-object noun phrase is ____. |
>   *à Paul*

  e In the indirect-object noun phrase, *Paul* is preceded by the preposition ____. |
>   *à*

6 In French, the indirect-object pronouns *lui* and *leur* usually replace the preposition *à* + a noun or noun phrase. Read the pairs of sentences below. Write the phrase from the first sentence that is replaced by *lui* or *leur* in the second.

a Je téléphone à Robert et à Alain. Je leur téléphone. |

> *à Robert et à Alain*

b Elle parle à son copain et à sa copine. Elle leur parle. |

> *à son copain et à sa copine*

c Vous donnez un disque à la cousine de Claire? Vous lui donnez un disque? |

> *à la cousine de Claire*

7 Answer each question below. Begin with *Oui* and use *lui* or *leur* in your responses.

a Est-ce que tu téléphones à Brigitte? |

> *Oui, je lui téléphone.*

b Est-ce que tu donnes un livre à Robert et à Jean? |

> *Oui, je leur donne un livre.*

c Vous parlez à cet homme? |

> *Oui, je lui parle.*

d Vous donnez des stylos à vos copains? |

> *Oui, je leur donne des stylos.*

3 Writing a dialogue

Complete the dialogue based on *Têtu comme une mule* that you began in class, and be prepared to hand in a copy of it in your next class. Be sure to check carefully for spelling, punctuation, and accents.

4 Practice with commands

1 The *vous-* and *nous-*commands of most verbs are identical to the present-tense *nous-* and *vous-* forms. Is the *tu*-command of an *-er* verb identical to the *tu*-form of the present tense? |

> no (The *tu*-command of an *-er* verb drops the final *s;* the *tu*-command of most other verbs is identical to the *tu*-form of the present tense.)

2 Form *tu-, nous-* and *vous-*commands with the following infinitive phrases.

> Modèle: manger de la viande |
>
> *Mange / Mangeons / Mangez de la viande.*

a montrer les photos à Marc |

> *Montre / Montrons / Montrez les photos à Marc.*

b venir à deux heures |

Viens / Venons / Venez à deux heures.

3 Below are statements about what people ought to do. Change each to a *tu-, nous-,* or *vous*-command.

Modèle: Tu dois manger vite à midi. |

Mange vite à midi.

a Tu dois acheter cette jolie veste! |

Achète cette jolie veste!

b Vous devez venir avant midi. |

Venez avant midi.

c Nous devons manger avant le concert. |

Mangeons avant le concert.

d Il fait frais; tu dois mettre ton cardigan. |

Il fait frais; mets ton cardigan.

1 *Indirect-object pronouns: all forms*

In Preparation 84 you practiced using the indirect-object pronouns *lui* and *leur.* This section will give you practice with all the forms of the indirect-object pronouns.

1 Read the following two-line conversations. Then answer the questions based on them.

–Qu'est-ce que tu montres à ta cousine?
–Je lui montre les photos de mon voyage.

–Qu'est-ce que tu montres au professeur?
–Je lui montre les photos de mon voyage.

–Qu'est-ce que tu montres aux parents de ton camarade?
–Je leur montre les photos de mon voyage.

a The phrases *à ta cousine* and *au professeur* are replaced by the indirect-object pronoun ____. |

lui (*Lui* replaces *à* + a noun or noun phrase referring to either a male or a female.)

b The phrase *aux parents de ton camarade* is replaced by the indirect-object pronoun ____. |

leur (*Leur* replaces *à* + a noun or noun phrase referring to more than one person.)

c Do *lui* and *leur* precede or follow the verb form *montre?* |

precede

2 There are four other indirect-object pronouns besides *lui* and *leur*. See if you can find them in the following sentences.

Mélanie me donne son numéro de téléphone. *Tu nous montres les photos.*
Je te téléphone demain. *Pierre vous parle de son voyage.*

   a The four indirect-object pronouns in the sentences above are ____. I
           me, te, nous, vous

   b Give the English equivalents of *me, te, nous,* and *vous.* I
           (to) me, (to) you, (to) us, (to) you

   c Do the indirect-object pronouns *me, te, nous,* and *vous* precede or follow the verb form? I
           precede

3 An indirect-object pronoun usually answers the question *to whom?*

   a Use *to* to write the English equivalent of *Elle me chante une chanson.* I
           She is singing a song to me.

   b Write a second English equivalent, without using *to.* I
           She is singing me a song.

4 Write two English equivalents for *Il nous donne de l'eau.* I
           He's giving some water to us./He's giving us some water.

5 Write a French equivalent for each sentence below.

   a I'm talking to you. (Use the object form of *vous.*) I
           Je vous parle.

   b He's talking to me. I
           Il me parle.

   c They're talking to us. I
           Ils/Elles nous parlent.

   d She's talking to you. (Use the object form of *tu.*) I
           Elle te parle.

6 Compare the indirect-object and direct-object pronouns.

DIRECT	me	te	nous	vous	le, la, l', les
INDIRECT	me	te	nous	vous	lui, leur

The indirect-object pronouns are identical in form to the direct-object pronouns except for ____ and ____. I
           lui, leur

7 In a negative sentence, *ne* precedes both the indirect-object pronoun and the verb form, and *pas* follows them. For practice, rewrite *Il me parle* in the negative. I
           Il ne me parle pas.

8 Answer the following questions in the negative.

      Modèle: Est-ce que vous me parlez? I
           Non, je ne vous parle pas.

   a Est-ce qu'il me parle? I
           Non, il ne te/vous parle pas.

b Est-ce qu'elle nous parle? **|**

Non, elle ne vous / nous parle pas.

c Est-ce que tu me parles? **|**

Non, je ne te parle pas.

NOTE ❋ *Marie-Antoinette and the French Revolution*

Marie-Antoinette, daughter of the Austrian emperor Francis I and queen Maria-Theresa, was married to the French crown prince Louis in 1770 to strengthen the alliance between Austria and France. They were not a well-matched couple: Marie-Antoinette was impulsive; Louis XVI was indecisive.

When Louis XVI came to the throne in 1774, France's rising middle class (the **bourgeoisie**) was clamoring for reform. Marie-Antoinette's childish and irresponsibly extravagant way of life angered the **bourgeoisie,** who suffered under heavy taxation while the nobility and clergy paid no taxes at all. Inspired by liberal ideas from England (like that of the English constitutional system, which guaranteed representation of all the people), the French people were becoming more and more dissatisfied with their lot.

Marie-Antoinette's unpopularity increased as she became involved in court intrigues with the nobles who resisted reforms. Her name was linked to the courtly extravagance that was considered to be one cause of the disastrous financial situation in France. If the king had not hesitated to carry out the financial reforms presented by his minister Turgot, he might have saved the monarchy. His wife, however, had no conception of the need for reform and economy. History has recorded her complete lack of understanding of the starvation menacing her people, shown by this remark: **"S'ils n'ont pas de pain, qu'ils mangent de la brioche!"** ("If they have no bread, let them eat pastry!") **Brioche,** a roll rich in eggs and butter, was something a poor person could not buy in the best of times, much less when bread was scarce.

The tide of history abruptly turned against Marie-Antoinette on July 14, 1789, when the Parisians stormed the Bastille prison, which had long been a symbol of the monarchy's authority. Several weeks later, the Parisian townspeople took over the Tuileries palace and imprisoned the royal family. Marie-Antoinette tried several times to escape, but without success. Louis XVI was executed in January 1793. After a brief trial on October 14, 1793, Marie-Antoinette was sentenced to death. She was guillotined on the **Place de la Révolution** two days later. Eyewitnesses reported that she was calm and dignified as she went to her fate.

2 Practice with indirect quotations

1 Compare the following sentences about what Paul says.

Paul dit: J'ai faim.   *Paul dit qu'il a faim.*

a Which of the sentences above is an indirect quotation? |

Paul dit qu'il a faim.

b The linking word *que* becomes ____ before *il* or *elle.* |

qu' (because of elision)

c When you report what someone else says, it's often necessary to change the subject pronoun and verb form. In the examples above, *J'ai* changes to ____. |

il a

2 Suppose you report to a friend what color Jeanne says her bicycle is. You could say *Jeanne dit: Mon vélo est jaune* or *Jeanne dit que son vélo est jaune.* When you turn the direct quotation into an indirect quotation, the marker *mon* becomes ____. |

son (You have to remember to change the possessive marker so that the new sentence makes sense.)

3 Now try your hand at reporting what the following people say. Remember to make all the appropriate changes. Answers are in the answer key.

     Modèle: Alain: Il fait très beau.

                 Roger: Mais non, il fait mauvais. |

Alain dit qu'il fait très beau.   Roger dit qu'il fait mauvais.

a Nanette: Mes cousins viennent demain.
      Philippe: Ma tante Lucie vient ce soir.
b Barbara: J'aime parler espagnol.
      Robert: Je préfère parler français.
c Pierre: Mon cardigan est vert.
      Renée: Mon pull est bleu.

CHECK-UP **Part 1**	Write French equivalents. **1** They show me their clothes. **2** He's talking to us about his trip. **3** I'm speaking to you (*formal*).

VOCABULARY

LA FÊTE DU MARDI GRAS   The Mardi Gras celebration

déjà   already
le costume   costume
deviner   to guess
le velours   velvet
la soie   silk
ça ne veut rien dire!   that doesn't
    mean anything
une perruque   wig

comprendre   to understand
je ne comprends rien du tout!
    I don't understand anything at all!
important   important
un bal   ball, danse
comme ça   like that
je te dis   I tell you
la guillotine   guillotine

1 More on object pronouns

This part will help you decide when to use the direct-object pronouns *le,* *la, les* and when to use the indirect-object pronouns *lui, leur.*

1 Read the following question and the two responses.
> –*Tu donnes ce gilet à ton frère?*   –*Oui, je le donne à mon frère.*
> –*Oui, je lui donne ce gilet.*

a Which noun phrase does *le* replace—*à ton frère* or *ce gilet?* |
ce gilet

b Does *ce gilet* follow the verb directly or does it follow the preposition *à?* |
It follows the verb directly. (In French, direct-object noun phrases usually follow the verb.)

c Which question does the direct-object pronoun *le* answer—*what* (*qu'est-ce que*) or *to whom* (**à qui**)? |
what (–*Qu'est-ce que tu donnes à ton frère?*   –*Ce gilet.*)

2 Look at the example at the beginning of frame 1 again.
a Which noun phrase does *lui* replace—*ce gilet* or *à ton frère?* |
à ton frère

b Does *ton frère* follow the verb directly? |
no (In French, most indirect-object noun phrases follow a form of the preposition *à.*)

c Which question does the indirect-object pronoun *lui* answer—*what* (*qu'est-ce que*) or *to whom* (**à qui**)? |
to whom (–*À qui donnes-tu ce gilet?*   –*À mon frère.*)

3 Rewrite each of the following sentences, substituting the appropriate object pronoun—*le, la, les* or *lui, leur*—for the italicized noun phrase.

> Modèle: Ma mère parle *à son ami Michèle.* |
> *Ma mère lui parle.*

a Je donne *ces trois disques* à mon ami Yves. |
Je les donne à mon ami Yves.

b Ils montrent le film *aux petits garçons.* |
Ils leur montrent le film.

c J'achète *cette chemise rouge.* |
Je l'achète.

d Elizabeth chante une chanson *à son petit frère.* |
Elizabeth lui chante une chanson.

4 Compare the French phrases with their English equivalents.
écouter quelque chose	to listen *to* something
chercher quelque chose	to look *for* something
regarder quelque chose	to look *at* something.

a Write the English equivalent of this sentence: ***J'écoute la radio.*** |

I'm listening to the radio.

b The English equivalent contains the preposition *to*. Does the French sentence contain a preposition? |

no (The French verbs *écouter*, *chercher*, and *regarder* all take *direct* objects.)

5 Write the French equivalents for each pair of sentences below.

a I'm looking for Nancy's dog. I'm looking for it. |

Je cherche le chien de Nancy. Je le cherche.

b We're listening to Jean's records. We're listening to them. |

Nous écoutons les disques de Jean. Nous les écoutons.

c He's looking at that old bicycle. He's looking at it. |

Il regarde ce vieux vélo. Il le regarde.

6 Now look at this list of French verbs and their English equivalents.

*téléphoner **à** quelqu'un*	to call someone (on the phone)
*montrer quelque chose **à** quelqu'un*	to show someone something (to show something to someone)
*donner quelque chose **à** quelqu'un*	to give someone something (to give something to someone)
*demander **à** quelqu'un si...*	to ask someone if . . .

a Write the English equivalent of this sentence: ***Je téléphone à mes parents.*** |

I'm calling my parents.

b The English equivalent has no preposition. Which preposition does the French sentence contain? |

à (The French verbs in the list above take *indirect* objects.)

7 Write the French equivalent of the sentences below. Remember that indirect-object pronouns replace noun phrases that follow a form of the preposition ***à***.

a Mme Prévot is calling the lawyer. |

Mme Prévot téléphone à l'avocat.

b Margot is showing him a book. |

Margot lui montre un livre.

c Georges is giving them these shoes. |

Georges leur donne ces chaussures.

d We call her often. |

Nous lui téléphonons souvent.

8 Now answer the following questions with the cue in parentheses and the appropriate object pronoun.

Modèle: Qu'est-ce que Jacques donne à Mathieu? (sa guitare) |

Il lui donne sa guitare.

a Qu'est-ce que vous montrez à vos grands-parents? (un joli livre) |

Je leur montre un joli livre.

b À qui est-ce qu'il montre ses devoirs? (au professeur) **|**

Il les montre au professeur.

c À qui donnent-elles cette jupe? (à Mlle Vérin) **|**

Elles la donnent à Mlle Vérin.

2 *Practice with* acheter *and* préférer

Do you remember how to spell the present-tense forms of *acheter* and *préférer?* If not, refer to the chart in Preparation 78.

1 Which subject pronouns match the following forms of *acheter?*

a *achète* and *achètent* **|**

j', on, il, and *elle* match *achète; ils* and *elles* match *achètent*

b *achetons* and *achetez* **|**

nous matches *achetons; vous* matches *achetez*

c *achètes* **|**

tu matches *achètes*

2 Complete each of the following sentences with the correct form of *acheter* and the names of the nouns represented by the drawings.

Modèle: Ma mère ＿＿ des  et des ＿ .**|**

Ma mère achète des pommes et des cerises.

a Ces hommes ＿＿ des  noirs et des ＿ marron. **|**

Ces hommes achètent des pantalons noirs et des chaussures marron.

b Jeanne et moi, nous ＿＿ trois  et une ＿ . **|**

Jeanne et moi, nous achetons trois chemisiers et une jupe.

c Je n' ＿＿ pas ces  et ce ＿ . **|**

Je n'achète pas ces croissants et ce fromage.

d Est-ce que vous ＿＿ une  ou un ＿ ? **|**

Est-ce que vous achetez une auto ou un vélomoteur?

3 Which subject pronouns match these forms of *préférer?*

a *préfère* and *préfèrent* |

> *je, on, il,* and *elle* match *préfère; ils* and *elles* match *préfèrent*

b *préférons* and *préférez* |

> *nous* matches *préférons; vous* matches *préférez*

c *préfères* |

> *tu* matches *préfères*

4 State which items the following people prefer. Use the first choice.

> Modèle: Georges: les chansons américaines ou les chansons françaises? |
> *Georges préfère les chansons américaines.*

a ces jeunes filles: les chaussures italiennes ou les chaussures espagnoles? |

> *Ces jeunes filles préfèrent les chaussures italiennes.*

b David et toi: les films italiens ou les films américains? |

> *David et toi (vous) préférez les films italiens.*

5 Ask which activity the following people like to do. Use questions with inversion.

> Modèle: (Roger) jouer aux boules / faire une promenade |
> *Préfère-t-il jouer aux boules ou faire une promenade?*

a (Annette) jouer de la guitare / danser |

> *Préfère-t-elle jouer de la guitare ou danser?*

b (Guy et Yves) faire du bateau / aller à un concert |

> *Préfèrent-ils faire du bateau ou aller à un concert?*

c (Jean et toi) faire une promenade / jouer aux cartes |

> *Préférez-vous faire une promenade ou jouer aux cartes?*

Les souks (bazars dans les pays arabes) à Tunis

3 Practice with markers and food

You know that in French, several kinds of noun markers are used with nouns referring to food, depending on the meaning of the sentence. This part will review the meanings and uses of the various kinds of markers.

1 Each item below begins with a question. Read the French sentences that follow, and choose the marker that answers the question.

> Modèle: Which marker is used to refer to something that has already been mentioned in the conversation?
> –Y a-t-il du beurre?
> –Oui, le beurre est sur la table. |
>> *le* (definite marker)

a Which marker is used to make a general statement?
> *Les fraises sont rouges.*
> *Comme dessert, je voudrais des fraises.* |
>> *les* (definite marker)

b Which marker is used to identify an item for the listener?
> *–Tu veux une poire?*
> *–Non, merci. Je n'aime pas les poires.* |
>> *une* (indefinite marker)

c Which marker is used with a count noun to indicate *some?*
> *–J'adore les frites.*
> *–Tu veux des frites avec ton steak?* |
>> *des* (indefinite marker)

d Which marker is used with a measure noun to indicate *some?*
> *Le beurre et les fromages de Normandie sont très bons.*
> *Je dois acheter du beurre et du fromage.* |
>> *du* (partitive marker)

2 In negative statements, a certain word replaces *du, de la, de l', un, une,* and ***des.*** Which word is missing from these sentences?
> *Non, merci, je ne veux pas ____ tomates.*
> *Je ne mange jamais ____ tomates.* |
>> *de, de*

3 The Lefranc family has gathered ***chez tante Monique*** for a Sunday dinner, and everyone is saying how good the food is. Write the definite marker that completes each exclamation below. Answers occur after item **d.**
> **a** Que ____ cidre est bon!
> **b** Que ____ pommes de terres sont bonnes!
> **c** Que ____ poulet est bon!
> **d** Que ____ tarte aux pommes est bonne! |
>> a *le* b *les* c *le* d *la*

4 Write a phrase to ask for some of each food below. Use the appropriate marker—*un, une, des* or *du, de la, de l'.* Follow the model. Answers occur after item **d**.

    Modèle: poire |

        Une poire, s'il vous plaît.

a bonbons   **c** poisson
b pêche   **d** glace à la vanille |

        a *Des bonbons, s'il vous plaît.* b *Une pêche, s'il vous plaît.* c *Du poisson, s'il vous plaît.* d *Une/De la glace à la vanille, s'il vous plaît.*

5 Write a phrase to say that you don't want any of what is being offered. Answers are in the answer key.

    Modèle: des carottes |

        Pas de carottes, merci.

a du café   **c** de l'eau
b des cerises   **d** un fruit

PREPARATION 87

1 *Commands with direct-object pronouns*

You learned in Phases 3 and 4 how to use direct-object pronouns in affirmative and negative statements: ***Je l'achète. Je ne l'achète pas.*** In this section you'll learn how to use direct-object pronouns with commands.

1 Do you remember how to form ***tu*-commands?**

    Tu-form: *Tu*-command:
    Tu regardes   *Regarde*
    Tu achètes   *Achète*

The ***tu*-command** of an *-er* verb is the same as the ***tu*-form** of the present tense, minus the final ___. |

        s

2 The ***tu*-command** of most other verbs is identical to the ***tu*-form** of the present tense.

    Tu-form: *Tu*-command:
    Tu viens   *Viens*
    Tu prends   *Prends*

Give the ***tu*-command** of ***voir, mettre,*** and ***faire.*** |

        vois, mets, fais

3 The *tu*-command of **aller** is usually *va* (without an *s*). Tell a friend to go to the library this afternoon. ▮

Va à la bibliothèque cet après-midi.

4 *Vous*-commands are easy to form. They are almost always identical to the *vous*-form of the present tense.

Vous-form:	*Vous*-command:
Vous regardez	*Regardez*
Vous venez	*Venez*

Give the **vous**-command of **mettre, montrer,** and **acheter.** ▮

mettez, montrez, achetez

5 *Nous*-commands are also easy to form. They are almost always identical to the *nous*-form of the present tense.

Nous-form:	*Nous*-command:
Nous regardons	*Regardons*
Nous allons	*Allons*

Give the **nous**-command of **donner, téléphoner,** and **faire.** ▮

donnons, téléphonons, faisons

6 Some verbs, like **regarder,** take a direct object in French. The direct object answers the question *what.* Compare these commands.

Regarde le vélo.	*Regarde-le.*
Regarde la bicyclette.	*Regarde-la.*
Regarde les vélomoteurs.	*Regarde-les.*

a When you use a direct-object pronoun with a command, does it precede or follow the verb? ▮

it follows (just as it does in English)

b In writing, what mark of punctuation is used between the verb form and the direct-object pronoun? ▮

a hyphen

7 You and a friend are out shopping. You see a handsome cardigan sweater in the display window, and you wish to call your friend's attention to it.

a Tell your friend to look at the sweater, by using a direct-object pronoun. ▮

Regarde-le!

b Another friend arrives. Tell them both to look at it. ▮

Regardez-le!

c Include yourself in the command. ▮

Regardons-le!

8 Suppose you're trying to convince a friend to buy a second-hand automobile your older brother wants to sell.

a Tell your friend to buy it. ▮

Achète-la!

b Try to convince two friends to buy it. ▮

Achetez-la!

c Include yourself in the command. ▮

Achetons-la!

2 Practice with indirect quotations

See if you can write the correct answers to all frames in this section in less than three minutes. Remember to change the subject pronoun, verb form, and possessive markers, if necessary.

1 Rewrite the following direct quotations as indirect quotations.
  a Jean: J'ai une grande sœur. ▌

> *Jean dit qu'il a une grande sœur.*

  b Marianne: Je suis l'aînée de la famille. ▌

> *Marianne dit qu'elle est l'aînée de la famille.*

  c Gilles: Mes parents habitent à Grenoble. ▌

> *Gilles dit que ses parents habitent à Grenoble.*

2 Report what Alain, Jules, and Renée say they are going to do this afternoon.

> *Alain:*   *Je vais au cinéma avec mon cousin.*
> *Jules:*   *Je vais jouer aux boules avec mon grand-père.*
> *Renée:*   *Je vais faire du patin avec mes copines.*

  a Que dit Alain? ▌

> *Alain dit qu'il va au cinéma avec son cousin.*

  b Que dit Jules? ▌

> *Jules dit qu'il va jouer aux boules avec son grand-père.*

  c Que dit Renée? ▌

> *Renée dit qu'elle va faire du patin avec ses copines.*

3 Practice with object pronouns

This part will give you practice using all the object pronouns.

1 Answer the following questions, using indirect-object pronouns.

> Modèle: Tu parles à Guy en anglais? (non) ▌
> *Non, je ne lui parle pas en anglais.*

  a Vous montrez les photos à vos copines? (oui)
  b Vous parlez souvent à votre grand-père? (non, nous...)
  c Tu demandes à Catherine si elle vient ce soir? (oui)
  d Elles te téléphonent demain? (oui)
  e Vos enfants vous montrent leurs dessins, M. et Mme Grammond?
(non, ils...) ▌

> **a** *Oui, nous leur montrons les photos.*   **b** *Non, nous ne lui parlons pas souvent.*   **c** *Oui, je lui demande si elle vient ce soir.*   **d** *Oui, elles me téléphonent demain.*   **e** *Non, ils ne nous montrent pas leurs dessins.*

2 Give the French equivalents of these sentences. Some sentences will need direct-object pronouns, others will need indirect-object pronouns.

a She's talking to them. ▌
Elle leur parle.

b She's looking at them, too. ▌
Elle les regarde aussi. (Remember that *regarder* takes a direct object.)

c He's listening to me. ▌
Il m'écoute.

d We're telephoning her. ▌
Nous lui téléphonons.

e We're listening to her. ▌
Nous l'écoutons.

f I'm looking at him. ▌
Je le regarde.

g They (*ils*) are talking to her. ▌
Ils lui parlent.

CHECK-UP
Part 1

Write French equivalents for these pairs of sentences.

1 Look at this photo. Look at it.

2 Look at that coat. Look at it.

3 Look at those shoes. Look at them.

1 *Practice with* devoir

In doing this part of the Preparation, remember that ***devoir*** has various meanings (*to have to, must, be supposed to,* etc.), depending on the tone of voice and the situation. If you think you've forgotten the forms of ***devoir,*** look back at Preparation 76, Part 1, before you begin frame 1.

1 Rewrite the following sentences, using the appropriate form of ***devoir.***

> Modèle: Je vais chez le dentiste demain. |
> > *Je dois aller chez le dentiste demain.*

a Est-ce que vous faites vos devoirs ce soir? |
> *Est-ce que vous devez faire vos devoirs ce soir?*

b Tu vas à la bibliothèque ce matin? |
> *Tu dois aller à la bibliothèque ce matin?*

c Paul et Philippe achètent des vêtements. |
> *Paul et Philippe doivent acheter des vêtements.*

d Nous déjeunons avec tante Germaine. |
> *Nous devons déjeuner avec tante Germaine.*

e Ta mère travaille à mi-temps. |
> *Ta mère doit travailler à mi-temps.*

2 Tell the persons indicated that they must or must not do the activities mentioned.

> Modèle: Hélène: prendre du lait / prendre du café |
> > *Tu dois prendre du lait. Tu ne dois pas prendre de café.*

a Henri: parler français / parler anglais |
> *Tu dois parler français. Tu ne dois pas parler anglais.*

b Georges et Gilles: dîner à six heures / dîner à neuf heures |
> *Vous devez dîner à six heures. Vous ne devez pas dîner à neuf heures.* ·

c Jeanne et Julie: travailler ce matin / travailler ce soir |
> *Vous devez travailler ce matin. Vous ne devez pas travailler ce soir.*

2 *Practice with commands*

Review the formation of commands in Preparation 87, Part 1. Then see if you can complete this section in less than one minute.

1 Rewrite the statements below as ***tu-, nous-,*** or ***vous-***commands.

> Modèle: Tu dois regarder ce film. |
> > *Regarde ce film.*

a Vous devez acheter ces légumes. ❚

Achetez ces légumes.

b Tu dois aller au bureau. ❚

Va au bureau.

c Nous devons jouer aux cartes chez Nanette. ❚

Jouons aux cartes chez Nanette.

d Tu dois faire les commissions à quatre heures. ❚

Fais les commissions à quatre heures.

e Vous devez faire du camping cet été. ❚

Faites du camping cet été.

3 *Writing practice*

Tell what articles of clothing Sylvie, Michel, and their friends put on in order to do certain activities. Form complete sentences according to the numbered cues indicated. Be sure to put the adjectives in column A *before* the noun, and the adjectives in column C *after* the noun.

A	B	C	D
1 joli	1 pantalon	1 blanc	1 aller au théâtre
2 petit	2 veste	2 jaune	2 faire de la voile
3 grand	3 maillot	3 marron	3 jouer au tennis
4 vieux	4 costume	4 noir	4 aller au restaurant
5 élégant	5 chemise	5 rouge	5 faire une promenade
	6 chapeau	6 violet	6 aller au bureau
	7 manteau	7 bleu	7 aller à la plage

Modèle: Raoul: 4 1 4 2 ❚

Raoul met un vieux pantalon noir pour faire de la voile.

a Sylvie: 1 7 6 1 ❚

Sylvie met un joli manteau violet pour aller au théâtre.

b Michel: 5 4 4 6 ❚

Michel met un élégant costume noir pour aller au bureau.

c Anne: 4 1 3 5 ❚

Anne met un vieux pantalon marron pour faire une promenade.

d Jeanne: 2 6 1 3 ❚

Jeanne met un petit chapeau blanc pour jouer au tennis.

e Pauline: 1 3 7 7 ❚

Pauline met un joli maillot bleu pour aller à la plage.

f Pierre: 5 2 5 4 ❚

Pierre met une élégante veste rouge pour aller au restaurant.

g Georges: 4 5 1 2 ❚

Georges met une vieille chemise blanche pour faire de la voile.

1 Pre-test practice: adjectives

Answers for all pre-test practice sections are in the answer key. If you want to review what you have learned about adjectives, refer to the Summary beginning on p. 381 or to Preparations 76, 77, and 79.

1 Each item in frame 1 consists of a noun phrase and two adjectives. One adjective belongs *before* the noun and one adjective belongs *after* it. Write complete sentences, beginning each with **C'est** or **Ce sont.**

> Modèle: une femme (allemand, gentil) |
>
> *C'est une gentille femme allemande.*

a les chaussures (vieux, marron) **d** un homme (jeune, jaloux)
b une pomme (rouge, gros) **e** une maison (jaune, petit)
c un chapeau (rose, joli)

2 Decide whether the adjective in parentheses belongs before or after the noun. Write the complete sentence on your worksheet.

> Modèle: Mon frère a une ____ voiture ____ . (vieux) |
>
> *Mon frère a une vieille voiture.*

a Moi, je préfère la ____ robe ____. (bleu)
b Le directeur est un ____ homme ____. (sympathique)
c À mon avis, elle porte des ____ chaussures ____. (laid)
d M. Delisle habite dans un ____ appartement ____. (petit)
e Yvette a une ____ amie ____. (martiniquais)

2 Pre-test practice: verbs

If you need to refresh your memory about the present tense of the verbs **manger, commencer, acheter,** and **préférer,** refer to Preparations 63 and 78.

1 The verb **manger** has only one spelling change in the present tense. That change occurs in the **nous**-form, which is spelled ____.

2 The verb **commencer** also has only one spelling change in the present tense. That change occurs in the **nous**-form, which is spelled ____.

3 The verb **acheter** adds accents on a number of the present-tense forms. Write the forms that match each subject pronoun.

a j' ____, vous ____, elle ____
b ils ____, tu ____, elles ____
c nous ____, on ____, il ____

4 The verb *préférer* has accents on every single present-tense form, but they are not always the same ones. Write the forms that match each subject pronoun.

    a tu ____, on ____, je ____

    b il ____, nous ____, elle ____

    c elles ____, vous ____, ils ____

5 Complete the negative answers to the following questions. Use the appropriate form of *manger, commencer, acheter,* or *préférer* in your responses.

    a –Alice et vous, vous mangez chez vous ce soir?
        –Non, nous ____ chez ma tante.

    b –Robert et vous, vous commencez vos devoirs à dix heures?
        –Non, nous les ____ à huit heures.

    c –Tu achètes cette chemise jaune pour ton frère?
        –Non, je l' ____ pour mon père.

    d –Où est-ce que votre sœur et vous achetez vos vêtements?
        –Nous les ____ au Printemps.

    e –Monsieur, préférez-vous le pull gris ou le pull marron?
        –Je ____ le pull marron.

    f –Quelle robe préférez-vous, Anne et Jeanne?
        –Nous ____ cette robe bleue.

NOTE ❋

How the French feel about clothes

Paris is one of the fashion capitals of the world, and travelers from all over like to shop for clothes there. **Haute couture** (high fashion) refers to the very expensive, one-of-a-kind creations by designers like Christian Dior, Pierre Cardin, Yves Saint-Laurent, Courrèges, Chanel and others. Only the rich can afford to buy an article of clothing that costs as much as a car. However, these **grands couturiers** also produce collections of **prêt-à-porter** (ready-to-wear clothes), as well as accessories such as scarves, jewelry, eyeglasses, luggage, etc. These can be bought in **boutiques** (small shops that specialize in high-quality clothing or accessories) and in most of the **grands magasins.**

For a French person, good taste means well-cut clothing with relatively simple lines and somewhat subdued colors. Quite a number of women are willing to pay several thousand francs (several hundred dollars) for a suit, a dress, or a sport coat bearing the **griffe** (signature) of one of the big names in **haute couture.** One can also buy less expensive clothes in the category of **prêt-à-porter;** still, it is not easy to find a simple "good" dress for a modest price, even in a small dress shop. Thus, most French people are careful in selecting the clothes they buy, and look for good quality as much as for style.

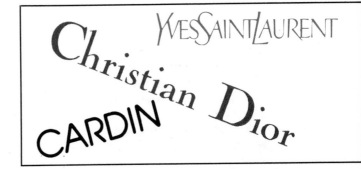

3 Pre-test practice: indirect quotations

If you need help with indirect quotations, see Preparation 83.

1 Report what each of the following persons is saying. Use the linking word *que.*

a M. Gérard: Nous devons acheter une maison à Paris.
b Marianne: Je veux voyager en Europe cet automne.
c Véronique: Mes parents aiment la musique classique.
d Mme Leclerc: Mon fils et ma fille vont à l'université.

2 Report what Michel and Carole say about the movie at the Odéon theater.

Michel: *Le film est très bon.*
Carole: *Au contraire, le film est très mauvais.*

"One who dresses well, lives well."

4 Pre-test practice: negative expressions

Ne...rien, ne...personne, and *ne...jamais* were presented in Preparation 81.

1 Give logical responses to the questions below with *ne...rien, ne...personne,* or *ne...jamais.* Write complete answers.

Modèle: Ils veulent quelque chose? ▌

Non, ils ne veulent rien.

a M. et Mme Vincent, vous achetez quelque chose aujourd'hui?
b Est-ce qu'il y a quelqu'un chez toi?
c Fais-tu souvent du ski?
d Elle connaît quelqu'un à Paris?
e Tu vois les Bertrand là-bas?
f Il y a quelque chose dans cette boîte?
g Est-ce que Madeleine achète un pantalon?

2 Give one-word answers with *rien, personne,* or *jamais* to the questions below.

a Qu'est-ce que tu vois?
b Allez-vous souvent au théâtre?

c Qui est là?

1 Pre-test practice: indirect-object pronouns

Indirect-object pronouns were presented in Preparations 84, 85, and 86.

1 Answer the following questions in the affirmative, and use an indirect-object pronoun in your responses.

> Modèle: Tu donnes un crayon à *Louis?* |
> *Oui, je lui donne un crayon.*

   a Est-ce qu'elle *te* donne un appareil-photo?
   b Il donne un cadeau *à son fils?*
   c Nous téléphonons *à Roger* ce soir?

2 Answer these questions in the negative, and use an indirect-object pronoun in your responses.

> Modèle: Vous parlez à Nathalie? |
> *Non, je ne lui parle pas.*

   a Vous donnez des fraises aux enfants?
   b Est-ce qu'elle te téléphone aujourd'hui?
   c Ils vous montrent les photos de leurs vacances?

2 Pre-test practice: commands

Commands were presented in Preparations 78, 80, 87, and 88.

1 Change the following ***vous*-commands** to ***tu-*** or ***nous*-commands**, according to the cues.

> Modèle: Prenez du pain. (tu) |
> *Prends du pain.*

   a Montrez ces photos à Laure. (nous)   **c** Allez à la librairie. (tu)
   b Faites vos devoirs. (tu)   **d** Chantez avec lui. (nous)

2 Write ***nous-, vous-,*** or ***tu*-commands**, according to the cues.

> Modèle: Il faut regarder le tableau. (vous) |
> *Regardez le tableau!*

   a Il faut venir avec René. (tu)   **c** Il faut commencer à dîner. (nous)
   b Il faut manger le poisson. (vous)   **d** Il faut faire un gâteau. (tu)

Getting ready for a test

In your next class you are going to have a progress test. To see how much you have accomplished, look back at the objectives listed at the beginning of the phase. This Preparation will give you practice with the kinds of questions you can expect on the test. Go through it carefully, write your answers on your worksheets, and check your answers with the answer key.

1 In Part A, you will hear *twice* a series of short conversational exchanges in French between two teenagers, Robert and Chantal. For each exchange, you will see on your answer sheet a question in English. You are to write a brief answer in English to each question. For example, you hear:

> (Robert): *J'aime beaucoup ces chaussures noires.*
> (Chantal): *Moi, je préfère ces chaussures marron.*

You see: What color shoes does Chantal prefer?
You answer: Brown.
Now try the following sample test items:

> (Robert): *Tu peux venir avec moi aux Trois Quartiers? Je veux acheter un cadeau pour Madeleine.*
> (Chantal): *Oui, d'accord.*

What are Robert and Chantal going to do?

> (Robert): *Tu peux aller au cinéma ce soir?*
> (Chantal): *Non, ma mère dit que je dois faire mes devoirs.*

Why can't Chantal go to the movies tonight?

2 In Part B, you will see a series of pictures representing articles of clothing, and the printed names of colors. You will hear a statement in French that mentions one of the articles of clothing and a color. You are to write the letter of the picture and word that the statement refers to. For example, you see:

 A   vert   B   vert   C   bleu

You hear: **Cet imperméable vert est très beau.**
You write: ____.

3 In Part C, you are to complete a set of sentences with the correct forms of **acheter, manger, préférer,** and **commencer**.

  a (acheter) Est-ce que tu ____ une cravate?
  b (manger) Nous ____ souvent des fruits.
  c (préférer) ____-vous le pull rouge ou le pull vert?
  d (commencer) Nous ____ nos devoirs maintenant.

4 In Part D, you are to change some direct quotations to indirect quotations. Remember to use a linking *que* or *qu'* in each indirect quotation.

    a Françoise dit: J'ai soif.

    Françoise dit ___.

    b Jean-Paul dit: Je dois aller au lycée maintenant.

    Jean-Paul dit ___.

    c Thérèse dit: On va dîner à neuf heures.

    Thérèse dit ___.

5 In Part F, you are to read a dialogue in French. Then you are to write short answers in English to some questions based on the dialogue.

SYLVIE	Je vais au cinéma après le dîner. Tu veux venir avec moi?
MARIE	Malheureusement, je ne peux pas. Je dois aider ma mère.
SYLVIE	Alors, tu peux aller au cinéma cet après-midi?
MARIE	Ah, non, je dois aller aux Galeries Lafayettes avec ma mère.
SYLVIE	Qu'est-ce que tu vas acheter?
MARIE	Je vais acheter une jupe marron et un chemisier rose. Et peut-être des chaussures.
SYLVIE	Oh, là là, quelle chance! Tu vas être très élégante!

    a What does Sylvie want to do this afternoon?

    b Why can't Marie go with Sylvie?

    c What is Marie going to buy?

6 In Part F, you are to write the correct form of *devoir* for each subject.

    a Vous ne ___ pas regarder la télévision.

    b ___-nous faire nos devoirs tout de suite?

    c Est-ce que tu ___ faire des commissions cet après-midi?

7 In Part G, you will see a series of questions in French. You are to write appropriate answers in the affirmative, replacing words in italics with the appropriate indirect-object pronoun.

    a Est-ce que vous donnez un livre *à Paul*?

    b Nous téléphonons *à M. et Mme Ledoux* maintenant?

    c Tu *me* parles?

8 In Part H, you are to supply the appropriate form of *mettre* for each subject.

    a Est-ce que Jean ___ ses livres sur la table?

    b ___-vous votre chemise bleue aujourd'hui?

    c Quand il fait froid, je ___ mon gros manteau.

9 In Part I, you will first be asked to change *vous*-commands to *tu*- or *nous*-commands, according to the cues given.

    a Regardez le tableau! (tu)

    b Mangez les légumes! (nous)

Then you will be asked to change sentences that contain *Il faut* + infinitive to commands with *nous, vous,* or *tu.*

    c Il faut acheter du pain. (vous)

d Il faut commencer à travailler. (tu)

e Il faut chanter. (nous)

10 In Part J, you will be asked to complete sentences with the correct form of the adjective.

    a (jeune) La ___ fille s'appelle Jeanne.

    b (français) M. Boudet est un photographe ___.

    c (beau) Regarde cette ___ voiture.

11 In Part K, you will be asked to write complete sentences telling what each person indicated is putting on in order to do a certain activity. You will be expected to use *mettre* and cues from the following columns:

A	B	C	D
1 élégant	1 le chapeau	1 marron	1 faire du ski
2 joli	2 la chemise	2 violet	2 aller à la discothèque
3 vieux	3 la robe	3 blanc	3 faire une promenade
4 grand	4 un pull	4 bleu	4 aller à l'usine

    a Mireille: 2 3 4 2

    b Edouard: 3 1 1 4

12 In Part L, you will be expected to contradict statements by using *ne...jamais, ne...personne,* and *ne...rien.*

    a Je prends un fruit comme dessert.

    b Il y a deux garçons là-bas.

    c Denise joue toujours au tennis avec Mireille.

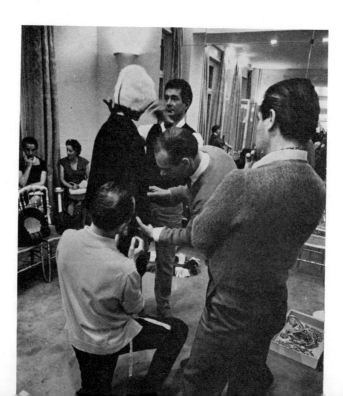

SUMMARY

1 The present tense of devoir (*Preparation 76*)

je	doi	s
tu	doi	s
on / il / elle	doi	t
ils / elles	doiv	ent
nous	dev	ons
vous	dev	ez

a. *Devoir* has three stems in the present tense: *doi-, doiv-,* and *dev-.*

b. *Devoir* can have several English equivalents. The meaning depends on the context.

	I have to	
	I must	
Je dois faire mes devoirs.	I should	do my homework.
	I'm supposed to	
	I've got to	

2 The present tense of acheter and préférer (*Preparation 78*)

j'	achèt	e	je	préfèr	e
tu	achèt	es	tu	préfèr	es
on / il / elle	achèt	e	on / il / elle	préfèr	e
ils / elles	achèt	ent	ils / elles	préfèr	ent
nous	achet	ons	nous	préfér	ons
vous	achet	ez	vous	préfér	ez

a. *Acheter* has two stems in the present tense: *achèt-* and *achet-.*

b. *Préférer* has two stems in the present tense: *préfèr-* and *préfér-.*

c. The stems *achet-* and *préfér-* occur in the *nous-* and *vous-* forms, when the verb ending is pronounced.

3 Devoir and il faut + infinitive (*Preparation 77*)

a. *Devoir* and *il faut* are commonly used to express obligation. *Il faut* is usually used to make a general statement. *Devoir* is usually used to make a statement directed toward a specific person. Both *devoir* and *il faut* can express many shades of obligation, depending on the context and the tone of voice of the speaker.

b. Both *devoir* and *il faut* are followed by an infinitive. The forms of *devoir* change to match the subject noun or pronoun. *Il faut* never changes form.

Tu dois partir.   Nous devons partir.   Il faut partir.

4 More about placement and agreement of adjectives (*Preparations 76, 77, 79*)

    a. In French most adjectives, including those of nationality and color, follow the nouns they describe.

        *Jean parle avec **le professeur italien.***
        *J'achète **une jupe verte.***

    b. Some commonly used adjectives often precede the noun.

beau (bel), belle	*gros, grosse*	*mauvais, mauvaise*
bon, bonne	*jeune, jeune*	*petit, petite*
grand, grande	*joli, jolie*	*vieux (vieil), vieille*

    c. The adjectives ***beau*** and ***vieux*** become ***bel*** and ***vieil*** when they precede a masculine singular noun beginning with a vowel sound.

        *C'est un **bel** enfant.*   *C'est un **vieil** homme.*

    d. The adjectives of color ***marron*** and ***orange*** are invariable. They do not change form in the feminine or in the plural.

*un chapeau **marron***	*une chemise **marron***	*des gants **marron***
*un pull **orange***	*une jupe **orange***	*des pantalons **orange***

5 Tu-, nous-, and vous-commands (*Preparations 78, 80*)

    a. Subject pronouns are not used with commands.

    b. ***Tu*-commands** of *-er* verbs are the same as the *tu*-form of the present tense, minus the final *-s.* ***Tu*-commands** of most other verbs are identical to the *tu*-form of the present tense. The *tu*-command of ***aller*** is usually ***va***.

Tu regardes la photo?	***Regarde** la photo.*
Tu prends un café?	***Prends** un café.*
Tu vas au cinéma?	***Va** au cinéma.*

    c. Most ***nous-*** and ***vous*-commands** are identical to the ***nous-*** and ***vous*-forms** of the present tense.

Nous achetons une moto rouge.	***Achetons** une moto rouge.*
Vous achetez une voiture bleue.	***Achetez** une voiture bleue.*

    d. The usual English equivalent of a ***nous*-command** is expressed with *let's.*

        ***Allons** au cinéma!*   Let's go to the movies!

6 Negative expressions (*Preparation 81*)

    a. The negative expressions ***ne...rien***, ***ne...personne***, and ***ne...jamais*** function in many ways like the negative expression ***ne...pas***. In the present tense, the particle ***ne (n')*** precedes the verb form, ***pas*** follows it.

*Je **ne** suis **pas** pressé.*	I'm not in a hurry.
*Je **n'**écoute **personne**.*	I don't listen to anybody.
*Je **ne** vois **rien**.*	I don't see anything.
*Je **ne** vais **jamais** au théâtre.*	I never go to the theater.

b. **Rien, personne,** and **jamais** may be used alone as a response.

–Qu'est-ce que tu vois?   –Rien.

c. **Jamais de** may be used like **pas de** with count and measure nouns.

Il ne prend jamais de bonbons.

7 *Present tense of* mettre   (*Preparation 82*)

je	met	s
tu	met	s
on/il/elle	met	
ils/elles	mett	ent
nous	mett	ons
vous	mett	ez

Mettre has two stems in the present tense: ***met-*** and ***mett-*.**

8 *Indirect quotations*   (*Preparation 83*)

Indirect quotations in French are always introduced with the connecting word **que.** Changes in subject pronoun, verb form, and possessive marker may be necessary.

M. Rolland dit: J'aime mes enfants.
*M. Rolland dit **qu'il** aime ses enfants.*

9 *Indirect-object pronouns*   (*Preparations 84, 85*)

DIRECT-OBJECT PRONOUNS	INDIRECT-OBJECT PRONOUNS
me, m'	me, m'
te, t'	te, t'
le, la, l'	lui
les	leur
nous	nous
vous	vous

a. The indirect-object pronouns are identical in form to the direct-object pronouns except for **lui** and **leur.**
b. Indirect-object pronouns usually precede a conjugated verb form. They come between a conjugated verb form and a following infinitive.

*Je **leur** donne les crayons*
*Je vais **lui** donner le cahier.*

10 *Commands with direct-object pronouns*   (*Preparation 87*)

Direct-object pronouns follow affirmative command forms. A hyphen is inserted between the verb form and the pronoun.

*Prenez-**le,** s'il vous plaît.*	Take it, please.
*Mettons-**les** là-bas.*	Let's put them over there.
*Invite-**la** à notre fête.*	Invite her to our party.

Parlons mode!

Histoire de chaussures

La scène se passe dans un grand magasin parisien, les Galeries Lafayette. Nous sommes au rayon des chaussures. Nous voyons une cliente et une jeune vendeuse. Oh là là ... toutes ces boîtes! Une, deux, trois, cinq, dix boîtes de chaussures ... Et la cliente n'est pas contente:

5   CLIENTE   Non, non, non, Mademoiselle! Ces chaussures sont trop grandes, je vous dis.

VENDEUSE   Mais Madame, c'est votre pointure... Vous prenez un 38 environ.

CLIENTE   Un 38! Jamais de la vie! Je prends un 37 au maximum, vous entendez, Mademoiselle, MA-XI-MUM!

10   VENDEUSE   Bien, Madame. Voilà un 37. Donnez-moi votre pied droit, s'il vous plaît.

CLIENTE   Aïe! Mais c'est trop petit, voyons!

VENDEUSE   Vous voyez, Madame, vous devez prendre un 38, au moins.

CLIENTE   Un 38? Au moins? Ça alors, c'est trop fort! Eh bien, gardez-les, vos chaussures, Mademoiselle! Au revoir!

15   VENDEUSE   Je regrette, Madame. Au revoir, Madame.

CLIENTE   (*en sortant*) Oh là là, ces vendeuses! Qu'elles sont stupides!

VENDEUSE   (*à mi-voix*) Oh là là, ces clientes! J'en ai marre!

Têtu comme une mule!

Aux Galeries Lafayette, au rayon des vêtements pour hommes. Une femme et son mari regardent des costumes, des imperméables, des vestes de sport. La femme voit une veste. Elle l'aime beaucoup, mais son mari ne l'aime pas du tout.

5   MARI   Non, je n'aime pas cette veste, je te dis! Regarde toutes ces couleurs, elles sont horribles.

FEMME   Au contraire, elles sont à la mode maintenant.

MARI   À la mode? Pour des étudiants comme Jean-Louis, mais pas pour moi.

FEMME   Mais si, pour toi! Regarde, elle est parfaite avec ton pantalon marron.

10   MARI   Jamais de la vie! Elle est parfaite pour Jean-Louis. Achetons-lui cette veste pour son anniversaire.

FEMME   Jean-Louis! Tu plaisantes. Il porte seulement des blue jeans et des vieux pulls.

MARI   Et cette veste, à mon âge? Tu plaisantes toi aussi!

15   FEMME   Mais, voyons, on doit changer de temps en temps.

MARI   Pourquoi «on doit»? Moi, je ne veux pas changer.

FEMME   Oh toi! Tu es têtu comme une mule...

La Fête du Mardi Gras

Isabelle et Bertrand, environ 16 ans.

BERTRAND	Tu viens à la fête du Mardi Gras?
ISABELLE	Bien sûr! J'ai déjà mon costume.
BERTRAND	Ah oui? Qu'est-ce que tu vas être?
5 ISABELLE	Devine! Je vais porter une veste de velours et un pantalon de soie.
BERTRAND	Ça ne veut rien dire! Tu peux être un homme ou une femme!
ISABELLE	Tu as raison. Alors, je vais être un homme, avec une magnifique perruque blonde.
BERTRAND	Un homme? Avec une perruque? Je ne comprends rien du tout!
10 ISABELLE	Écoute. Tu vas comprendre tout de suite. Je suis très important et très célèbre. J'ai une femme très belle, qui adore les fêtes et les bals.
BERTRAND	Je ne connais personne comme ça...
ISABELLE	Mais si, tu connais, je te dis! Écoute. Qui dit: «S'ils n'ont pas de pain, qu'ils mangent de la brioche!»?
15 BERTRAND	Ah, Marie Antoinette, bien sûr! Alors tu vas être Louis XVI?
ISABELLE	C'est ça! Tu peux être Marie-Antoinette, si tu veux!
BERTRAND	Non, merci! Je préfère être la guillotine!

XERCICES

1 Sound-spelling correspondences

1 important	4 impertinent	7 indifférent
2 impatient	5 imprudent	8 intelligent
3 imposant	6 intéressant	9 instrument

2 Comparisons with animals

le bœuf	ox	*le pinson*	finch
la carpe	carp (large fish)	*le renard`*	fox
l'oie (f.)	goose	*la taupe*	mole
le paon	peacock	*la tortue*	tortoise

1. *Il est fort comme un bœuf.* He's as strong as . . .
2. *Elle est muette comme une carpe.* She's as silent as . . .
3. *Il est bête comme une oie.* He's as . . . as a goose.
4. *Elle est fière comme un paon.* She's as . . . as a peacock.
5. *Il est gai comme un pinson.* He's as happy as . . .
6. *Elle est rusée comme un renard.* She's as . . . as a fox.
7. *Il est myope comme une taupe.* He's as blind as . . .
8. *Elle est lente comme une tortue.* She's as slow as . . .

3 Indirect quotations

a. Le mari dit: –Ces couleurs sont horribles.
b. *Le mari dit que ces couleurs sont horribles.*
c. Le mari dit: –Je n'aime pas cette veste.
d. *Le mari dit qu'il n'aime pas cette veste.*

1. Le vendeur dit: –Ces couleurs sont à la mode.
   Qu'est-ce qu'il dit? Il dit ...
2. Claudine dit: –La vendeuse n'aime pas la cliente.
   Qu'est-ce qu'elle dit? Elle dit ...
3. Marianne dit: Le film commence à huit heures.
   Qu'est-ce qu'elle dit? Elle dit ...

4 Practice with liaison

1. C'est un disque.
   C'est mon disque.
2. Nous voyons une voiture.
   Nous achetons une voiture.
3. Ils ont beaucoup d'argent.
   Ils parlent beaucoup.
4. Où sont vos amis?
   Où sont vos chaussures?

5. Je vois dix girafes.
   Je vois dix éléphants.
6. Tu connais mon cousin?
   Tu connais mon oncle?
7. Sommes-nous intelligents?
   Est-il intelligent?
8. Prends-tu le métro?
   Prennent-ils le métro?

5 Practice with devoir *and the possessive markers*

Les Corot ont quatre enfants. Toute la famille va chez les grands-parents pour le week-end. Qu'est-ce qu'ils doivent (ou ne doivent pas) prendre avec eux?

1. Papa veut faire des photos. Il _____ appareil-photo.
2. Maman et Lisette veulent nager. Elles _____ maillots de bain.
3. Grand-mère n'aime pas la musique rock. Nous ne _____ pas _____ disques.
4. Lisette veut jouer au tennis. Elle _____ raquette (f.).
5. Il va faire froid le soir. Nous _____ manteaux.

6 Visual-lingual drill: direct- and indirect-object pronouns

1 Je	1 parler à	1 Angélique
2 Tu	2 écouter	2 les élèves
3 Yvette	3 téléphoner à	3 Léonard et à moi
4 Simone et Denis	4 regarder	4 Julien et à toi
5 Guy et moi, nous	5 voir	5 la radio
6 Vous	6 donner un cadeau à	6 la télévision

7 Sound-symbol correspondences: closed /o/ vs. open /ɔ/

/o/		/ɔ/	
1 beau	4 pauvre	1 école	4 bonne
2 rose	5 jaune	2 porte	5 Paul
3 chaud	6 beaucoup	3 pomme	6 téléphone

EN AFRIQUE

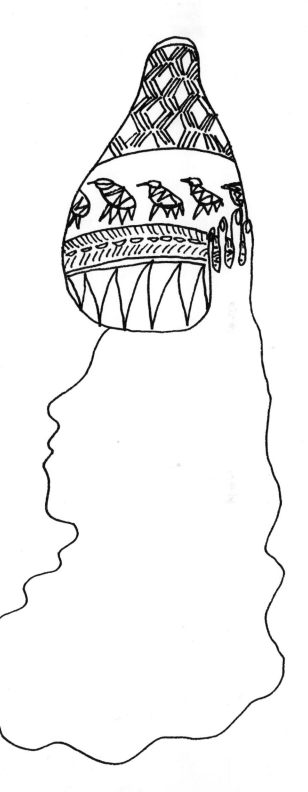

PHASE SEVEN OBJECTIVES

In this Phase, you will learn to talk about things that happened in the past, about geography, and about different means of transportation. You will listen to and read a story about a young Frenchman who is going to live in Senegal, a French-speaking country in West Africa. You will also begin working with a group of classmates to explore the culture of a French-speaking country. By the end of this Phase, you should be able to:

1 Compare one person or thing to another, using the comparative expressions **aussi...que, plus...que, moins...que** with adjectives and adverbs.

2 Combine two statements about a person or thing, using the relative pronoun **que.**

3 Talk about things that happened in the past, using the **passé composé** forms of **-er** verbs, **faire,** and **voir.**

4 Talk about writing to people and sending them things, using **écrire** (to write) and **envoyer** (to send).

5 Describe quantities, using the expressions **beaucoup de, trop de,** and **assez de.**

6 Describe someone's activities by using adverbs.

✳ The cultural notes will describe various aspects of **Sénégal:** its history, its ethnic composition, the weather, the food, what a rural village is like, what **un griot** is, and who Léopold Senghor is.

Qu'est-ce que vous savez sur le Sénégal?

1 If you think of the United States, many images may come to mind: the Statue of Liberty, the Grand Canyon, hot dogs, baseball, TV commercials, and so forth. List ten things that you associate with the U.S. Your teacher will talk with you and your classmates about the things you thought of.

2 The English equivalent of *Qu'est-ce que vous savez sur le Sénégal?* is *What do you ___ about ___?*

know, Senegal

3 In Phase 7 you will be learning about *Sénégal,* a French-speaking country in West Africa. You may already know something about West Africa because of television, the movies, and magazines you've seen. List five things you can think of in association with West Africa.

4 Below is a list of French words that you will see in Phase 7. See if any of the words refer to things you know something about already. By the end of this Phase, all of them should have some meaning for you.

un griot	des cacahuètes	un tam-tam
la Coopération	Léopold Senghor	un kora, un balafon
une concession	le baobab	le couscous
une case	un palabre	le mil
Dakar	un boubou, un pagne	Ouolof

1 *The relative pronouns* qui *and* que

1 A relative pronoun combines information about a person, thing or idea with information in another statement. The example below shows the relative pronoun *qui* (which you learned about in Phase 2) connecting two statements.

> *Je connais cette femme. **Elle** travaille là-bas.*
>
> *Je connais la femme **qui** travaille là-bas.*

a Write the English equivalent of ***Je connais la femme qui travaille là-bas.*** ▌

> I know the woman who works over there.

b ***Qui*** replaces the word ***elle.*** Is ***elle*** the subject or the direct object of ***travaille?*** ▌

> subject (The relative pronoun *qui* replaces the subject in the second statement.)

2 Write one sentence that combines both statements below. Use ***qui*** to relate the second statement to the first.

a Voilà une voiture. Cette voiture est chère (*expensive*). ▌

> *Voilà une voiture qui est chère.*

b Je ne connais pas le jeune homme. Ce jeune homme parle avec Mimi. ▌

> *Je ne connais pas le jeune homme qui parle avec Mimi.*

3 Now look at the example below that shows the relative pronoun ***que*** connecting two statements.

> *Voilà une belle moto. Je voudrais acheter **cette moto.***
>
> *Voilà une belle moto **que** je voudrais acheter.*

a Give an English equivalent for ***Voilà une belle moto que je voudrais acheter.*** ▌

> There's a beautiful motorcycle (that) I would like to buy.

b In the example above, ***que*** replaces ***cette moto.*** Is ***cette moto*** the subject or the direct object of the second sentence? ▌

> direct object (The relative pronoun *que* replaces a direct-object noun phrase or pronoun.)

4 Read the sentences below.

> *Tu connais la jeune fille que François invite à la fête?*
>
> Do you know the girl (whom) François is inviting to the party?

a Can a relative pronoun refer to people as well as to things? ▌

> yes (In English, one may omit the relative pronoun when connecting two sentences. In French, the relative pronoun may not be omitted.)

b Now read this sentence.

> *Tu connais la jeune fille qu'Eric va inviter au cinéma?*

What form does ***que*** take when it precedes a word beginning with a vowel sound, like ***Eric?*** ▌

> qu'

bienvenue au senegal

5 The relative pronoun *que* changes to *qu'* before a vowel sound. The relative pronoun *qui,* however, never changes form. Connect these sentence fragments with *qui: Thierry est un garçon / a beaucoup d'amis.* |

Thierry est un garçon qui a beaucoup d'amis.

6 Combine each pair of statements below into one statement. Use *que* or *qu'* to connect the second statement to the first by replacing the direct object in italics.

Modèle: C'est un vieil ami. J'aime beaucoup *ce vieil ami.* |

C'est un vieil ami que j'aime beaucoup.

a C'est une jolie robe. Elle porte souvent *cette jolie robe.* |

C'est une jolie robe qu'elle porte souvent.

b Il a deux frères. Je ne connais pas *ses deux frères.* |

Il a deux frères que je ne connais pas.

c C'est un chien très gentil. Toute ma famille aime beaucoup *ce chien.* |

C'est un chien très gentil que toute ma famille aime beaucoup.

7 Use the cues below to write French equivalents of the English sentences. Use the appropriate relative pronoun—*qui* or *que.*

Modèle: Georges sees a red vest that he wants to buy.

Georges / voir / gilet rouge / il veut acheter. |

Georges voit un gilet rouge qu'il veut acheter.

a Adeline is a young Haitian woman who wants to work in the United States. *Adeline / être / jeune Haïtienne / veut travailler aux Etats-Unis.* |

Adeline est une jeune Haïtienne qui veut travailler aux Etats-Unis.

b Where's the blue jacket Philippe likes so much? *Où / être / veste bleue / Philippe aime tellement?* |

Où est la veste bleue que Philippe aime tellement?

c I know something you don't know. *Je / savoir / quelque chose / tu ne sais pas.* |

Je sais quelque chose que tu ne sais pas.

d There's a bike that's very expensive. *Voilà / vélo / est très cher.* |

Voilà un vélo qui est très cher.

History of Senegal

The first Europeans arrived in Senegal around 1445, when Portuguese navigators landed at **le Cap vert** (Cape Verde)—the peninsula on which Dakar, the capital, is now situated. The French came nearly 200 years later, and built a trading post at the mouth of the Senegal River in 1638. They influenced Senegalese history to a much greater extent than any other European people.

Like most of western Africa, the area that is now Senegal was heavily exploited as a source for slaves. Men and women were kidnapped and shipped across the Atlantic. Those who survived the nightmarish conditions of the voyage were sold in North America and in the Caribbean.

In the 1800's, the French governor Faidherbe established colonial authority more firmly, built roads, and made it possible for civilization as the French knew it to begin to develop in Senegal. During this period, French authorities encouraged the colonists to raise and export **les cacahuètes** (peanuts), a valuable crop which plays an important role in the economy of Senegal today.

Many Senegalese riflemen (**les tirailleurs sénégalais**) fought for the Allies in World War I, and after World War II, French citizenship was granted to all Senegalese. In 1960, Senegal became independent of France, and is today **la République du Sénégal.**

Senegal produces mostly peanuts, cotton, rice, and sugar cane. The commercial fishing industry is expanding. The mineral wealth of the country consists of phosphates, salt, copper, and iron. Dakar is the cultural center as well as the political capital of the country. In addition to the university, museum, and center for folk arts, there are two film societies and a national theater (the **Théâtre National Daniel Sorano**) which promotes performances by Senegalese musicians, dancers, and actors.

SÉNÉGAL

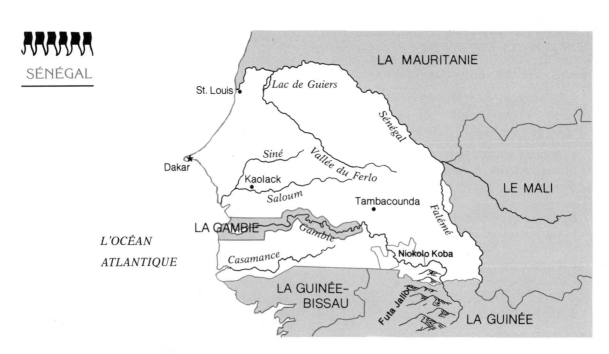

2 Practice with direct and indirect objects

You learned in Phase 6 that in French, a direct object usually answers the question *what?* or *whom?* and an indirect object usually answers the question *to whom?*

1 Here are two questions:

> *Qu'est-ce que Jacques montre à Marie?*
> *À qui est-ce que Jacques montre ses photos du Sénégal?*

a Which question asks *what?*—the question beginning with ***Qu'est-ce que...?*** or the one beginning with ***À qui...?*** |

the one beginning with *Qu'est-ce que...?*

b The question that asks *to whom?* begins with the words ____. |

À qui...

2 Here is a sentence that answers both questions above.

> *Jacques montre ses photos du Sénégal à Marie.*

a Write the phrase that answers the question ***Qu'est-ce que Jacques montre à Marie?*** |

ses photos du Sénégal (This is a direct-object noun phrase.)

b Write the phrase that answers the question ***À qui est-ce que Jacques montre ses photos?*** |

à Marie (This is an indirect-object noun phrase.)

c In French, an indirect-object noun or noun phrase is usually preceded by a form of the preposition ____. |

à

3 Look at the following question and answer.

> *–Qui invites-tu à ta fête?*   *–J'invite Michel.*

Does the direct-object noun ***Michel*** answer the question ***qui...?*** or ***qu'est-ce que...?*** |

qui...?

4 Below are some incomplete questions and their answers. Look at the answers, then decide which phrase belongs in the question: ***qui, qu'est-ce que,*** or ***à qui.***

a – ____ voyez-vous là-bas?   –Je vois la jeune secrétaire qui habite près du lycée. |

Qui

b – ____ est-ce que Jacques invite à la fête?   –Jacques invite ses amis à la fête. |

Qui

c – ____ ils regardent?   –Ils regardent un vieux film américain à la télé. |

Qu'est-ce qu'

d – ____ montrez-vous le film de votre voyage en Afrique?   –Je le montre à ma famille et à mes camarades. |

À qui

e – ____ téléphones-tu ce soir?   –Je téléphone à Jacques. |
À qui

5 Pronouns are useful because they let a speaker refer to a person or thing without saying the name over and over. If you don't remember the object pronouns in French, look for a moment at the chart in the Summary, p. 383.

a In French, the same pronouns are used for *me, you, us* and *to me, to you, to us*. These pronouns are *m __, t __, n __, v __*. |
me, te, nous, vous

b The pronouns that are used to mean *him, her, it,* or *them* are *l __, l __, l __*. |
le, la, les

c The pronoun that is used to mean *to him* or *to her* is *l __*. |
lui

d The pronoun that means *to them* is *l __*. |
leur

6 You are planning a slide show for some friends. Your parents want to make sure you've thought of everything and they keep asking you questions about what you're doing. Answer according to the cue in parentheses, and use an object pronoun to replace each italicized phrase. Answers are in the answer key.

Modèle: Tu invites *ta petite sœur et ses copines?* (Non...) |
Non, je ne les invite pas.

a Tu invites *la jeune Américaine qui habite chez tante Marthe?* (Oui...)
b Est-ce qu'elle a *notre adresse?* (Non...)
c Tu montres *les diapos de nos vacances en Bretagne?* (Non...)
d Alors, tu montres *à tes amis* nos diapos de l'Espagne? (Oui...)
e Tu téléphones *à ton oncle* pour emprunter (*borrow*) son écran? (Oui...)
f Tu mets *les diapos* en ordre samedi? (Non, vendredi).

7 Some French verbs use a preposition that the English equivalent doesn't use. Some English verbs use a preposition that the French equivalent doesn't use.

Look at the English and French equivalents below. Write each French phrase on your worksheet, including the preposition where needed. Answers are in the answer key.

a *to look at something:* regarder ____ quelque chose
b *to call someone:* téléphoner ____ quelqu'un
c *to show someone something:* montrer ____ quelque chose ____ quelqu'un
d *to ask someone if. . . :* demander ____ quelqu'un si...
e *to listen to someone:* écouter ____ quelqu'un
f *to look for something:* chercher ____ quelque chose
g *to give someone something:* donner ____ quelque chose ____ quelqu'un

VOCABULARY

Many of the new words in this Phase are cognates, and should be easy for you to learn. Take a couple of minutes to look at the French and think of the English equivalent. Then look at the English and try to think of the French.

le soldat soldier   *le marin* sailor

LE SERVICE DE LA COOPÉRATION   Alternate military service

l'armée de l'air (f.) air force	*difficile* difficult
l'armée de mer (f.) navy	*mémorable* memorable
l'armée de terre (f.) army	*obligatoire* compulsory
un caméraman cameraman	*passionnant, -e* exciting
un examen exam, test	*d'abord* first, at first
un institut technique technical institute	*enfin* at last
le service militaire military service	

PREPARATION 94

1 *Comparison of adjectives*

In this section, you'll learn how to express comparisons in French; for example *taller than, as tall as, less tall than.*

1 Compare the following sentences, which contrast Jean and Guy.
    Jean est plus petit que Guy.   Jean is shorter than Guy.
    Jean est plus sportif que Guy.   Jean is more athletic than Guy.
a In the comparisons above, French uses the word pattern ___ + adjective + ___. I
            plus...que
b English uses either the pattern adjective + *-er* + *than* or the pattern ___ + adjective + ___. I
            more . . . than
2 Suppose you and a business partner are arguing about whom to hire. Say that Paul is more qualified than David in some respects.

    Modèle: –David est gentil. I
            –Oui, mais Paul est plus gentil que David.

a –David est intelligent. I
            –Oui, mais Paul est plus intelligent que David.
b –David est sympathique. I
            –Oui, mais Paul est plus sympathique que David.
c –David est consciencieux. I
            –Oui, mais Paul est plus consciencieux que David.

3 Now compare sentences, which contrast Hélène and Monique.

> *Hélène est moins petite que Monique.*   Hélène is less short than Monique.
> *Hélène est moins sportive que Monique.*   Hélène is less athletic than Monique.

a In the comparisons above, French uses the word pattern ___ + adjective + ___. |

> *moins...que*

b English uses the pattern ___ + adjective + ___. |

> less . . . than

4 Now pretend that you and a friend are arguing about whether Yvette or Barbara should play center on the basketball team. Say that Yvette is less qualified in certain respects than Barbara. Remember to make each adjective agree with the subject noun.

> Modèle: –Yvette est grande. |
>
> > –Oui, mais elle est moins grande que Barbara.

a –Yvette est forte (*strong*). |

> > –Oui, mais elle est moins forte que Barbara.

b –Yvette est consciencieuse. |

> > –Oui, mais elle est moins consciencieuse que Barbara.

5 Now read the French and English sentences below, comparing Henriette and Julie.

> *Henriette est aussi grande que Julie.*   Henriette is as tall as Julie.

a In the comparison above, French uses the word pattern ___ + adjective + ___. |

> *aussi...que*

b English uses the pattern ___ + adjective + ___. |

> as . . . as

6 You and your friend Alice are each making a film. When Alice says that her film is better in certain respects than yours, reply that yours is as good as hers.

> Modèle: –Mon film est plus intéressant que ton film. |
>
> > –Mais non! Mon film est aussi intéressant que ton film.

a –Mon film est plus original que ton film. |

> > –Mais non! Mon film est aussi original que ton film.

b –Mon film est plus long que ton film. |

> > –Mais non! Mon film est aussi long que ton film.

c –Mon film est plus beau que ton film. |

> > –Mais non! Mon film est aussi beau que ton film.

7 Sometimes the people or things you want to compare are different in gender and number.

> *Laure et Julie sont aussi gentilles que Léonard.*
> *Mon pantalon est plus élégant que mes chaussures.*

Does the adjective agree with the subject, or with the noun that follows the word *que?* |

> It agrees with the subject.

8 Complete each sentence below with the appropriate form of the adjective.

    a Ces femmes sont plus (*grand, grandes*) que M. Moraud. |

             grandes

    b Cette photo est moins (*belles, belle*) que les autres. |

             belle

    c Ces jeunes filles sont aussi (*maigres, maigre*) que ce garçon. |

             maigres

    d Les légumes sont aussi (*importants, important*) que la viande. |

             importants

NOTE ❋

Le riz, le mil et le couscous

Three kinds of grain form an important part of the diet in Senegal: **le riz, le mil** (millet) and **le couscous** (tiny pellets of milled wheat). In rural villages, women prepare **le mil** for cooking by pounding it briskly in a wooden bowl. Often several women work together and sing to the rhythm made by the drumming of the wooden pestle in the bowl. **Le couscous** frequently accompanies a tasty meat or fish stew. Dishes with **couscous** are featured in many African restaurants in other parts of the world.

2 *Practice with the relative pronouns* qui *and* que

This part gives you practice using the relative pronouns *qui* and *que* to combine two related statements.

1 Compare the two sentences below.

    Je vois un garçon qui joue au basket.

    C'est un garçon que je ne connais pas.

    a Write English equivalents for each sentence. |

             I see a boy (who is) playing basketball.

             He's a boy (whom) I don't know.

    b Is *qui* the subject or object of *joue?* |

             Qui is the subject of *joue.* The verb usually follows *qui* immediately.

c Is *que* the subject or object of *je ne connais pas?* |

    Que is the object of *je ne connais pas.*

d In the clause *que je ne connais pas,* which word is the subject of *connais?* |

    je (The relative pronoun *que* is usually followed immediately by the noun or pronoun that is the subject of the relative clause.)

2 Complete each sentence below with the information in the second sentence. Use the appropriate relative pronoun to connect the two. Use *qui* to replace a subject in italics; use *que* to replace an object in italics.

    Modèle: Voilà une jeune fille _____. (*Elle* joue au basket.) |

    Voilà une jeune fille qui joue au basket.

    Voilà une jeune fille _____. (Je *la* trouve sympathique.) |

    Voilà une jeune fille que je trouve sympathique.

a Voilà la jeune fille _____. (*Elle* invite mon frère à une petite fête.)
Voilà la jeune fille _____. (Mon frère *la* trouve sympathique.) |

    Voilà la jeune fille qui invite mon frère à une petite fête.
    Voilà la jeune fille que mon frère trouve sympathique.

b J'aime bien les bonnes crêpes _____. (On fait *de bonnes crêpes* en Bretagne.)
J'aime bien ces crêpes _____. (*Ces crêpes* ont beaucoup de confiture.) |

    J'aime bien les bonnes crêpes qu'on fait en Bretagne.
    J'aime bien ces crêpes qui ont beaucoup de confiture.

c Hélène a un cours de maths _____. (*Le cours* est difficile.)
C'est un cours _____. (Elle *le* trouve passionnant.) |

    Hélène a un cours de maths qui est difficile.
    C'est un cours qu'elle trouve passionnant.

3 Jeanne and Albert are talking about various people they know. Each time Jeanne makes a statement, Albert disagrees and gives his own opinion. Complete Albert's statements with the relative pronoun *qui* or *que.*

    a Jeanne: Cette jeune fille là-bas va être journaliste, n'est-ce pas?
          Albert: Mais non, c'est l'étudiante _____ va être ingénieur. |

          qui

    b Jeanne: Paul Lévêque n'est pas gentil.
          Albert: Mais si, Paul est un garçon _____ je trouve très sympathique! |

          que

    c Jeanne: Tout le monde dit que tu aimes Monique. C'est vrai?
          Albert: Mais non, Monique est une jeune fille _____ je ne trouve pas du tout sympathique! |

          que

    d Jeanne: Laurent me dit qu'il est au régime.
          Albert: Impossible! C'est un garçon _____ mange tout le temps. |

          qui

Write a French equivalent for each sentence.

Marie-Hélène is taller than Jacques.

Jacques is as intelligent as Marie-Hélène.

Write the relative pronoun *qui* or *que* that correctly completes each sentence.

–Tu connais le garçon _____ porte le pull bleu?

–Oui, c'est un copain _____ je vais inviter à jouer au tennis.

VOCABULARY

LE SERVICE DE LA COOPÉRATION (2)

un domaine area (of interest)

un habitant inhabitant

un pays country, nation

exotique exotic, foreign

fascinant, -e fascinating

intéressant,-e interesting

varié,-e a variety of; various

aider to help, aid

avoir besoin de to need

envoie (envoyer) send (to send)

remplacer to substitute, replace

généralement usually, generally

pendant for, during

en même temps at the same time

PREPARATION 95

1 Stressed pronouns

You learned in Phase 5 that stressed pronouns have many uses in French. One common use is to give emphasis to a subject pronoun or noun; for example, *Moi, je n'aime pas la musique classique.* Another common use is after the preposition *chez;* for example *Nous allons chez lui cet après-midi.* In this Preparation, you'll learn some additional uses of stressed pronouns.

1 Here is a comparison of the stressed pronouns with the subject pronouns.

Subject pronouns: **je, tu, il, elle, ils, elles, nous, vous**

Stressed pronouns: **moi, toi, lui, elle, eux, elles, nous, vous**

a Four of the subject pronouns and the stressed pronouns are identical in form: _____, _____, _____, and _____. ▮

elle, elles, nous, vous

b Four of the stressed pronouns have forms that are different from the subject pronouns: _____, _____, _____, and _____. ▮

moi, toi, lui, eux

2 You have used stressed pronouns after *chez.* They are used after the other prepositions also. This frame will give you practice using them after *pour, avec,* and *sans* (for, with, without).

Imagine that you are having a dream in which you are a soldier named Dupont, who is being sent on a dangerous mission. You can't quite believe it, and simply echo the end of each statement you hear. Give your responses by repeating the preposition and using the appropriate stressed pronoun. Note that officers usually address non-commissioned soldiers as *tu.*

Modèle: Dupont, tu dois parler avec le capitaine. ▮
         Avec lui?

a Oui. Nous avons une mission dangereuse pour toi. ▮
         Pour moi?

b Oui. C'est un message secret pour le Président. ▮
         Pour lui?

c Oui. Tu vas aller au palais avec Leduc et Poiret. ▮
         Avec eux?

d Oui. Tu vas aller au Palais avec eux mais tu vas délivrer le message sans eux. ▮
         Sans eux?

e Oui. Ensuite tu dois revenir ici avec Mme X, la fameuse espionne. ▮
         Avec elle?

f Oui. Il y a grand danger pour elle et pour toi. ▮
         Pour nous? (–Oui. Bonne chance, Dupont!)

3 Some prepositions describe the position of one thing in relationship to another; for example, *devant, derrière,* and *entre.*

Where is the dog in the drawings below in relation to the persons shown? Use stressed pronouns in your responses.

Modèle: Le chien est devant la femme? ▮
         Non, il est derrière elle.

a Le chien est derrière l'homme? ▮
         Non, il est devant lui.

b Le chien est derrière la fille et le garçon? ▮
         Non, il est entre eux.

AIR AFRIQUE

L'Afrique Noire, c'est notre affaire.

4 Some prepositions describe relative position in time; for example, *avant* and *après.* In the sentences below, indicate who arrives *after* whom.

    Modèle: J'arrive avant lui. ▌

                    Il arrive après moi.

a Elle arrive avant eux. ▌

                    Ils arrivent après elle.

b Tu arrives avant elle. ▌

                    Elle arrive après toi.

5 Another common use of stressed pronouns is after the expression *être à* to show ownership. The English equivalent is *to belong to.*

    –Est-ce que cette voiture est à Roger?   –Does that car belong to Roger?
    –Non, elle est à moi.   –No, it belongs to me.

a Give the English equivalent of the following sentence.

    Cet électrophone est à eux. ▌

                    That record player belongs to them.

b Give the French equivalent of the following sentence.

    That record belongs to me. ▌

                    Ce disque est à moi.

6 Answer the questions below to say that the articles of clothing belong to the people indicated.

    Modèle: Les chaussettes sont à Léonard? ▌

                    Oui, elles sont à lui.

a Ce cardigan est à Barbara? ▌

                    Oui, il est à elle.

b La chemise est à Georges? ▌

                    Oui, elle est à lui.

c Ces manteaux sont à vous, Jacqueline et Marie? ▌

                    Oui, ils sont à nous.

d Les vestes sont à Christian et à Roger? ▌

                    Oui, elles sont à eux.

2 Adverbs ending in -ment

You've been using adverbs since the beginning of the course. Adverbs usually answer the question **comment? quand?** or **où?** In this section, you'll learn how to form a large group of adverbs that end in **-ment,** which usually answers the question **comment?**

1 In English, many adverbs are formed by adding the ending *-ly* to the base form of the adjective. For example:

careful   *carefully*   regular   *regularly*

Look at the adverbs below. What is the base form of the adjectives to which the ending *-ly* is added?

easily   actually   quickly I

easy, actual, quick

2 In French, many adverbs are formed by adding **-ment** to the feminine singular form of the adjective. All feminine singular adjectives end in **-e.** For example:

M.	F.	ADVERB
sérieux	sérieuse	sérieusement
naturel	naturelle	naturellement
rare	rare	rarement

For each adverb below, what is the base form to which **-ment** is added?

heureusement   seulement   nécessairement I

heureuse, seule, nécessaire

3 It's easy to guess the meaning of most adverbs ending in **-ment,** because they usually have an English equivalent ending in *-ly*. What do the adverbs in **-ment** mean in the following sentences?

  a Je mange rapidement parce que je dois faire mes devoirs. I

rapidly, quickly

  b Ils travaillent tranquillement toute la journée. I

quietly

4 Complete the second sentence in each pair with the adverb in **-ment** that corresponds to the adjective.

Modèle: Dans le désert l'eau est *rare*. Il pleut ＿＿. I

rarement

  a En *général,* nous passons nos vacances à la plage. ＿＿ nos cousins viennent avec nous. I

Généralement

  b Mon frère est *sérieux*. Il travaille ＿＿. I

sérieusement

  c Mon père trouve le français *difficile*. Il le parle ＿＿. I

difficilement

d Ma mère trouve le français *facile* (easy). Elle le parle ____. |

facilement

5 Compare the following sentences.

> *C'est **vrai**. Cette veste est **vraiment** belle.*

a *Vraiment* (*really*) ends in *-ment.* Is the *-ment* added to the masculine or feminine singular form of the adjective? |

masculine singular (If the masculine adjective ends in a vowel sound, it is used to form the adverb. *Vraiment* is one example: *vrai + ment.*)

b Write a sentence to say that Didier dances really well. |

Didier danse vraiment bien.

3 Practice with commands and direct-object pronouns

In doing this section, remember that a direct-object noun or pronoun answers the question *what* or *whom.* An indirect-object noun or pronoun usually answers the question *to whom.*

1 Compare the word order in these sentences.

> *Montre la photo à Jean-Marc.*
> *Montre-la à Jean-Marc.*

a Where does a direct-object pronoun occur in an affirmative command—before or after the verb? |

after

b Which punctuation mark links the verb form and the direct-object pronoun? |

a hyphen

c Write the English equivalent of ***Montre-la à Jean-Marc.*** |

Show it to Jean-Marc. (The word order in French is the same as that in English.)

2 Rewrite each of these affirmative commands with the direct-object pronouns *le, la,* or *les.* Remember to include the hyphen.

a Montre la chemise à Henri. |

Montre-la à Henri.

b Montre le manteau à Gilliane. |

Montre-le à Gilliane.

c Montre les chaussures à Bernard. |

Montre-les à Bernard.

3 Complete the commands below with the appropriate direct-object pronouns.

Modèle: Vous connaissez cette chanson? Chantez- ____ . |

Chantez-la

a Tu as un chapeau? Mets- ____ . |

Mets-le.

b Voilà M. Feydeau. Regarde- ___. |
                     Regarde-le.

c Cette tarte est délicieuse. Mangeons- ___. |
                     Mangeons-la.

d Ces chaussures sont belles. Achetez- ___. |
                     Achetez-les.

CHECK-UP **Part 1**	Write the French equivalent for these sentences. **1** That camera belongs to me. **2** This car belongs to them (to Roger and Catherine Ledoux).
Part 2	Form adverbs in *-ment* with the adjectives indicated. **1** Jean est *sérieux.* Il travaille ___. **2** Ces devoirs sont *faciles.* On peut les faire ___.
Part 3	Give the French equivalents. Use the *tu*-command. **1** Show it (*the book*) to your grandfather. **2** Give them (*the pencils*) to your sister.
VOCABULARY	*ensuite* then, afterwards, next *puis* then, afterwards, next *tout le temps* often *tout à l'heure* in a little while *facile* easy

1   *The concept of tense*

You know how to talk in French about things that are happening right now by using the present tense of the verb; for example, ***J'écris à Louis*** (I'm writing to Louis). This section will begin to explain how to talk about things that have happened in the past.

1 In both English and French, verbs have different forms to indicate the different times at which an action takes place *in relation to the moment of speaking.* Suppose, for example, you're talking with a classmate about your hard-working friend Jeanne. For each verb phrase below, write *present, past,* or *future* to indicate the time of the action.

      Modèle: she worked **|**
                    past

a she was working **|**
               past

b she's working **|**
             present

c she will work **|**
             future

d she did work **|**
             past

e she works **|**
             present

f she has worked **|**
             past

2 An expression of time like *tomorrow, yesterday, soon, at 2 p.m.* may help tell whether the action is present, past, or future in relation to the moment of speaking. Complete the following sentences about George, who is a great football player. Use the correct tense of the verb *to play.*

  a George ＿＿ ball tomorrow afternoon. **|**
                will play

  b George ＿＿ ball last week. **|**
              played

  c George ＿＿ ball yesterday when he turned his ankle. **|**
              was playing

  d George ＿＿ ball right now. **|**
             is playing

3 The French sentences below have adverbs indicating various times. Write *present, past,* or *future* to indicate the time of the action.

  a Jean travaille maintenant. **|**
             present

b Jean va travailler demain. |
  future

c Jean a travaillé hier. |
  past (The meaning of *hier* is a clue that *a travaillé* means *worked*.)

4 Below are expressions of time that may be used with actions in the past. Take a moment to study any that you don't know. Look at the French expression, then glance up from the page and try to recall the English equivalent. Then look at the English, glance up, and try to recall the French.

hier	yesterday	*la semaine dernière*	last week
hier matin	yesterday morning	*le mois dernier*	last month
hier après-midi	yesterday afternoon	*l'année dernière*	last year
hier soir	yesterday evening, last night		

2   Comparison of adverbs

If you remember how to make comparisons with adjectives, you'll find it easy to learn how to make comparisons with adverbs. The language patterns are similar.

1 Read the following sentences containing comparisons with adverbs.

Henri mange plus vite que Guy.   Henri eats faster than (more quickly than) Guy.

Paulette voyage moins souvent que Claire.   Paulette travels less often than Claire.

Ma mère marche aussi rapidement que mon père.   My mother walks as rapidly as my father.

a The French expressions of inequality are ____. |
  plus vite que, moins souvent que

b The French expression of equality is ____. |
  aussi rapidement que

2 Give the English equivalents of the following sentences.
a Je travaille plus vite que ma sœur. |
  I work faster than (more quickly than) my sister.

b Yves fait la cuisine moins souvent que toi. |
  Yves does the cooking less often than you (do). (In French, the stressed form of a pronoun is used at the end of a comparison.)

c Alain joue du piano aussi bien que Jean. |
  Alain plays the piano as well as Jean.

3 Tell how quickly Renée works in comparison to Anne, Marguerite, and Gilliane. Use the adverb *vite.*
  a She works more quickly than Anne. |
    Elle travaille plus vite qu'Anne.

b She works less quickly than Gilliane. |
Elle travaille moins vite que Gilliane.

c She works as quickly as Marguerite. |
Elle travaille aussi vite que Marguerite.

4 In items **a–e**, compare the activities of the two people mentioned. Use *plus...que, moins...que,* or *aussi...que* with the adverb in parentheses. Answers are in the answer key.

Modèle: Gertrude va à Paris en février, en mai, en septembre et en décembre. Monique va à Paris en juin. Monique va à Paris _____. (souvent) |
Monique va à Paris moins souvent que Gertrude.

a Nanette arrive à 9h. Gauthier arrive à 10h. Gauthier arrive _____. (tard)
b Marcel commence son déjeuner à 1h, et il le termine à 2h. André commence son déjeuner à 1h, et il le termine à 1h 30. Marcel mange _____. (lentement)
c Roger peut nager 100 mètres en une minute et trente secondes. Delphine peut nager 100 mètres en une minute et trente secondes. Delphine nage _____. (rapidement)
d Les parents d'Yves prennent du vin tous les soirs. Les parents de Robert prennent du vin le dimanche seulement. Les parents de Robert prennent du vin _____. (souvent)
e Marie-Thérèse va arriver chez nous à 8h. Sylvie va arriver chez nous à 7h. Marie-Thérèse va arriver _____. (tôt)

3 *The present tense of* envoyer

You have recently been introduced to the verb *envoyer* (to send). Take a moment to look at the chart, and notice especially the stems.

j'	envoi	e
tu	envoi	es
on/il/elle	envoi	e
ils/elles	envoi	ent
nous	envoy	ons
vous	envoy	ez

1 The endings of *envoyer* are those of any regular *-er* verb.
a The stem, however, has two forms. What are they? |
envoi-, envoy-

b The stem *envoy-* occurs in the infinitive and two other forms. What are they? |
nous-form and vous-form (The stem envoy- occurs in the forms that have a pronounced ending.)

c Which form of the stem matches the *je-, tu-, on/il/elle-,* and *ils/elles-*forms? |
envoi-

2 Write French equivalents for each sentence below.

   Modèle: You're sending them a card (*une carte*). |
   Vous leur envoyez une carte.

a We're sending them a card.

b She's sending them a card.

c I'm not sending them a card.

d They (*ils*) aren't sending them a card. |

   a *Nous leur envoyons une carte.* b *Elle leur envoie une carte.* c *Je ne leur envoie pas de carte.* d *Ils ne leur envoient pas de carte.*

HOTEL TERANGA . DAKAR
Nous vous y souhaitons un séjour agréable

CHECK-UP
Part 2

Complete the following comparisons, using the French equivalent of the expressions in parentheses.

1 (as quickly as) Georges fait ses devoirs _____ Albert.

2 (less often than) Alice voyage _____ son frère.

3 (later than) J'arrive toujours à l'université _____ les autres étudiants.

VOCABULARY

Since this list is short, you might want to take a few minutes to review the words at the ends of Preparations 93 and 94. See if, this time, you can look at the English definition and recall the French.

le nord	north	*au nord de*	(to the) north of	*près de*	near
le sud	south	*au sud de*	(to the) south of	*loin de*	far from
l'est	east	*à l'est de*	(to the) east of	*une carte*	postcard
l'ouest	west	*à l'ouest de*	(to the) west of		

OÙ ALLER? Where to go?

le froid cold weather

une partie part

décidé settled, decided

poser une question to ask a question

1 *The* passé composé *with* avoir

There are a number of tenses in French that express action in the past.
One of the past tenses commonly used in conversation is the *passé
compose* (compound past). It is called *passé composé* because the verb
forms of this tense consist of more than one part. The *passé composé* is
usually made up of the present-tense forms of the verb *avoir* and a past
participle. To review the forms of *avoir*, read frame 1.

1 Charles and his friends are about to take a train and they check to see
if everyone has a ticket. Read the statements made by the group.

    –J'ai un billet, et toi, tu as un billet?
    –Oui, et mon frère a un billet aussi.
    –Henri et Marcel, vous avez vos billets?
    –Oui, nous avons nos billets et Nadine et sa sœur ont leurs billets aussi.

a Which forms of *avoir* are used in the above statements? |
      ai, as, a, avez, avons, ont

b Now write the complete phrases, using the form of *avoir* that
matches each subject pronoun.

    j' ___, tu ___, il ___, on ___, nous ___, vous ___, elles ___ |
      j'ai, tu as, il a, on a, nous avons, vous avez, elles ont

2 Yesterday M. Martin and his boss worked late. He tells his wife about
it. Read their conversation.

    –Hier, j'ai travaillé tard.
    –Oui, tu as travaillé tard. Et ton patron (boss)*?*
    –Il a travaillé tard aussi. Nous avons travaillé très tard.

a Which phrase is the French equivalent of *I worked late?* |
      j'ai travaillé tard (Notice that the equivalent verb in English is only one word.)

b Which word in *j'ai travaillé* is related to the infinitive *travailler?* |
      travaillé (Travaillé is the past participle of travailler.)

c The past participle is a verb form that is used in combination with
another verb form in a compound tense. In the sentences above, the
passé composé verbs contain present-tense forms of the verb ___ plus
the past participle ___. |
      avoir; travaillé (Avoir is often called the auxiliary or helping verb. It "helps" by
      telling the person—je, nous, etc.—while the past participle gives the meaning.)

d In the phrases *j'ai travaillé* and *tu as travaillé,* do the forms of *avoir*
change according to the subject? |
      yes

e Does the past participle change form according to the subject? |
      no

3 Write the subject and the complete *passé composé* form of *travailler* for these items. Use the form of *avoir* that matches the subject.

a toi et moi, nous ____ travaillé |

toi et moi, nous avons travaillé

b Jacques et Denis ____ travaillé |

Jacques et Denis ont travaillé

c tu ____ travaillé |

tu as travaillé

d Brigitte ____ travaillé |

Brigitte a travaillé

e vous ____ travaillé |

vous avez travaillé

f j' ____ travaillé |

j'ai travaillé

4 Roger is telling Marie about what he did earlier in the day.

–*Aujourd'hui, j'ai joué au bridge*   –Today, I played bridge
avec des amis, puis nous   with some friends, then we
avons dîné dans un restaurant.   ate dinner in a restaurant.

a The two *passé composé* verbs used above are ____. |

j'ai joué, nous avons dîné

b *Joué* is the past participle of the verb *jouer*. *Dîné* is the past participle of the verb ____. |

dîner

c The past participle of an *-er* verb is formed with the infinitive stem (*dîn-*, for example) and the ending ____. |

é

5 Write the past participle of each *-er* verb below.

parler   écouter   chercher   donner   regarder   visiter |

parlé, écouté, cherché, donné, regardé, visité

6 Rewrite the following sentences in the *passé composé,* and begin each sentence with *hier aussi.*

Modèle: Je visite des monuments historiques. |

Hier aussi, j'ai visité des monuments historiques.

a Nous parlons à nos grands-parents au téléphone.
b Serge et Cécile regardent des danseurs à la télévision.
c Alain danse avec Mireille.
d Tu manges du poulet pour le dîner.
e Je montre des photos à mon frère. |

a Hier aussi, nous avons parlé à nos grands-parents au téléphone.   b Hier aussi, Serge et Cécile ont regardé des danseurs à la télévision.   c Hier aussi, Alain a dansé avec Mireille.   d Hier aussi, tu as mangé du poulet pour le dîner.   e Hier aussi, j'ai montré des photos à mon frère.

7 Write the French equivalent of *Yesterday I played volleyball.* |

Hier, j'ai joué au volley-ball.

NOTE ✳ *Languages, ethnic groups, and religion in Senegal*

French is the official language of Senegal, providing a single language in which the affairs of the nation can be conducted. The people of Senegal comprise a number of ethnic groups, each with its own oral language—Ouolof, Serère, Peul, Toucouleur, Diola, Mandingue, Maure. Of these, the **Ouolof** (Wolof) group is the largest. Here are some phrases in **Ouolof:**

Bonjour: **Diam 'ngam** (literally, "Do you have peace?")

Bonsoir: **Diame nga yendou** ("Have you spent the day in peace?")

Au revoir: **Diam ac diam** ("Peace.")

In addition to native Senegalese people and Europeans, there are a number of Syrian and Lebanese people living in Senegal.

The Islamic religion has been established in West Africa for several hundred years, and most Senegalese are Moslems (**musulmans**). Many men can read and recite verses in Arabic from the Koran, the Islamic holy book. The most impressive mosque is in Touba, a town in the interior, and once a year there is a great pilgrimage to Touba. There are many Catholics in Dakar and among the Serère people. In addition, many people in the interior of the country are animists. An animist believes that inanimate objects, like trees and rocks, and phenomena, like rain and wind, have souls.

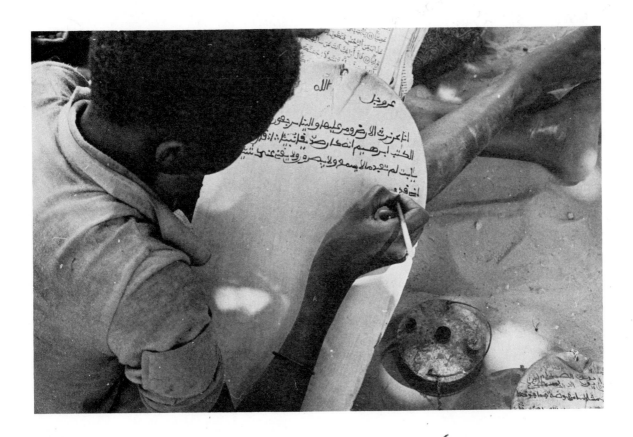

2 *The comparative form of the adverb* **bien**

Recently you have been learning to compare people and things. You've learned that comparisons using adverbs and those using adjectives are formed in the same way. In this section, you will use an adverb—*bien*—that has a special irregular form when it is used in a comparison.

1 Most adverbs in French and English have regular comparative forms.
 a Which word is missing in the following comparison?
>Pierre eats his lunch in half an hour.
>Laura eats her lunch in an hour.
>Laura eats ____ slowly than Pierre. |
>> more

 b Which word is missing in the French equivalent below?
>*Pierre mange son déjeuner en une demi-heure.*
>*Laura mange son déjeuner en une heure.*
>*Laura mange ____ lentement que Pierre.* |
>> plus

 c Denise and Thomas play tennis once a week. How would you say in French that Denise plays tennis as often as Thomas? ***Denise joue au tennis ____ Thomas.*** |
>> aussi souvent que

 d Write the French equivalent of the sentence *I play tennis less often than my brother.* |
>> Je joue au tennis moins souvent que mon frère.

2 Read the comparative sentences below in which the adverb *bien* (well) is used.
>*Denise chante aussi bien qu'Angélique.*   Denise sings as well as Angélique.
>*Bertrand chante moins bien que Laurent.*   Bertrand sings less well than Laurent.

 a Are the *aussi...que* and *moins...que* forms of the comparative used with *bien* regular? |
>> yes

 b Suppose you think that Denise sings well, but you feel that Angélique's singing is superior to Denise's. You probably wouldn't say that Angélique sings more well than Denise. Instead, you'd say *Angélique sings ____ than Denise.* |
>> better

 c Here is the French equivalent of *Angélique sings better than Denise: **Angélique chante mieux que Denise.*** What is the word that expresses the meaning *better?* |
>> mieux

 d Write the English equivalents of the French sentences below.
>*Tu nages mieux que ton cousin.*
>*Ils patinent mieux que nous.* |
>> You swim better than your cousin. They skate better than we do (better than us).

3 With the information below, say that the first person does something better than the other.

> Modèle: Tu / nager / moi ▌
>> *Tu nages mieux que moi.*

a Nathalie / patiner / Eric
b Paul / jouer du violon / moi
c le jeune garçon / parler anglais / son père ▌

> a *Nathalie patine mieux qu'Eric.* b *Paul joue du violon mieux que moi.* c *Le jeune garçon parle anglais mieux que son père.*

4 Write the French equivalent for each sentence.
a Hélène sings less well than Nancy.
b René and Serge swim better than Thomas.
c You play the guitar as well as Alain. ▌

> a *Hélène chante moins bien que Nancy.* b *René et Serge nagent mieux que Thomas.* c *Tu joues (Vous jouez) de la guitare aussi bien qu'Alain.*

CHECK-UP
Part 1

Write these sentences in the *passé composé*.
1 Il téléphone à son père.
2 Nous écoutons des chansons folkloriques du Sénégal.

Part 2

Use the sentence fragments to say that your brother does something better than you.

> Mon frère / travailler / bien / moi

VOCABULARY

il/elle court   he/she runs

OÙ ALLER? (2)
une décision   decision
une demande   request
agréable   pleasant
parler de   to talk about
penser à   to think about
supposer   to suppose
naturellement   of course,
   naturally
sérieusement   seriously
bonne chance!   good luck!
il paraît   apparently,
   so it seems

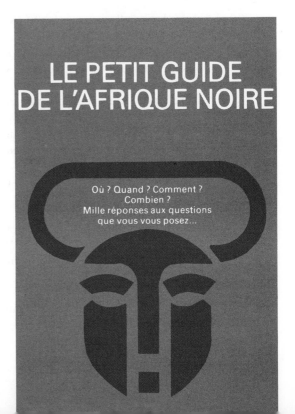

LE PETIT GUIDE
DE L'AFRIQUE NOIRE

Où ? Quand ? Comment ?
Combien ?
Mille réponses aux questions
que vous vous posez...

1 *Practice with relative pronouns* qui *and* que

If you need to refresh your memory about the use of *qui* and *que*, turn back to Preparations 93 and 94.

1 The sentences in this frame will tell you two facts about Pierre. Combine each pair of ideas, using the relative pronoun *qui.* Insert the *qui*-clause in the middle of the sentence.

> Modèle: Mon ami Pierre a dix-huit ans. Il est plus grand que moi. |
> *Mon ami Pierre, qui est plus grand que moi, a dix-huit ans.*

a Mon ami Pierre nous invite souvent pour le week-end. Il habite dans un petit village. |

> *Mon ami Pierre, qui habite dans un petit village, nous invite souvent pour le week-end.*

b Mon ami Pierre écrit des chansons. Il est très intelligent. |

> *Mon ami Pierre, qui est très intelligent, écrit des chansons.*

2 Now use the relative pronoun *que* to say two things about Pierre's relatives. Write a complete sentence from the cues, as in the model.

> Modèle: la tante de Pierre / j'aime bien / arrive bientôt chez lui |
> *La tante de Pierre, que j'aime bien, arrive bientôt chez lui.*

a son grand-père / il voit tous les jours / l'aide à faire ses devoirs |

> *Son grand-père, qu'il voit tous les jours, l'aide à faire ses devoirs.* (Did you remember that *que* becomes *qu'* before a subject beginning with a vowel?)

b sa cousine Louise / tu vois là-bas / vient de Montréal |

> *Sa cousine Louise, que tu vois là-bas, vient de Montréal.*

c son frère aîné / je ne connais pas très bien / est ingénieur |

> *Son frère aîné, que je ne connais pas très bien, est ingénieur.*

3 To check your understanding, write the English equivalent of *Son frère aîné, que je ne connais pas très bien, est ingénieur.* |

> *His older brother, whom I don't know very well, is an engineer.*

4 In this frame you will read about Louise's favorite hobby, photography, and find out what she is planning to do. Complete each sentence with either *qui* or *que.*

a Louise est une jeune fille ____ fait de la photographie. |

> *qui*

b Voilà l'appareil-photo ____ Louise veut acheter pour son voyage au Sénégal. |

> *que*

c Pour elle, le voyage ____ elle va faire au Sénégal est plus intéressant qu'un voyage aux Etats-Unis. |

> *qu'*

5 Write the English equivalent of ***Pour elle, le voyage qu'elle va faire au Sénégal est plus intéressant qu'un voyage aux Etats-Unis.*** |

For her, the trip (that) she's going to take to Senegal is more interesting than a trip to the United States. (Notice that the word *que/qu'* has more than one meaning in French. It means *that* or *whom* when it is used as a relative pronoun. When it is used in a comparison, it means *than*.)

2 The present tense of écrire

In this section, you'll practice using the present-tense forms of the verb *écrire* (to write).

1 Here is a chart showing the present-tense forms of *écrire.*

j'	écri	s
tu	écri	s
on/il/elle	écri	t
ils/elles	écriv	ent
nous	écriv	ons
vous	écriv	ez

    a How many forms does the present-tense stem have? |
            two forms
    b One form of the stem ends with the letter *v: écriv-.* Does this form occur with singular subjects or with plural subjects? |
            plural subjects

2 Complete these sentences with the present-tense form of *écrire* that matches the subject. Refer to the chart to check your answers.
    a Nous ____ des lettres à nos parents.
    b Il faut ____ *France* avec un *F* majuscule.
    c M. Perreault ____ des articles excellents pour un journal.
    d Je lui ____ tous les samedis.
    e Tu lui ____ souvent?
    f Avant de commencer votre examen, ____ votre nom sur votre feuille.

3 Answer the following questions according to the cues given.
    a Est-ce qu'elles t'écrivent souvent? (oui) |
            Oui, elles m'écrivent souvent.
    b Tu écris des lettres à tes amis? (non) |
            Non, je n'écris pas de lettres à mes amis. / Je ne leur écris pas de lettres.
    c Est-ce que j'écris aussi bien qu'un poète? (non) |
            Non, tu n'écris pas (vous n'écrivez pas) aussi bien qu'un poète.

4 Write the French equivalents.
    a She's writing a letter.
    b Let's write a postcard to Hélène. |
            a *Elle écrit une lettre.* **b** *Écrivons une carte à Hélène.*

In a developing nation like Senegal, modern industrialized cities like Dakar, Saint-Louis, and Rufisque coexist with very simple rural villages.

In a city, people live in buildings like those in any European or American city, and an inhabitant isn't likely to know most of the other people in the neighborhood. In a village, houses are made of locally-available building materials. In a coastal village, the paths are paved with crushed shells. In an interior village, houses are made of sticks and mud, with a thatched roof. Each house is called **une case,** and each family (consisting of several generations of people) has a number of **cases** gathered together in a group called **une concession.** The chickens, sheep, and goats of the village are not fenced in, but wander at random. Villagers live very close to nature and have great respect for the power of a drought, storm, or illness to influence their lives.

In most parts of a city there is running water and electricity. In a village, water is drawn from a well that the men have dug together, and kerosene lamps and candles provide illumination after dark.

In a city, people's lives run by the clock. In villages, where clocks are often rare, time is measured in more general units, like "tomorrow afternoon."

In a city, many people adopt industrialized values. They compete with each other for better-paying jobs. In a village, people fish or farm with very simple equipment. They cooperate in work in order to survive. They also value friends highly and treat conversation as a skill and as an important means of maintaining personal relationships.

In Dakar, government officials try to persuade village farmers to increase their production of peanuts **(les cacahuètes)** for export. In the villages, where it takes hard labor to produce enough food for local consumption, peo-ple are reluctant to depend on cash from the sale of a large peanut crop for buying food. They would rather use the land to produce cereal grains and just enough peanuts for themselves.

Like many developing nations, Senegal must try to reconcile the consequences of industrial development with the need to maintain stable cultural values.

3 Practice with the passé composé

You were introduced to the *passé composé* in Preparation 97. See if you can complete the exercises in this section without looking back at the Preparation.

1 Read each of the following sentences aloud, and write an English equivalent.

a Nous avons mangé des légumes pour le dîner. |
               We ate some vegetables for dinner.

b Les enfants ont donné de la viande au chien. |
               The children gave some meat to the dog.

c Ma sœur a visité Paris l'année dernière. |
               My sister visited Paris last year.

d Tu as parlé à Jacqueline aujourd'hui? |
               Did you talk to Jacqueline today?

2 Complete these sentences with the *passé composé* of the verb in parentheses. Write the complete verb phrase.

a Georges ____ ses amis à une petite fête. (inviter)
b Vous ____ une carte à Guy, n'est-ce pas? (envoyer)
c L'été dernier, je/j' ____ dans une station de télévision. (travailler) |

        a *Georges a invité*   b *Vous avez envoyé*   c *j'ai travaillé*

3 Restate in the *passé composé.*

     Modèle: Je parle anglais avec M. Brown. |
               J'ai parlé anglais avec M. Brown.

a Mme Décibelle chante une aria italienne.
b M. Cassepied danse avec Mlle Lapauvre.
c Tu écoutes le concert à la radio, n'est-ce pas?
d Vous fermez les fenêtres? |

        a *Mme Décibelle a chanté une aria italienne.*   b *M. Cassepied a dansé avec Mme Lapauvre.*   c *Tu as écouté le concert à la radio, n'est-ce pas?*   d *Vous avez fermé les fenêtres?*

4 The questions in this frame ask whether someone is doing something today. Say no, the person or persons did it yesterday.

     Modèle: Marie et toi, vous mangez au Café Florence aujourd'hui? |
               Non, nous avons mangé au Café Florence hier.

a Est-ce que tu joues au tennis cet après-midi?
b Le professeur montre un film aujourd'hui?
c Les enfants nagent ce matin?
d René et Maryse, vous téléphonez à tante Mathilde maintenant? |

        a *Non, j'ai joué au tennis hier.*   b *Non, il a montré un film hier.*   c *Non, ils ont nagé hier.*   d *Non, nous avons téléphoné à tante Mathilde hier.*

5 You have now learned how to say what someone *is doing* now, what someone *is going to do* in the future, and what someone *did* in the past. This frame will give you practice in deciding whether to use the present, the *futur proche,* or the *passé composé.*

Assume that it's 3:00 in the afternoon. Use the cues indicated to say what you did, are doing, or are going to do.

Modèles: Demain soir ____. (téléphoner à ma copine Simone) ▮
Demain soir je vais téléphoner à ma copine Simone.

Hier matin ____. (envoyer une lettre à Pierre) ▮
Hier matin j'ai envoyé une lettre à Pierre.

a Hier soir ____. (parler à mon oncle au téléphone)
b En ce moment ____. (regarder la télévision)
c Hier après-midi ____. (envoyer un cadeau d'anniversaire à un ami à Dakar)
d La semaine prochaine ____. (chercher un appartement)
e La semaine dernière ____. (acheter un vélo)
f Je regarde un western et, en même temps, je ____. (manger du chocolat) ▮

a Hier soir j'ai parlé à mon oncle au téléphone. b En ce moment je regarde la télévision. c Hier après-midi j'ai envoyé un cadeau d'anniversaire à un ami à Dakar. d La semaine prochaine je vais chercher un appartement. e La semaine dernière j'ai acheté un vélo. f Je regarde un western et, en même temps, je mange du chocolat.

CHECK-UP
Part 1

Complete the sentences with the correct relative pronoun, *qui* or *que.*
1 Est-ce que Maryse est l'amie ____ va déjeuner avec toi?
2 Est-ce que Maryse est l'amie ____ tu invites à aller au cinéma?

Part 2

Write the French equivalents of these two sentences.
1 They're writing to their parents.
2 Write your name on this paper.

Afrique... *continent en transition*

Technologie,

artisanat,

Contrastes

1 Reports on Francophone countries

During this Phase and the next, some class time and parts of the Preparations will be used to help you prepare a report in French on a country in the French-speaking world. The purpose of this activity is to help you learn more about the French-speaking world, to help you practice working on a project over a period of time, and to give you an opportunity to use the French you've learned so far in giving a report. Each student will be expected to do a portion of the research, to write a complete report (using information supplied by the other members of the group), and to give part of the oral report.

You will work with a group of about five to seven other students. Each of you will be responsible for finding part of the information about the country, which you will give to the other members of your group. Over a period of time, the Preparations will help each student write short paragraphs in French using the information. For instance, the student who finds out about geography will give the information to the rest of the group, so that each one can write a paragraph about the geography of the group's Francophone country.

Below is a list of the topics to be researched and the Preparations for which the information is needed. Think about which Francophone country you might like to learn more about (see the map of the French-speaking world on p. 500). Then look at the list and think about which topics you would like to research. In a forthcoming class each group will get together to plan the report.

PREPARATION 102
Geography: boundary countries; mountains, principal rivers, plains, lakes; capital and principal cities; number of inhabitants; size in comparison with your state

PREPARATION 103
Climate: seasons; amount of rain and snow; comparison with the climate where you live; maximum and minimum temperature; effect on agriculture

PREPARATION 105
Economy: mostly agricultural or mostly industrial?; agricultural and industrial products the country is noted for; exports and imports
Government: kind of government; old or young nation; names of current heads of state

2 Écrire, envoyer *and indirect-object pronouns*

This section will give you practice using indirect-object pronouns with the two verbs you have learned recently, *écrire* and **envoyer.** To remind yourself which verb form matches each subject, take a quick look at the chart in the Summary, p. 455.

1 Mélanie is writing some cards to some friends.

a How would you say in French *Mélanie is writing a card to Louise?* |

Mélanie écrit une carte à Louise.

b What is the indirect-object noun in the French sentence? |

Louise

c Rewrite the English sentence *Melanie is writing a card to Louise* and replace *Louise* with a pronoun. |

Mélanie is writing a card to her. / Mélanie is writing her a card.

d The French equivalent of that sentence is **Mélanie lui écrit une carte.** What is the indirect-object pronoun? |

lui

2 Suppose Mélanie were writing to Louis.

a How would you say in French *Mélanie is writing to him?* **Mélanie ____ écrit.** |

lui

b Can the indirect-object pronoun **lui** refer to a male as well as to a female? |

yes

3 Marcel is on a world tour, but he takes time out in Dakar to write several letters. To a friend he writes **Je t'écris de Dakar.** To his cousins he writes **Je vous écris de Dakar.**

a What do the French sentences mean? |

I'm writing (to) you from Dakar.

b Which two object pronouns are used in the sentences? |

t' and vous

4 *Me, te, nous,* and *vous* function as either direct or indirect-object pronouns. They probably are easy for you to use, but you may need help in distinguishing *le, la,* and *les* from *lui* and *leur.* You also need to remember to put the preposition *à* before a noun phrase that follows verbs like *écrire, envoyer, téléphoner,* etc. The next frames will give you more practice using *écrire* and *envoyer.*

Rewrite each of the following sentences, replacing the indirect object noun phrase by the appropriate indirect-object pronoun.

a J'écris à mes parents.

b Nous écrivons à notre voisin.

c Ils écrivent à notre sœur et à nous.

d Vous écrivez à Jean et à moi? |

a *Je leur écris.* b *Nous lui écrivons.* c *Ils nous écrivent.* d *Vous nous écrivez?*

5 Laurence and Claire are sending gifts to friends and relatives for Christmas. Read their conversation, and complete what Claire says, using the appropriate object pronoun and form of *envoyer.*

Laurence: *Est-ce que tu envoies quelque chose à tes grands-parents pour Noël?*

Claire: *Oui, je _____ un beau livre de photographie.*

Laurence: *Est-ce qu'ils t'envoient quelque chose pour Noël?*

Claire: *Oui, ils _____ toujours quelque chose pour Noël.* |

leur envoie; m'envoient

6 Answer the following questions with *oui* or *non* as indicated. Answers are in the answer key.

Modèle: Est-ce qu'ils vous envoient vos billets? (non) |

Non, ils ne nous envoient pas nos billets.

a Est-ce qu'ils vous envoient le journal de Dakar? (non)

b Est-ce qu'elles vous écrivent tous les jours? (non)

c Est-ce que vous leur envoyez des cadeaux? (oui)

3 Pre-quiz practice: the passé composé

During the next class, you'll have a quiz to find out how well you know how to use *passé composé* forms of *-er* verbs. If you want to review the formation of the *passé composé* before you do the practice frames below, look back at Preparation 97.

1 Hubert loves to talk about what he has read in the morning paper. He discusses the news with Vincent, a fellow worker.

Vincent: *Tu as acheté le journal ce matin?*

Hubert: *Oui, et j'ai regardé la page des sports tout de suite. Notre équipe de football a gagné* (won) *le match hier soir.*

Vincent: *Ah oui! C'est formidable!*

Hubert: *Oui, je suis très content.*

a Which *passé composé* verb forms are used in the above sentences? |

as acheté, ai regardé, a gagné

b The *passé composé* of most *-er* verbs is made up of the present-tense forms of the verb ____ plus a past participle ending in ____. |

avoir; é

2 Rewrite the following sentences in the *passé composé.* Answers are in the answer key.

    a Vous écoutez les chanteurs.

    b Il envoie des cartes à ses amis.

    c Nous demandons au professeur la date de l'examen.

    d Ils cherchent leurs gants dans la voiture.

PREPARATION **100**

1 *Reading comprehension:* **Un An plus tard (1)**

1 Michel is now working at the television station in Dakar. Today he writes a letter. Read the first part to find out to whom he is writing and why.

Michel est maintenant «coopérant» à Dakar. Il travaille à la station de télévision avec des techniciens sénégalais. Aujourd'hui, il écrit une lettre à son amie Thérèse qui va avoir dix-huit ans bientôt.

Chère°Thérèse,
Joyeux anniversaire°! Dix-huit ans déjà°! Dis donc, tu es vieille! J'espère° que tu vas bien et que tu ne travailles pas trop° au lycée!

dear
happy birthday / already
I hope / too much

    a Michel is in the *service de la Coopération.* He is a ____ in Dakar. |

coopérant

    b What is the English equivalent of the sentence *Thérèse va avoir dix-huit ans bientôt?* |

Thérèse will be eighteen years old soon.

    c What's one way to say *Happy Birthday!* in French? |

Joyeux anniversaire!

2 Write a brief answer in French to each question below. Refer to the letter if necessary.

    a Avec qui travaille Michel? |

avec des techniciens sénégalais

    b Est-ce que Thérèse est lycéenne? |

oui

SÉNÉGAL TOURS

3 Write the French equivalents for these English sentences. Look at the last two lines of the letter if you need to.

    a I hope you're well. |

            J'espère que tu vas bien.

    b I hope that you're not working too hard at school. |

            J'espère que tu ne travailles pas trop au lycée.

4 Michel works hard at his job. How does he like his work? What does he say about Dakar in his letter? Does he find any interesting contrasts in the city? Read the second part for the answers to these questions.

Moi, je travaille beaucoup mais je suis très heureux au Sénégal. Dakar est une ville d'environ° 390 000 habitants. Elle est européenne et africaine, et les contrastes sont très intéressants. Il y a des immeubles° très modernes, des avenues avec des arbres°, des jardins publics°, des cinémas, des stades de sport, et une grande université. Mais il y a aussi des quartiers° très vieux et très pauvres.

                                           approximately

                                           buildings

                                         trees/parks

                                           neighborhoods

    a Une personne qui habite dans une ville est un ___ de cette ville. |

            habitant

    b Rewrite in French: *There are some very modern buildings.* |

            Il y a des immeubles très modernes.

5 Write a brief answer to each of the following questions.

    a Est-ce que Michel est heureux ou malheureux au Sénégal? |

            Il est heureux.

    b Qu'est-ce qu'il trouve de très intéressant à Dakar? |

            les contrastes

    c Est-ce qu'il y a une grande université à Dakar? |

            oui

6 Read the following statements. Write *vrai* if the statement is true, *faux* if the statement is false.

    a Dakar est une ville moderne.

    b Il y a des cinémas et des stades de sport.

    c Il n'y a pas d'avenues.

    d Il n'y a pas de vieux quartiers.

    e C'est une ville complètement africaine. |

            a *vrai* **b** *vrai* **c** *faux* **d** *faux* **e** *faux*

2 Practice with comparisons

Each frame in this part shows drawings of two or more people. Write sentences comparing them, using **plus...que, moins...que,** or **aussi...que** and the subjects and adjectives indicated.

Constantin   Alphonse

Modèles: Constantin / Alphonse (fort) ▌
          Constantin est plus fort qu'Alphonse.

          Alphonse / Constantin (fort) ▌
          Alphonse est moins fort que Constantin.

M. Lepoids   M. Bâton   Mme Bâton

1 Mme Bâton / M. Lepoids (gros) ▌
   Mme Bâton est moins grosse que M. Lepoids.
2 M. et Mme Bâton / M. Lepoids (maigre) ▌
   M. et Mme Bâton sont plus maigres que M. Lepoids.
3 Mme Bâton / M. Bâton (maigre) ▌
   Mme Bâton est aussi maigre que M. Bâton.

Charles   Charlotte

4 Charles / Charlotte (intelligent) ▌
   Charles est aussi intelligent que Charlotte.
5 Charlotte / Charles (intelligent) ▌
   Charlotte est aussi intelligente que Charles.

3 La géographie de votre région

In preparation for talking about the geography of the place where you live, read the following questions aloud. Answer them orally in complete French sentences. You may find it helpful to write your answers before you practice saying them, but the most important thing is to be confident about giving the information orally.

　　Your answers will depend on what part of the country you live in. The ones given are just possibilities.

1 Est-ce qu'il y a des montagnes dans l'état où vous habitez? ❙
　　　Oui, il y a des montagnes dans l'état où j'habite.

2 Habitez-vous près de l'océan? ❙
　　　Oui, j'habite près de l'océan Atlantique (Pacifique).

3 Votre état est au nord (au sud, à l'est, à l'ouest) de quel autre état? ❙
　　　Mon état est au nord de l'Iowa.

4 Quels grands fleuves y a-t-il dans votre région? ❙
　　　Il y a le Missouri et le Kansas.

5 Y a-t-il des collines près de votre ville? ❙
　　　Non, il n'y a pas de collines près de ma ville.

6 Y a-t-il des lacs dans votre état? Près de chez vous? ❙
　　　Oui, il y a des lacs dans mon état, mais il n'y a pas de lac près de chez moi.

7 Est-ce que votre ville est sur un plateau? Près d'un fleuve? ❙
　　　Ma ville n'est pas sur un plateau. Elle est près d'un fleuve.

L'Afrique vous attend

4 *Working on your report*

The factual information needed for your report can be found easily in an encyclopedia or almanac. However, you should also try to use books, magazines, pamphlets—and if possible, people who have lived or visited in the country—as sources for interesting information and pictures. Ask your teacher where you can find these sources. As you work on your report, be sure to keep a record of the sources you have used.

　　When it's your turn to have information ready, either make a copy for the other members of the group or write neatly enough for them to copy it in class. Information on geography should be ready to give to the other members of the group two classes from now.

1 *Double verbs with direct-object pronouns*

Part 1 of this Preparation gives practice using direct-object pronouns in sentences that contain two verbs.

1 You already know how to use direct-object pronouns in French sentences that contain one verb, as in the following example.

> *Je visite le musée.*   I'm visiting the museum.
> *Je le visite.*   I'm visiting it.

In French, does the object pronoun precede or follow the verb of which it is an object? **l**

> it precedes (The single exception is that of affirmative commands: *Visite-le.*)

2 Now look at the following example containing a sentence with a double verb and an object pronoun.

Jeanne and Nicole plan to go to the museum, and Jeanne asks Denis if he would like to join them.

> *Il y a une belle exposition au musée. Tu veux la voir avec Nicole et moi?*

a What are the two verb forms in *Tu veux la voir avec Nicole et moi?* **l**

> *veux, voir*

b Which verb is in the infinitive form? **l**

> *voir* (*Veux* is a present-tense form of the infinitive *vouloir.*)

c What is the English equivalent of *Tu veux la voir?* **l**

> Do you want to see it?

d The pronoun *la* refers to *l'exposition.* Is *la* the object of *veux* or of *voir?* **l**

> of *voir* (There's a difference between asking *Tu la veux?*—Do you want it?—and *Tu veux la voir?*—Do you want to see it?)

e When an infinitive has an object pronoun, does the pronoun precede or follow the infinitive? **l**

> it precedes

3 Answer the following question. Begin with *Oui,* and use an object pronoun. *Tu veux voir le match de football samedi prochain?* **l**

> *Oui, je veux le voir.*

4 Luc and Françoise like to eat peas with butter, but Lucie and Annick don't.

> *Ils aiment les manger avec du beurre.*   *Elles n'aiment pas les manger avec du beurre.*

a In the negative statement above, which verb is negated—the present-tense form or the infinitive? **l**

> the present-tense form

b Suppose that your little sister has asked you to finish some cookies so that she can ask your parents to buy a new box. Say that you don't want to eat them. **l**

> *Je ne veux pas les manger.*

5 The verbs below are often used with a second verb that is in the infinitive form. Use them in the situation that follows.

   aimer *aller* *devoir* *pouvoir* *vouloir*

Various people are looking at shoes in a store. Write what some of them are thinking as they examine the shoes.

    Modèle: I want to buy them in this store. **I**
          Je veux les acheter dans ce magasin.

 a I'm going to buy them in this store. **I**
       Je vais les acheter dans ce magasin.

 b I mustn't buy them in this store. **I**
       Je ne dois pas les acheter dans ce magasin.

 c I like to buy them in this store. **I**
       J'aime les acheter dans ce magasin.

 d I can't buy them in this store. **I**
       Je ne peux pas les acheter dans ce magasin.

6 Write a French equivalent for each statement.

 a I'm going to invite them.   **c** He isn't going to invite us.
 b I'm going to invite you.   **d** He isn't going to invite me. **I**

    a Je vais les inviter. *b Je vais t'inviter. / Je vais vous inviter.* *c Il ne va pas nous inviter.* *d Il ne va pas m'inviter.*

2 Prepositions with cities and countries

1 Look at the patterns below and note the different words French uses to express *in* and *to* with the names of cities and countries.

Je vais / Je suis	à Paris.	(**À** is used with the names of most cities.)
	en France.	(**En** is used with most countries having feminine names.)
	au Canada.	(**Au** is used with most countries having masculine singular names.)
	aux Etats-Unis.	(**Aux** is used with countries having plural names.)

The preposition **en** is used more frequently with countries than **au** and **aux** because the majority of countries have feminine singular names.
Tell a friend that you're going to **la Belgique.** **I**

    Je vais en Belgique.

2 Now look at the following patterns and note the words used to express *from* with the names of cities and countries.

J'arrive	de Paris.	(**De/d'** is used with the names of most cities.)
	de France.	(**De/d'** is used with most countries having feminine names.)
	du Canada.	(**Du** is used with countries having masculine singular names.)
	des Etats-Unis.	(**Des** is used with countries having plural names.)

Say that Bernard is arriving from **Italie** (f.) tomorrow. **I**

    Bernard arrive d'Italie demain.

3 Imagine that you're on a film crew that is touring Senegal. One of the other people on the crew asks you which city the crew is going to visit on different days of the month. Answers are in the answer key.

> Modèle: Où va-t-on le six? (Saint-Louis) ▮
>   *Le six, on va à Saint-Louis.*

a Où va-t-on le dix? (Thiès)
b Où va-t-on le quinze? (Dakar)

c Où va-t-on le vingt? (Tambacounda)

4 Tell which cities M. Santini's grandchildren are coming from to celebrate his seventieth birthday. Answers are in the answer key.

> Modèle: Louise / Grenoble ▮
>   *Louise vient de Grenoble.*

a Janine / Montpellier
b Hervé / Arles

c Annette / Toulon
d Stéphanie / Avignon

5 The husbands and wives below will be spending the next week apart. Say where the second person in each pair is going.

a M. Durand va en Suisse; sa femme ____. (Allemagne)
b Mme Lambert va aux îles Baléares; son mari ____. (Etats-Unis)
c Mme Cressier va au Maroc; son mari ____. (Canada) ▮

> a *sa femme va en Allemagne*   b *son mari va aux Etats-Unis*   c *son mari va au Canada*

6 Tell what time the following people are arriving at the airport from their country of departure.

a Mme Joly arrive (Allemagne) à 17h 30.
b M. Clément arrive (Etats-Unis) à 15h.

c M. Levant arrive (Canada) à midi.
d M. Johnson arrive (France) à 20h. ▮

> a *Mme Joly arrive d'Allemagne à 17h 30.*   b *M. Clément arrive des Etats-Unis à 15h.*   c *M. Levant arrive du Canada à midi.*   d *M. Johnson arrive de France à 20h.*

NOTE ✳

Le Griot

Since tribal languages are not written, village and tribal history has been passed on by word of mouth to each new generation. A **griot,** or oral historian, was trained to recount in detail the history of his region for a period of several hundred years.

The **griot** travelled from village to village, learning news, and bringing news or folk tales to tell. His vivid descriptions were accompanied by music on the **kora** (a kind of lute), the **balafon** (a kind of xylophone), and the **tam-tam**

(drums). Many in the audience knew the songs that the **griot** wove through the narration, and young and old joined in singing the refrain. In modern-day Africa, the role of the **griot** is primarily that of a dramatic narrator of folk tales.

3 *Reading comprehension:* **Les Sénégalais**

The reading below tells a little about the people of Senegal. Do you know what sorts of entertainment they like, or what kinds of clothes they wear? Read the passage below to find out.

Les jeunes Sénégalais adorent le cinéma, surtout les westerns américains ... doublés° en français, comme en France! Ils adorent aussi danser, et ils dansent non seulement° les danses africaines mais aussi le rock. Ils aiment beaucoup le football et, le dimanche, le stade est plein de monde°.

    Les Sénégalais aiment porter des vêtements confortables. Ces vêtements sont généralement en coton° imprimé de couleurs vives°. Les hommes portent des tuniques ou robes longues et flottantes° qu'on appelle° *boubous.* Dans les grandes villes, ils portent en général un pantalon et une chemise flottante, avec toutes sortes° de fleurs° et de dessins°.

    Les femmes portent une blouse avec *un pagne.* Le pagne est un long morceau d'étoffe° que la femme drape comme une jupe. Souvent les femmes portent un turban gracieusement° drapé sur la tête.

    Dans les villes on voit des vêtements variés—robes, tailleurs, complets européens, ou vêtements africains.

	dubbed
	not only
	full of people
	cotton / printed in bright colors
	loose
	calls
	all kinds / flowers
	designs
	piece of cloth
	gracefully

REMINDER

Information about the climate of your Francophone country should be ready to be given to the other members of the group two classes from now. Your library can offer a number of sources for information. Consult a world almanac or an encyclopedia. You can also ask the librarian to suggest other books and travel magazines.

VOCABULARY

UN AN PLUS TARD   A year later
un arbre   tree
une avenue   avenue, wide street
un contraste   contrast
un immeuble   building
un jardin public   public garden, park
un quartier   neighborhood
européen, européenne   European
espère: espérer   to hope
bientôt   soon
déjà   already
environ   about, approximately
joyeux anniversaire!   happy birthday!

1 *Reading comprehension:* Un an plus tard (2)

1 This is a continuation of Michel's letter to Thérèse in which he is telling about his life in Senegal. With whom is he living? What is his apartment like? Has he made new friends? Read this part of his letter to find out the answers to these and other questions.

J'habite avec un autre° coopérant français dans un appartement agréable, avec eau courante° et électricité. Nous avons beaucoup d'amis sénégalais. Ils sont gentils, accueillants°, et ils parlent le français aussi bien que nous. Plusieurs° pays d'Afrique ont des dialectes différents, et le français est la seule° langue° de communication entre eux.

other
running water
friendly, warm
a number of, several
only / language

Now write a brief answer to the questions below.

a Qui habite avec Michel, un Sénégalais ou un Français? |
    un Français

b Est-ce qu'il y a l'eau courante et l'électricité dans l'appartement de Michel? |
    oui

c Comment sont ses amis sénégalais, gentils ou désagréables? |
    gentils

2 Michel encloses a photograph in his letter. What is it a picture of? Why doesn't Michel drive a car in Senegal? What does he ask Thérèse to do for him? Read the last part of his letter to find out the answers.

Je t'envoie une photo de la station de télévision. Devant la porte, c'est moi avec mon vélo! Ici les autos, même les petites deux chevaux°, sont très chères°. Et moi, je ne suis pas riche! Alors, je circule° en vélo, comme° tout le monde.

    Je te quitte°, maintenant, ma chère Thérèse. Le vélo et le boulot° m'attendent°. Dis° bonjour de ma part° à tout le monde. Et encore, bon anniversaire°!

small French car
expensive / get around
like
leave / work (slang)
wait for / say / for me
happy birthday
love

Affectueusement°,

Michel

Now write a brief answer to each question below.

a Sur la photo, qui est devant la porte? |
    Michel

b Qu'est-ce qui est aussi sur la photo? |
    le vélo

c Qui circule en vélo au Sénégal? |
    Michel; tout le monde

3 Complete each statement below with the appropriate phrase from those in parentheses.

a Michel habite avec ____. (plusieurs coopérants, un autre coopérant français)

b Les amis sénégalais de Michel parlent le français ____. (aussi bien que lui, moins bien que lui)

c La seule langue de communication entre certains pays africains est ____. (un dialecte, le français)

d Les autos au Sénégal ____. (sont chères, ne sont pas chères)

e Michel doit quitter Thérèse parce que ____ l'attend. (le boulot, une fête) ▌

a un autre coopérant français   b aussi bien que lui   c le français   d sont chères   e le boulot

NOTE

A statesman's poetry

Léopold Sédar Senghor, the first president of Senegal, is also a well-known poet and essayist in French. In his writings, he celebrates the warmth and humanity of African societies—qualities which he feels have been lost in many industrial cultures. His poetry combines both French and African artistic traditions. Some of his works are intended to be read aloud to the accompaniment of traditional African music played on the **kora, balafon,** and **tam-tam.** Here is part of the poem **Nuit de Sine** (excerpted from **Chants d'ombre,** copyright Editions du Seuil, 1945), and an English translation.

Là-haut, les palmes balancées qui bruissent dans la haute
    brise nocturne
À peine. Pas même la chanson de nourrice.
Qu'il nous berce, le silence rythmé.
Écoutons son chant, écoutons battre notre sang sombre,
    écoutons
Battre le pouls profond de l'Afrique dans la brume des villages
    perdus.

Above, swaying palms that rustle in the high night breeze
Almost not at all. Not even a lullaby.
Let the rhythmic silence cradle us.
Let us listen to its song, let us listen to the drumming
    of our dark blood,
Let us listen
To the deep pulse of Africa beating in the mist of villages
    forgotten.

2 Faire *and* voir *in the* passé composé

1 You have learned that the ***passé composé*** of most verbs is composed of the present tense of ***avoir*** plus the past participle of the main verb. It's easy to know the past participle of an ***-er*** verb, but some verbs have irregular past participles. Read the statements below made by a group of people who visited Senegal and are talking about what they saw.

> *Nous avons vu l'université à Dakar.*
> *J'ai vu la Maison des Esclaves* (slaves) *à Gorée.*
> *Mes frères ont vu des villages de pêcheurs* (fishing villages) *et des pirogues* (brightly decorated small fishing boats).

a What is the English equivalent of the first sentence? |
   We saw the university at Dakar.

b What is the past participle that appears with a form of ***avoir*** in each statement? |
   vu

c ***Vu*** is the past participle of the verb ____. |
   voir

d Write the French equivalent of *We saw some fishing villages.* |
   Nous avons vu des villages de pêcheurs.

2 The sentences below talk about what people are seeing at the moment. Rewrite the sentences to tell or ask what they saw in the past. Write the time phrase at the beginning of your answer.

> Modèle: Ils voient la voiture que tu veux acheter. (hier soir) |
>   Hier soir ils ont vu la voiture que tu veux acheter. / Ils ont vu hier soir la voiture que tu veux acheter. (The time phrase may occur in more than one location.)

a Ma sœur et ses amis voient un très bon film. (hier soir)
b Tu vois les clowns? (hier)
c Vous voyez toutes les autos sur la route? (ce soir)
d Je vois sa vieille voiture. (ce matin) |
   a *Hier soir, ma sœur et ses amis ont vu un très bon film.* / *Ma sœur et ses amis ont vu un très bon film hier soir.* b *Tu as vu les clowns hier?* / *Hier, est-ce que tu as vu les clowns?* c *Vous avez vu toutes les autos sur la route ce soir?* d *J'ai vu sa vieille voiture ce matin.*

3 Chantal was busy this morning. She tells a friend what she did.

> *Ce matin, j'ai fait des commissions.*   This morning, I did some errands.

a ***J'ai fait*** is a ***passé composé*** form of the infinitive ____. |
   faire

b Write the French for *This morning my brother did some errands.* |
   Ce matin mon frère a fait des commissions.

4 Below are some statements in English about people who did some errands. Write the French equivalent of these statements.

a My father and my sister did some errands Saturday morning. |
   Mon père et ma sœur ont fait des commissions samedi matin.

b We did errands all day. |
Nous avons fait des commissions toute la journée.

5 Ask what the people below saw and did in the locations where they were. Answers are in the answer key.

Modèle: vous / en Afrique |
Qu'est-ce que vous avez vu en Afrique? Qu'est-ce que vous avez fait en Afrique?

a Georges et Hélène / à New York   **b** toi / au zoo

3 La Géographie de votre pays francophone

By now you have probably chosen a Francophone country to study. In this section, you will be asked to write about its location and geography. Below is a sample paragraph using New Hampshire as an example. A number of French-speaking people, mainly of French-Canadian origin, live there. Read the sample, then write your own paragraph according to the instructions below.

Le New Hampshire est en Amérique du Nord. Il est près de l'océan Atlantique. Au sud du New Hampshire, il y a le Massachusetts, à l'est il y a le Maine, et à l'ouest, il y a le Vermont. Au nord, il y a le Canada. Quelle province du Canada est au nord du New Hampshire? Le Québec. La capitale du New Hampshire est Concord. Les autres villes importantes sont Manchester, Nashua, Berlin et Portsmouth. Les montagnes dans le New Hampshire sont les White Mountains. Les principaux fleuves sont le Connecticut et le Merrimack.

Now write answers to the questions below, but don't number your sentences. You will then have a paragraph that you can use in your final report.
1 Est-ce que votre pays est en Europe, en Afrique, en Asie ou en Amérique?
2 Est-il près de l'océan?
3 Quels pays y a-t-il au nord, au sud, à l'est et à l'ouest de votre pays?
4 Quelle est la capitale? Quelles sont les autres villes importantes?
5 Est-ce qu'il y a des montagnes dans votre pays? Quelles sont les principales montagnes?
6 Quels sont les principaux fleuves dans votre pays?

REMINDER
If you are the one who is to supply the information about the economy of your Francophone country, look ahead to Part 3 of Preparation 105 to see what information is needed. Plan time to find the information and write it down for your classmates.

1 *Adverbs of quantity*

In this part you will learn how to use the adverbs of quantity *beaucoup, assez,* and *trop* with *de* + a noun.

1 People use adverbs of quantity to measure *how much* or to count *how many.* You are already acquainted with the adverb of quantity *beaucoup.*

a For example, when someone says, *J'aime beaucoup patiner,* you know that the meaning of that statement is *I like skating ____.* ▌

a lot/very much

b A teacher may say to a particularly talkative student *Vous parlez trop!* Which word is the adverb that means *too much?* ▌

trop

c Eight-year old Claire is rough-housing with her big brother, who suddenly locks her in an unescapable hold and starts tickling her. She giggles, struggles, and finally calls out *Arrête! Assez!* What do you think is the English equivalent of what she says? ▌

The equivalent is *Stop! Enough! (Was your guess close in meaning to the exact answer?)*

2 Henri is teaching his younger sister to make *crêpes.* Read the instructions that he gives her.

Ne mets pas trop de sucre. Il n'y a pas assez de farine. Il faut beaucoup d'œufs.

a Write an English equivalent for each statement above. ▌

Don't put in too much sugar. There's not enough flour. You need a lot of eggs.

b When adverbs of quantity are used with nouns, a preposition is used in the phrase. Which preposition? ▌

de (d' before a vowel sound)

3 Adverbs of quantity may be used with either singular nouns or plural nouns. Rewrite each sentence below, and add the information in parentheses.

Modèle: Yves a des disques. (beaucoup) ▌

Yves a beaucoup de disques.

a Tu as des fraises? (assez)
b Paul m'envoie des cartes d'Afrique. (beaucoup)
c Cet élève n'a pas de papier. (assez)
d J'ai mangé du chocolat! (trop) ▌

a *Tu as assez de fraises?* b *Paul m'envoie beaucoup de cartes d'Afrique.*
c *Cet élève n'a pas assez de papier.* d *J'ai mangé trop de chocolat!*

4 You and a couple of friends are planning a back-packing trip. Here are some of the things you are taking.

> *des pulls*   *de l'eau*
> *des chaussettes*   *du lait en poudre*
> *du chocolat*

As leader of the excursion you are checking the supplies. Say the following things in French.

a We don't have enough water. (Use **On n'a pas...**) ▮
> *On n'a pas assez d'eau.*

b We have too much chocolate. ▮
> *On a trop de chocolat.*

c There's a lot of powdered milk. ▮
> *Il y a beaucoup de lait en poudre.*

d Do you (**tu**) have enough socks? ▮
> *Est-ce que tu as assez de chaussettes?*

e I have too many sweaters. ▮
> *J'ai trop de pulls.*

2 *Practice using* ne...rien, ne...personne

1 To review the meanings of *rien* and *personne,* read each brief dialogue below, and write the English equivalents.

a –Qu'est-ce que tu fais ce soir?   –Rien. ▮
> —What are you doing this evening?   —Nothing.

b –Qui va au cinéma avec toi?   –Personne. ▮
> —Who's going to the movies with you?   —No one. (Nobody).

2 Answer the following questions with **ne...rien** or **ne...personne.** Answers are in the answer key.

> Modèle: Qui vois-tu là-bas? ▮
> > *Je ne vois personne là-bas.*
>
> Achètes-tu quelque chose dans ce magasin? ▮
> > *Non, je n'achète rien dans ce magasin.*

a Y a-t-il quelqu'un chez toi?

b Qu'est-ce que Nicole mange?

c M. et Mme Bernard, connaissez-vous quelqu'un à Londres?

d Est-ce que Marie invite quelqu'un pour son anniversaire?

e Qu'est-ce que tu regardes?

f Qu'est-ce qu'ils prennent comme dessert?

3 Vocabulary practice

The story **Séjour au Sénégal** has a lot of French words that are new to you. This part will give you a chance to practice using some of them.

Here is a list of words and phrases that fit into the numbered blanks of the paragraph below. To review the meaning of each phrase, say it aloud and think of its English equivalent. If there are some words you don't remember, look them up in the French-English vocabulary at the end of the book. Then write the phrase that belongs in each numbered blank below. Answers are in the answer key.

des examens difficiles	*pendant*
un jour mémorable	*les habitants*
un travail intéressant	*remplacer*
passionnant	*le service national*
un autre pays	*son service militaire*

Aujourd'hui est ____1____ pour Michel Bertrand. Après ____2____, il est caméraman. Il voudrait trouver ____3____ mais d'abord il doit faire ____4____. Pas très ____5____. Il a une idée: on peut ____6____ le service militaire par ____7____. On vous envoie ____8____ seize mois dans ____9____ où vous travaillez avec ____10____.

4 Le Climat de votre pays francophone

Read the following paragraphs concerning the climate of Senegal. You should be able to understand them fairly easily. Then use the questions that follow to help you write similar paragraphs about your Francophone country.

Le Sénégal, sur la côte° ouest de l'Afrique, est un pays qui a un climat chaud. La température maximum est de 29 degrés° et la température minimum est de 18 degrés°. Il fait moins chaud en janvier qu'en juillet.

Il y a deux saisons principales: une saison pluvieuse° et une saison sèche°. En été de mai à octobre, c'est la saison pluvieuse, qu'on appelle° l'hivernage. La saison sèche dure° de novembre à avril. Le climat n'est pas très bon pour l'agriculture parce qu'il y a trop de pluie° pendant l'hivernage, et pas assez de pluie pendant la saison sèche.

coast
84°F
64°F
rainy
dry / calls
lasts
rain

Write answers to the questions below, and arrange the sentences in a passage similar to the one above. This will go in the report.

1 Est-ce que votre pays a un climat froid, chaud, ou modéré (*temperate*)?
2 Combien de saisons y a-t-il?
3 Quelle est la température minimum, maximum et moyenne (*average*)?

4 Est-ce qu'il neige plus ou moins dans votre pays francophone que chez vous?

5 Ce climat est-il bon ou mauvais pour l'agriculture?

6 En général, est-ce que vous trouvez ce climat agréable?

VOCABULARY

l'autobus city bus
l'autocar bus, motor coach
l'avion airplane
le bateau boat

le train train
à pied on foot
voyager en travel by (car, boat, etc.)

UN AN PLUS TARD (2)

affectueusement love (closing a letter)
le boulot job, work (slang)
une deux chevaux small French car
un dialecte dialect
l'eau courante (f.) running water
l'électricité (f.) electricity
une langue language
accueillant, -e friendly, hospitable
autre other
cher, chère expensive; dear
différent, -e different

plusieurs several; a number of
seul, -e only; alone
circuler to get around
dire bonjour to say "hi"
quitter to leave someone
beaucoup de a lot of
encore again
bon anniversaire happy birthday
de ma part from me
tout le monde everybody

PREPARATION **104**

1 More on double verbs with object pronouns

In Preparation 101 you practiced using direct-object pronouns in double-verb constructions, as in **Je vais le voir** (I'm going to see him). Indirect-object pronouns also occur in double-verb constructions, as you'll discover in this section.

1 Read the following sentence, which has a double-verb construction with an indirect-object pronoun.

    Nous allons leur écrire ce soir.

  a Write an English equivalent. ▎

      We're going to write to them this evening.

  b In the French sentence, does the pronoun precede or follow the infinitive? ▎

      it precedes (Object pronouns in a double-verb construction precede the verb of which they are an object.)

bijoux filigranes d'afrique...

2 Write the complete French equivalent of each sentence.

a He's going to write me tomorrow. ***Il va ___ demain.*** ▌

       Il va m'écrire demain.

b You have to call him. ***Tu dois ___.*** ▌

       Tu dois lui téléphoner.

3 Say that Mireille wants to speak to the following people. Use the appropriate indirect-object pronoun in your response.

    Modèle: à sa tante ▌

        Elle veut lui parler.

a à son grand-père   **c** à toi

b à ses amies   **d** à vous et à moi ▌

        a Elle veut lui parler.   *b Elle veut leur parler.*   *c Elle veut te parler.*   *d Elle veut nous parler.*

4 Now review the use of direct-object and indirect-object pronouns in double-verb constructions, by completing the second line in each conversation below.

a –Vous allez parler à vos parents?

    –Oui, je vais ___ parler ce soir.

b –Tu dois écrire à ta cousine, n'est-ce pas?

    –Oui, je dois ___ écrire une lettre bientôt.

c –Tu vas voir ton grand-père demain?

    –Non, je vais ___ voir la semaine prochaine.

d –Est-ce que Roger va acheter cet électrophone?

    –Oui, il dit qu'il va ___ acheter demain.

e –Vous aimez regarder la télévision, mademoiselle?

    –Oui, j'aime ___ regarder le samedi. ▌

        a leur   *b lui*   *c le*   *d l'*   *e la*

5 Say that it's necessary to buy or do the following things right away. Use the appropriate direct- or indirect-object pronoun in your responses.

    Modèle: acheter ce chapeau ▌

        Il faut l'acheter tout de suite.

a écrire à votre père   **c** inviter tes cousins

b téléphoner à tes parents   **d** mettre ce manteau ▌

        a Il faut lui écrire tout de suite.   *b Il faut leur téléphoner tout de suite.*   *c Il faut les inviter tout de suite.*   *d Il faut le mettre tout de suite.*

2 *Reading comprehension:* **Moyens de transport**

Each frame in this section is a riddle about one kind of transportation. There is a good bit of new vocabulary. However, many of the new words are cognates. English equivalents are given for new words you might not be able to guess.

The word **ça** means *it* or *that*. French speakers use **ça** in riddles because **ça** doesn't give away the gender of the unnamed thing, as **il** or **elle** would.

Moyens de transport (Means of transportation)
l'autocar (m.)   le train
l'avion (m.)   le vélo (la bicyclette)
le bateau   le vélomoteur
la moto

Read each paragraph carefully. Then identify the method of transportation you think is described. Answers are in the answer key.

1 Ça n'a pas de moteur. Ça a une place pour une personne seulement. C'est moins rapide que les autres moyens de transport, mais c'est moins cher° aussi. Pour aller à l'école, pour faire des commissions, ou pour une promenade, c'est formidable. Qu'est-ce que c'est?

expensive

2 Ça a deux roues° comme une bicyclette. Mais ça a aussi un petit moteur; alors, c'est plus rapide et moins fatigant° qu'une bicyclette. Mais quand il pleut ou quand il fait froid, ça n'est pas très agréable. Qu'est-ce que c'est?

wheels
tiring

3 Ça a deux roues comme une bicyclette ou un vélomoteur. Ça a aussi un moteur puissant° et bruyant°. Mais est-ce que c'est dangereux? Ça dépend du chauffeur. Qu'est-ce que c'est?

powerful / noisy

4 Si vous voulez voyager d'une ville à une autre, vous pouvez utiliser ce mode de locomotion. Ça a un grand moteur. Ça a assez de places pour un grand nombre de passagers. Ça roule° rapidement sur les autoroutes. Qu'est-ce que c'est?

travels, "rolls"

5 Ça peut naviguer sur les océans, les lacs ou les rivières. Parfois°, ça a un moteur; parfois ça a des voiles°. Ça n'est pas très rapide, mais si vous n'êtes pas pressé, c'est la manière idéale de voyager. Qu'est-ce que c'est?

sometimes
sails

6 Vous prenez le petit déjeuner à New York, et vous voulez être à San Francisco pour le déjeuner? Oui, c'est possible. Pendant le voyage, vous pouvez regarder un film ou vous pouvez dormir. Qu'est-ce que c'est?

7 Ça n'est pas aussi rapide qu'un avion, mais c'est plus rapide qu'une voiture. Vous faites un long voyage? Pas de problème, parce qu'il y a un restaurant et même des wagons-lits°. Qu'est-ce que c'est?

sleeping cars

1 *Practice with the* passé composé

In this section you'll practice telling what happened or didn't happen in the past.

1 Ask your friend Maryse whether she did the following things last night. Use the cues indicated. Answers are in the answer key.

> Modèle: écouter la radio I
> > *Tu as écouté la radio hier soir?*

a envoyer un cadeau à Jeanne
b faire tes devoirs
c voir le vieux film à la télé

2 Maryse replies that she didn't happen to see the old movie last night.
> *Non, je n'ai pas vu le vieux film hier soir.*

a In a negative sentence in the past tense (*passé composé*), where do **ne** and **pas** occur—around the helping verb **avoir** or around the past participle? I
> around the helping verb *avoir*

b Make this statement negative: *J'ai vu Jeanne hier.* I
> *Je n'ai pas vu Jeanne hier.*

3 Rewrite each sentence below in the negative.
a Vous avez parlé français avec eux? I
> *Vous n'avez pas parlé français avec eux?*

b Ils ont trouvé cette ville très intéressante. I
> *Ils n'ont pas trouvé cette ville très intéressante.*

c J'ai fait des amis là-bas. I
> *Je n'ai pas fait d'amis là-bas.* (The markers *un, une, des* usually become *de* or *d'* in a negative *passé composé* sentence, just as they do in a negative present-tense sentence.)

d Elles ont vu des quartiers pauvres là-bas. I
> *Elles n'ont pas vu de quartiers pauvres là-bas.*

4 The following people had a terrible day yesterday because they didn't accomplish what they originally wanted to do. Make complete statements, using the cues indicated. Answers are in the answer key.

> Modèle: Georges / regarder la télé I
> > *Georges n'a pas regardé la télé.*

a nous / patiner avec nos copains
b mon père / commencer son régime
c je / faire une promenade
d Sara et Luc / terminer leurs devoirs

2 Pre-test practice: indirect-object pronouns

Indirect-object pronouns were practiced in Preparations 93 and 99.

1 One of your parents asks you if you're doing certain things, and you say that you are doing them now. Use indirect-object pronouns and the phrase *tout de suite* in your answers. Answers for frames 1–4 are in the answer key.

> Modèle: Tu téléphones à ta tante Marie? |
>> *Oui, je lui téléphone tout de suite.*

a Tu envoies une carte d'anniversaire à ton oncle Albert?
b Tu parles à Mimi et à Roger de tes projets de vacances?

2 Answer each question below with a negative statement.
a Vous m'écrivez avant le week-end?
b Tu me donnes ton pull gris pour ce soir?
c Vous et Madeleine, vous nous téléphonez plus tard?

3 Tell a friend that he or she should do the following things. Use an indirect-object pronoun in your answers.

> Modèle: envoyer une carte à Jean et à Marguerite |
>> *Tu dois leur envoyer une carte.*

a écrire à ton amie Françoise
b téléphoner tout de suite à tes parents

4 Your teacher asks if you want to do the following things. Tell her that you don't want to, and use an indirect-object pronoun in your answer.

> Modèle: Vous voulez demander à votre sœur si elle peut vous aider? |
>> *Non, je ne veux pas lui demander si elle peut m'aider.*

a Vous voulez montrer vos diapos à vos camarades de classe?
b Vous voulez demander à Mme Cooper si elle veut venir nous parler?

3 L'Économie et le gouvernement de votre pays

The purpose of this section is to help prepare you to talk about the economy and government of your Francophone country. Below are two paragraphs about a few aspects of the economy of France. First read the material straight through to get the general idea of the content. Then read it again slowly, and concentrate on the unfamiliar words.

La France est un pays où l'agriculture est très importante. La culture du blé (*wheat*) est importante dans la Beauce, une grande plaine au sud de Paris. En Normandie, on élève (*raise*) des vaches (*cows*) pour avoir du lait, de la crème, du beurre et du fromage. Le vin est un produit qui a une importance énorme en France. Les Français exportent beaucoup de vin.

Mais il y a aussi beaucoup de régions industrielles en France. À Billancourt, près de Paris, il y a une usine d'automobiles Renault. On fabrique (*manufacture*) des vélos Peugeot dans une usine à Valentigney, près de la Suisse. La ville de Lyon, par exemple, est renommée (*famous*) pour l'industrie de la soie (*silk*) et du pétrole.

Write answers to the questions below and arrange them in paragraph form. This section will be part of your final report. Use the passage above as a guide for the section on the economy.

1 Quelle sorte de gouvernement y a-t-il dans votre pays? C'est une république, une monarchie, ou un empire?
2 Qui le gouverne (*governs it*)—un président? un premier ministre? un roi (*king*) ou une reine (*queen*)? un empereur?
3 Est-ce qu'il y a un parlement?
4 C'est un pays vieux ou un pays jeune?
6 Est-ce que l'agriculture est importante dans votre pays?
7 Quelles sont les régions agricoles et les régions industrielles?
8 Quels sont les principaux produits de votre pays?
9 Qu'est-ce qu'on exporte? Quels produits faut-il importer?

PREPARATION **106**

1 *Pre-test practice: relative pronouns*

In a few days you'll have another progress test. If you need to review relative pronouns, check the Summary on page 454 or turn back to Preparations 93 and 94. Remember that answers for all pre-test sections are in the answer key.

1 The relative pronoun ____ is the subject of a relative clause.
2 The relative pronoun ____ is the direct object of the verb in a relative clause.
3 Complete the sentences with a *qui-* or a *que*-clause based on the information given in parentheses.

> Modèle: La petite fille ____ est ma sœur. (Tu vois la petite fille.) |
> *La petite fille que tu vois est ma sœur.*

a Les pays d'Afrique ____ sont fascinants. (Tu vas visiter ces pays.)
b Cette jeune fille, ____, est professeur à Paris. (Elle va venir nous voir.)

c Les diapos ___ sont excellentes. (Vous montrez les diapos aux étudiants.)

d Mon père, ___, aime faire des promenades en auto. (Il est assez vieux.)

2 Pre-test practice: giving commands

1 Tell your friend Yves to do the following things. Use a direct-object pronoun in your commands.

> Modèle: Tu dois mettre tes gants. |
> *Mets-les.*

a Tu dois chercher ton cahier.
b Tu dois acheter ces disques.
c Tu dois écrire ces cartes postales.
d Tu dois prendre cette salade.

2 Tell your friends Maurice and Claire to do the following things.

a Vous devez envoyer cette carte.
b Vous devez manger votre dîner.
c Vous devez acheter ces chaussures marron.

3 Suggest to your friends that you all do the following things. Use the *nous*-form of the verb.

a Il faut écouter ces disques.
b Il faut prendre le train.
c Il faut faire cet exercice.
d Il faut manger ces crêpes.

VOCABULARY   Take a few minutes to review the vocabulary on p. 442.

fort, -e   strong
sauter   to jump

1 *Pre-test practice:* **passé composé**

For additional help with the *passé composé* see the Summary on page 455 or Preparations 97, 102, and 105. Answers for all pre-test sections are in the answer key.

1 The *passé composé* is a compound tense made up of a form of a helping verb (like *avoir*) and ___ of a main verb.
2 The past participle of *-er* verbs is formed by substituting the ending ___ for the *-er* ending.
3 The past participles of *faire* and *voir* are irregular. The past participle of *faire* is ___, and the past participle of *voir* is ___.
4 Write what the following people did last night, using the cues indicated.

> Modèle: mes grands-parents: écouter la radio **|**
>
> *Mes grands-parents ont écouté la radio.*

a nous: faire une promenade
b tu: envoyer une lettre à Nicole
c elles: parler avec leurs copains
d il: commencer son travail
e vous: voir un film à la télévision.
f je: dîner à neuf heures

5 In items **a–e** you are told to do certain things. Say that you did them yesterday.

> Modèle: Il faut voir ce film. **|**
>
> *Mais j'ai vu ce film hier!*

a Regarde ces photos.
b Vous devez téléphoner au médecin.
c Achète des fruits.
d Tu dois faire des commissions.
e Donne un disque à Albert.

2 *Pre-test practice: writing practice*

Write complete sentences in French according to the instructions below. Be sure you remember to make verbs match their subjects, and make adjectives and markers match their nouns. Remember to include capital letters, punctuation, and accents.

1 Say that your aunt is buying you a record-player.
2 Ask your mother whether you can play tennis.
3 Tell Louise to show you her movie camera.
4 Say that you telephoned your friend Roger yesterday afternoon.
5 Ask the principal of the school if he or she wants to see you at three o'clock.

1 Pre-test practice: double verbs, object pronouns

Turn to the Summary or Preparations 101 and 104 if you need to review the use of object pronouns with double verbs. Answers for pre-test sections are in the answer key.

1 Direct- and indirect-object pronouns usually precede a conjugated verb form, for example *Je lui écris.* When there is a double-verb construction, however, as in *Je vais lui écrire,* where is the object pronoun?
2 Answer the following questions in the affirmative. Replace the italicized words with the appropriate object pronouns.

    a Tu aimes écouter *la musique moderne?*
    b Vous allez donner ce disque *à votre frère?*
    c Ton père veut dire bonjour *aux voisins?*
    d Est-ce que tes parents vont écrire *au directeur du lycée?*
    e Est-ce que Jeanine va voir *ses amis sénégalais* au restaurant?
    f Tu préfères acheter *ces chaussures marron,* n'est-ce pas?

2 Pre-test practice: écrire

You can review the present-tense forms of *écrire* in the Summary.

1 Give the negative forms of the following verb phrases.
    a j'écris, tu écris   **c** ils écrivent, Lucie et Anne écrivent
    b il écrit, on écrit   **d** nous écrivons, vous écrivez
2 Complete the following sentences with the appropriate form of *écrire.*
    a Nous allons ____ à nos copains.
    b Ils nous ____ une carte tous les dimanches.
    c Je n' ____ jamais à mes cousins.
    d Est-ce que vous ____ souvent à Jean?
    e Tu ____ quelque chose à Henriette?
    f Roger n' ____ pas de cartes aujourd'hui.

3 Vocabulary round-up

Complete the following excerpt based on Michel's letter to Thérèse, using the words from the list below. Answers are in the answer key.

accueillants	bien	immeubles	plusieurs
africaine	contrastes	jardins	quartiers
agréable	coopérant	parlent	sénégalais
arbres	courante	pauvres	seule
au	dialectes		ville
beaucoup	environ		

Moi, je travaille __1__, mais je suis content __2__ Sénégal. Dakar est une ville __3__ d' __4__ 390 000 habitants. Elle est européenne et __5__, et les __6__ sont très intéressants. Il y a des __7__ modernes, des avenues avec des __8__ et des __9__ publics. Il y a aussi des __10__ très vieux et très __11__.

J'habite avec un autre __12__ français dans un appartement __13__, avec eau __14__ et électricité. Nos amis __15__ sont gentils, __16__, et ils __17__ le français aussi __18__ que nous. __19__ pays d'Afrique ont des __20__ différents, et le français est la __21__ langue de communication entre eux.

Getting ready for a test

Study this Preparation to make sure you understand the types of questions you will be asked in Progress Test 7. Write your answers on your worksheet. Then check your answers in the answer key.

1 Parts A, B, and C will test how well you understand spoken French. Part A consists of six groups of pictures. As you look at each group, you will hear a statement describing one picture. You are to write on your answer sheet the letter that corresponds to the picture. For example:

A   B   C

You hear: *Nous avons fait une promenade hier matin.*
You write the letter ___.

2 In Part B, you will see a pair of French sentences. You will hear one of the sentences. You are to circle the letter that corresponds to the French sentence you hear. For example:

You see: A Mon petit frère a deux ans.
          B Mon petit frère a douze ans.
You hear: Mon petit frère a douze ans.

You circle the letter ____.

3 In Part C, you will hear a series of statements about someone. You will hear each statement twice. On your answer sheet you will see a question in English about what you have just heard. You are to answer the question in English in the space provided. For example:

> *Nathalie aime voyager. Elle parle bien anglais. Elle veut aller aux Etats-Unis en décembre avec son amie Marie.*

What does Nathalie plan to do in December?

4 In Part D, you are to compare pairs of people, using the expressions *plus...que, aussi...que,* and *moins...que.* In your comparisons, you are to use the name of the person on the left first. For example:

a You see:

Jacques   Hélène   (grand)

You write: ____.

b You see:

M. Ledoux   Mme Ledoux   (maigre)

You write: ____.

5 Part E consists of a reading selection followed by questions in English. For practice, read the following dialogue. Then answer, in English, the two questions based on it.

> *Maurice: Bonjour, Edouard, où vas-tu?*
> *Edouard: À la bibliothèque. Je vais chercher des livres pour un examen de littérature.*
> *Maurice: Moi, j'ai un examen de biologie. Bon, alors, à demain.*
> *Edouard: Oui, à demain.*

a Why does Edouard have to go to the library?
b What kind of exam does Maurice have?

6 In Part F, you will be asked to write *tu-, vous-,* and *nous*-commands with direct-object pronouns.
Write *tu*-commands based on the information given below.

a Tu dois chercher ton vélo.   **b** Tu dois regarder l'écran.

Write *vous*-commands based on the following information.

c Vous devez écouter la radio.   **d** Vous devez envoyer ces lettres.

Write ***nous***-commands based on the following information.

    e Il faut chanter les chansons.   **f** Il faut manger tout le poisson.

7 In Part G, you will be asked to write the forms of ***écrire*** that match the corresponding subjects. Complete these two sentences:

    a Mes cousines m'____ souvent.   **b** Tu ____ une lettre à Thérèse?

8 Part H will test you on your ability to use indirect-object pronouns in affirmative statements. Your friend René tells you to do certain things. Tell him that you are doing them right away.

    Modèle: Parle aux enfants! **I**
              Bon, je leur parle tout de suite.

    a Écris à ton oncle!   **b** Envoie ces cadeaux à Gilliane et à Anne.

9 In Part I, you are to complete sentences with a relative clause. Complete these two sentences with a clause that begins with ***qui*** or ***que.***

    a Ces jeunes filles sont mes sœurs. (Les jeunes filles parlent là-bas.)

    Ces jeunes filles ____ sont mes sœurs.

    b Dans la lettre je parle de mes vacances. (Je vais envoyer cette lettre à Michel.)

    Dans la lettre ____, je parle de mes vacances.

10 In Part J, you will write sentences in the ***passé composé.*** Write what the following people did yesterday.

    a Pierre: jouer au tennis.   **b** tu: faire du camping

Now write what the following people did not do yesterday.

    c nous: voir M. Didier   **d** Solange: téléphoner à ses parents.

11 In Part K, you will be asked to use double-verb constructions with object pronouns. Answer the following questions in the affirmative, replacing the italicized phrase with an object pronoun.

    a Est-ce qu'Annette va envoyer une carte *à sa copine?*

    b Vous voulez acheter *ce maillot de bain?*

12 Part L tests your ability to compare adverbs. You will see a drawing and some cues. In your comparisons, use the name on the left first.

    Write sentences comparing the activity of the three people below.

    Modèle: Roger / Marianne (vite) **I**
              Roger court moins vite que Marianne.

           Roger   Henri   Marianne

    a Roger / Henri (vite)

    b Henri / Marianne (lentement)

13 In Part M, you are to write complete sentences in French according to instructions given you in English.

    a Say that Mme Delacroix is going to go to Baton Rouge next week.

    b Ask your friend Charles if he wants to play tennis tomorrow.

Summary

1 Relative pronoun que (*Preparations 93, 94, 98*)

a. The relative pronoun *que* connects two statements about a person, thing, or idea. It replaces a direct-object noun or noun phrase.

*Dakar est une ville africaine. J'aime beaucoup **Dakar.***
*Dakar est une ville africaine **que** j'aime beaucoup.*

b. The relative pronoun *que* must be used in French. Its English equivalent may be omitted.

*Le garçon **que** je vois là-bas joue au football.*	The boy (whom) I see over there is playing football.
*Je sais quelque chose **que** tu ne sais pas.*	I know something (that) you don't know.

c. Before a vowel sound, ***que*** becomes ***qu'.***

*Voilà la jeune fille **qu'**Henri va inviter.*

2 Formation of adverbs in -ment (*Preparation 95*)

Many adverbs are formed by adding ***-ment*** to the feminine singular form of the adjective. These adverbs often correspond to English adverbs ending in *-ly*.

ADJECTIVE		ADVERB
sérieux	*sérieuse*	*sérieusement* (seriously)
régulier	*régulière*	*régulièrement* (regularly)
rare	*rare*	*rarement* (rarely)

One exception is ***vraiment*** (really), formed from the masculine singular adjective ***vrai,*** which already ends in a vowel.

3 Comparisons of adjectives and adverbs (*Preparations 94, 95*)

a. In French, comparisons of adjectives and adverbs are usually made using the following expressions: ***plus...que, aussi...que, moins...que.***

Ma tante Louise est plus riche que mon oncle Roger.	My Aunt Louise is richer than my Uncle Roger.
Mais elle voyage moins souvent que lui.	But she travels less often than he (does).

b. The adverb ***bien*** (well) has an irregular comparative form: ***mieux*** (better).

Laure danse mieux qu'Yves.	Laure dances better than Yves.

c. Stressed pronouns may be used after ***que*** in comparisons.

Je suis moins riche que toi.	I'm less rich than you (are).

4 The present tense of envoyer *and* écrire (*Preparations 96, 98*)

j'	envoi	e	écri	s
tu	envoi	es	écri	s
on/il/elle	envoi	e	écri	t
ils/elles	envoi	ent	écriv	ent
nous	envoy	ons	écriv	ons
vous	envoy	ez	écriv	ez

a. The *nous-* and *vous-*forms of *envoyer* retain the infinitive stem *envoy-*. This stem changes to *envoi-* in the forms whose endings are not pronounced.

b. *Écrire* has two present-tense stems. The stem *écri-* is used in the *je-, tu-,* and *on/il/elle-*forms of the verb. The stem *écriv-* is used in the *ils/elles-, nous-,* and *vous-* forms.

5 Object pronouns in a double-verb construction (*Preparations 101, 104*)

In many double-verb constructions, the second verb (the infinitive) may have an object. When this object is a pronoun, it is placed right before the infinitive.

Je vais donner le stylo à Gilbert.	I'm going to give the pen to Gilbert.
Je vais le donner à Gilbert.	I'm going to give it to Gilbert.
Je vais lui donner le stylo.	I'm going to give him the pen.

6 The passé composé (*Preparations 97, 102, 105*)

a. The *passé composé* of most verbs is formed with the present tense of *avoir* and the past participle of the main verb.

j'	ai	parlé	
tu	as	parlé	
on/il/elle	a	parlé	
ils/elles	ont	parlé	à M. Barre.
nous	avons	parlé	
vous	avez	parlé	

b. The past participle of *-er* verbs is formed by adding *é* to the infinitive stem.

INFINITIVE	STEM	PAST PARTICIPLE
parler	parl-	parlé
travailler	travaill-	travaillé

c. The *passé composé* is used to refer to or describe an action that happened in the past. It has several English equivalents.

J'ai travaillé ce matin.   I worked (have worked, did work) this morning.

d. In negative *passé composé* sentences, *n'* occurs before the conjugated form of *avoir* and *pas* occurs after it.

Je n'ai pas travaillé ce matin.	I didn't work this morning.
Ils n'ont pas parlé avec nous.	They haven't spoken with us.

Séjour au Sénégal

Le Service de la Coopération

PARTIE A   Aujourd'hui est un jour mémorable pour Michel Bertrand. Après deux ans dans un institut technique et des examens difficiles... enfin!... il est caméraman! Il est très heureux. Maintenant il peut travailler dans une station de télévision. Mais d'abord, il doit faire son service militaire.... Armée de terre? armée de mer? armée de l'air? Pas très passionnant pour un jeune homme qui veut faire de la photographie, de la télévision, des films... Mais le service militaire est obligatoire, alors...

PARTIE B   Michel a une idée: on peut remplacer le service militaire par le service national, dans la «Coopération»! On vous envoie généralement pendant seize mois dans un pays pour «coopérer» avec ses habitants. Là, vous travaillez avec eux dans des domaines variés: médecine, éducation, technique, etc. Vous travaillez beaucoup mais vous aidez des personnes qui ont besoin de vous et, en même temps, vous visitez des pays exotiques et fascinants. C'est très intéressant.

Où aller?

PARTIE A   C'est décidé, Michel voudrait être «coopérant». Oui, mais où? Voilà la question.... Son ami, Gérard Lemarchand, est coopérant au Canada, à Québec. Hier soir Michel a téléphoné à Mme Lemarchand, la mère de Gérard, pour lui poser quelques questions. Voici une partie de leur conversation.

MICHEL   Comment va Gérard? Il est content dans la «Coopération»?

MME LEMARCHAND   Oui, très content. Vous aussi, vous voulez aller au Canada comme coopérant?

MICHEL   Oh, non! Moi, je déteste la neige et le froid! Je préfère les pays chauds.

MME LEMARCHAND   L'Afrique alors?

MICHEL   Oui, peut-être. La Côte d'Ivoire, le Dahomey, le Sénégal...Je ne sais pas.

PARTIE B	
MME LEMARCHAND	Un ami de Gérard est à Dakar. Il dit que c'est une ville très agréable.
MICHEL	Oui, il paraît. Je pense sérieusement à Dakar. Je vais peut-être faire une demande pour le Sénégal.
MME LEMARCHAND	Il faut la faire très vite, vous savez.
MICHEL	Oui, je suppose...Mais d'abord, je dois parler de cette question avec mes parents.
MME LEMARCHAND	Oui, naturellement, c'est une décision importante. Alors, bonne chance!
MICHEL	Merci beaucoup, Madame.

Un An plus tard

PARTIE A   Michel est maintenant «coopérant» à Dakar. Il travaille à la station de télévision avec des techniciens sénégalais. Aujourd'hui, il écrit une lettre à son amie Thérèse qui va avoir 18 ans bientôt.

PARTIE B   Chère Thérèse,
Joyeux anniversaire! Dix-huit ans déjà? Dis donc, tu es vieille! J'espère que tu vas bien et que tu ne travailles pas trop au lycée!
Moi, je travaille beaucoup mais je suis très heureux au Sénégal. Dakar est une ville d'environ 390 000 (trois cent quatre-vingt-dix mille) habitants. Elle est européenne et africaine, et les contrastes sont très intéressants. Il y a des immeubles très modernes, des avenues avec des arbres, des jardins publics, des cinémas, des stades de sport et une grande université. Mais il y a aussi des quartiers très vieux et très pauvres.

PARTIE C   J'habite avec un autre coopérant français dans un appartement agréable, avec eau courante et électricité. Nous avons beaucoup d'amis sénégalais. Ils sont gentils, accueillants, et ils parlent le français aussi bien que nous. Plusieurs pays d'Afrique ont des dialectes différents et le français est la seule langue de communication entre eux.

PARTIE D   Je t'envoie une photo de la station de télévision. Devant la porte, c'est moi avec mon vélo! Ici les autos, même les petites deux chevaux, sont très chères. Et moi, je ne suis pas riche! Alors, je circule en vélo, comme tout le monde.
Je te quitte maintenant, ma chère Thérèse. Le vélo et le boulot m'attendent! Dis bonjour de ma part à tout le monde. Et encore, bon anniversaire!

Affectueusement,

Michel

EXERCICES

1 Spot dictation

Aujourd'hui est ___1___ pour Michel Bertrand. Après deux ans dans un ___2___ technique et ___3___ ...enfin!...il est caméraman! Il est très heureux. Maintenant il peut travailler dans une station de télévision. Mais ___4___ il doit faire ___5___ .... Armée de terre? armée de mer? armée de l'air? Pas très ___6___ pour un jeune homme qui veut ___7___, de la télévision, des films... Mais le service militaire est obligatoire, alors...

Michel ___8___: on peut remplacer le service militaire par le service national, dans la «Coopération»! ___9___ généralement pendant seize mois dans un pays pour «coopérer» avec ___10___. Là, vous travaillez ___11___ dans des ___12___: médecine, éducation, technique, etc. Vous travaillez beaucoup mais vous aidez ___13___ et, en même temps, vous visitez des pays exotiques et ___14___. C'est très intéressant.

2 Geographical cognates

un océan	une péninsule	une montagne	une île	un glacier
une rivière	une plaine	une vallée	un lac	un plateau

3 Visual-lingual drill: relative pronoun que

1 Le/Les sport/s		1 mon ami préfère...
2 Le cours		2 ma copine préfère...
3 La profession	que	3 je préfère...
4 La/Les couleur/s		4 je déteste...
5 La/Les chose/s		5 je trouve passionnant/e/s...
6 Le/Les vêtement/s		6 je voudrais acheter...

4 Reading comprehension: la nourriture sénégalaise

J'aime bien la nourriture sénégalaise. Il n'y a pas beaucoup de viande au Sénégal mais il y a beaucoup de poisson, surtout à Dakar. Le plat° national est le riz au poisson, que j'aime beaucoup. Comme fruits, il y a surtout des mangues° et des bananes. Bien sûr, il y a beaucoup de cacahuètes°. Les autres fruits sont importés et ils sont chers.

dish

mangoes

peanuts

1 Est-ce que Michel aime la nourriture sénégalaise?
2 Est-ce qu'il y a beaucoup de viande et de poisson au Sénégal?
3 Il y a beaucoup de poisson, surtout à Dakar. À votre avis, pourquoi?
4 Quel plat aime-t-il?
5 Il n'y a pas beaucoup de mangues et de bananes, n'est-ce pas?
6 Est-ce que les mangues et les bananes sont importées?
7 Les autres fruits sont chers. À votre avis, pourquoi?

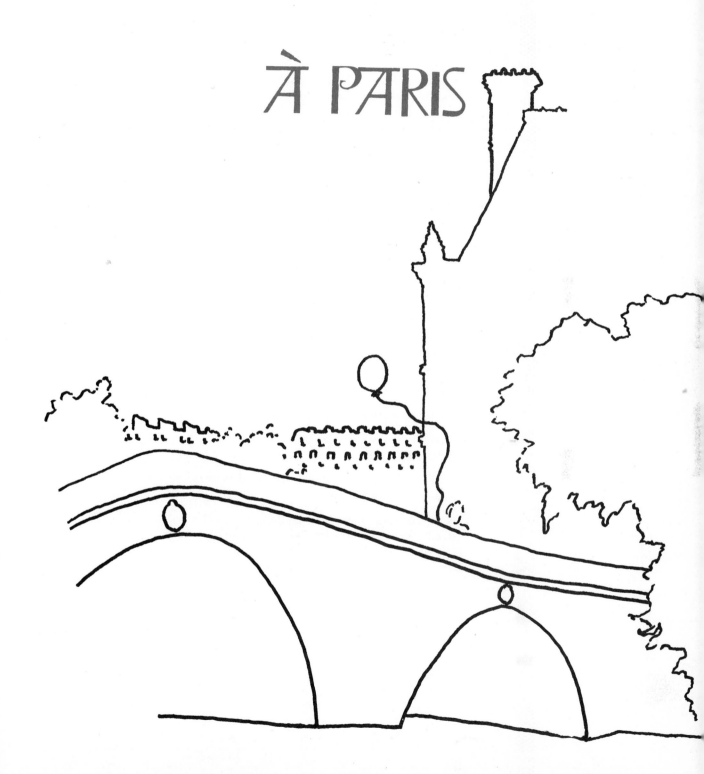

PHASE EIGHT OBJECTIVES

In this final Phase of the course, you will read about Michel Bertrand's return home to Paris from his stay as a **coopérant** in Sénégal. You will become familiar with some of the famous landmarks of the city and some of the benefits and disadvantages of living in Paris. By the end of this Phase, you should be able to:

1 Talk about events that happened in the past, using additional **-er** verbs and **écrire, prendre,** and **mettre** in the **passé composé.**

2 Tell what people are saying or have said, using all forms of the verb **dire** in the present and **passé composé** tenses.

3 Talk about what someone has **not** bought, written, eaten, etc., using the **passé composé** with the structure **pas de.**

4 Use indirect-object pronouns in **passé composé** sentences.

5 Refer to a location by using the pronoun **y.**

6 Refer to a portion of something by using the pronoun **en.**

7 Talk about **all** or **the whole,** using all forms of the adjective **tout.**

✿ The cultural notes describe Paris as a modern city, as a center for intellectual and artistic activities, and as a city where it is possible to stroll leisurely down tree-lined boulevards and enjoy boat trips on the Seine River.

Writing about your Francophone country (*1*)

Write a few sentences in French about the topics discussed below. You can write about each of them separately or combine them in a short paragraph, using the questions as a guide. Try to use only vocabulary and structures that you already know. Keep your sentences short and simple. During the next few classes there will be time when the teacher can help you with the French.

1 Décrivez une ville ou région importante de votre pays francophone. Cette ville ou région est connue pour quelles choses?

2 Écrivez quelques phrases sur les sujets suivants:

a un monument ou personnage (*character*) célèbre, important, ou historique de ce pays.

b un écrivain, musicien, ou peintre (*painter*) de ce pays.

3 Répondez aux questions suivantes:

a Dans votre pays francophone, est-ce qu'il y a des fêtes (*holidays; festivals*) importantes? Décrivez une de ces fêtes.

b Est-ce que les habitants de votre pays francophone portent des costumes folkloriques? Comment sont ces costumes?

4 Read the following sample paragraph about Geneva, which may help you write about your Francophone country.

En Suisse on parle plusieurs langues, et il y a une région où on parle français. La Suisse est mon pays francophone et Genève est une ville très importante de ce pays. Située° au bord° du Lac Léman, Genève est une jolie ville connue° pour toutes les organisations internationales (comme La Croix Rouge) qui y° sont installées°. C'est aussi la ville où est né° Jean-Jacques Rousseau, grand écrivain et philosophe du dix-huitième siècle°.

    La fête nationale de la Suisse est le 1er août. Ce soir-là° il y a beaucoup de monde° dans les rues et des feux d'artifices sur le lac.

    Les Suisses portent parfois° des costumes folkloriques pour certaines occasions. Mais pour la vie de tous les jours°, les vêtements ne sont pas différents des vêtements qu'on porte dans toutes les grandes villes européennes.

located / on the edge
known
there / established / born

18th century
that evening
people
sometimes
everyday life

... PARIS RAYONNE DANS LE MONDE ...

Paris: city for strolling

If you are blessed with curiosity and boundless energy, strolling through Paris will provide the excitement and challenge you're looking for—both narrow, winding streets, with buildings that are hundreds of years old, and huge parks and **places** (squares). There are palaces, museums, and other impressive monuments, but also high-rise buildings and shopping centers. Paris is a city where you can stroll for hours without being bored. Along the **grands boulevards,** there are many stores, theaters, movies, **discothèques,** and fine restaurants. The **boulevard St.-Michel (Boul' Mich)** in the **Quartier latin** has many book stores and cafés, where students sit for hours, reading and talking. You can stop at **Le Louvre**—once a royal palace, now one of the world's greatest museums. Then go out and walk in **le jardin des Tuileries,** a large formal park with **allées** (wide gravel paths), large fountains, and statues. Then stroll up **les Champs-Elysées** (literally, "Elysian Fields")—the long, wide, elegant avenue leading to the **Arc de Triomphe**—or follow the Seine, the meandering river that poets picture as the heart of Paris. You can cross one of its many bridges to get to **l'île de la Cité** and **Notre Dame de Paris** or to other famous landmarks.

You can climb the narrow, twisting streets of quaint **Montmartre,** where the dazzling **Sacré-Cœur** church overlooks the hillside and sidewalk artists do portraits and scenes of Montmartre as souvenirs for tourists. Near where the huge market **Les Halles** used to be, there is now an exciting new museum complex—**Le Centre Pompidou** (also called **Le Centre Beaubourg**)—with exhibits of contemporary art, an open-stack reading room, a lounge for listening to tapes and records, a center for children's art classes, a center for musical and acoustical research, and a restaurant. For a rest, you can always sit as long as you like, talking, reading, or watching other visitors.

2 Practice with negation in the passé composé

This section will show you how to use the expression *ne...pas de* in *passé composé* sentences.

1 Read these sentences:

Pierre fait du ski. Il **ne** fait **pas de** vélo.

Anne a fait du bateau. Elle **n'**a **pas** fait **de** camping.

a In a sentence with the *passé composé,* are *ne* and *pas* placed around the auxiliary verb or the past participle? |

the auxiliary verb

b After a negative verb, the markers *du, de la, de l', un, une,* and *des* usually become ____. |

de

2 Answer the following questions with a negative sentence in the passé composé.

Modèle: Tu as envoyé des lettres à ta famille? |

Non, je n'ai pas envoyé de lettres à ma famille.

a Tu as donné ton numéro de téléphone à Philippe? |

Non, je n'ai pas donné mon numéro de téléphone à Philippe.

b Il a invité ses amis pour vendredi soir? |

Non, il n'a pas invité ses amis pour vendredi soir.

c Vous avez fait un gâteau pour son anniversaire? |

Non, nous n'avons pas fait de gâteau pour son anniversaire.

d Philippe a donné des fleurs à Marie-Hélène? |

Non, il n'a pas donné de fleurs à Marie-Hélène.

e Gérard et Guy ont pris un taxi pour venir? |

Non, ils n'ont pas pris de taxi pour venir.

3 Georges is going to be in a circus and is putting together a clown costume. He decides to buy clothes he would never ordinarily wear. Say that he has never bought the following clothes before. Answers are in the answer key.

Modèle: acheter un pantalon de velours |

Il n'a jamais acheté de pantalon de velours.

a un chapeau jaune

b des chaussures rouges

c une chemise rose

d des gants gris

VOCABULARY

SUR LES CHAMPS-ÉLYSÉES, PARTIE A

l'absence (f) absence

les Champs-Elysées long boulevard

la place de la Concorde handsome esplanade

été (past participle of *être*) been

oublier to forget

penser à to think of, to think about

immense immense, large

long, longue long

loin away, far

pendant during

1 *Writing about your Francophone country* (2)

1 This is the last section that you will write for the final report on your Francophone country. Before you tell whether you'd like to visit this country or not, write brief answers to the following questions about languages, food, and sports. The sample answers apply to the French-speaking province of Quebec in Canada.

    a Quelles langues ou quels dialectes est-ce qu'on parle là-bas? ▌
        On parle français et anglais.

    b Quelle sorte (*kind*) de nourriture mange-t-on le plus souvent? ▌
        On mange des légumes, de la viande et du poisson.

    c Y a-t-il un plat (*dish*) national ou régional? Si «oui», décrivez ce plat. ▌
        On mange beaucoup de steak-frites. On prépare des plats français comme le coq au vin. Il y a aussi des restaurants chinois, italiens, comme aux Etats-Unis.

    d Quels sont les sports populaires? ▌
        Les sports populaires sont le hockey sur glace (ice), le baseball et le football européen (pas américain).

2 By now you know enough about your Francophone country to answer these questions: ***Voudriez-vous visiter ce pays ou non? Pourquoi?*** Write a few sentences to give your opinion. You may wish to read the following paragraph written by a student from the northeast part of the United States and use it as a sample.

Le Québec est une province francophone au Canada. Je voudrais le visiter parce que c'est un monde° différent du monde que je connais.   world
Là-bas on parle français et je voudrais rencontrer° des gens qui parlent   meet
français. On dit que la ville de Québec est très différente des villes
américaines. Je voudrais savoir comment elle est différente! Je voudrais
aussi aller à la campagne voir les vieilles fermes° en pierre° qui sont près   farms / stone
du Saint-Laurent. Il paraît° que c'est très joli. Le Québec n'est pas trop   seems
loin de chez moi: je voudrais aller le visiter un jour°.   some day

2 *The present tense of* dire

Here is a chart showing the present-tense forms of ***dire*** (to say, to tell). Take a moment to see which forms go with each subject pronoun.

je	dis
tu	dis
on/il/elle	dit
ils/elles	disent
nous	disons
vous	dites

1 The present-tense forms of *dire* are irregular. They cannot be predicted from the infinitive. Which form of *dire* matches each subject pronoun or set of pronouns below?

a ils/elles

b nous

c je, tu

d vous

e on/il/elle

a disent b disons c dis d dites e dit

2 Tell what the following people have to say about a painting they are looking at. Use the cues given below and the appropriate present-tense forms of *dire.*

Modèle: Marie-Hélène: laid

Marie-Hélène dit que c'est laid.

a nous: très intéressant

Nous disons que c'est très intéressant.

b tu: un ballon

Tu dis que c'est un ballon.

c vous: une grosse tomate

Vous dites que c'est une grosse tomate.

d Philippe: une orange

Philippe dit que c'est une orange.

e ils: une blague (*joke*)

Ils disent que c'est une blague.

f je: amusant (*funny*)

Je dis que c'est amusant.

3 Give English equivalents for the last three items in frame 2.

Philippe says (that) it's an orange. They say (that) it's a joke. I say (that) it's funny (amusing).

CHECK-UP
Part 2

Write French equivalents for these sentences.

1 I say (that) I don't like coffee.

2 They (*on*) say (that) it's nice out today.

VOCABULARY

SUR LES CHAMPS-ELYSÉES, Partie B

un aspect aspect

la circulation traffic

l'esprit (m.) mind, spirit

les gens people

un poète poet

la pollution pollution

un prix price

astronomique astronomical

désagréable unpleasant

difficile difficult

impressionnant, -e impressive

courent (from *courir*) (they) run

revu (past participle of *revoir*) seen again

vouloir dire to mean

par exemple for example, for instance

quoi? what?

1 *The pronoun* y

The pronoun *y* (there) can replace locative expressions introduced by a preposition such as *à, chez, dans, devant,* etc. In this section you'll learn how to use *y* in affirmative and negative sentences.

1 Read the following pairs of sentences. Write the prepositional phrases that *y* replaces.

    a –Tu vas à Lyon?

      –Oui, j'y vais la semaine prochaine. ▌

              à Lyon

    b –Le cahier est dans le tiroir?

      –Oui, il y est. ▌

              dans le tiroir

    c –Tu manges à la cantine scolaire?

      –Non, je n'y mange pas. ▌

              à la cantine scolaire

2 Look back at frame 1. In affirmative and negative statements, does *y* precede or follow the verb? ▌

              it precedes

3 In English, if someone asked you *Are you going to the station?*, you might respond simply with *Yes* or with complete sentences such as *Yes, I'm going there,* or *Yes, I'm going,* or *Yes, I am.* You don't need to include the word "there." In French, if someone asks you ***Tu vas au stade?*** you may likewise answer with just ***Oui*** or with complete sentences. In French, however, you must always include the word *y* in a complete sentence.

    Answer the following questions with a complete sentence, and write an English equivalent of your answer.

    a Tu vas en Suisse? ▌

          Oui, j'y vais. Yes, I'm going (there) / Yes, I am.

    b Roger va à l'aéroport? ▌

          Oui, il y va. Yes, he's going (there). / Yes, he is.

4 Write complete answers to these questions according to the cues. Be sure to use *y* in each response.

      Modèle: Jean va au supermarché? (oui, à deux heures) ▌

          Oui, il y va à deux heures.

    a Vos parents vont en Europe? (oui, en août) ▌

          Oui, ils y vont en août.

    b Tu travailles à Bordeaux? (non) ▌

          Non, je n'y travaille pas.

c Ton frère arrive tard au lycée, n'est-ce pas? (non, tôt) ▌

Non, il y arrive tôt.

d On va au match avec Paul? (non, avec Gilles) ▌

Non, on y va avec Gilles.

5 Write this dialogue in French.

−Does Alice go to school by subway?
−No, she goes on foot. ▌

−Alice va au lycée en métro?
−Non, elle y va à pied.

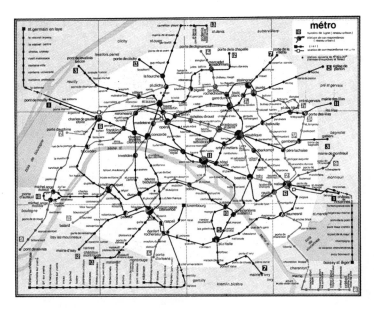

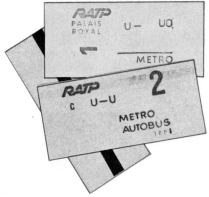

2 Writing the report on your Francophone country

Begin writing your final report. First, organize the materials you prepared for Preparations 102, 103, 105, and 110 so that the ideas lead reasonably from one to the other. Be sure to include a complete bibliography of the book and magazine sources you used for the section of the report that you researched.

Everyone is to turn in a *complete* written report. Each group will then present the report orally to the class, and you will participate in your group's oral presentation. To illustrate your oral report, have some photographs and/or hand-drawings, maps, diagrams, or other appropriate visuals ready for your classmates to look at when they listen.

CHECK-UP
Part 1

Write the French equivalents of this dialogue.
−Is he going to the airport? −Yes, he is.

Paris: city of light

Paris is sometimes called **la ville lumière.** This title refers to its role as a center for intellectual and artistic activity. For centuries, noted writers, philosophers, scholars, poets, scientists and artists—French and foreign alike—have gone to Paris to share in the stimulating discussions and activities available there.

Ville lumière also refers to the physical beauty of Paris. Many monuments and **places** are illuminated at night, with lights that play on graceful **jets d'eau** (fountains), and throw the beautiful sculptures on historic buildings into relief. One can take a sightseeing tour at night to see the imposing reminders of the city's historic past. The **colonne de la Bastille** commemorates the French revolution of 1789. The **Place de la Concorde** offers the viewer classical fountains and a handsome Egyptian obelisk placed by Napoleon, as well as splendid views of famous buildings in every direction. During the French revolution, it was here that Louis XVI and his queen Marie Antoinette were guillotined. **Notre Dame de Paris,** one of the world's most famous Gothic cathedrals, is a witness to eight centuries of history. Here, along the Seine, one can watch a **son-et-lumière** presentation, in which colored spotlights and a recorded narration recount the history of the cathedral and its city, ending with a fireworks display.

Paris, **la ville lumière,** is truly a unique city.

Completing your report

Finish writing the report on your Francophone country. Prepare a clean final version (either typewritten or neatly handwritten).

Practice reading aloud the section of the report that you will be giving to the class with the other members of your group. Try to read it distinctly phrase by phrase rather than word by word. Look up from the page as you speak—it's easier for people to hear you, and it helps to keep you from talking too fast.

Finish preparing any visuals you want to use to illustrate your talk.

In the next class period you will be given time to work with your group to organize and practice your oral presentation.

1 Passé composé: prendre, mettre, dire, écrire

In Phase 7 you learned how to use the *passé composé* of *faire, voir,* and regular *-er* verbs. In this section you'll learn how to use the *passé composé* of *prendre, mettre, dire,* and *écrire.*

1 Read each sentence below, and write the past participle of the verb. Then say the English equivalent of the sentence to be sure you understand its meaning.

   a Pour le dîner, j'ai pris du poulet et du riz. ▮

               pris / For dinner, I had chicken and rice.

   b Richard a mis son chapeau. ▮

               mis / Richard put on his hat.

   c Nous avons dit bonjour à la vendeuse. ▮

               dit / We said good morning (hello) to the saleslady.

   d Est-ce que vous avez écrit à vos parents? ▮

               écrit / Did you write/Have you written to your parents?

2 Look at the past participles of *prendre, mettre, dire,* and *écrire,* and say them aloud.

      prendre: **pris**   *mettre:* **mis**   *dire:* **dit**   *écrire:* **écrit**

   Do all four past participles end in the same *vowel* sound? ▮

               yes (They end in the vowel sound /i/. The final consonants *s* and *t* are not pronounced.)

3 Practice using these new verb forms by rewriting each verb phrase in the *passé composé.*

> Modèle: Nous prenons du café. **I**
>> *Nous avons pris*

a Je mets mon pull. **I**
>> *J'ai mis*

b Louise et Claude prennent de la glace. **I**
>> *Louise et Claude ont pris*

c Il dit au revoir à sa copine. **I**
>> *Il a dit*

d Vous écrivez une lettre à votre ami? **I**
>> *Vous avez écrit*

4 Answer the following questions according to the cues.

> Modèle: Est-ce qu'elle a dit où elle habite? (oui) **I**
>> *Oui, elle a dit où elle habite.*

a Est-ce que Serge a mis son imperméable? (non) **I**
>> *Non, il n'a pas mis son imperméable.*

b Ton père et toi, vous avez pris des croissants? (oui) **I**
>> *Oui, nous avons pris des croissants.*

c Est-ce que les élèves ont dit bonjour au professeur? (non) **I**
>> *Non, ils n'ont pas dit bonjour au professeur.*

d Tu n'as pas écrit à ta cousine? (si) **I**
>> *Si, j'ai écrit à ma cousine.*

5 Write the French equivalents of the following sentences, using the past participles you have just learned.

a I put on my gloves.

b Brigitte wrote a letter to her aunt.

c You did not say good-by to Pierre.

d We had eggs for breakfast. **I**

>> *a J'ai mis mes gants.* **b** *Brigitte a écrit une lettre à sa tante.* **c** *Tu n'as pas dit / vous n'avez pas dit au revoir à Pierre.* **d** *Nous avons pris des œufs pour le petit déjeuner.*

2 Practice with the pronoun y

In doing this section, remember that in affirmative and negative sentences, the pronoun **y** (there) precedes the verb form. Remember also that in French, you *must* include **y** when you answer in a complete sentence.

1 Look at the following sentences.

> Nous chantons *la Marseillaise.*   Je parle *à Michel.*   Roland va *à l'école.*

Which italicized phrase could you refer to with the pronoun **y?** **I**

>> *à l'école (Y can be used to refer to phrases that name a location.)*

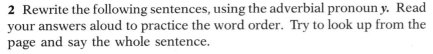

Brasserie Pont Mirabeau

L'ambiance, le service et toutes les spécialités
d'une brasserie parisienne.

Ouvert tous les jours de 7 h 00 à 24 h 00.
61, quai de Grenelle - 75015 Paris. Tél. 575.62.62.

2 Rewrite the following sentences, using the adverbial pronoun *y*. Read your answers aloud to practice the word order. Try to look up from the page and say the whole sentence.

> Modèle: Roger va chez le médecin à deux heures.
> *Roger y va à deux heures.*

a Nous allons à la montagne pour faire du camping.
> *Nous y allons pour faire du camping.*

b Je ne vais pas au club ce soir.
> *Je n'y vais pas ce soir.*

c Mes grands-parents vont en Europe cet été.
> *Mes grands-parents y vont cet été.*

d Vous n'allez pas à la campagne en hiver.
> *Vous n'y allez pas en hiver.*

e On va à Grenoble pour faire du ski.
> *On y va pour faire du ski.*

3 Answer in the affirmative or negative, according to the cue. Answers are in the answer key.

> Modèle: Tu vas à Québec? (oui)
> *Oui, j'y vais.*

a Tu vas au cinéma? (non)
b Est-ce que Véronique va au match de football? (oui)
c Elles ne vont pas au supermarché, n'est-ce pas? (si)
d Tes amis et toi, vous allez au parc? (non)
e Ta mère est chez le dentiste? (oui)

VOCABULARY

À LA PLACE DE LA CONCORDE (Partie A)

un accident accident
l'argent money
un chauffeur de taxi taxi driver
une foule crowd
un hold-up hold-up
un revolver revolver
écraser to run over

kidnapper to kidnap
armé, -e armed
encore un/une another, one more
beaucoup de monde a lot of people
il y a eu (*passé composé* of *il y a*)
    there was
sans doute probably

1 Practice with dire

1 Look at each pronoun below and write the form of **dire** that matches it.

a je   **c** ils   **e** tu
b elle   **d** nous   **f** vous |

               a *dis* b *dit* c *disent* d *disons* e *dis* f *dites*

2 Béatrice wants to know what the following people have to say about Paris. Write complete sentences, using the correct form of **dire** and the cues indicated. Give English equivalents for the first three sentences. Answers are in the answer key.

      Modèle: son père / la circulation est très difficile |
                 Son père dit que la circulation est très difficile.

a Charles et Diane, vous / les gens courent toujours à Paris
b sa mère et sa tante / les prix sont astronomiques
c tu / il y a beaucoup de musées
d nous / c'est une belle ville
e je / c'est une ville moderne

2 The pronoun en

Pronouns are very useful because they keep sentences from becoming cumbersome. Here's one more useful French pronoun: **en** (some, any). It is often used to replace a partitive noun phrase.

1 Read this question and answer.
      –Ton amie veut du chocolat?
      –Oui, elle en veut.
a Which phrase does *en* replace? |
             du chocolat
b Does *en* precede or follow the verb? |
             it precedes
2 Now read this conversational exchange.
      –Ton amie veut de la glace?
      –Non, elle n'en veut pas.
a Which phrase does *en* replace? |
             de la glace
b Does *en* precede or follow the verb? |
             it precedes (*En* precedes a verb in an affirmative or negative statement.)

3 Write English equivalents for *Elle en veut* and *Elle n'en veut pas.* |

She wants some (of it). She doesn't want any (of it).

4 Write the words that *en* refers to in the following pairs of sentences.

a –Je veux du café.
–Moi aussi, j'en veux.

c –Avez-vous de l'eau?
–Oui, nous en avons.

b –Vous prenez de la salade?
–Oui, j'en prends.

d –Tu ne prends pas de dessert?
–Non, je n'en prends pas. |

a *du café* b *de la salade* c *de l'eau* d *de dessert*

5 Answer the following questions according to the cues.

Modèle: Est-ce que ta sœur a des disques? (oui) |
Oui, elle en a.

a Tu voudrais du poisson? (oui)
b Isabelle prend de la viande? (non)
c Vous deux, vous achetez des fruits? (non)
d Tu ne manges pas de pain? (si) |

a *Oui, j'en voudrais.* b *Non, elle n'en prend pas.* c *Non, nous n'en achetons pas.* d *Si, j'en mange.*

6 In French, the pronoun *en* must usually be expressed in a response, if the speaker doesn't repeat the noun. For example:

–Tu veux des bananes?
–Oui, j'en veux.

–Do you want some bananas?
–Yes, I do. (Yes, I want some.)

–Il prend du thé?
–Non, il n'en prend pas.

–Is he having tea?
–No, he isn't. (No, he's not having any.)

Write French equivalents for these dialogues.

a –Is your mother having coffee?
–No, she isn't. |

–(Est-ce que) ta mère prend du café?   *–Non, elle n'en prend pas.*

b –Does your brother want dessert?
–Yes, he does. |

–(Est-ce que) ton frère veut du dessert?   *–Oui, il en veut.*

CHECK-UP
Part 1

Write French equivalents for these dialogues. Use the subject pronoun *tu.*

1 –Would you like some chicken?
–Yes, I would.

2 –Aren't you having tea?
–No, I'm not.

VOCABULARY

À LA PLACE DE LA CONCORDE (Partie B)
un gangster gangster
un motocycliste motorcyclist
un problème problem
arrêter to arrest
renverser to knock over
circulez! keep moving!
s'il vous plaît please

dans un décor
Belle Epoque...

LE CAFÉ
FRANÇAIS

1 *The* passé composé *with indirect-object pronouns*

1 At a family reunion, Mme Lambert wants to make sure that everybody has dessert. Her daughter Monique helps serve the guests. Read their conversation.

> –*Monique, tu as donné de la glace à ta grand-mère?*
> –*Oui, je lui ai donné de la glace.*
> –*Et à tes oncles?*
> –*Oui, je leur ai donné de la glace aussi.*

a The indirect object of the first question is ____. |
   ta grand-mère

b What is the English equivalent of the answer? |
   Yes, I gave her some ice cream.

c In the second question, ***tes oncles*** is the ____ object. |
   indirect

d Which indirect-object pronoun replaced ***tes oncles*** in the answer? |
   leur

e Do the indirect-object pronouns ***lui*** and ***leur*** occur immediately before or after the ***passé composé*** verb form? |
   immediately before

f Answer affirmatively in French: ***Tu as donné de la glace à ton père?*** |

   Oui, je lui ai donné de la glace.

2 Hélène and Guy are talking about a friend on vacation.

> –*Ta copine t'a écrit?*
> –*Oui, elle m'a écrit et m'a envoyé des photos.*

a Which indirect-object pronouns are used in the question and answer? |

   t', m'

b What is the English equivalent of the question? |
   Has your friend written (to) you?

c In the French sentences, do the indirect-object pronouns occur before or after the ***passé composé*** verb forms? |
   before

3 Gilbert, who's ten years old, is telling his grandmother what happened today. Rewrite the sentences, using indirect-object pronouns.

   Modèle: Alain a parlé à Suzanne et à moi de son voyage. |
      Alain nous a parlé de son voyage.

a Ma mère a donné dix francs à mon frère. |
   Ma mère lui a donné dix francs.

b J'ai téléphoné à mes cousins. ▮
Je leur ai téléphoné.

c J'ai envoyé une carte postale à Marianne. ▮
Je lui ai envoyé une carte postale.

4 Answer the following commands by saying that you have already done what you are being asked to do. Use indirect-object pronouns in your responses.

Modèle: Demande de l'argent à ton père. ▮
Je lui ai déjà demandé de l'argent.

a Montre tes dessins (*drawings*) à tes professeurs. ▮
Je leur ai déjà montré mes dessins.

b Envoie une lettre à ta tante. ▮
Je lui ai déjà envoyé une lettre.

c Parle-nous de ton travail. ▮
Je vous ai déjà parlé de mon travail.

d Envoie des cartes à tes amis américains. ▮
Je leur ai déjà envoyé des cartes.

DEUX CONCERTS EXCEPTIONNELS • 15 ET 16 JUIN   A 21 H
AU PROFIT DES CHANTIERS DU CARDINAL
NOTRE-DAME DE PARIS

2 Reading comprehension

Do large cities have anything in common? How would you describe Paris as a city? What are Paris's most famous parks like? If you are fond of shopping, where would you go? Read the selection below for the answers to these and other questions.

Toutes les grandes villes ont des problèmes, mais toutes les grandes villes ne sont pas belles! Paris est une ville très belle et très intéressante.

    Par exemple, si on veut faire une promenade à pied, on peut aller aux Tuileries ou au Luxembourg. Là, on peut admirer° les fleurs°, les arbres, les bassins°, les grandes allées° avec leurs statues magnifiques. Si on veut voir des magasins élégants, on peut aller à pied ou en autobus aux Champs-Elysées ou sur les grands boulevards.

admire / flowers
fountains / wide paths

1 Complete the following sentences based on the passage above.
  a Une grande ville n'est jamais sans ___ . ▮
     problèmes

  b Le contraire de **laide** est ___ . ▮
     belle

  c On peut dire que ___ est une ville très belle et très intéressante. ▮
     Paris

2 Complete each statement below with the appropriate phrase chosen from those in parentheses.

a Les Tuileries et le Luxembourg sont ＿＿. (deux parcs, deux musées, deux grands magasins) ┃

- deux parcs

b Aux Tuileries et au Luxembourg il y a des ＿＿ splendides. (des magasins et des livres, des arbres et des fleurs) ┃

des arbres et des fleurs

c Aux Champs-Elysées on peut ＿＿. (acheter de belles choses, nager) ┃

acheter de belles choses

d On peut aller sur les grands boulevards ＿＿. (en autobus, en taxi, en bateau) ┃

en autobus, en taxi

CHECK-UP
Part 2

Write the French equivalent of each sentence below.
Write to your grandparents. I already wrote to them.

1 Practice with the pronoun en

In this section you'll practice using the pronoun *en.* Remember that in affirmative sentences, *en* means *some* or *any* (*of it/of them*).

1 Compare the following pairs of sentences.

Je prends du lait.	*Elle achète des haricots.*	*Il ne veut pas de poisson.*
J'en prends.	*Elle en achète.*	*Il n'en veut pas.*

a Which words does the pronoun *en* replace? ┃

du lait, des haricots, de poisson

b Give the English equivalents of ***J'en prends, Elle en achète, Il n'en veut pas.*** ┃

I'm having some (of it). She buys some (of them). He doesn't want any (of it).

c In negative and affirmative sentences, does *en* precede or follow the verb? ┃

precede

2 Rewrite the following sentences, using the pronoun *en* to replace the noun phrase. Write an English equivalent for each sentence.

a Nous achetons des poires. ┃

Nous en achetons. We're buying some.

b Tu as du fromage? ┃

Tu en as? Do you have any/some?

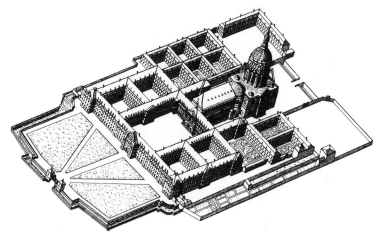

c Ils ne veulent pas de dessert. ▌
      Ils n'en veulent pas.   They don't want any.

3 The pronoun *en* is often used with the expression *il y a.*

–Il y a des chaises dans la classe?	–Are there any chairs in the classroom?
–Oui, il y en a.	–Yes, there are.
–Il y a des bancs?	–Are there some benches?
–Non, il n'y en a pas.	–No, there aren't.

Notice that in the English equivalents the words *some* or *any* may be omitted, but the pronoun *en* must be expressed in French.

4 Answer the following questions with *Oui, il y en a,* or *Non, il n'y en a pas,* according to the cues.

    Modèle: Est-ce qu'il y a des montagnes en Floride? (non) ▌
             Non, il n'y en a pas.

a Est ce qu'il y a des grandes villes en France? (oui) ▌
      Oui, il y en a.

b Est-ce qu'il y a de la neige en hiver chez vous? (non) ▌
      Non, il n'y en a pas.

c Il n'y a pas de pluie en été chez vous, n'est-ce pas? (si) ▌
      Si, il y en a.

d Est-ce qu'il y a des fruits dans le réfrigérateur? (non) ▌
      Non, il n'y en a pas.

5 Compare the following questions and answers.

    Combien de filles y a-t-il dans la classe?   How many girls are there in the classroom?
    Il y en a treize.   There are thirteen (of them).

In French, the pronoun *en* must be used in statements of quantity to refer to the item being counted. In English, the reference is often understood without being stated.

    Tell how many of the following items you have, according to the cued numbers. Say each answer aloud before you write it, and look up from the page as you speak. Answers are in the answer key.

    a Combien de manteaux avez-vous? (2)   **c** Combien de livres avez-vous? (22)
    b Combien de crayons avez-vous? (13)   **d** Combien de frères avez-vous? (3)

2 Reading comprehension

Do you like art? The museums of Paris contain some of the world's finest art treasures. Would you like to see artists at work? Would you like to meet students from many other countries? Read below to see where art lovers, students, writers, and artists like to spend their time in Paris.

Si on aime la peinture°, on peut visiter plusieurs musées célèbres ou, simplement, faire une promenade à Montmartre. Là, dans toutes les rues, on peut voir des artistes plus ou moins bons en train de peindre° des tableaux° plus ou moins bons. Si on veut parler avec des étudiants de tous les pays, on peut aller au Quartier latin. Là, il y a aussi des restaurants et des cafés très connus° où viennent des écrivains et des artistes de tous les pays.

    Oui, bien sûr...la circulation, la pollution, l'inflation...: Paris a tous ces problèmes. Mais, malgré° tout, Paris est une ville intéressante, merveilleuse, unique.

painting

in the act of painting
pictures

known

in spite of

1 Answer the following questions based on the passage above.
   a How do you say in French *«if one loves painting...»?* |
     si on aime la peinture

   b What is the English equivalent of ***des artistes plus ou moins bons?*** |
     more-or-less good artists

   c How would you say in French: *more-or-less good paintings?* |
     des tableaux plus ou moins bons

   d *Être en train de faire quelque chose* means *to be in the act of doing something.* Rewrite in French: *They are in the act of painting pictures.* |
     Ils sont en train de peindre des tableaux.

2 Write a brief answer in French to each question below. Refer to the reading selection if necessary.
   a Que peut-on visiter pour voir des objets d'art? |
     des musées

   b Où peut-on aller pour voir des artistes en train de peindre des tableaux? |
     à Montmartre

   c Qui aime aller dans les restaurants et les cafés du Quartier latin? |
     les étudiants, les écrivains, les artistes de tous les pays

   d Comme toutes les grandes villes, Paris a des problèmes. Quels sont ces problèmes? |
     la circulation, la pollution, l'inflation

Paris, *ville aux mille richesses…*

Ville intime

Ville unique!

1 Object pronouns in double-verb constructions

In this part you'll review the use of object pronouns with double-verb constructions. Say each answer aloud before you write it.

1 To refresh your memory, look at the pairs of sentences below.

> *Je voudrais acheter **ce maillot de bain.***   *Renée va parler **à Maryse.***
> *Je voudrais **l'**acheter.*   *Renée va **lui** parler.*

What are the English equivalents of *Je voudrais **l'**acheter* and *Renée va **lui** parler?* |

> I would (I'd) like to buy it. Renée is going to talk to her.

2 Look once more at the example in frame 1. When the first verb (***voudrais***) is followed by a second verb (***acheter***), where is the object pronoun placed—before the first verb or the second verb? |

> before the second verb

3 Answer the following questions in the affirmative, and use an object pronoun in each response.

   a Est-ce que vous voudriez visiter les grandes villes d'Europe? |

> *Oui, je voudrais les visiter.*

   b Aimes-tu regarder les matchs de basket à la télé? |

> *Oui, j'aime les regarder.*

   c Est-ce que vous devez téléphoner à votre copain ce soir? |

> *Oui, je dois lui téléphoner ce soir.*

4 Now answer the following questions in the negative, and use an object pronoun in each response. Again, you can increase your fluency in speech by saying your answers aloud before you write them.

> Modèle: Tu aimes parler à ton professeur? |
> > *Non, je n'aime pas lui parler.*

   a Est-ce que vous voulez voir le Musée du Louvre? |

> *Non, je ne veux pas le voir.*

   b Pouvez-vous aider vos parents avec leur travail? |

> *Non, je ne peux pas les aider.*

   c Est-ce qu'on va montrer les diapos du voyage en Afrique? |

> *Non, on ne va pas les montrer.*

5 Answer the following questions in the affirmative or negative, according to the cues.

> Modèle: Doit-elle vous écrire, Paul? (oui) |
> > *Oui, elle doit m'écrire.*

   a Maman, papa va me donner de l'argent? (non) |

> *Non, papa ne va pas te donner d'argent.*

b Pouvez-vous nous aider? (oui) **|**

    Oui, nous pouvons vous aider.

c Va-t-elle vous voir demain? (non) **|**

    Non, elle ne va pas nous voir demain.

d Viennent-ils dire au revoir aux enfants? (oui) **|**

    Oui, ils viennent leur dire au revoir.

Second floor of the **Louvre**

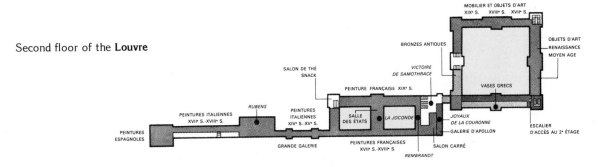

2 *The adjective* tout

The adjective *tout* is used in many expressions in French, sometimes with the meaning *all* or *the whole,* sometimes with the meaning *every* or *each.* In this part, you'll practice *tout* meaning *all* or *the whole.*

1 Read the following passage about Mother Hubbard, and notice especially the forms of the adjective *tout.*

    Mme Hubbard arrive chez elle un jour et voit que le réfrigérateur est vide (empty). *Pourquoi? Parce que:*

    M. Hubbard, son mari, a mangé tout le gigot. Yvette, sa fille, a mangé tous les fruits. François, son fils, a mangé toutes les pommes de terre. Socrate, le chien, a mangé toute la glace.

Now write the form of *tout* that is used with each of these nouns.

a le gigot **|**

    tout   (*Tout* is used with a masculine singular noun.)

b la glace **|**

    toute   (*Toute* is used with a feminine singular noun.)

c les fruits **|**

    tous   (*Tous* is used with a masculine plural noun.)

d les pommes de terre **|**

    toutes   (*Toutes* is used with a feminine plural noun.)

2 The adjective *tout* is usually followed by a marker and a noun.

  a Write the markers that follow forms of *tout* in these noun phrases:

  toutes ces voitures, tous mes amis, tout le gâteau, toute la classe. **|**

    ces, mes, le, la

  b Write an English equivalent for each phrase. **|**

    all these (those) cars; all my friends; the whole cake; the whole class

3 Complete the following sentences with the appropriate forms of *tout,* and give an English equivalent for each sentence.

Modèle: ____ les petites villes de France sont jolies. ▮
Toutes / All the small towns in France are pretty.

a Je connais bien la France; ____ le pays est intéressant et agréable. ▮
tout / I know France well; the whole country is interesting and pleasant.

b Mais Paris est vraiment spécial; ____ la ville est magnifique. ▮
toute / But Paris is truly special; the whole city is magnificent.

c Bien sûr, ____ les immeubles et ____ les maisons ne sont pas beaux. ▮
tous, toutes / Of course, all the buildings and all the houses aren't beautiful.

3 Pre-test practice: the pronoun y

The pronoun **y** was presented in Preparations 111 and 115. Remember that answers to pre-test practice sections are in the answer key.

1 Read the following pairs of questions and answers. Write the word(s) in each question that are replaced by the pronoun *y.*
  a –Tu vas à Lyon?
  –Oui, j'y vais la semaine prochaine.
  b –M. Nadeau est au bureau en ce moment?
  –Oui, il y est.
  c –Tu manges à la cantine scolaire?
  –Non, je n'y mange pas.

2 Write French equivalents for the pairs of questions and answers below.
  a –Are you going to the movies with Gisèle?
  –No, I'm going with my brother.
  b –Is Anne going to school today?
  –No, she's not going today.
  c –Are we going to the park?
  –Yes, we're going by bus.

CHECK-UP
Part 1

How would you say the following sentences in French?
1 We must write to them.
2 I can help her tomorrow.

Part 2

Write French equivalents of the following noun phrases.
1 the whole country
2 all the buildings
3 all the small towns
4 the whole city

1 Pre-test practice: *the* passé composé

By now, you have had a lot of practice talking about things that happened in the past, using the *passé composé.* This part will give you practice using indirect-object pronouns and *ne...pas de* in the *passé composé* with the verbs you've learned so far. Remember that answers to pre-test sections are in the answer key. Information on the *passé composé* was presented in Phase 7 (see the Summary beginning on p. 454) and in Preparations 110, 114, and 116 of Phase 8.

1 To form the past participle of an *-er* verb, what do you add to the infinitive stem?

2 The three columns below list possible subjects, verbs, and objects from which sentences can be made. Write sentences in the *passé composé,* using the items that correspond to the numbers you are given. Make your sentences affirmative or negative as indicated.

Subjects	*Verbs*	*Objects*
1 Je	1 chanter	1 mes amis
2 Vous	2 manger	2 trop de frites
3 Nous	3 acheter	3 Georges
4 Tu	4 écouter	4 une chanson
5 Mme Drouin	5 inviter	5 assez de sandwichs
6 Jean et Claire	6 chercher	6 des disques

Modèle: 6–5–1 (negative) |
                Jean et Claire n'ont pas invité mes amis.

a 1–2–2 (affirmative)
b 2–3–5 (negative)
c 3–1–4 (affirmative)
d 5–5–3 (negative)

3 To be sure that you understand the meaning of what you just wrote, write an English equivalent for each answer in frame 2.

4 You are also familiar with a number of irregular verbs and their past participles. Use the phrases in parentheses to write complete French equivalents for each English sentence below.

a Paul and Gérard went camping. (*faire du camping*)
b I wrote my brother. (*écrire à mon frère*)
c We said good-by to the neighbors. (*dire au revoir aux voisins*)
d Julie saw M. Lille this morning. (*voir M. Lille ce matin*)
e They (*on*) didn't put any salt in the soup. (*mettre du sel dans la soupe*)
f Did Henri take this photograph? (*prendre cette photo*)

5 Read these sentences:

> *Albert et Denise ont pris du café.*   *Ils n'ont pas pris de dessert.*

a Give the English equivalents.

b In a negative sentence, do **ne (n')** and **pas** occur around auxiliary verb **avoir,** or around the past participle?

c When the markers **du, de la, de l',** and **un, une, des** occur after a negative verb, they usually become ___.

6 Mme Drouin finds her kitchen in complete disorder and asks her children if they are responsible for the mess. Respond to her questions in the negative, using the *passé composé.*

> Modèle: Bernard, tu as mis du beurre sur la chaise? |
> *Non, je n'ai pas mis de beurre sur la chaise.*

a Anne-Marie et Julie, vous avez pris des petits gâteaux?

b Julie, tu as mangé de la glace?

c Alain, tu as pris du jus d'orange?

d Vous avez mis des yaourts dans le réfrigérateur?

e Alain, tu as fait une omelette?

7 Now read these sentences:

> *J'ai écrit à Dominique.*   *Je lui ai écrit hier.*   *Je ne lui ai pas téléphoné.*

a In a sentence that is in the *passé composé,* does the indirect-object pronoun occur directly before the auxiliary verb or the past participle?

b When a negative sentence is in the *passé composé* and contains an indirect object pronoun, **ne** and **pas** are placed around the auxiliary verb and the ___.

8 You and your friends are asked to do certain things. Say that you did do them, according to the cues. Use the *passé composé* in your answers and replace all indirect-object noun phrases with indirect-object pronouns.

> Modèle: Tu n'as pas téléphoné à tes parents? (si) |
> *Si, je leur ai téléphoné.*

a Tu as écrit à Jeanne et Guy? (oui)

b Maryse a donné un cadeau à Chantal? (oui)

c Vous n'avez pas envoyé le livre aux Drouin? (si)

9 Your mother tells you to do the following things. Say that you did them yesterday. Use the *passé composé* and the indirect-object pronouns where appropriate.

> Modèle: Fais tes devoirs! |
> *Mais j'ai fait mes devoirs hier!*

a Tu dois téléphoner à ta tante Jeanne.

b Mets ton nouveau (*new*) pantalon!

c Écris à ton oncle François!

d Achète de la glace pour le dessert!

Paris: modern city

Until recent years, most residential and office buildings were about five to seven stories high. Within the last ten years or so, however, the number of skyscrapers or towers **(des gratte-ciel ou des tours)** has mushroomed in Paris. To many Parisians the building of **la Tour Montparnasse,** now the tallest building in Paris, marked the beginning of a new era. The American influence is especially evident in the covered shopping mall within the building. An example of the "new" Paris is **La Défense,** a high-rise complex of office buildings and apartments that is visible beyond the Arc de Triomphe. Many Parisians regret the impersonal flavor of such complexes when compared to the intimate character of a traditional neighborhood.

Outside of Paris, **des villes-dortoirs** (bedroom communities) have sprung up in recent years. These consist of many blocks of apartment buildings and duplexes, and some old residential areas, generally with shopping facilities and schools. The people living here commute to Paris by train or subway.

2 *Pre-test practice: the pronoun* en

En replaces direct-object nouns that are used with the markers *un, une, du, de la, de l', des,* or *de.* In most affirmative and negative sentences *en* occurs directly before the verb. The pronoun *en* was presented in Preparations 115 and 117.

1 In the sentences below, replace all direct-object nouns with *en.* For practice in speaking, say your answers aloud before you write them.

> Modèle: Ils prennent de la salade. ▮
> *Ils en prennent.*

a Roger a du lait.
b Nous n'avons pas de pain.
c Ils cherchent du beurre.
d Je veux de la glace.
e Vous ne prenez pas de poulet?
f Tu n'achètes pas de légumes?

2 Write English equivalents for your answers to a, c, and e above.

1 Pre-test practice: Reading comprehension

Read the rather fanciful passage below. Then answer the questions that follow.

	Une conversation dans une salle° du musée du Louvre...	room
UN VISITEUR	Excusez-moi...	
LE GARDIEN°	Oui, monsieur?	guard
VISITEUR	Cette statue là-bas m'a parlé tout à l'heure.	

(Le gardien tourne le dos° à la statue en question.) back

5   GARDIEN   *(Sarcastique)* Ah oui, vraiment? Et qu'est-ce qu'elle vous a dit?

VISITEUR   Elle m'a demandé une cigarette.

GARDIEN   *(Toujours° sarcastique)* Pas possible! Et alors, vous lui avez donné une cigarette?   still

10   VISITEUR   Mais, monsieur, je lui ai dit qu'il est interdit° de fumer° au Louvre.   forbidden / to smoke

GARDIEN   Monsieur, vous avez beaucoup d'imagination, mais je peux vous assurer que nos statues ne parlent pas. Au Musée d'Art moderne, peut-

15   être, mais ici, jamais.

(Le visiteur continue à parler.)

VISITEUR   Et puis elle m'a dit, «Je vais faire une petite promenade. Je veux voir les autres salles.»

GARDIEN   Mais monsieur, vous êtes fou! Je vous dis que

20   cette statue...

(Le gardien tourne la tête° et voit que la statue n'est pas là.)   head

Mais où est-elle? Elle n'est pas là! Au voleur°! Au voleur!   Stop, thief!

25   VISITEUR   Mais monsieur, je vous ai dit qu'elle fait une promenade. Elle ne va pas aller trop loin.

GARDIEN   Quelqu'un a kidnappé notre magnifique statue italienne. Au voleur! Au voleur!

VISITEUR   Italienne? Ah, ça explique° son accent. Mais   that explains

30   magnifique? Ah non, alors! Moi, je la trouve plutôt° laide.   rather

UN DES PORTRAITS   Peut-être, monsieur. Mais elle est très gentille, vous savez.

Now answer the following questions in French, using complete sentences. If you have difficulty finding the correct answers, the line numbers in parentheses at the end of each question will help you find them. Answers are in the answer key.

Modèle: Que dit le visiteur au gardien? (ll. 1–3)

Il dit qu'une statue lui a parlé.

1 Qu'est-ce que la statue a demandé au visiteur? Et qu'est-que le visiteur lui a répondu (*answered*)?   (ll. 7–11)

2 Est-ce que le gardien croit (*croire:* to believe) le visiteur?   (ll. 12–15)

3 Le gardien assure le visiteur qu'il n'y a pas de statues qui parlent au Louvre. Où trouve-t-on peut-être des statues qui parlent?   (l. 14)

4 Pourquoi la statue a-t-elle quitté la salle? Qu'est-ce qu'elle a voulu (*voulu:* past participle of *vouloir*) faire?   (ll. 17–18)

5 Quand le gardien voit que la statue n'est pas là, que pense-t-il? (ll. 27–28)

6 La statue vient de quel pays?   (l. 28–29)

7 Qui pense que la statue est très gentille?   (ll. 32–33)

2   *Pre-test practice:* **dire**

The present tense of **dire** was presented in Preparations 111 and 115. The *passé composé* of **dire** was presented in Preparation 114. Answers are in the answer key.

1 Complete the following sentences with the correct form of **dire**.

   a Mais je te ____ que je dois travailler demain!

b Je lui ai ___ où j'habite, mais je ne lui ai pas donné mon numéro de téléphone.

c Nous ___ bonjour à notre voisin quand nous le voyons.

d Si vous ___ à l'agent où vous voulez aller, il peut vous aider.

e Mes parents ___ qu'il faut manger des légumes.

f Tu ___ que tu n'as pas faim, mais tu as mangé tout mon dessert!

g Est-ce que tu peux me ___ pourquoi il y a un chimpanzé dans la cuisine?

h Quand Robert ___ «peut-être», il veut ___ «non».

2 Give the English equivalents of the first three sentences in frame 1.

Getting ready for a test

Tempus fugit (that's Latin, not French, for *time flies*), and once again it's time to brush up on your test-taking technique. In your next class you will have a progress test on the skills you have been working with in Phase 8. This Preparation will tell you what kinds of questions to expect. It will also give you a bit of practice. Write your answers on your worksheet and check them against the answer key.

1 Parts A and B will test your listening comprehension ability. In Part A, you will hear a series of conversational exchanges between Caroline and Alain. On your answer sheet you will see questions in English. After hearing each exchange, you are to write the answer in English. For example:

You hear: Alain: J'ai visité Paris la semaine dernière.
              Caroline: Est-ce que tu as vu tous les musées?
You read: What does Caroline ask Alain about his visit to Paris?
You write: ___.

2 In Part B, you will hear a series of recorded questions. On your answer sheet, you will see three possible answers for each question. Make a check mark in the box next to the logical answer. (For now, write the letter of the logical answer.) For example:

You hear: ***Tu vas au jardin public en autobus?***
You see these three possible answers: A Non, je ne prends pas la voiture.
                                        B Non, j'y vais en métro.
                                        C Non, j'y vais en autobus.

Which letter did you write? ___

une semaine de paris
pariscop

3 Part C tests your reading comprehension ability. You will read a dialogue in French between a French girl and an American girl, and then answer questions about it in English.
For example:

CHANTAL	Est-ce que tu as envoyé des photos de Paris à ta famille?
JANET	Oui, et je leur ai écrit que c'est une ville magnifique.
CHANTAL	Moi, je connais bien l'Europe. Maintenant je voudrais visiter les États-Unis.
JANET	Ah oui? Tu vas y aller bientôt?
CHANTAL	J'espère. Peut-être l'été prochain. Mais pour avoir assez d'argent, je dois travailler pendant les vacances de Noël.

a How has Janet shared her visit to Paris with her family? What has she told them about Paris?
b What does Chantal hope to do? When?
c What must Chantal do in order to achieve this goal?

4 Part D calls for the use of the *passé composé*. You will see a subject and a verb phrase. For the first items, you are to write sentences indicating what the subject did yesterday.

Modèle: Paul: déjeuner à la cantine
Paul a déjeuné à la cantine.

a On: faire du ski
b Thérèse et Georges: voir un film intéressant
For the last items, you are to write sentences saying what the subjects did *not* do yesterday.

Modèle: Elles: faire des commissions
Elles n'ont pas fait de commissions.

c Je: acheter des livres
d Nous: écrire des lettres

5 In Part E, you will be asked to complete sentences with the correct present-tense form of the irregular verb *dire.* For example:
a Vous ____ que vous ne pouvez pas venir?
b Mes amis ____ qu'ils ne vont pas à la plage aujourd'hui.

6 Part F tests your ability to use the pronoun *y.* You will be asked to answer questions in the affirmative or negative, according to the cues *oui* on *non.*

> Modèle: Tu vas au cinéma? (oui) |
> *Oui, j'y vais.*

a Elles travaillent à Marseille? (oui)
b On va à la plage? (non)

7 In Part G, you will be expected to write sentences using indirect-object pronouns with the *passé composé.* Respond to the following statements by saying that you did yesterday whatever you are asked to do now.

> Modèle: Écris à ton oncle. |
> *Je lui ai écrit hier.*

a Tu dois parler à tes professeurs cet après-midi.
b Écris à ta tante Geneviève pour son anniversaire.

8 Part H tests your ability to use the pronoun *en.* Answer the following questions, using *en* in your responses.

> Modèle: Vous voulez des haricots? (oui) |
> *Oui, j'en veux.*

a Est-ce que ton frère prend de la salade? (oui)
b Il y a de la neige à Dakar? (non)

9 In Part I you will be asked to use double-verb constructions with object pronouns. Answer the following questions, replacing the italicized words with the correct object pronoun.

> Modèle: Suzanne va téléphoner *à l'ami de Paul* demain? |
> *Oui, Suzanne va lui téléphoner demain.*

a Tu veux voir *la maison de M. et Mme Neuilly?*
b Est-ce que Paul va envoyer des journaux *à sa sœur?*

10 In Part J you will be asked to write sentences in the *passé composé,* using the cues provided. Tell what you did yesterday, using the words given to form complete sentences.

> Modèle: prendre / lait / avec / croissants |
> *J'ai pris du lait avec des croissants.*

a mettre / un chapeau / et / des gants
b écrire / lettre / mon grand-père

If you did this Preparation carefully and if you understood all parts of it, you should do well on the test. If you had difficulty with any of the frames, go back now and figure out where and why you went wrong. You might want to look back at some of the earlier Preparations to help yourself get ready for the test.

Bonne chance!

SUMMARY

1 The pronoun y (*Preparations 112, 114*)

    a. The pronoun *y* replaces expressions of location introduced by a preposition such as *à, chez, dans, devant,* etc.

    b. *Y* must always be expressed in French, even though the equivalent expression *there* may be omitted in English.

–Paul est chez lui?	–Is Paul home?
*–Oui, il **y** est.*	–Yes, he is (there).
*–Non, il n'**y** est pas.*	–No, he isn't (there).

2 The pronoun en (*Preparations 115, 117*)

    a. The pronoun *en* replaces nouns introduced by *de* and used in a partitive or in an indefinite sense. It means *some (of it, of them),* and *any (of it, of them).*

    b. *En* must always be expressed in French.

–Tu veux du poulet?	–Do you want some chicken?
*–Oui, j'**en** veux.*	–Yes, I do (want some).
*–Non, je n'**en** veux pas.*	–No, I don't (want any).
–Combien de pommes y a-t-il?	–How many apples are there?
*–Il y **en** a cinq.*	–There are five (of them).

3 The present tense of dire (*Preparations 111, 115*)

je	dis
tu	dis
on/il/elle	dit
ils/elles	disent
nous	disons
vous	dites

4 More about the passé composé (*Preparations 114, 116*)

    a. The past participles of *écrire, dire, mettre,* and *prendre* are irregular: *j'ai écrit, j'ai dit, j'ai mis, j'ai pris.*

    b. In negative *passé composé* sentences, the markers *un, une, des, du, de la,* and *de l'* usually become *de* before a noun: *Je n'ai pas écrit de lettres.*

    c. Object pronouns precede the auxiliary verb: *Je **lui** ai parlé hier.*

5 The adjective tout (*Preparation 118*)

    a. The forms of *tout* are often followed by a noun marker.

tout le gâteau	the whole cake	*tous mes amis*	all my friends
toute la classe	the whole class	*toutes ces villes*	all these cities

    b. Forms of *tout* occur in idiomatic expressions like *tout le monde* (*everyone*) and *tout de suite* (*immediately*).

Retour à Paris

SCÈNE 1   ***Sur les Champs-Elysées***

Michel et Thérèse sont sur les Champs-Elysées, près de la Place de la Concorde.

THÉRÈSE   Alors, comment trouves-tu Paris après ta longue absence?

MICHEL   Merveilleux! Et grand!

5   THÉRÈSE   Comment, grand? Mais Paris a toujours été grand!

MICHEL   Oui, mais quand on est loin, on oublie... Maintenant, après Dakar, je trouve Paris immense.

THÉRÈSE   Tu as pensé à Paris pendant ton séjour au Sénégal?

MICHEL   Oui, bien sûr! Dans mon esprit, j'ai souvent revu les Champs-Elysées, par exemple, mais jamais tellement beaux, tellement impressionnants.

10   THÉRÈSE   Dis donc, tu parles comme un poète! Tu as oublié les aspects désagréables de Paris...

MICHEL   Quoi? Tu veux dire toute cette circulation...

THÉRÈSE   Oui, la circulation difficile, les gens qui courent toujours, et aussi la pollution, les prix astronomiques...

15

SCÈNE 2   ***À la Place de la Concorde***

Michel et Thérèse sont maintenant à la Place de la Concorde. Il y a beaucoup de voitures, beaucoup de monde...

MICHEL   Oh là là! Qu'est-ce que c'est, toute cette foule? Et tous ces agents de police?

5   THÉRÈSE   Je ne sais pas! Encore un accident, sans doute.

FEMME 1   Oui, un taxi a écrasé une femme et deux enfants.

HOMME 1   Mais non, un chauffeur de taxi a kidnappé deux enfants.

FEMME 2   Pas du tout! Il y a eu un hold-up dans un taxi. Une femme armée d'un revolver a pris l'argent du chauffeur.

10   AGENT   Allons, allons, circulez, circulez!

HOMME 2   On a arrêté les gangsters?

AGENT   Quels gangsters? Il n'y a pas eu de gangsters. Un taxi a renversé un motocycliste, c'est tout... Allez, allez, circulez, s'il vous plaît.

THÉRÈSE   Alors, Michel, comment trouves-tu Paris maintenant?

15   MICHEL   Quoi? Paris a des problèmes? Bien sûr, comme toutes les grandes villes!

Lecture

Toutes les grandes villes ont des problèmes, mais toutes les grandes villes ne sont pas belles! Paris est une ville très belle et très intéressante.

Par exemple, si on veut faire une promenade à pied, on peut aller aux Tuileries ou au Luxembourg. Là, on peut admirer les fleurs, les arbres, les bassins, les grandes allées avec leurs statues magnifiques. Si on veut voir des magasins élégants, on peut aller à pied ou en autobus aux Champs-Elysées ou sur les grands boulevards.

Si on aime la peinture, on peut visiter plusieurs musées célèbres ou, simplement, faire une promenade à Montmartre. Là, dans toutes les rues, on peut voir des artistes plus ou moins bons en train de peindre des tableaux plus ou moins bons. Si on veut parler avec des étudiants de tous les pays, on peut aller au quartier Latin. Là, il y a aussi des restaurants et des cafés très connus où viennent des écrivains et des artistes de tous les pays.

Oui, bien sûr... La circulation, la pollution, l'inflation...: Paris a tous ces problèmes. Mais, malgré tout, Paris est une ville intéressante, merveilleuse, unique.

SCÈNE 3   *Une promenade en bateau-mouche*

MICHEL	Une promenade en bateau-mouche°, c'est toujours sensationnel!	type of sightseeing boat
THÉRÈSE	Oui, tu as raison... Le Louvre, Notre Dame, tous les monuments sont vraiment très impressionnants.	
MICHEL	Et la Seine est toujours belle!	
THÉRÈSE	Oh, Michel! Tu veux voir seulement les beaux aspects de Paris. Tu as oublié qu'il y a des rues sales° et tristes°...	dirty streets / sad
MICHEL	Et des appartements où le soleil° n'entre jamais? Non, je n'ai pas oublié. Mon appartement est sombre°, microscopique, et dans un quartier plutôt° pauvre.	sun / dark / rather
THÉRÈSE	Comment? Tu n'habites pas chez tes parents, dans leur bel appartement?	
MICHEL	Mais non, j'ai préféré être indépendant. Ce n'est pas facile° sans travail et sans beaucoup d'argent.	easy
THÉRÈSE	Alors, Paris n'est pas tellement beau, après tout!	
MICHEL	Mais si, c'est beau; c'est très, très beau. Tu sais, après une longue absence, on l'apprécie!	

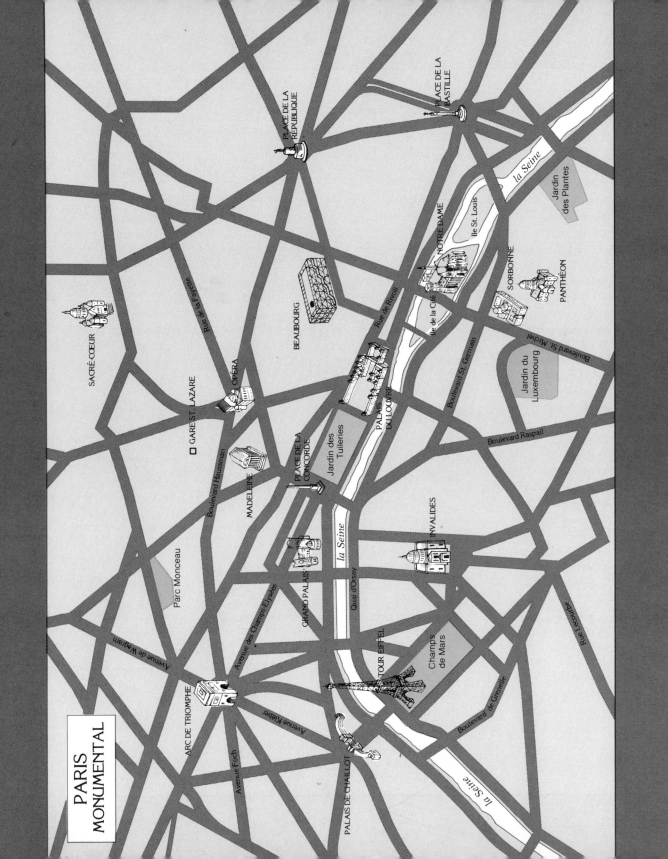

PARIS
MONUMENTAL

ARC DE TRIOMPHE

PALAIS DE CHAILLOT

TOUR EIFFEL

Champs
de Mars

Boulevard de Grenelle

la Seine

Rue Lecourbe

INVALIDES

GRAND PALAIS

Quai d'Orsay

la Seine

Avenue Foch

Avenue Kléber

Avenue des Champs-Elysées

Avenue de Wagram

Parc Monceau

Boulevard Haussman

MADELEINE

PLACE DE LA
CONCORDE

Jardin des
Tuileries

PALAIS
DU LOUVRE

Boulevard Raspail

Jardin du
Luxembourg

PANTHÉON

SORBONNE

Boulevard St. Michel

Boulevard St. Germain

Rue de Rivoli

BEAUBOURG

OPÉRA

GARE ST. LAZARE

Rue de la Fayette

SACRÉ-CŒUR

PLACE DE LA
RÉPUBLIQUE

NOTRE DAME

Île de la Cité

Île St. Louis

la Seine

Jardin
des Plantes

PLACE DE LA
BASTILLE

1 l'Algérie
2 la Belgique
3 le Bénin (le Dahomey)
4 le Burundi
5 le Cameroun
6 le Congo
7 la Corse
8 la Côte d'Ivoire
9 le Djibouti
10 l'Empire Centrafricain
11 la France
12 le Gabon
13 la Guadeloupe
14 la Guinée
15 la Guyane française
16 Haïti
17 la Haute Volta
18 le Cambodge
19 le Laos
20 la Louisiane
21 le Luxembourg
22 Madagascar
23 le Mali
24 le Maroc
25 la Martinique
26 la Mauritanie
27 le Niger
28 la Nouvelle-Calédonie
29 la Polynésie française
30 **le Québec**
31 la Réunion
32 le Ruanda
33 le Sénégal
34 la Suisse
35 le Tchad
36 le Togo
37 la Tunisie
38 le Zaïre

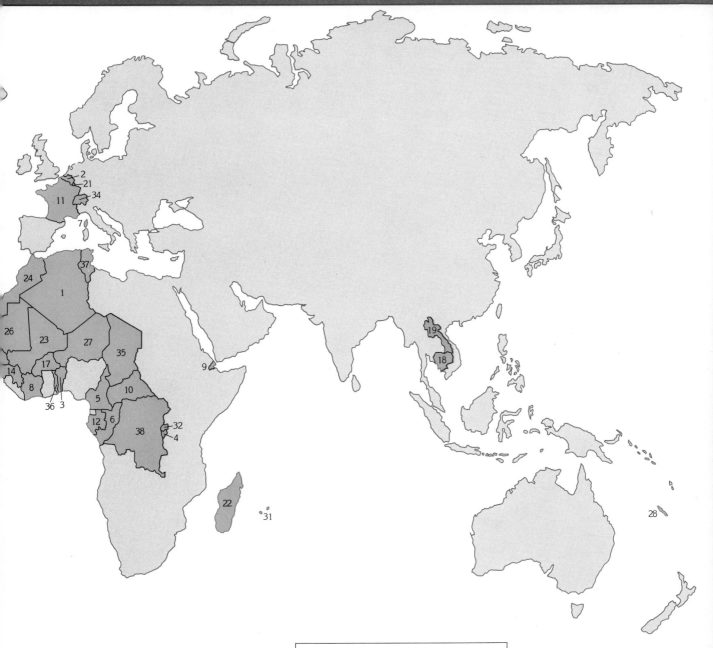

LE MONDE FRANCOPHONE

L'ANGLETERRE

Londres

LA MANCHE

Bruxelles

Lille

LA BELGIQUE

L'ALLEMAGNE

Le Havre

la Seine

Reims

LE LUXEMBOURG

Strasbourg

LES VOSGES

Le Rhin

Paris

Brest

la Loire

Nantes

Tours

LE JURA

LA SUISSE

Genève

L'OCÉAN ATLANTIQUE

LE MASSIF CENTRAL

Lyon

ALPES

Bordeaux

Grenoble

L'ITALIE

LES

Le Rhône

la Garonne

Montpellier

Nice

Toulouse

L'ESPAGNE

Marseille

LA FRANCE

LA MER MÉDITERRANÉE

LES PYRÉNÉES

PHASE 1

Preparation 4
2 3 a. Jeanne est de Chicago.
    b. Nous sommes d'Ivry.
    c. Tu es très en retard!
    d. Jeanne et Paul Dupont sont d'Ivry.
    e. Vous êtes Monsieur Chardin?
    f. Je suis très pressé!
3 3 a. un disque
    b. une règle
    c. un transistor
    d. une affiche
    e. une caméra
    f. un morceau de craie
    g. un stylo
    h. un cahier
    i. une feuille de papier

Preparation 5
2 1 C'est un crayon.
  2 C'est un bureau.
  3 C'est une bande.
  4 C'est un morceau de craie.
  5 C'est un écran.
  6 C'est une table.
  7 C'est une feuille de papier.
  8 C'est un tableau.
  9 C'est une cassette.

Preparation 6
2 1 a. est
    b. sommes
    c. es
    d. sont
    e. suis
    f. êtes
  2 a. suis
    b. êtes
    c. est
    d. sommes
    e. sont
    f. es

Preparation 7
2 4 a. C'est la caméra d'Alain.
    b. C'est le transistor de Valérie.
    c. C'est l'affiche d'Alice.
3 4 a. Nous ne sommes pas en retard.
    b. Je ne suis pas Sylvie Lemaître.

    c. Paul et Jean ne sont pas de Paris.
    d. Le cadeau n'est pas sur la table.

Preparation 8
3 5 a. Non, nous ne cherchons pas l'écran.
    b. Non, Robert n'est pas devant le tableau.
    c. Non, le crayon et la feuille de papier ne sont pas sur le bureau.
4 2 a. la (radio), le (transistor)
    b. la (fille), l'(enfant), le (garçon)
    c. le (garçon), l'(homme)
    d. la (chaise)
    e. l'(homme)
    f. l'(écran)
    g. la (bande)
    h. le (morceau de craie)
    i. l'(affiche)
    j. le (bureau)
    k. la (feuille de papier)
    l. la (table)

Preparation 9
1 1 je cherche
  2 André cherche
  3 M. et Mme Dupont cherchent
  4 vous cherchez
  5 Marie et Hélène cherchent
  6 Marc cherche
  7 tu cherches
  8 nous cherchons
2 9 a. Mlle Bonnard est pressée aujourd'hui.
    b. Philippe est très grand.
    c. Catherine n'est pas très gentille.
    d. Sheila n'est pas française.

Preparation 10
1 1 a. caméra, présent, pressé, télévision
    b. français, garçon, ça alors!, ça va?
    c. mathématiques, géographie, géométrie, américaine
    d. bien sûr!, vous êtes, bête
    e. où est...?, règle, très bien, à demain

    f. élève
  2 a. C'est le stylo de Philippe.
    b. Ce n'est pas une gomme.
    c. Je cherche l'affiche de Marie.
    d. Je cherche un crayon.

Preparation 11
1 1 a. vous
    b. je
    c. tu
    d. elle
  2 a. cherche
    b. cherches
    c. cherchez
    d. cherche
  3 a. Non, je ne suis pas de Versailles.
    b. Non, je ne suis pas français.
    c. Oui, ils cherchent une bande.
    d. Oui, je cherche le cahier d'Isabelle.
2 1 a. une, un
    b. une
    c. un, un
    d. un
    e. un
    f. un
  2 a. La femme cherche l'enfant.
    b. Nous cherchons le livre de Martine.
    c. L'homme n'est pas en retard aujourd'hui.
    d. La feuille de papier est sous la chaise.
4 1 a. L'homme est grand.
    b. Anne est française.
    c. Monsieur Martelli n'est pas pauvre.
    d. Madame Martelli est riche.
    e. La fille est petite.
    f. Elizabeth n'est pas présente aujourd'hui.
  2 a. Jacques n'est pas pauvre.
    b. La femme est grande.

Preparation 12
1 1 a. C'est l'affiche de Martine.
    b. C'est le disque d'Annick.
    c. C'est l'enfant de M. Marteau.

1 1 d. C'est la caméra de Bernard.
2 a. Où est la gomme de Jacques?
b. Je cherche la caméra de M. Teyssier.
c. Tu ne cherches pas la bande de Mme Legrand?
2 1 a. Je ne suis pas de Boston.
b. Elles ne cherchent pas le disque d'Hélène.
c. La télévision de M. Moreau n'est pas très grande.
d. Nous ne cherchons pas le transistor.
2 a. They are not looking for Hélène's record.
b. Mr. Moreau's television set is not very big.
3 a. Non, je ne cherche pas le disque de Monique.
b. Non, le stylo et la feuille de papier ne sont pas sur la table.
c. Non, nous ne cherchons pas M. Legrand.
d. Non, vous n'êtes pas en retard.
3 1 vous
2 tu
3 vous
4 tu
5 vous
6 vous
7 tu
8 vous
9 tu
10 vous
4 1 a
2 c
3 a
4 b

Preparation 13
1 a. B
b. A
2 a. A
b. C
3 a. Non, je suis américain.
b. C'est Pierre.
4 a. il, elle
b. vous
5 a. cherches
b. cherchent
6 a. un
b. une
7 a. l'
b. la
8 a. tu
b. vous
8 c. vous

9 a. Hélène est grande.
b. Le garçon est français.
c. Madeleine est gentille.
10 a. Béatrice ne cherche pas le livre.
b. Il n'est pas sur le bureau.
11 a. C'est le cadeau de Bernard.
b. C'est le cahier d'Annette.
12 a. Un homme cherche l'enfant.
b. Elle n'est pas américaine.
c. La caméra de Chantal est là.

PHASE 2
Preparation 14
3 6 a. Monique aime le français, mais elle déteste l'espagnol.
b. Jean et moi, nous aimons l'algèbre, mais nous détestons l'histoire.
c. Antoine et Michel aiment la physique, mais ils détestent la biologie.

Preparation 15
1 7 a. Ils n'aiment pas l'histoire.
b. Georges n'aime pas la géographie.
c. Anne et moi, nous n'aimons pas l'espagnol.
d. Vous n'aimez pas tricoter, Madame?
2 7 a. Tu aimes Marie-Hélène?
b. Nous cherchons Robert.
c. Il n'aime pas Marc.
d. Etienne et Charles, vous cherchez Anne?
e. Ils ne cherchent pas Guillaume.

Preparation 16
1 4 a. vous chantez
b. Elle habite
c. Nous n'écoutons pas
d. habiter
5 a. Jean-Claude et Philippe écoutent la radio.
b. Richard et Martine ne dansent pas le rock.
c. Tu aimes danser?
d. Marc déteste le jazz.
6 a. Oui, je cherche un disque.
b. Non, elles n'aiment pas la vie à la campagne.
c. Non, nous n'habitons pas à Saint-Louis.

1 6 d. Oui, il aime habiter à Ivry.
2 3 a. Nathalie aime un garçon. Le garçon est américain.
b. Eric habite dans une ville. La ville est en France.
c. Je cherche une affiche. L'affiche est de San Francisco.
d. Nous écoutons un transistor. Le transistor est très petit.

Preparation 17
1 3 a. écoutons
b. nages
c. ne dansent pas
d. ne mange pas
e. patiner
f. tricotez
g. aiment
h. regardes

Preparation 21
3 4 a. Cette
b. Cet
c. Cette
d. Ce
e. Ce
f. Cette
g. Cet
h. Ce
5 a. Cet homme est ouvrier.
b. Cette actrice est belle.

Preparation 24
1 1 ce, cet, cette
2 this, that
3 cet
4 cet écran, cet écrivain
5 ce
6 ce musicien, ce dentiste, ce comptable
7 cette
8 cette actrice, cet écrivain, cet écran, cette école, cet/cette enfant
9 a. Ce garçon est blond.
b. Cette fille est rousse.
c. Cette femme est grande.
d. Cet enfant est beau.
2 1 a. Elle parle italien?
b. Ils parlent allemand?
c. Tu parles anglais?
d. Robert habite à New York?
e. Pierre et Jean aiment patiner?
f. Vous regardez la télévision?

2 1 g. Elle écoute la radio/le transistor.

h. Elles mangent maintenant?

3 1 a. Renée est rousse aussi.

b. Renée est grosse aussi.

c. Renée est jeune aussi.

d. Renée est belle aussi.

e. Renée est jalouse aussi.

f. Renée est gentille aussi.

2 a. Non! Il est italien.

b. Non! Elle est bête.

c. Non! Elle est laide.

d. Non! Elle est martiniquaise.

Preparation 25

1 1 a. Mardi, j'écoute la radio avec Gabrielle.

b. Jeudi, je regarde la télévision avec Jean-François.

c. Dimanche, je patine avec Daniel et Sylvie.

2 Je ne danse pas.
Je ne patine pas.
Je ne tricote pas.

3 a. dentiste

b. comptable

c. photographe

d. professeur

e. écrivain

4 martiniquaise, grande, maigre, intelligente

5 anglais, petit, beau, roux, gentil

6 infirmière, actrice, musicienne, chanteuse, ouvrière, danseuse

7 canadien, italien, anglais, belge, suisse

2 1 vowel

2 écouter, habiter

3 a. j'écoute

b. je danse

c. je n'écoute pas

d. je regarde

e. je ne danse pas

f. je ne regarde pas

g. j'habite

h. je n'habite pas

4 a. Oui, j'aime tricoter.

b. Non, je n'aime pas nager.

3 1 b

2 a

3 b

Preparation 26

1 a. A

b. A

c. B

2 a. B

b. A

2 c. A

3 a. C

b. A

4 b

5 a. roux

b. intelligente

c. anglaise

6 a. Cet

b. Cette

c. Ce

d. Cette

7 a. Je

b. J'

c. Je

d. J'

8 a. vous

b. ils, elles

c. je, il, elle

d. tu

e. nous

9 a. êtes

b. sommes

c. sont

10 a. Jeannette cherche un disque?

b. Tu aimes le français?

c. Ils aiment nager?

11 a. La dame qui nage est espagnole.

b. Ce garçon n'aime pas l'histoire.

c. Vous regardez la télévision aujourd'hui?

PHASE 3

Preparation 27

1 5 a. Oui, j'ai une sœur.

b. Oui, elle a une sœur.

c. Oui, nous avons une sœur.

d. Oui, ils ont une sœur.

2 10 a. Le professeur a des cahiers.

b. Le professeur a des gommes.

Preparation 28

1 8 a. Non, ce sont les chaises de M. Roger.

b. Non, ce sont les sœurs d'Henri.

2 13 a. Non, il n'y a pas de crocodiles dans le tiroir.

b. Non, il n'y a pas de lion sous la chaise.

Preparation 29

3 1 a. Mme Perrier a un grand bureau.

b. J'ai des sœurs.

c. M. et Mme Victor ont deux enfants.

3 1 d. Vous avez quel âge?

2 a. Mais nous n'avons pas de feuilles de papier!

b. Mais nous n'avons pas de crayons!

c. Mais nous n'avons pas de gomme!

3 a. Le petit Jérôme n'a pas quinze ans, il a cinq ans!

b. Chantal n'a pas vingt-quatre ans, elle a quatorze ans!

Preparation 30

2 1 Nous avons des grands-parents.

2 J'ai une tante qui a vingt ans.

3 Vous n'avez pas trente ans.

4 Tu as un morceau de craie?

5 Elles ont un chien et un chat.

6 Il a dix-neuf ans, n'est-ce pas?

7 Je n'ai pas de frères.

8 Guy et Henri n'ont pas de sœur.

Preparation 31

1 7 a. La tante d'André est vieille, mais les oncles d'André ne sont pas vieux.

b. Guy est jaloux, mais Yvette et Lise ne sont pas jalouses.

9 a. beau

b. beaux

c. belle

d. belles

Preparation 32

2 1 Il y a cinquante-cinq chiens en tout.

2 Il y a trente-six lions en tout.

3 Il y a soixante-neuf personnes en tout.

Preparation 33

1 8 a. Je n'aime pas ces magnétophones.

b. Je n'aime pas ces électrophones.

2 2 a. Je travaille.
Tu travailles.
Michèle travaille.

b. Dany et Monique travaillent.

2 2 c. Toi et moi, nous travaillons.
    d. Annick et toi, vous travaillez.
    4 a. Tu trouves le magnétophone?
      b. Je porte une grosse boîte.
      c. Nous aidons M. et Mme Peyre, qui sont très vieux.
      d. Hélène et Lucie ferment la porte.
      e. Tu fermes la fenêtre?
      f. Je ne trouve pas mon cahier.
3 3 a. Ces élèves ont des crayons et des cahiers.
      b. Ces vieilles femmes sont très sympathiques.
      c. Les fils de M. Poirier sont beaux.
      d. Nous ne sommes pas riches.
      e. Elles ne sont pas grandes.

Preparation 34
3 1   –Tu connais ces deux filles qui parlent avec ta sœur?
      –Oui, bien sûr, ce sont mes cousines.
      –Tes cousines! Oh là là, elles sont bien!
      –Oui, pas mal. Et très gentilles.
      –Elles sont étudiantes?
      –Non, elles sont musiciennes.

Preparation 35
1 6 a. mon
      b. ta
      c. son
      d. mes
      e. ses
      f. ton
      g. son
      h. tes
      i. ma
2 2 a. Angélique et Jeanne connaissent cet avocat.
      b. Tu connais cette ville?
      c. Paul ne connaît pas ma tante.
      d. Je connais cette mécanicienne.
    3   Tu connais ma copine Sara?
      Ils ne connaissent pas Sara.

Preparation 36
1 5 a. Je vois cinq serpents.

1 5 b. Marc et Robert voient trois souris.
      c. Georges et moi, nous voyons une voiture/une auto.
      d. Ils voient deux vélos.
      e. M. Lafayette voit quatre saxophones.
      f. Les enfants voient deux pianos.

Preparation 37
2 2 a. C'est la guitare de son camarade Guy.
      b. C'est le cahier de sa sœur.
      c. Nous connaissons leur tante.
    3 a. Est-ce que votre dentiste est gentil?
      b. Notre docteur est français.
      c. Leur professeur est intelligent.

Preparation 38
1 4 a. Est-ce qu'elles connaissent son frère?
      b. Est-ce qu'il connaît nos tantes?
      c. Est-ce que nous connaissons leurs oncles?

Preparation 40
1 1 a. Je le vois.
      b. Je les vois.
      c. Je les vois.
      d. Je la vois.
    2 a. Nous le connaissons.
      b. Ils la cherchent.
      c. Elle le voit.
      d. Il l'aime.
      e. Vous les écoutez.
2 1 H: Tu connais ce garçon là-bas?
      R: Bien sûr. C'est mon cousin Jean-Pierre.
      H: Il est médecin, n'est-ce pas?
      R: Mais non! Il est ingénieur.
      H: Ah oui? Où est-ce qu'il travaille?
      R: Chez Renault.
    2 a. Il connaît New York et Paris, n'est-ce pas?
      b. L'infirmier écoute des médecins célèbres.
      c. Ces danseuses sont grandes, maigres et jolies.

      d. Est-ce que le père cherche ses enfants?
      e. L'architecte qui travaille dans mon bureau est espagnol.
    3 a. nos
      b. votre
      c. mon
      d. leurs
      e. leur
      f. ma
      g. sa
      h. ton
4 1 a. il y a
      b. Voilà
      c. Voilà
      d. Il y a

Preparation 41
1 1 a. Cet
      b. Ce
      c. Cette
      d. Ces
    2 a. Je connais cet homme.
      b. Nous connaissons ces garçons.
      c. Ils connaissent ce professeur.
      d. Elle connaît cette ville.
2 1 a. vois
      b. voyez
      c. voit
      d. voyons
      e. voient
      f. vois
    2 a. travaille
      b. travailles
      c. travaille
      d. travaillez
      e. travaillent
      f. travaillons
3 1   Ils ne sont pas américains.
    2   Ces filles sont blondes.
    3   Mes oncles habitent à Québec.
    4   Ils voient Mme Lautrec.
    5   Ses sœurs sont gentilles.

Preparation 42
1 a. P
    b. S
2   C
3 a. C
    b. B
4 a. Ces filles ont dix-sept ans.
    b. Ce sont des écrans.
5 a. Je les vois.
    b. Je la vois.
    c. Je les écoute.
    d. Je l'écoute.

6 a. Cet
b. Ce
7 a. travaille
b. travaillons
8 a. connaissez
b. connaissons
c. connais
9 a. Est-ce qu'il aime la géographie?
b. Ils sont anglais, n'est-ce pas?
10 a. a
b. avons
11 a. Non, je n'ai pas de clarinette.
b. Non, je n'ai pas de cousins.
12 a. vois
b. voyez
13 a. ma, mes, mon
b. son
c. vos
14 a. Est-ce qu'elles habitent chez Louise?
b. Il n'est pas jeune.

PHASE 4

Preparation 45

4 1 a. veux
b. veux
c. voulez
d. veut
2 a. Qui veut faire une promenade?
b. On ne veut pas jouer aux échecs.
c. Est-ce que Paul et Marie veulent jouer au volleyball demain?
d. Nous ne voulons pas habiter à New York.

Preparation 46

3 1 Allô, André? C'est Pierre.
2 On joue au basket cet après-midi, n'est-ce pas?
3 À deux heures, si tu veux.
4 Bon, d'accord. À tout à l'heure.

Preparation 47

1 5 Il neige à Montréal.
6 Il fait beau à Miami.
7 À Chicago il fait du vent.
8 Il pleut à Vancouver.
9 À Denver il fait mauvais.
10 Il fait frais à San Francisco./Il fait du vent à San Francisco.

Preparation 48

1 5 a. Tu veux écouter la radio mainenant, mais tu ne peux pas.
b. Vous voulez aller au cinéma, mais vous ne pouvez pas.
3 3 no
4 gender; number
5 a. mon, ma, mes
b. ton, ta, tes
c. son, sa, ses
d. notre, nos
e. votre, vos
f. leur, leurs
6 a. mes
b. son
c. leur
d. notre
e. leurs
f. ses

Preparation 49

2 2 a. Paul et moi, nous allons voir un film samedi.
b. Tu vas tricoter samedi.
c. Tante Geneviève va faire une promenade samedi.
3 1 a. un hôpital.
b. un appartement
c. un supermarché
d. une station-service
2 a. une maison
b. un magasin
c. un stade
d. un bureau
e. une librairie

Preparation 51

3 4 a. J'aime jouer du piano.
b. J'aime jouer au football.
c. Tu aimes jouer de la batterie?
d. Tu aimes jouer aux cartes?

Preparation 52

2 1 a. le tennis, le ping-pong
b. le volley-ball
c. le football
d. le hockey
2 a. les cartes
b. les échecs
c. les boules
3 a. le piano
b. l'accordéon
c. le violon
d. la batterie
e. la flûte
f. la trompette
4 a. Il fait chaud.

2 4 b. Il fait beau.
c. Il fait du vent.
d. Il fait froid./Il neige.
e. Il pleut.
3 4 a. du, aux, au
b. au, de l'

Preparation 53

1 7 a. eux
b. nous
c. elle
d. lui
e. elles

Preparation 54

2 2 a. vais
b. va
c. vont
d. vont
e. allons
3 a. Demain je vais travailler avec Michèle.
b. Demain les ouvriers vont faire des chaises.
c. Demain vous allez aller à la plage.
4 a. M. Belcourt va à la station-service dans sa voiture.
b. Les élèves vont au zoo avec leurs amis.
c. Le docteur Pasquier et l'infirmier vont à l'hôpital.

Preparation 55

3 1 faux
2 vrai
3 faux
4 faux
5 vrai

Preparation 56

1 1 a. va
b. allons
c. vont
d. aller
2 a. vais
b. vas
c. allez
d. vont
3 a. Tu fais (vous faites) des projets?/Est-ce que tu fais (vous faites) des projets?
b. Qu'est-ce qu'il fait?
c. Nous faisons des crêpes aujourd'hui.
d. (Est-ce qu') ils font du camping en septembre?

1 4 a. savez
b. savoir
c. sais
d. sais
e. savent
2 1 aux
2 au
3 à l'
4 à l'
5 à la
6 aux
3 1 Mon sport préféré est le tennis.
2 Le samedi je fais mes devoirs, je joue de la guitare et je visite le musée avec une amie.
3 Au printemps j'aime faire des promenades.

Préparation 57
1 1 a. Ce musicien ne peut pas aller à Bruxelles en juin.
b. Thierry et Mathieu ne peuvent pas faire du/de ski en Suisse.
c. Tu ne peux pas regarder le match de basket à la télé.
d. Nos voisins ne peuvent pas faire des/de crêpes ce soir.
2 a. Elles veulent chanter en allemand.
b. Je veux jouer au ping-pong.
c. Mon frère et moi, nous voulons faire du bateau.
2 1 a. savoir
b. connaître
c. savoir
d. connaître
e. savoir
f. savoir
2 a. connais
b. savent
c. connaît
d. sais

Préparation 58
1 1 a. Oui, je le regarde.
b. Oui, le petit garçon (il) l'écoute.
c. Oui, nous les invitons à la fête.
d. Oui, les chats les aiment.
2 a. Non, il ne me connaît pas bien.
b. Non, je ne t'écoute pas.
c. Non, mes sœurs ne me cherchent pas.

1 2 d. Non, je ne la regarde pas le matin.
2 1 a. Nicole et Martine jouent du piano.
b. Je joue de l'accordéon.
c. Tu joues des cymbales et de la batterie.
d. Le petit Maurice joue du violon.
e. Vous jouez de la trompette.
f. Françoise joue du saxophone.
2 a. Ce sont les trois chiens de la femme.
b. C'est la voiture du médecin.
2 c. C'est le restaurant des sœurs Bourget.
d. C'est le vélo de l'enfant.
3 1 a. Est-ce que tu fais des commissions cet après-midi?
b. Elles vont au match de football.
c. Je ne peux pas trouver mes livres.
2 a. Marie-Jeanne connaît Yvonne, une jeune musicienne qui joue de la flûte.
b. On aime être à la plage en août, n'est-ce pas?

Préparation 59
1 a. B
b. C
2 a. C
b. B
3 a. faux
b. vrai
c. faux
4 a. faites
b. veulent
c. vas
5 a. savent
b. connais
6 a. Oui, ils la connaissent.
b. Non, je ne l'aime pas.
7 a. à l'
b. au
8 a. de la
b. du
9 a. Thérèse et moi, nous allons jouer au tennis.
b. Tu ne vas pas au supermarché avec nous?
10 a. Samedi après-midi je vais au cinéma avec ma sœur.
b. Il fait très beau aujourd'hui.

PHASE **5**
Préparation 62
2 4 a. Nous voulons, Nous pouvons
b. Tu veux, Tu peux
c. Elles veulent, Elles peuvent
d. Il veut, Il peut

Préparation 65
1 3 a. de, les
b. de, de, la, le
c. du, des, des, du
d. le, les, les, le
3 2 a. Elle, elle mange.
b. Nous, nous commençons nos devoirs.
c. Eux, ils font une promenade.
d. Toi, tu vas au café.
e. Vous, vous mangez.
f. Moi, je vais au cinéma.

Préparation 66
1 4 a. Il fait beau.
b. Il fait froid.
c. Il ne fait pas mauvais aujourd'hui.
d. Il ne fait pas chaud.
5 a. Nous avons faim.
b. Je n'ai pas soif.
c. Patricia a raison.
d. Ils ont très froid.
e. Thierry a quinze ans.
2 5 a. sa maison
b. son vélomoteur
2 5 c. leurs enfants
d. sa guitare
e. ses disques
f. sa trompette
g. leur restaurant

Préparation 68
2 8 a. Tu viens jouer aux cartes.
b. Vous venez chez nous.

Préparation 69
2 2 a. Nous allons au lycée à huit heures et quart/ huit heures quinze.
b. Le médecin va à l'hôpital à onze heures moins cinq.
c. Les ouvrières vont à l'usine à six heures moins le quart/cinq heures quarante-cinq.
d. Le comptable va au bureau à huit heures vingt.

3 2 a. C'est son vélo.
3 2 b. C'est leur voiture.
    c. C'est sa flûte.
    d. C'est sa guitare.
    e. C'est leur caméra.
    f. Ce sont leurs chiens.
    g. Ce sont ses singes.
    h. C'est son poisson.

Preparation 72
2 2   allez
      fait
      avez
      êtes
      suis

Preparation 73
1 1   prends
   2   prennent
   3   prenons
   4   prendre
   5   prends
   6   prenez
2 1   le, le
   2   la, de
   3   de, les
   4   les, des, du
   5   les, une
   6   le, du
   7   les, une
   8   le, de
   9   l', de l'
  10   des, de
3 1   Lui, il fait des commissions
   2   Moi, je fais mes devoirs.
   3   Vous, vous écoutez la radio.
   4   Toi, tu chantes.
   5   Eux, ils vont au cinéma.
   6   Elles, elles jouent aux échecs.
4 1   b
   2   c
   3   b
   4   c
   5   b
   6   a

Preparation 74
1 1   viens
   2   vient
   3   venir
   4   vient
   5   venez
   6   vient
   7   viens
   8   venons
   9   viennent
2 1   son
   2   sa

   3   leur
   4   ses
2 5   leur
3 1   c lycéenne
   2   c jolie
   3   b stupide
   4   b maigre
   5   b manger son petit déjeuner
   6   a à midi
   7   c poisson
   8   c du pain et du chocolat
   9   a oui
  10   c n'a pas faim

Preparation 75
1 a. He's going to Valerie's house.
    b. He's beginning his diet.
2 a. H, B
    b. E, C
3 a. A
    b. B
4 a. du/un
    b. des
    c. une
    d. de
5 a. prenez
    b. prennent
    c. prendre
    d. prends
6 a. viennent
    b. Venez
    c. vient
    d. viens
7 a. a
    b. fait
7 c. suis
    d. vas
8 a. Son
    b. Sa
    c. Ses
9 a. moi
    b. lui
    c. elles
    d. eux
10 a. B
    b. C
11 a. Je préfère des œufs et du pain grillé comme petit déjeuner.
     b. Ce soir je vais manger du poisson pour le dîner.

PHASE 6
Preparation 82
2 4   I am putting on (put on) a heavy brown pullover.
   5   a. Il met un costume.
       b. Nous mettons des maillots de bain.

     c. Vous mettez des chaussettes.
2 5 d. Ils mettent des imperméables.
     e. Tu mets un short et une chemise.

Preparation 83
1 7 a. Maryse dit que sa voiture est belle.
     b. Marcel dit qu'il doit travailler.
     c. Jacques dit que nous pouvons aller à la plage.
3 3 a. C'est mon vieil oncle Georges.
     b. C'est une belle tomate.
     c. Il y a un joli parc là-bas.
     d. Ce sont deux gros poulets.
     e. C'est une bonne idée.
     f. J'ai une vieille moto.
   4 a. Ce sont mes grands-parents canadiens.
     b. Je ne mange jamais de pommes vertes.
     c. C'est un avocat célèbre.
     d. Renée est une jeune fille jalouse.
     e. Je préfère les pulls blancs.

Preparation 85
2 3 a. Nanette dit que ses cousins viennent demain. Philippe dit que sa tante Lucie vient ce soir.
     b. Barbara dit qu'elle aime parler espagnol. Robert dit qu'il préfère parler français.
     c. Pierre dit que son pull est vert. Renée dit que son pull est bleu.

Preparation 86
3 5 a. Pas de café, merci.
     b. Pas de cerises, merci.
     c. Pas d'eau, merci.
     d. Pas de fruit, merci.

Preparation 89
1 1 a. Ce sont de vieilles chaussures marron.
     b. C'est une grosse pomme rouge.
     c. C'est un joli chapeau rose.

d. C'est un jeune homme jaloux.

e. C'est une petite maison jaune.

2 2 a. Moi, je préfère la robe bleue.

b. Le directeur est un homme sympathique.

c. À mon avis, elle porte des chaussures laides.

d. M. Delisle habite dans un petit appartement.

e. Yvette a une amie martiniquaise.

2 1 mangeons

2 commençons

3 a. j'achète, vous achetez, elle achète

b. ils achètent, tu achètes, elles achètent

c. nous achetons, on achète, il achète

4 a. tu préfères, on préfère, je préfère

b. il préfère, nous préférons, elle préfère

c. elles préfèrent, vous préférez, ils préfèrent

3 a. mangeons

b. commençons

c. achète

d. achetons

e. préfère

f. préférons

3 1 a. M. Gérard dit que nous devons (qu'ils doivent) acheter une maison à Paris.

b. Marianne dit qu'elle veut voyager en Europe cet automne.

c. Véronique dit que ses parents aiment la musique classique.

d. Mme Leclerc dit que son fils et sa fille vont à l'université.

2 Michel dit que le film est très bon. Carole dit qu'au contraire, le film est très mauvais.

4 1 a. Non, nous n'achetons rien.

b. Non, il n'y a personne chez moi.

c. Non, je ne fais jamais de/du ski.

d. Non, elle ne connaît personne à Paris.

e. Non, je ne vois personne là-bas.

f. Non, il n'y a rien dans cette boîte.

g. Non, elle n'achète rien.

2 a. Rien.

4 2 b. Jamais.

c. Personne.

Preparation 90
1 1 a. Oui, elle me donne un appareil-photo.

b. Oui, il lui donne un cadeau.

c. Oui, nous lui téléphonons ce soir.

2 a. Non, je ne leur donne pas de fraises./Nous ne leur donnons pas de fraises.

b. Non, elle ne me téléphone pas aujourd'hui.

c. Non, ils ne me (nous) montrent pas les photos de leurs vacances.

2 1 a. Montrons ces photos à Laure.

b. Fais tes devoirs.

c. Va à la librairie.

d. Chantons avec lui.

2 a. Viens avec René.

b. Mangez le poisson.

c. Commençons à dîner.

d. Fais un gâteau.

Preparation 91
1 They're going to buy a present for Madeleine. Her mother says she has to do her homework.

2 A

3 a. achètes

b. mangeons

c. Préférez

d. commençons

4 a. (Françoise dit) qu'elle a soif.

b. (Jean-Paul dit) qu'il doit aller au lycée maintenant.

c. (Thérèse dit) qu'on va dîner à neuf heures.

5. a. Sylvie wants to go to the movies.

b. Marie can't go because she has to help her mother, and also go to Galeries Lafayette with her.

c. Marie is going to buy a brown skirt and a pink blouse and maybe some shoes.

6. a. devez

b. Devons

c. dois

7 a. Oui, je lui donne un livre.

b. Oui, nous (vous) leur téléphonons (téléphonez).

c. Oui, je te parle.

8 a. met

b. Mettez

c. mets

9 a. Regarde le tableau!

b. Mangeons les légumes!

c. Achetez du pain.

d. Commence à travailler.

e. Chantons.

10 a. jeune

b. français

c. belle

11 a. Mireille met une jolie robe bleue pour aller à la discothèque.

b. Edouard met un vieux chapeau marron pour aller à l'usine.

12 a. Je ne prends jamais de fruit comme dessert./Je ne prends rien comme dessert.

b. Il n'y a personne là-bas.

c. Denise ne joue jamais au tennis avec Mireille.

PHASE 7
Preparation 93
2 6 a. Oui, je l'invite.

b. Non, elle ne l'a pas.

c. Non, je ne les montre pas.

d. Oui, je leur montre nos diapos de l'Espagne.

e. Oui, je lui téléphone pour emprunter son écran.

f. Non, je les mets en ordre samedi.

7 a. regarder quelque chose

b. téléphoner à quelqu'un

c. montrer quelque chose à quelqu'un

d. demander à quelqu'un si

e. écouter quelqu'un

f. chercher quelque chose

g. donner quelque chose à quelqu'un

Preparation 96
2 4 a. Gauthier arrive plus tard que Nanette.

b. Marcel mange plus lentement qu'André.

c. Delphine nage aussi rapidement que Roger.

d. Les parents de Robert

prennent du vin moins souvent que les parents d'Yves.

2 4 e. Marie-Thérèse va arriver moins tôt que Sylvie.

Preparation 99
2 6 a. Non, ils ne nous envoient pas le journal de Dakar.
b. Non, elles ne nous écrivent pas tous les jours.
c. Oui, nous leur envoyons des cadeaux.

3 2 a. Vous avez écouté les chanteurs.
b. Il a envoyé des cartes à ses amis.
c. Nous avons demandé au professeur la date de l'examen.
d. Ils ont cherché leurs gants dans la voiture.

Preparation 101
2 3 a. Le dix, on va à Thiès.
b. Le quinze, on va à Dakar.
c. Le vingt, on va à Tambacounda.

2 4 a. Jeanine vient de Montpellier.
b. Hervé vient d'Arles.
c. Annette vient de Toulon.
d. Stéphanie vient d'Avignon.

Preparation 102
2 5 a. Qu'est-ce que Georges et Hélène ont vu à New York? Qu'est-ce que Georges et Hélène ont fait à New York?
b. Qu'est-ce que tu as vu au zoo? Qu'est-ce que tu as fait au zoo?

Preparation 103
2 2 a. Non, il n'y a personne chez moi.
b. Elle ne mange rien.
c. Non, nous ne connaissons personne à Londres.
d. Non, Marie n'invite personne pour son anniversaire.
e. Je ne regarde rien.
f. Ils ne prennent rien comme dessert.

3 1 un jour mémorable
2 des examens difficiles
3 un travail intéressant
4 son service militaire
5 passionnant

6 remplacer
7 le service national
8 pendant
9 un autre pays
10 les habitants

Preparation 104
2 1 le vélo (la bicyclette)
2 le vélomoteur, la moto
3 la moto
4 l'autocar
5 le bateau
6 l'avion
7 le train

Preparation 105
1 1 a. Tu as envoyé un cadeau à Jeanne hier soir?
b. Tu as fait tes devoirs hier soir?
c. Tu as vu le film à la télé hier soir?

4 a. Nous n'avons pas patiné avec nos copains.
b. Mon père n'a pas commencé son régime.
c. Je n'ai pas fait de promenade.
d. Sara et Luc n'ont pas terminé leurs devoirs.

2 1 a. Oui, je lui envoie une carte d'anniversaire tout de suite.
b. Oui, je leur parle de mes projets de vacances tout de suite.

2 a. Non, je ne vous écris pas avant le week-end./Non, nous ne vous écrivons pas avant le week-end.
b. Non, je ne te donne pas mon pull gris pour ce soir.
c. Non, nous ne vous téléphonons pas plus tard.

3 a. Tu dois lui écrire.
b. Tu dois leur téléphoner tout de suite.

4 a. Non, je ne veux pas leur montrer mes diapos.
b. Non, je ne veux pas lui demander si elle veut venir nous parler.

Preparation 106
1 1 qui
2 que
3 a. Les pays d'Afrique que tu vas visiter sont fascinants.
b. Cette jeune fille, qui va

venir nous voir, est professeur à Paris.

1 3 c. Les diapos que vous montrez aux étudiants sont excellentes.
d. Mon père, qui est assez vieux, aime faire des promenades en auto.

2 1 a. Cherche-le.
b. Achète-les.
c. Écris-les.
d. Prends-la.

2 a. Envoyez-la.
b. Mangez-le.
c. Achetez-les.

3 a. Écoutons-les.
b. Prenons-le.
c. Faisons-le.
d. Mangeons-les.

Preparation 107
1 1 the past participle
2 é
3 fait; vu
4 a. Nous avons fait une promenade.
b. Tu as envoyé une lettre à Nicole.
c. Elles ont parlé avec leurs copains.
d. Il a commencé son travail.
e. Vous avez vu un film à la télévision.
f. J'ai dîné à neuf heures.

5 a. Mais j'ai regardé ces photos hier!
b. Mais j'ai téléphoné au médecin hier!
c. Mais j'ai acheté des fruits hier!
d. Mais j'ai fait des commissions hier!
e. Mais j'ai donné un disque à Albert hier!

2 1 Ma tante m'achète un électrophone.
2 Est-ce que je peux jouer au tennis?
3 Montre-moi ta caméra.
4 J'ai téléphoné hier après-midi à mon ami Roger.
5 Voulez-vous (Est-ce que vous voulez) me voir à trois heures?

Preparation 108
1 1 directly before the infinitive
2 a. J'aime l'écouter.
b. Je vais lui donner ce disque.

c. Mon père veut leur dire
bonjour.

1 2 d. Mes parents vont lui
écrire.
e. Jeanine va les voir au
restaurant.
f. Je préfère les acheter.

2 1 a. Je n'écris pas.
Tu n'écris pas.
b. Il n'écrit pas.
On n'écrit pas.
c. Ils n'écrivent pas. Lucie
et Anne n'écrivent pas.
d. Nous n'écrivons pas. Vous
n'écrivez pas.

2 a. écrire
b. écrivent
c. écris
d. écrivez
e. écris
f. écrit

3 1 beaucoup
2 au
3 agréable
4 environ
5 africaine
6 contrastes
7 immeubles
8 arbres
9 jardins
10 quartiers
11 pauvres
12 coopérant
13 moderne
14 courante
15 sénégalais
16 accueillants
17 parlent
18 bien
19 Plusieurs
20 dialectes
21 seule

Preparation 109
1 B
2 B
3 She plans to go to the
United States in December
with her friend Marie.
4 a. Jacques est moins grand
qu'Hélène./Hélène est
plus grande que Jacques.
b. M. Ledoux est aussi
maigre que Mme Ledoux.
5 a. He has to go to the library to look for some books
for a literature exam.
b. a biology exam.
6 b. Cherche-le.
b. Regarde-le.
c. Ecoutez-la.

d. Envoyez-les.
e. Chantons-les.
6 f. Mangeons-le.
7 a. écrivent
b. écris
8 a. Bon, je lui écris tout
de suite.
b. Bon, je leur envoie ces
cadeaux tout de suite.
9 a. qui parlent là-bas.
b. que je vais envoyer à
Michel
10 a. Pierre a joué au tennis
hier.
b. Tu as fait du camping
hier.
c. Nous n'avons pas vu
M. Didier hier.
d. Solange n'a pas téléphoné
à ses parents hier.
11 a. Oui, elle va lui envoyer
une carte.
b. Oui, je veux l'acheter.
12 a. Roger court moins vite
qu'Henri.
b. Henri court plus lentement que Marianne.
13 a. Mme Delacroix va aller
à Baton Rouge la semaine
prochaine.
b. Charles, veux-tu jouer au
tennis demain après-midi?

PHASE 8
Preparation 110
2 3 a. Il n'a jamais acheté de
chapeau jaune.
b. Il n'a jamais acheté de
chaussures rouges.
c. Il n'a jamais acheté de
chemise rose.
d. Il n'a jamais acheté de
gants gris.

Preparation 114
2 3 a. Non, je n'y vais pas.
b. Oui, elle y va.
c. Si, elles y vont.
d. Non, nous n'y allons pas.
e. Oui, elle y est.

Preparation 115
1 2 a. Vous dites que les gens
courent toujours à Paris.
You say that people are
always running (in a
hurry) in Paris.
b. Sa mère et sa tante
disent que les prix sont
astronomiques.

Her mother and her aunt
say that the prices are
astronomical.
c. Tu dis qu'il y a beaucoup
de musées.
You say that there are
many museums.
d. Nous disons que c'est
une belle ville.
e. Je dis que c'est une
ville moderne.

Preparation 117
1 5 a. J'en ai deux.
b. J'en ai treize.
c. J'en ai vingt-deux.
d. J'en ai trois.

Preparation 118
3 1 a. à Lyon
b. au bureau
c. à la cantine scolaire.
2 a. Est-ce que tu vas au
cinéma avec Gisèle?/Tu
vas au cinéma avec Gisèle?
Non, j'y vais avec mon
frère.
b. Est-ce qu' Anne va au
lycée aujourd'hui?/Anne
va au lycée aujourd'hui?
Non, elle n'y va pas
aujourd'hui.
c. Est-ce que nous allons au
jardin public/parc?/Nous
allons au jardin public
(parc)?
Oui, nous y allons
en autobus.

Preparation 119
1 1 é
2 a. J'ai mangé trop de fruits.
b. Vous n'avez pas acheté
de disques.
c. Nous avons chanté une
chanson.
d. Mme Drouin n'a pas invité
Georges.
3 a. I ate too much fruit.
b. You didn't buy any
records.
c. We sang a song.
d. Mme Drouin didn't invite
Georges.
4 a. Paul et Gérard ont fait
du camping.
b. J'ai écrit à mon frère.
c. Nous avons dit au revoir
aux voisins.
d. Julie a vu M. Lille ce
matin.

e. On n'a pas mis de sel dans la soupe.

f. Est-ce qu'Henri a pris cette photo?

1 5 a. Albert and Denise had some coffee. They didn't have any dessert.

b. avoir

c. de

6 a. Non, nous n'avons pas pris de petits gâteaux.

b. Non, je n'ai pas mangé de glace.

c. Non, je n'ai pas pris de jus d'orange.

d. Non, nous n'avons pas mis de yaourts dans le réfrigérateur.

e. Non, je n'ai pas fait d'omelette.

7 a. the auxiliary verb (before the verb *avoir*)

b. indirect-object pronoun

8 a. Oui, je leur ai écrit.

b. Oui, elle lui a donné un cadeau.

c. Si, je leur ai envoyé le livre.

9 a. Mais je lui ai téléphoné hier!

b. Mais j'ai mis mon nouveau pantalon hier!

c. Mais je lui ai écrit hier!

d. Mais j'ai acheté de la glace hier!

2 1 a. Roger en a.

b. Nous n'en avons pas.

c. Ils en cherchent.

d. J'en veux.

e. Vous n'en prenez pas?

f. Tu n'en achètes pas?

2 Roger has some.
They're looking for some.
You aren't having any?

Preparation 120

1 1 La statue a demandé une cigarette au visiteur. Le visiteur lui a dit qu'il est interdit de fumer au Louvre.

2 Non, le gardien ne croit pas le visiteur.

3 On trouve peut-être des statues qui parlent au Musée d'art moderne.

4 La statue a quitté la salle parce qu'elle a voulu faire une petite promenade et voir les autres salles.

5 Il pense que quelqu'un a volé la statue.

6 La statue vient d'Italie.

7 Un des portraits la trouve très gentille.

2 1 a. dis

b. dit

c. disons

d. dites

e. disent

f. dis

g. dire

h. dit, dire

2 But I'm telling you that I have to work tomorrow! I told him/her where I live, but I didn't give him/her my telephone number.
We say hello to our neighbor when we see him.

Preparation 121

1 She asks him if he saw all the museums.

2 B

3 a. She sent pictures of Paris to her family and wrote that it's a magnificent city.

b. She hopes to visit the United States next summer.

c. She has to work during Christmas vacation.

4 a. On a fait du ski.

b. Thérèse et Georges ont vu un film intéressant.

c. Je n'ai pas acheté de livres.

d. Nous n'avons pas écrit de lettres.

5 a. dites

b. disent

6 a. Oui, elles y travaillent.

b. Non, on n'y va pas.

7 a. Je leur ai parlé hier.

b. Je lui ai écrit hier.

8 a. Oui, il en prend.

b. Non, il n'y en a pas.

9 a. Oui, je veux la voir.

b. Oui, il va lui envoyer des journaux.

10 a. J'ai mis un chapeau et des gants.

b. J'ai écrit une lettre à mon grand-père.

VOCABULAIRE FRANÇAIS-ANGLAIS

A

à in; at, to; with

l'absence (*f.*) absence

absent, -e absent

un accident accident

un accordéon accordion

accueillant, -e friendly, hospitable

acheter to buy; **achetons-lui** let's buy (something) for him

un acrobate acrobat

un acteur, une actrice actor, actress

admirable admirable

admirer to admire

adorer to like a lot

un aéroport airport

les affaires business; **prenez vos affaires** pick up your things

affectueusement love (closing a letter); affectionately

une affiche poster

affreux, affreuse awful, terrible

âge: quel âge avez-vous? how old are you?

un agent de police police officer

agréable pleasant, nice

ah bon! oh! oh?

ah non, alors! oh, no!

aider to help, aid

aïe! ouch!

aimer to like; to love

l'aîné, -e the oldest one

l'algèbre (*f.*) algebra

allée: une grande allée wide path

l'Allemagne (*f.*) Germany

allemand, -e German; **l'allemand** (*m.*) German language

aller to go; **aller voir** to visit (a person); **allons-y!** Let's go!; **comment allez-vous?** how are you feeling?

alors then; well... (stalling for time)

américain, -e American

un ami, une amie close friend

amuse: on s'amuse they have a good time

anglais, -e English **l'anglais** (*m.*) English language; **en anglais** in English

l'Angleterre (*f.*) England

animation: avec animation excitedly

l'anniversaire (*m.*) birthday; **bon/joyeux anniversaire** happy birthday

une antilope antelope

août August

un appareil-photo camera

un appartement apartment

appelle: je m'appelle my name is; **on appelle** one calls

appétit: bon appétit! enjoy your meal!

apprécier to appreciate

après after; **après-demain** day after tomorrow

l'après-midi (*m.*) afternoon; in the afternoon

un arbre tree

un architecte architect

l'argent (*m.*) money

armé, -e armed

l'armée de l'air (*f.*) air force; **l'armée de mer** navy; **l'armée de terre** army

arrêter to stop someone (from doing something); to arrest

arriver to arrive, come

un artiste artist

un aspect aspect

asseyez-vous sit down

assez enough; somewhat

astronomique astronomical

attendre to wait (for)

attirer l'attention to attract attention

au contraire on the contrary

aujourd'hui today; **aujourd'hui, c'est...** today is

au maximum at most

au moins at least

au revoir good-by

aussi also; **moi aussi** me, too; **aussi...que** as...as

un autobus city bus

un autocar bus, motor coach

l'automne (*m.*) autumn, fall; **en automne** in the fall

autre other

avant before; **avant-hier** day before yesterday

avec with

une avenue avenue

un avion airplane; **en avion** by plane

avis: à mon avis in my opinion

un avocat, une avocate lawyer

avoir to have; **avoir besoin de** to need; **avoir chaud** to be hot; **avoir faim** to be hungry; **avoir froid** to be cold; **avoir raison** to be right; **avoir soif** to be thirsty
avril April

B

un bal dance, ball
une banane banana
une bande tape recording
une banque bank
une barbe beard
le basket-ball (basket) basketball
un bassin fountain
un bateau boat; **faire du bateau (à voile)** to go boating (sailing)
un bateau-mouche Parisian sightseeing boat
la batterie drums
beau, belle handsome, beautiful
beaucoup a lot; many; **pas beaucoup** not much; **beaucoup de** a lot of; **beaucoup de monde** a lot of people
belge Belgian
la Belgique Belgium
la belle-mère mother-in-law
besoin: avoir besoin de to need
bête stupid, dumb; **que tu es bête!** how dumb you are!
le beurre butter
une bibliothèque library
bien well; **bien sûr** of course; certainly; **ça va bien?** are things OK?; **il est bien** he's good-looking; **je ne vais pas bien** I'm not feeling well; **très bien**

very well; fine; **pas très bien** not too well (good)
bientôt soon
la biologie biology
blanc, blanche white
le blé wheat
bleu, -e blue
blond, -e blond
un blue-jean blue jeans
le bœuf beef
bof! (indifference or mild impatience) well...!
boire to drink
une boisson drink, beverage
une boîte box
bon, bonne good; **bon anniversaire** happy birthday; **bon appétit** enjoy your meal; **bonne chance!** good luck!; **bonne idée!** good idea!
un bonbon piece of candy
bonjour hello, good morning; **dire bonjour à** to say hello to
bonsoir good evening; good night
les boules French game
le boulot (slang) job, work
brun, -e brown; brown-haired
un bureau desk; office

C

ça that; **ça alors!** (surprise or exasperation) good grief! **ça fait** that makes; **ça ne veut rien dire!** that doesn't mean anything! **ça va** how's it going? O.K.; **oh, ça va, ça va!** (exasperation) O.K., enough! **où ça?** where?
une cacahuète peanut
un cadeau present
le café coffee; **un café**

coffee house, restaurant, bar; cup of coffee
un cahier notebook
un/une camarade friend, pal
une caméra movie camera
un caméraman cameraman
la campagne country
le Canada Canada
canadien, canadienne Canadian
la cantine scolaire school cafeteria
un cardigan cardigan sweater
une carotte carrot
une carte card
une cassette cassette recording
c'est it/this is, he/she is; **ce n'est pas** it isn't, this isn't; **c'est trop fort!** that's too much! **c'est vrai** that's true
ce/cet, cette this, that
ce sont these/those are; they are
célèbre famous
cent hundred
un centimètre centimeter ·
une cerise cherry
ces these, those
une chaise chair
une chambre room
un champignon mushroom
un chandail heavy pullover
changer to change
chanter to sing
un chanteur, une chanteuse singer
un chapeau hat
chaud hot; **avoir chaud** to be hot, warm; **faire chaud** to be hot (weather)
un chauffeur de taxi taxi driver
une chaussette sock
une chaussure shoe
une chemise man's shirt
un chemisier woman's blouse or shirt

cher, chère expensive, dear
chercher to look for
chez at, to (someone's) house; **chez moi** (at) home; **chez Renault** at the Renault factory
un chien dog
le chocolat au lait hot chocolate; **le chocolat chaud** hot chocolate
le cidre cider
le cinéma movies; movie theater
cinq five
cinquante fifty
la circulation traffic
circuler to get around; **circulez!** keep moving!
une clarinette clarinet
classique classical
un client, une cliente customer
le climat climate
un coiffeur, une coiffeuse hairdresser
un collant pantyhose
combien de...? how many...? **combien de...y a-t-il?** how many...are there?
comme like, as; **comme ça** like that; **comme dessert** for dessert
commencer to begin
comment how; **comment dit-on...?** how do you say...? **comment allez-vous?** how are you?
comprendre to understand; **je ne comprends rien du tout!** I don't understand anything at all!
un comptable accountant
la confiture jam, preserves
connaître to know, to be acquainted with
connu, -e known
consciencieux, consciencieuse reliable, conscientious

content, -e happy
un contraste contrast
coopérer to cooperate; to be a **coopérant**
un copain, une copine buddy, friend
un costume costume; man's suit
un coup de téléphone telephone call
la cour courtyard
courent: ils courent they run, are running
court: il/elle court he/she runs, is running
un cousin, une cousine cousin
un crayon pencil
la crème cream
un crocodile crocodile
crois: je crois I think
un croissant crescent roll
la culture cultivation; culture
une cymbale cymbal

D

d'abord first, at first
d'accord O.K.; **être d'accord** to agree; to think something is all right
dans in
une danse dance; **danser** to dance
un danseur, une danseuse dancer
de/d' of; from
debout standing; **debout!** get up!
début: au début at the beginning
décembre December
décidé settled, decided
une décision decision
déjà already
déjeuner to eat lunch; **le déjeuner** lunch; **le petit déjeuner** breakfast

demain tomorrow; **demain, c'est...** tomorrow is...; **à demain** see you tomorrow
une demande request; **faire une demande** to request
demie: huit heures et demie eight-thirty
un/une dentiste dentist
depuis since; for
dernier last
derrière behind, in back of
des some; of (the)
désagréable unpleasant
le dessert dessert
un dessin drawing
détester to hate
deux two
une deux chevaux small French car
devant before, in front of
deviner to guess
devoir ought to, must, should; to have to; **les devoirs** (*m.*) homework
un dialecte dialect
une diapo slide (from **une diapositive**)
diététique dietetic
différent, -e different
difficile difficult
dimanche Sunday
dire to say; **dire bonjour à** to say "hello" to (someone); **il/elle dit** he/she says; **dis donc...** say...; **dites** say, tell
un directeur, une directrice principal; director
une discothèque discotheque
un disque record
distraitement inattentively

dix ten
dix-huit eighteen
dix-neuf nineteen
dix-sept seventeen
un domaine area (of interest)
dommage: quel dommage! what a pity!
donc: dis donc... say...
donner to give; **donnez-moi** give me
dormir to sleep
douze twelve
droit, -e right

E

l'eau (*f.*) water; **l'eau courante** running water
les échecs (*m.*) chess
l'école (*f.*) school
écouter to listen (to)
un écran screen
écraser to run over; crush
un écrivain writer; author
l'éducation (*f.*) education
l'électricité (*f.*) electricity
un électrophone record-player
élégant, -e elegant
un éléphant elephant
un/une élève pupil
élever to raise (animals)
elle/elles she; they
en in; to (a country); by (car, plane, etc.); **en anglais** in English; **en même temps** at the same time; **en retard** late; **en sortant** while leaving; **en tout** altogether; **en train de** busy; in the act of
encore again; still; **encore un/une** one more; **encore un peu** a little more; **encore une fois** again

un/une enfant child
enfin at last, finally
énorme enormous, huge
ensuite then, afterwards, next
entendez: vous entendez you hear, understand
entre between
entrer to enter
environ about, approximately
envoyer to send
l'Espagne (*f.*) Spain
espagnol, -e Spanish **l'espagnol** (*m.*) Spanish language
espérer to hope
un espion, une espionne spy
l'esprit (*m.*) mind, spirit
l'est (*m.*) east; **à l'est de** (to the) east of
et and
une étagère bookcase; shelf
été been (past participle of **être**)
l'été (*m.*) summer; **en été** in the summer
être to be; **être à** to belong to
un étudiant, une étudiante university student
européen, européenne European
eux they, them (stressed)
un examen exam, test
excusez-moi! excuse me!
un exercice homework; exercise
exotique exotic; foreign

F

fabriquer to manufacture
facile easy
faim: avoir faim to be hungry
faire to do, to make; **il fait beau** it's nice (weather); **il fait**

chaud it's warm, hot; **il fait frais** it's cool; **il fait froid** it's cold; **il fait mauvais** the weather's bad; **il fait du vent** it's windy; **faire du camping** to go camping; **faire des commissions** to do errands; **faire du bateau (à voile)** to go boating (sailing); **faire une petite fête** to have a small party; **faire du patin** to go skating; **faire des projets** to make plans; **faire une promenade** to go for a walk; **faire une promenade en vélo** to take a bike ride; **faire du ski** to go skiing; **faire les vendanges** to harvest grapes; **faire de la voile** to go sailing; **faire un voyage** to take a trip
la famille family
fascinant, -e fascinating
faut: il faut it is necessary, you have to, you must
faux, fausse false; fake
une femme woman; wife
une fenêtre window
fermer to close
une fête festival, holiday; **petite fête** party
une feuille de papier sheet of paper
février February
une fille girl; daughter
un film movie
un fils son
une fleur flower
une flûte flute
le football soccer
formidable! great!
fort, -e strong

fou, folle crazy, mad
une foule crowd
une fraise strawberry
français, -e French; **le français** French language;
  en français in French
un frère brother
les frites (*f.*) French fries
le froid cold weather;
  avoir froid to be cold;
  faire froid to be cold (weather)
le fromage cheese
le fruit fruit; **un fruit** piece of fruit

G

un gant glove
un garage garage
un garçon boy
gardez-les! keep them!
le gâteau cake
généralement usually, generally
les gens people; **les jeunes gens** young people
gentil, gentille nice
la géographie geography
la géométrie geometry
un gilet vest
une girafe giraffe
la glace ice cream
une gomme eraser
le goût taste; **à chacun son goût** each to his/her own taste
un gramme gram
grand, -e big, large, tall; **un grand magasin** department store
la grand-mère grandmother
le grand-père grandfather
les grands-parents grandparents
gris, -e gray
gros, grosse fat; heavy
une guitare guitar
la gymnastique gym

H

un habitant inhabitant
habiter à to live in (a place)
haché: le steak haché ground beef
un hamburger hamburger
les haricots verts (*m.*) green beans
hein? isn't it? huh?
une heure hour; **à quelle heure?** what time? when? **quelle heure est-il?** what time is it? **à tout à l'heure** see you later, in a little while
heureux, heureuse happy
hier yesterday; **hier, c'était...** yesterday was...
l'histoire (*f.*) history; story; **histoire de chaussures** a question (matter) of shoes
l'hiver (*m.*) winter; **en hiver** in the winter
le hockey hockey
un hold-up hold-up
un homme man
un hôpital hospital
horrible horrible
un hot-dog hot dog
un hôtel hotel
huit eight

I

il/ils he; they
il y a there is; there are; **il n'y a pas de** there is/are no...; there isn't/aren't any...; **il y a eu** there was; **y a-t-il?** is/are there?
une île island
immense immense, huge
un immeuble building
un imperméable raincoat
important, -e important
impressionnant, -e impressive

indépendant, -e independent
industriel, industrielle industrial
un infirmier, une infirmière nurse
l'inflation (*f.*) inflation
les informations news
un ingénieur engineer
un institut technique technical college
intelligent, -e intelligent
intéressant, -e interesting
inviter to invite
l'Italie (*f.*) Italy
italien, italienne Italian; **l'italien** (*m.*) Italian language

J

jaloux, jalouse jealous
jamais never; ever; **jamais de la vie!** not on your life!
le jambon ham
janvier January
un jardin public public garden; park
jaune yellow
le jazz jazz
je/j' I
jeudi Thursday
jeune young; **les jeunes gens** young people
joli, jolie pretty
jouer (à/de) to play (a sport/a musical instrument)
un joueur, une joueuse player
le jour day
un journal newspaper
un/une journaliste reporter
joyeux anniversaire! happy birthday!
juillet July
juin June
une jupe skirt
le jus (de fruit) (fruit) juice

K

kidnapper to kidnap
un kilogramme kilogram

L

la the; her; it
là there; **là-bas** over there
un lac lake
laid, -e ugly
le lait milk
une laitue (head of) lettuce
une langue language
le the; him; it
un légume vegetable
lentement slowly
les the; them
leur to them; their; **leurs** their
une librairie bookstore
un lion lion
un livre book
loin away, far; **loin de** far from
les loisirs spare-time activities
long, longue long
lui to him, to her; he (stressed)
lundi Monday
le lycée high school
un lycéen, une lycéenne high-school student

M

ma my
madame Mrs.; ma'am
mademoiselle Miss
un magasin store; **un grand magasin** department store
un magnétophone tape recorder
magnifique magnificent
mai May
maigre thin, lean
un maillot de bain bathing suit
maintenant now

mais but; **mais non!** (strong disappointment) oh no!; **mais oui!** (emphatic) well, yes! of course! **mais si!** (contradictory) yes (it is!/ I can!/he does!)
une maison house, home
mal bad; **pas mal** not bad
malgré in spite of; **malgré tout** in spite of everything
malheureusement unfortunately
malheureux, malheureuse unhappy
manger to eat
un manteau coat
mardi Tuesday; **Mardi Gras** Shrove Tuesday
le mari husband
un marin sailor
marre: j'en ai marre! I'm fed up!
marron brown (clothing)
mars March
martiniquais, -e from Martinique
un match athletic contest
les mathématiques (f. pl.) mathematics; **les maths** math
le matin morning; in the morning
mauvais, -e bad
me me, to me
un mécanicien, une mécanicienne mechanic
un médecin doctor
même: en même temps at the same time
mémorable memorable
merci thanks, thank you
mercredi Wednesday
la mère mother
merveilleux, merveilleuse wonderful, marvelous
mes my
un message publicitaire commercial

mesurer to measure; to be...tall
la météo weather report
un mètre meter
microscopique tiny
midi noon; **à midi** at noon
mince slim, slender
minuit midnight; **à minuit** at midnight
mi-temps: à mi-temps part-time
mi-voix: à mi-voix softly, under one's breath
moche ugly; homely
la mode fashion; **à la mode** in fashion
moderne modern
moi me; I (stressed); **moi aussi** me, too; **moi non plus** me neither
moins less; **au moins** at least; **moins le quart** quarter to (the hour); **moins...que** less...than
un mois month
mon my
le monde world; **tout le monde** everyone; **beaucoup de monde** a lot of people
monsieur Mr.; sir; **un monsieur** a gentleman
une montagne mountain; **à la montagne** to/in the mountains
montrer to show; **montrez-moi** show me
un monument monument
un morceau de craie a piece of chalk
une moto motorcycle
un motocycliste motorcyclist
un musée museum
un musicien, une musicienne musician
la musique music

N

nager to swim
naturellement. of course, naturally
ne/n'...pas not; **ce n'est pas...** it's/that's not...; **ne... jamais** never; **ne...personne** no one; nobody; not anyone; **ne...rien** nothing; not anything
n'est-ce pas? isn't it? don't you? aren't they? etc.
nécessaire necessary
neiger to snow; **il neige** it's snowing
neuf nine
noir, -e black
non no; **non, alors!** oh, no! **moi non plus** me, neither; neither do I
le nord north; **au nord de** (to the) north of
notre/nos our
nourrissant, -e nourishing
la nourriture food
nous we; us; to us
nouveau, nouvelle new
novembre November

O

obligatoire compulsory
un océan ocean
octobre October
un œuf egg
oh là là! (surprise, pleasure, dismay, annoyance) oh my! wow!
on we; you; people
l'oncle (*m.*) uncle
onze eleven
orange orange; **une orange** orange
original, -e original
ou or
où where; **où aller?** where to go?
oublier to forget

l'ouest west; **à l'ouest de** (to the) west of
oui yes; **ah, oui?** oh? **mais oui** certainly, of course; **oh, oui alors!** oh, yes!
un ouvrier, une ouvrière worker

P

le pain bread; **du pain grillé** toast; **un petit pain** roll
un palais palace
un pamplemousse grapefruit
un pantalon pants
par by; **par exemple** for example
il paraît apparently; so it seems
un parc park
parce que because
pardon! excuse me!
les parents parents; relatives
parfait, -e perfect
parisien, parisienne Parisian
parler to speak, to talk; **parler français** to speak French; **parler de** to talk about
part: de ma part from me
une partie part
pas: pas beaucoup not much; **pas de/d'** not any; no; **pas mal** OK; not bad; **pas possible!** impossible! you're kidding! **pas tellement** not very much; **pas du tout** not at all; **pas très bien** not very well
passer to pass; to have, take (an exam); to spend (time); **se passer** to happen
passionnant, -e exciting
patiner to skate

pauvre poor
un pays country, nation
une pêche peach
peindre to paint
la peinture painting
pendant for; during
une péninsule peninsula
penser to think; **penser à** to think of (someone or something)
le père father
une personne person
peser to weigh
petit, -e little, small, short; **le petit déjeuner** breakfast
le pétrole oil
un peu a little
peut-être maybe
une photo photograph; **la photographie** photography; photograph
un/une photographe photographer
la physique physics
un piano piano
pied: à pied on foot
un pilote pilot
le ping-pong table tennis
une place city square; **la place de la Concorde** esplanade in Paris
une plage beach
une plaine plain
plaisanter to kid around; **tu plaisantes!** you're kidding!
plaisir: avec plaisir gladly, with pleasure
un plateau plateau
pleut: il pleut it's raining
plus more; **plus...que** more...than; **non plus** neither
plusieurs several; a number of
plutôt rather, somewhat
un poète poet
la pointure shoe size
une poire pear

pois: des petits pois (*m.*) peas
le poisson fish
le poivre pepper
la pollution pollution
une pomme apple
une pomme de terre potato
le porc pork
une porte door
porter to wear; to carry
poser une question to ask a question
poudre: en poudre dried, powdered
le poulet chicken
pour for; in order to
pourquoi why? why
pouvoir can, to be able
préférer to prefer
un premier ministre prime minister
près de near
présent, -e present
un président president
pressé, -e in a hurry
prêt, prête ready
le printemps spring; **au printemps** in the spring
un prix price; prize
un problème problem
un produit product
un professeur teacher, professor
projet: faire des projets to make plans
puis then, afterwards, next
un pull pullover, sweater

Q

quand when
quarante forty
quart: et quart quarter past (the hour); **moins le quart** quarter of
un quartier neighborhood
quatorze fourteen
quatre four; **quatre-vingt** eighty; **quatre-vingt-dix** ninety

que/qu' that, which; than; what...?; **que tu es bête!** how dumb you are! **que veut dire...?** what does...mean?
quel, quelle, quels, quelles which? what? **quel dommage!** what a pity! **quel âge a-t-elle?** how old is she? **quelle heure est-il?** what time is it? **quel jour est-ce?** what day is it? **quel temps fait-il?** what's the weather like?
quelque chose something
quelquefois sometimes
quelqu'un someone
qu'est-ce que...? what...? **qu'est-ce que tu cherches?** what are you looking for? **qu'est-ce que c'est?** what is it? **qu'est-ce qu'il y a...?** what is there...? what's the matter?
qui that, which, whom; who? **qui est-ce?** who is it?
quinze fifteen
quitter to leave (someone or something)
quoi? what?

R

la radio radio
raffiné, -e refined
raison: avoir raison to be right; **ne...pas avoir raison** to be wrong
rarement rarely
le rayon department or counter of a store
le recensement census
le recenseur the census-taker
un réfrigérateur refrigerator
regarder to watch, to look at

un régime diet; **au régime** on a diet
une région region
une règle ruler
regrette: je regrette I'm sorry
remplacer to substitute, replace
une Renault Renault car; **chez Renault** at the Renault factory
renommé, -e famous
renverser to knock over; to reverse
répond: il répond he answers
la résolution resolution
un restaurant restaurant
retard: en retard late
le réveil waking up
réveiller to wake (someone) up
revenir to return, come back
un revolver revolver
revu (past participle of **revoir**) seen again
riche rich
rien nothing; **ça ne veut rien dire!** that doesn't mean anything! **ne...rien** nothing; not anything
une rivière river
le riz rice
une robe dress
le rock rock music
rose pink
rouge red
roux, rousse red-haired
une rue street

S

sa his; her
un sac handbag
une saison season
une salade salad
sale dirty; **quel sale temps!** What awful weather!

salut! hi!

samedi Saturday

un sandwich sandwich

sans without; **sans blague!** no kidding! **sans doute** probably; **sans manger** without eating; **sans faute** without fail

sauter to jump

savoir to know (a fact); to know how to

un saxophone saxophone

la scène scene

la science-fiction science fiction

les sciences naturelles (*f. pl.*) natural science

scolaire: la cantine scolaire school cafeteria

un/une secrétaire secretary

seize sixteen

un séjour stay

le sel salt

la semaine week

sensationnel, sensationnelle sensational

sept seven

septembre September

sérieux, sérieuse serious; earnest; **sérieusement** seriously; earnestly

un serpent snake

le service de la coopération alternate military service; **le service militaire** military service

ses his; her

seul, -e only; alone

seulement only

un short shorts

si yes (in reply to a negative statement or question); if; **s'il vous plaît** please

simplement simply

un singe monkey

six six

une sœur sister

la soie silk

soif: avoir soif to be thirsty

le soir evening; in the evening

soixante sixty; **soixante-dix** seventy

un soldat soldier

le soleil sun

solitaire lonely; alone

sombre dark

son his; her

sonner to sound, to ring

soudain suddenly

sous under

souvent often

un stade stadium

une station-service service station

le steak haché ground beef

stupide stupid

un stylo pen; **un stylo à bille** ballpoint pen

le sucre sugar

le sud south; **au sud de** (to the) south of

suisse Swiss; **la Suisse** Switzerland

un supermarché supermarket

supposer to suppose

sur on

sûr: bien sûr! of course!

sympathique likeable, nice

T

ta your

une table table; student's desk

un tableau chalkboard; painting

un tailleur woman's suit

la tante aunt

tard late; **plus tard** later; **un an plus tard** a year later

une tarte tart, pie

un taxi taxicab

te you; to you

un technicien, une technicienne technician

technique technical

un téléphone telephone

téléphoner to call, to make a telephone call

la télévision (la télé) television (TV)

tellement so much; a lot; **pas tellement** not very much

tempéré temperate

le temps weather; time; **quel temps fait-il?** what's the weather like? **de temps en temps** from time to time; **en même temps** at the same time

le tennis tennis

terminer to end, finish

tes your

têtu, -e stubborn; **têtu comme une mule** stubborn as a mule

le thé tea

un théâtre theater, playhouse

tiens! (mild astonishment) hey! well!

un tigre tiger

un tiroir drawer

toi you (stressed); **toi aussi** you, too

une tomate tomato

ton your

toujours always; still

tout, toute, tous, toutes all; every; the whole; **tout à l'heure** in a little while; **tout de suite** right away; **toute l'année** all year; **toute la journée** all day; **tout le monde** everybody; **tout le temps** often, always; **toutes sortes** all kinds

le train train
un transistor transistor radio
le travail work
travailler to work
treize thirteen
trente thirty
très very; **très bien** very well; **très pressé** in a big hurry
tricoter to knit
trois three
une trompette trumpet
trop too much; **trop de** too many
trouver to find; **je la trouve...** I think she is...
tu you

U

unique unique
une usine factory

V

une vallée valley
varié, -e a variety of, various
un vélo bicycle
un vélomoteur motorized bicycle, moped

le velours velvet
un vendeur, une vendeuse salesperson
vendredi Friday
vert, -e green
une veste jacket
les vêtements (*m.*) clothing
la viande meat
la vie life; **la vie à la campagne** country living
vieux, vieille old
un village village; small town
une ville city; town
le vin wine
vingt twenty; **vingt et un** twenty-one; **vingt-deux** twenty-two
violet, violette purple
un violon violin
vite quickly
voilà there is/are...; **le voilà** there he/it is
voile: faire de la voile to go sailing
voir to see; **voyons!** (impatience) look here!

un voisin, une voisine neighbor
une voiture automobile, car
le volley-ball volleyball
votre/vos your
voudrais: je/tu voudrais I/you would like (from **vouloir**)
vouloir to want, to wish (for); **que veut dire...?** what does....mean?
vous you
un voyage trip; **voyager en** to travel by (car, etc.)
vrai true
vraiment really

W

un western Western (film)

Y

le yaourt yogurt

Z

un zèbre zebra
zéro zero
zut! darn it!